The Great Secession Winter

of 1860-61

AND OTHER ESSAYS

The Great Secession

AND OTHER ESSAYS

EDITED AND WITH AN INTRODUCTION

A Perpetua Book

Winter of 1860-61

BY HENRY ADAMS

BY GEORGE HOCHFIELD

A. S. BARNES AND COMPANY, INC.
NEW YORK

The Editor's Part

Is Dedicated to

Anna and Max Hochfield

Acknowledgments

Acknowledgment is here made to the Massachusetts Historical Society for permission to reprint "The Great Secession Winter of 1860-61," and to Houghton Mifflin Company for permission to quote from the following works: *A Cycle of Adams Letters, 1861-1865* (1920) and *Letters of Henry Adams* (Vol. I, 1930; Vol. II, 1938) edited by Worthington C. Ford; *The Education of Henry Adams* (1918); and *Henry Adams and His Friends* (1947) by Harold Dean Cater. I am indebted also to the Graduate School of The Ohio State University for a grant which helped defray the expense of preparing the manuscript. I have drawn upon Ernest Samuels' *The Young Henry Adams* for a good deal of biographical information.

Bibliographical Note

The essays of Henry Adams not included in this volume are: "British Finance in 1816" (*North American Review*, April, 1867), "The Bank of England Restriction" (*North American Review*, October, 1867), Review of Sir Charles Lyell's *Principles of Geology* (North American Review, October, 1868), "American Finance, 1865-1869" (*Edinburgh Review*, April, 1869), "Anglo-Saxon Courts of Law" in *Essays in Anglo-Saxon Law* ed. by Henry Adams (Boston, 1876), "Napoleon I at St. Domingo" in *Historical Essays*, 1891, "The Rule of Phase Applied to History" in *The Degradation of the Democratic Dogma* (MacMillan Co., 1919). This list does not include essays written while Adams was in college.

In some cases essays were reprinted twice during Adams' lifetime. The text used here is always that of the latest publication. All additions by the present editor are enclosed in brackets.

The best biography of Henry Adams is Ernest Samuels' *The Young Henry Adams;* the best study of his thought is William H. Jordy's *Henry Adams: Scientific Historian*. Adams' relation to the intellectual currents of his time is discussed in Henry Steele Commager's *The American Mind*. Other books of interest on Adams are J. C. Levenson's *The Mind and Art of Henry Adams*, Elizabeth Stevenson's *Henry Adams: A Biography*, and Robert A. Hume's *Runaway Star*.

Contents

Introduction by George Hochfield   xiii

The Great Secession Winter of 1860-61   1

Captaine John Smith   33

The Session   61

Civil Service Reform   95

The Legal-Tender Act   129

The New York Gold Conspiracy   157

The Session. 1869-70   191

Harvard College. 1786-1787   223

Von Holst's History of the United States   253

The "Independents" in the Canvass   289

Primitive Rights of Women   333

The Declaration of Paris. 1861   361

Count Edward de Crillon   391

The Tendency of History   415

Index   425

Introduction

THIS collection of essays is intended to serve two purposes. First, it provides a body of interesting material relevant to American political history, especially in the period following the Civil War. Even Henry Adams himself, who in his later years found it almost impossible to break the habit of self-denigration, admitted that "A good deal of authentic history slipped into these papers."

Second, the essays presented here should have the effect of modifying the image of their author so powerfully imposed upon readers by the *Education of Henry Adams.* I do not mean that something hitherto unknown is revealed in them, but simply that they have rarely been read as they ought to be read and as this book makes it convenient to read them—that is, as a single, related body of work. Viewed in this light, the essays—and I am thinking particularly of those published in 1869 and 1870—can be seen as constituting the first distinct phase of Henry Adams' literary career. It is not a juvenile phase; only "The Great Secession Winter" and "Captaine John Smith" were written before Adams was thirty. On the contrary, the essays show a mind that is quite mature in its poise, resourcefulness, and reasoning power. It is a mistake, therefore, to ignore what they say and to think of Adams exclusively in terms of his later accomplishments or of the picture he created of himself in his autobiography written at sixty-five. The essays, to be sure, do not contain in embryo either the accomplishments or the picture, but they provide, as Henry Adams might have said, the "fixed point" from which it is possible to measure accurately the development of his genius.

II

When Henry Adams returned to the United States from England in 1868, he was faced with the necessity of choosing an occupation and making a place for himself in the new America that had emerged from the Civil War. His position was one peculiarly vulnerable to a sense of detachment from his surroundings. He was thirty years old; he had been abroad for seven years and had picked up English manners and habits; and he had missed direct involvment in the crucial American experience of his generation, the Civil War. Furthermore, he had spent the past seven years largely in the shadow of his father, whom he had served in the American embassy in London, without official rank or reward, as private secretary. Thus his return to America was both a belated entry into manhood and a confronting of what must have seemed to him his "real world," the world in which, although he was something of a stranger to it, he must assume responsibility for his own life and find the means of making himself felt.

Inevitably, his whole upbringing and family inheritance drew him toward politics, but as he was totally unsuited for the usual sort of political career, he decided to "strike for the press." As a political writer he could capitalize on his talents and still hope to wield influence, even perhaps—though he never openly expressed the desire—to find some access to the tangible power of government itself. He settled, therefore, in Washington and entered upon a course of free-lance journalism, writing chiefly for two organs: the *Nation,* a weekly, and the *North American Review,* the country's oldest and most respectable quarterly. But this manner of life lasted only for about a year and a half. Without a definite status in the press and uncertain of his accomplishment, Adams let himself be persuaded to leave Washington and to accept a professorship in History at Harvard. Politics was not completely abandoned, since he also became editor of the *North American Review,* which he intended to use as a forum for liberal opinion. But practically, Adams' removal to Cambridge marked the end of his first career as journalist and the beginning of his second as historian.

Despite its brevity and inconclusiveness, his stay in Washington was a decisive experience for Adams. In the *Education* he classed it among his many "failures," an attempt to do what he was not fitted for in a time that was not fitted for him. But the four chapters of the *Education* devoted to Washington show how deep an impression this period left in his mind. It did so because Washington was the first real test he encountered of certain attitudes and assumptions about politics derived from his family background. This test had a permanent influence on his way of thinking because it resulted in a disillusionment that shook him loose from the family tradition and opened the way, ultimately, to a questioning of all values that pretended to give a meaning, not only to politics, but to history as well.

III

The role that Henry Adams undertook to perform in Washington was a special one, and this partly explains his insecurity in it. He was neither reporter nor correspondent, but what should probably be called a "critic of government," one who attempts to penetrate beneath the surface of the news to fundamental issues of policy and organization. Two standards of judgment motivated his criticism and gave the impetus to his reforming zeal. They were standards which he never explicitly defined and perhaps never even consciously thought about, but which he inherited almost as part of his biological make-up from the philosophic systems of his forebears. In the first place, he assumed, as John Quincy Adams had put it, that "The eternal and immutable laws of justice and morality are paramount to all human legislation." In accordance with this assumption, it followed that government was obliged to act in keeping with these laws; that legislation must be framed on them and policy guided by them; in short, that government was a moral agent designed to aid man in realizing the "good." Hence the final justification of governmental conduct was necessarily couched in moral terms, as were the criteria for evaluating that conduct. To Charles Francis Adams, Henry's father, it had been axiomatic that "The first and greatest qualification of a statesman . . . is the mastery of the whole theory of morals which makes the foundation of all human society." The "great and everlasting question," he thought, in political as well as private life, was the question of right and wrong.

It is this metaphysical assumption, however vague and ill-defined, which determines the character of Henry Adams' early criticism. Over and over the most conclusive and most damning argument he can think of against protectionism, or the spoils system, or legal tender is that they have the effect of breeding evil, of degrading the morals of the community. Government loses its highest sanction, its very *raison d'être*, when it permits and even propagates such forms of corruption. Above all, therefore, the duty of those who govern is to keep in mind their responsibility to "the principles upon which all government and all society must ultimately rest." To ignore this responsibility is to threaten with meaninglessness the whole enterprise of government itself.

The second assumption on which Adams' criticism of government was based concerns the role in American politics of the Constitution. To the Adamses the Constitution had always been, in John Quincy's words, a "revered instrument." During the Civil War, as Henry Adams watched the course of events from his post in England, one of his greatest fears was that the Constitution might suffer irreparable changes. At one point he wrote to his brother that when the war was over their task would be to bring the country "back to its true course," to a "respect for law and order and the Constitution," lest "we lose all our landmarks and go ahead like France with a mere blind necessity to get on, without a reason or a principle."

The virtue of the Constitution was that it embodied more perfectly than any other comparable document or system of government the moral law that for the Adamses transcended human legislation. It provided, therefore, a solid foundation for the happiness and well-being of the American union, since, as John Adams thought, "the virtues [of the best republics] have been the effect of [a] well-ordered constitution, rather than the cause." From the time that John Adams proclaimed the Constitution the result of "the greatest single effort of national deliberation that the world has ever seen," he and his descendants were committed to protecting its integrity and founding on it their highest national ambitions.

This attitude toward the Constitution was responsible for the form taken by many of Henry Adams' specific criticisms in his Washington essays. His denunciation of party machines, and his concern over the activities of great corporations like the Erie Railroad, come from his belief that their power was wholly extra-constitutional, hence a danger to the traditional structure of American government. Similarly, the decay of the executive power and the corruption of the legislature, which are alluded to in almost every one of the early essays, are viewed by Adams with the dismay of one who sees something like an ideal form dissolving before his eyes. There is an unholy conspiracy which Adams is repeatedly dragging out into the light, a conspiracy among senatorial ambition, parties, and special interest "rings" which threatens to reduce constitutional government to a mere shadow and to erect in its place, "without a reason or a principle," a system of irrational power. Thus Adams' criticism, in large measure, was a conservative attempt to redefine the Constitution in terms of the problems of his own age, while its reforming purpose was the eradication of all those immoral practices which had grown up like weeds in the cracks of the neglected Constitution.

IV

The disillusionment that began during his stay in Washington remained an active process in Henry Adams' mind for many years, and its consequences may be studied in such later works as *Democracy*, the *History of the United States . . . during the Administrations of Thomas Jefferson and James Madison*, and the *Education*. But its earliest manifestations are visible in some of the essays Adams wrote while still in Washington. Most significantly, what we see in these essays is the gradually hardening conviction, which is fully and explicitly stated in "The Session. 1869-1870," that the moral purport of the Constitution is being lost, probably for good and all. The implications of this discovery for Adams, as may easily be imagined, were far-reaching. In the first place, it was brought home to him that the Constitution had no special dispensation of Providence, that the ideal it had attempted to realize of a government powerless to encroach on the liberties of the people was "delusive" and "chimerical." But even more importantly, the failure of the Constitution threw into grave doubt the very basis of Adams' criticism. For if the moral order that the Constitution had tried to establish was impermanent and incapable of perfecting itself, what became then of the moral law transcending human legislation, the theory of which was supposed to be at the foundation of all human society? Evidently it was possible that society might not, after all, be grounded in moral law, and that the conception of transcendent principles to which human legislators were ultimately responsible might itself be delusive and chimerical. If this were so, what meaning was to be discerned in politics other than that contained in its superficial aspect, "the crash and war of jealous and hostile interests"? What ground existed outside the self on which the criticism and reform of politics might be firmly based?

Adams was forced to confront these disturbing questions by one notable deficiency in his critical point of view. When one searches his Washington essays for the ends implicit in them, the political objectives toward which they might be said to have been aiming, one is led to the conclusion that so far as Adams thought about the matter the only end he could conceive was simply the preservation of the Constitution in and for itself. Thus no alternatives were available to his mind once he became convinced that the Constitution was defunct. His ancestors, closer to the revolutionary vision of the early republic, combined their faith in the Constitution with a faith in the social and intellectual improvability of mankind under the beneficent influence of liberty and the guarantee of inalienable rights. An ideal of man in full realization of his human possibilities, "a being of loftier port, of larger dimensions, of infinitely increased and multiplied powers, and of heavier and deeper responsibilities," animated the republicanism of John Quincy Adams. But this clear outline was mostly lost to his grandson, for whom there remained only the moral compulsion inherent in such idealism without belief in the ideal itself; a sense of the necessity of commitment to principles without a clear idea of the object such principles were necessary for. In the absence of a well-defined end, and forced, as he thought, to acknowledge the collapse of the Constitution, Adams' vague and unexamined assumption of a moral order transcending human law was put to a test it could not possibly survive. The result was a loss, for the time being at any rate, of the critical motive, and a sense of life's meaninglessness in the absence of impersonal values that could legitimately claim the allegiance of faith and action. This state of mind is attested to by a variety of evidence: by Adams' relatively quick capitulation to the family pressure that favored his return from Washington to Boston; by remarks such as the following in his Washington letters, written at moments when he seemed to be quite happily embroiled in his journalistic adventures: "Personally I am still at a loss to know what the devil I want, or can possibly get, that would be an object, in case my friends came into power. . . . I want nothing and fight only for the amusement of fighting;" and by the feeling which emerged at this time and deepened over the years, particularly after the failure of the Independent movement, that politics in the usual sense was sheer anarchy, a senseless struggle for power.[1] In short, the outcome of Adams' "Washington experiment" was something in the nature of an intellectual crisis, not abrupt and violent, but subtle, protracted, and demanding of profound readjustments for its solution.

What that solution was, or whether it ever was achieved, are not questions properly dealt with here, since their answers lie far outside the frame of the essays. But something may be said concerning the effects of the Washington crisis on Adams' mind, effects which more or less conditioned his quest for a solution. In the first place, he was impelled towards history as a possible means of clarifying the disorder and unintelligibility of politics. Of course, his departure from Washington coincided with his acceptance of a History professorship, but having begun as a medievalist, within a few years his fascination with what had happened to him in Washington diverted his energies entirely to the study of the American past. History, for Adams, was the attempt to understand politics in terms of broad, underlying themes like the development of institutions or of national character; it was the discovery of orderly progression beneath the chaos of events. It need not, furthermore, be considered exclusively through moral spectacles; one might regard it with the detachment and impartiality of the scientist. Thus the study of American history was for him, at least partially, an effort to discover the inner meaning of what he had experienced in Washington, to locate the values hidden in that experience. The essays reveal two widely separated mo-

[1] This attitude is most clearly set forth, and in a tone of the strongest revulsion, in Adams' novel *Democracy*, one of the lessons of which is that the American government is "nothing more than government of any other kind."

ments in this quest. The first, Adams' review of Von Holst's *Constitutional and Political History of the United States,* shows a strikingly changed attitude toward the Constitution from that of his Washington pieces. Here the Constitution has no particular moral significance but is seen as a "practical machine" for the creation of nationality; it is an agency resembling a natural "law" in its relentless, irreversible operation. The Constitution, in other words, has become an ingredient of a larger historical context, no longer an end in itself but pointing to ends beyond itself. "The Tendency of History," however, written twenty years later, shows Adams on the verge of a new departure in his thinking. During the interval he had come to the conclusion that the ordinary forms of historical investigation were fruitless as means of ascertaining the nature of historical reality. What was necessary was a method capable of piercing to the bottom of the matter through all the layers of appearances, the method of the scientist whose objects of study were the fundamental constituents of reality. Only in this way could the historian learn the final and absolute truth contained in his material; only by making his work a branch of the physical sciences could he hope to arrive at something more than a relative and superficial interpretation of the meaning of events. Adams' quest, touched off, though certainly not wholly sustained, by the failure of his assumptions in Washington, ended in a kind of conversion of history into metaphysics in which the laws of matter ironically replaced the moral law transcending human legislation.

The second important effect of Adams' stay in Washington was the doubt engendered there of his adaptability to his own time. Every reader of the *Education* knows how troubled Adams was on this score; it became a major source of irony in the book written to expose what he called, with perverse insistence, his "failure." This sense of maladjustment goes back, I believe, to two things Adams learned in Washington: that a reasoned appeal to moral standards in politics is not necessarily persuasive—that government does, in fact, ignore moral responsibility—and that as a private individual, unallied with a party machine and armed only with the weapons of criticism, he was politically impotent. These two lessons, which are really opposite sides of the same coin, lie behind much of Adams' feeling of living in the wrong century. His consciousness of the ineffectuality of moral criticism combined with his inability to suppress his moral judgments produced the conviction that he was a member of an outmoded species, an anachronistic hold-over from the eighteenth century of John and John Quincy Adams. At the same time, his disgust with party organizations, which were in his eyes the great source of corruption in American politics, and his impotence in the face of them, led to an identification of them with human nature and finally to despair at the prospect of reforming either politics or human nature. "Masses of men," he concluded in the *Education,* "invariably follow interests in deciding morals," which is to say that morality is irrelevant to politics. His own inherited moral code, therefore, had been a "private and costly luxury," something that had gotten in the way of a true relation with his time and had prevented him from reacting "with vigor and economy" on the "lines of force" that attracted his world. Masses of men who followed their interests, on the other hand, seemed to him more and more as he grew older the blind, predestined agents of uncontrollable forces in history. The determinism of Adams' later years is remotely but unmistakably linked to the bafflement of his youthful hopes for reform and the forsaking of his social aspirations in response to the loss of his early faith.

One further observation is worth making with respect to the significance in Adams' career of the Washington episode. It has never been very clear why Adams, when he wrote as a professional historian, devoted himself exclusively to the period of Jeffersonian republicanism. Superficially there would appear to be little reason why in the mid-1870's Henry Adams, great-grandson of a Federalist president, grandson of a president who was evicted from office by men who considered themselves the true heirs of Jefferson, a New Englander to the core and hence almost instinctively distrustful of the South and West where Jefferson had found his strongest support and where his theories had had the greatest influence—why he should have become interested in the republican movement to the extent of fifteen years of labor, a nine-volume history, two biographies, and several volumes of edited papers.

The reasons are surely many and complicated, but a decisive one was the parallel Adams felt to exist between himself and the leaders of the first Republican party. As he interpreted them, the Republicans were the only true and distinctively American political idealists. They had tried to create, by means of concrete reforms and policies, a perfect governmental system and a new order of society in which the evils that had tormented human history would be ended and mankind set free to realize its highest natural capacities. In all of his books Adams gave the closest attention to these ideal hopes, and it is impossible not to feel in him a sympathetic identification with the men who held them. But in all of his books the same pattern of defeat and disillusionment is repeated, the chaos of events rises and sweeps away the frail structure of idealism, "circumstances" (as Adams called them in the *Life of Albert Gallatin*), in the form of intractable human nature and ineradicable social evil, triumph over "principles" helpless to control them. By the time he finished his *History,* Adams was certain that idealism in any form was illusory and doomed to such defeat.

It would be absurd, of course, to regard Adams as ever having been a Jeffersonian in politics, nor was he ever so wholehearted an idealist as he imagined the Republican leaders to have been, but the kinship he felt with them was based on a similarity of fate that was real—at least to his own mind. The whole of his youthful attitude toward politics rested on the belief that it was a struggle between right and wrong and that right must somehow triumph. Washington and the subsequent breakdown of the reform movement convinced him that he had been mistaken, and the shock of his disappointment, as his books testify, remained a powerful intellectual and emotional stimulus to the end of his life.

GEORGE HOCHFIELD

The Ohio State University

The Great Secession Winter

of 1860-61

In November, 1860, Charles Francis Adams was re-elected to Congress from the Third District of Massachusetts, and Henry Adams, then not quite twenty-three, accompanied him to Washington as his private secretary. During much of the subsequent winter, in addition to his regular duties, Henry acted as Washington correspondent for the Boston Advertiser. Writing anonymously in order not to compromise his father, he tried to explain and muster support for the policies of the moderate Republicans under the leadership of William H. Seward of New York and Charles Francis Adams. The correspondence ended in February, 1861, when the editor of the Advertiser came to Washington and assumed Henry's function himself.

"Tolerably well satisfied" with his winter's literary work, Henry next decided to write a full-dress article for the Atlantic Monthly which would restate and summarize his view of recent events. "The Great Secession Winter of 1860-61" was to be his contribution to the cause led by Seward and, not incidentally, an act of homage to Seward himself, whose "grand, broad ideas . . . would inspire a cow with statesmanship if she understood our language." However, when the article was finished, Adams decided it was "not worth printing." He sent it to his brother Charles in Boston, among whose papers it remained for many years until Charles recovered it and had it published in the Proceedings of the Massachusetts Historical Society.

W<small>HEN</small> Congress met at the beginning of December the country was in a condition of utter disorganization. A new question had been sprung upon it before men had had time to discover where they stood, or what the danger really was, or indeed whether any real danger in fact existed. In the extreme North the belief was general that the whole trouble was only sheer panic, which would be short-lived as it was violent, and it is no fair reproach to any good Republican that he should not have believed it possible for any body of reasoning men to take so wild and suicidal a course as that of the southern secessionists. In the middle States, however, there was great alarm. They knew their neighbors better. And as one passed southward, there could be no longer any doubt that the danger was real. The whole country was frantic in its coarse and drunken way with what it called its wrongs, and intoxicated with the prospect of the new Confederacy which was to be founded on slave labor and to draw its wealth from its harvests of cotton. In the city of Washington there was a strange and bewildering chaos, the fragments of broken parties and a tottering Government. Between the quiet New Englanders with their staid and Puritanical

[From the *Proceedings* of the Massachusetts Historical Society, 1909-1910, vol. 43, pp. 660-687. The footnotes not contributed by the present editor were evidently added by Charles Francis Adams, Jr. at the time of publication.]

ideas of duty and right, of law and religion, and the rough representatives of the Northwest, who swore by everything in the Heavens above and the Earth beneath that they would turn the rebel States into a wilderness, the difference of manner and idea was great enough. But the southerners were beyond all imagination demented. The more moderate, or the more astute, who followed the footsteps of the Virginia leaders, men like Senator Mason[1] and his colleague,[2] and Mr. Breckinridge, were all agog with the idea of a dissolution and a reconstruction of the Union with the anti-slavery element left out. But those from the cotton States abandoned at once all thought of uniting themselves again with the cold and repulsive North, and turned their minds from the recollection of their temporary alliance with barren New England, and degrading free labor, to the contemplation of fancies which were oriental in their magnificence. They talked enthusiastically of the new nation which was to be formed about the Gulf of Mexico, which should excel in its splendor and gorgeousness all those which had in old times made the Mediterranean the light of the world. In comparison with this the northern States would remain in a gloomy insignificance. Syria and Egypt, Carthage and Rome, Athens and Constantinople were to come to life again around the shores of the western Mediterranean; the commerce and wealth of Asia and Europe were to flow without an effort into this, their natural harbor; and the delights of the highest civilization were to be added to the luxuries of their tropical climate. It was useless to argue with men mad with such ideas; but so confident were they of their success, that they even met with open arms their old enemies, the Republicans, as men from whom they wished to part in kindness now that the time of separation had come.

Full of these various elements, mixed up in strange confusion, Congress came together. The crowds that for the first few days came up to the Capitol expecting to see some violent and probably bloody explosion, were disappointed and soon became thinner. The business of the country was taken up and continued with more than the usual quiet and industry, and except for the vagaries of some southern Senator there was little to see or hear. The field of action

[1] James M. Mason.
[2] Robert M. T. Hunter.

was at that time not in Congress but in the Cabinet. There the Union and Disunion parties were struggling for the control, and until that battle was decided, Congress could only look on. No party was disposed to hurry matters, for in spite of all their preparation, the explosion found the South unprepared for it as well as the North, and both sections stood in need of organization. Accordingly, instead of the theatrical and violent scenes and debates that had been expected, the House contented itself with referring the whole question of the national troubles to a large Committee,[1] and until the appropriation bills were passed and the session nearly half over, no general debate was permitted. In the Senate, where there is seldom life enough to stir up the languid atmosphere, the debate which could not be suppressed had little effect. Other events threw for a time the proceedings of Congress into the shade.

Meanwhile the whole nation was clamoring that something must be done; but at least in the city of Washington it seemed fairly agreed that nothing could be done at all. Through the whole month of December the panic there was terrible and always increasing. The rumors from the southern States were enough alone to create very great alarm, but that was not the greatest trouble. The greatest danger was in the Government itself, and so long as the disunionists had the control there, everything was to be feared. It was well known that three of the Cabinet officers were disunionists, and that the President was under their influence.[2] It was known to be their policy to keep him so, and it was said that they had placed him under a system of actual surveillance, so that he never was out of their sight. Visitors at the White House found him regularly hemmed in by these men, who poured into his ear all sorts of prayers and threats. On one side they besought him as a patriot and a Christian to avert the danger of civil war, and on the other warned him that a single step would bring on the most horrible calamities and blast his name as well as the country's hap-

---

[1] December 4, 1860.—Congressional Globe, 36th Congress, 2d Session, 6, 22. Charles Francis Adams was a member of this Committee.

[2] [The three were Howell Cobb of Georgia, Secretary of the Treasury; Jacob Thompson of Mississippi, Secretary of the Interior; and John B. Floyd of Virginia, Secretary of War.]

piness forever. He was threatened with assassination till he was said actually to believe that it would come if he moved a step from his position. But no sooner had the South by these means wrung from him some concession, than the North howled itself hoarse with execrations, and seized on the vacillating old man with a bitterness that made him aghast. Men high in station made no scruple of remonstrating in a most outspoken way, and with gestures that looked very like shaking their fists in his face. They held impeachment over him, and even went so far as to initiate the first steps toward it. Under these threats the President again wavered toward the northern side and allowed his former concessions to be wrung out of his hands. In this way he remained for months in a position that would have been ludicrous if it had not been tragical. It was a battle after the Homeric style. Mr. Cass and the North dragged him by the foot;[1] Mr. Cobb and the South by the head, and between impeachment and assassination, the feeble object of the furious contest could only weep with his ancient friends, and call upon the people to fast and pray.

While the result was as yet doubtful, and the disunionists still had practically the control of the Government, the news came of the action of Major Anderson.[2] This cut the knot of the difficulty, and gave the whole contest another aspect. Unable longer to resist the pressure, the President threw himself with all the energy of which he was capable, on the side of the Government, and the disunionists one after another were forced out of the Cabinet. To make their departure still more disgraceful, the discovery of a fraud in the Interior Department was made, and it was said at the time, that when the President received the new blow, he broke out into ejaculations much more energetic than they were polite. Little by little the new hands, to whom the country was now en-

[1] [Lewis Cass, Secretary of State. He resigned December 12, 1860.]
[2] [On the night of December 26, 1860, Major Robert Anderson, commander of the Federal garrison in Charleston harbor, secretly and without explicit orders, removed his men from their exposed positions at Fort Moultrie and Castle Pinckney to the more defensible Fort Sumter. The South Carolinians, who thought they had an agreement with President Buchanan that the military status of the harbor would not be changed without notice, were enraged and demanded Anderson's return to his original positions. He refused, and in the end Buchanan was forced by his cabinet to support him.]

trusted, patched up the rents that their predecessors had so skilfully made, and with extreme difficulty succeeded in weathering the immediate dangers. But the panic had already risen to fever heat. On the 1st of January the belief was universal in Washington that there would be fighting in the city within the month. The talk in the hotels, in Congress, and in private society, everywhere men met, was, that a collision was inevitable. Stories flew about and were generally believed, which to a stranger seemed the wildest absurdity. The most flagrant treason was openly proclaimed, accompanied by threats that reminded one of the days of Catiline. Clerks in the Government Departments mounted the disunion badge and talked openly of oaths they had taken never to permit the inauguration of Abraham Lincoln. Before that should happen Washington would be a heap of ashes. Some of them appeared in costumes of homespun, and announced that it was the uniform of a corps of five hundred who were bound by solemn oaths never to allow the election to be declared or the inauguration to be consummated. Persons whose business led them to keep late hours were alarmed by meeting bodies of men drilling at midnight in the environs of the city. Anonymous letters, and warnings not anonymous, came in numbers to persons in power all dwelling on designs of violence to be used against the Capitol. If this could have been made light of as a mere passing effect of accidental and unorganized influences, the alarm might not have risen to such a height; but the more closely the matter was examined, the more formidable it appeared. The disunionists, either confident temperamentally or extremely mendacious, asserted loudly and with one voice that they were certain of obtaining possession of Washington before the 4th of March. The War Department, the only power which could control them, was in the hands of their most unscrupulous tool, whose long course of dishonest administration, flagrant even compared with the general corruption under the last two Presidents, led naturally to the belief that he would scruple at no violence if by it he could cover his tracks and obtain a claim on the consideration of the new Confederacy. Some of his measures were known. In spite of the universal alarm, no means of defence were taken by him. All the Federal troops were kept as far as possible from Washington. Large quantities of Federal arms were transferred by his orders from the loyal States to the extreme South. Still larger quantities, it was said, had been sold by him at merely nominal prices to the southern States, and it was also said that he had received a commission on such sales. When the investigation into the matter of the abstracted bonds took place, it became still more evident why he should have wished at all hazards to destroy the record of his administration. Long known to be dishonest, and long suspected of being a traitor, his course during this winter would, in any other country or time, have cost him his life. With this man at the head of the War Department, pledged to effect by every means, honest or dishonest, the destruction of the Government, and conscious that on his success depended, not only his name and honor, which were already held in small esteem, but his power and future prospects and perhaps still more; with him and his confederates in power, it was no wonder that the people of Washington believed themselves lost.

A wide-spread and intricate conspiracy existed against the Government; so much was undoubted. Mr. Douglas and his friends denounced it openly, and traced it up to its source. For many years past there has been, it is true, a class of men in the southern States, as in the northern, who have wished for disunion as a thing good in itself. But this class was always small and could never have obtained the control of a single State as long as the slave power ruled the country. But, according to Mr. Douglas, when it became evident, at the dissolution of the Baltimore Convention in the spring of 1860, that the Democratic party were to lose their omnipotent voice in the affairs of the nation, the leading statesmen in the southern States framed a plan for the dissolution of the Union. They nominated Mr. Breckinridge for the Presidency, under the idea that they could combine on him the votes of every slave State, and having in this way carried Maryland and Virginia, they intended, or at least hoped, so to arrange the course of events that they might refuse to acknowledge the validity of the election, if the Republican candidate should be chosen, or in case of no choice by the people, that they might declare Mr. Breckinridge their President, obtain possession of Washington by means of their control of the Cabinet, and call upon all foreign Governments to recognize them as the Government *de facto*.

To defeat this conspiracy had been the object of Mr. Douglas's journey to Virginia and through the South. No one even at that time was wild enough to suppose that he expected to carry those States himself. Mr. Douglas was not so young nor so sanguine a politician as to expect a result like that. His object was to break up this southern combination and to throw the State of Virginia, on which great weight would evidently be laid, into the hands of the southern Whigs. His manoeuvre was only partially successful. His influence did, it is true, defeat and just defeat the Democrats in Virginia, but Maryland and North Carolina, both old Whig States, were carried by the Breckinridge party. Still the main object was gained, and the southern line broken so that it was impossible to carry out the original plan of the disunionist leaders. The large majority of Mr. Lincoln and the hasty action of South Carolina[1] disconcerted their plans and prevented that appearance of unity and combination that was necessary to make the explosion severe enough to overthrow the existing Government.

This was the conspiracy according to Mr. Douglas's views, openly declared in Washington and elsewhere. This coarse politician, whose animal features and bull-like voice make the admiration of the Senate galleries, revenged the insults that his old friends had heaped upon him, by striking at them in their own stronghold. How far mere patriotism led him to make this move, those who knew him best can judge. No man in the whole nation has done so much as he to degrade the standard of political morality and to further the efforts of the slave power. No man has suffered more from their resentment, and the harm he has done them during the last year may be some consolation to him for the bitterness of their persecution at that time when the President himself was not ashamed to lend the weight of his official position to shut the doors of his friends' houses in his face.

With all these facts and statements staring them in the face, it was reasonable enough that the people of Washington should be alarmed. They saw no way of escape, for both parties were at a deadlock and neither showed any sign of giving way. But with the purgation of the Cabinet, one most imminent danger was removed, though rather by the accidental boldness and honesty of

[1] [South Carolina seceded from the Union on Dec. 20, 1860.]

Major Anderson than by any exertion of statesmanship on the part of the North. It fell upon Congress to decide in what way this stroke of fortune should be improved or neglected.

In circumstances of such sudden emergency as this of disunion, Congress is far too unwieldy and unreliable a body to give much hope of its becoming an efficient agent for anything but further embroilment. It is strange to see how few men there are in such a body, where yet each must have some position or reputation for ability however small it may be, who are capable of rising to the level of any occasion be it ever so little above their ordinary mark.

At such times a few men make a reputation for a life-time; the rest will neither follow them nor take any decided steps themselves unless their constituents have already endorsed it. No branch of the Government has a greater power for good or evil than Congress in dangerous times, and yet it is generally reserved for the Executive or for the energy of single men to throw the decisive weight into the scales while Congress is still laboring after a decision.

So it was during the whole of this winter. With the Senate the case was desperate from the beginning. It was here that the whole disunion scheme had its origin and this was always its stronghold. Of all the southern Senators only two made even an effort to uphold the Government under which they had been born and to which, till a few months before, they had vowed the most unfaltering devotion. Mr. Crittenden, an old Whig, attempted to do something, but succeeded in little more than showing his own honesty and good intentions. He began his work at the wrong end. Wishing to obtain some foundation on which the North and South could unite, he was prevailed upon by his southern friends to offer measures to which it was impossible for the Republicans to accede. In this way the evil which he did became far greater than the good, for the real effect of his effort was to furnish a ground on which the disunionists could stand and make use of his name and influence in their own favor. He became practically an instrument of the secessionists. He himself soon perceived the false position he occupied, and did his best to correct the mistake. But the evil was already done and, before he could set himself right, far the greater part of the power which he might have exerted was expended.

It was not so with Andrew Johnson of Tennessee. Although a Democrat, and a follower of Mr. Breckinridge in the election, he would not yield to the tyranny which bound every other southern man in the Senate, more or less, as well as no small number of the northerners. He did not, like Mr. Crittenden, begin by practically siding with the secessionists. He limited himself to fighting disunion and treason and declaring a war of extermination with it, without putting a price on his services, but rather declaring that he was strong enough to vindicate his own rights in the Union, whoever might attack them. His bold and uncompromising attack was the first great blow that the disunionists suffered in Congress.[1] Jefferson Davis actually writhed under it, and listened with a look and an attitude of the bitterest hatred and disgust. It was a defection from their own ranks; a rebellion among their own slaves. It was a grave matter indeed when a Breckinridge Senator dared break through party lines and strike such a blow at the power which controlled all his friends.

These two men at least did stand up for the Union among the southern Senators, but the northern Democrats did not even rise as far as this. Not one of all that crew of peddling politicians ever took bold and honest ground on the new issue. Their Telamonian Ajax, Mr. Douglas, and all his herd of followers still avoided an honest avowal of a broad, unhesitating acquiescence in the new contest, and still left it doubtful which of the two they were really acting against, the disunionists or the Republicans. A true statesman, or even a high-minded man, would have seized the first opportunity to place himself above party on such a question as this. Mr. Douglas is neither the one nor the other. He, like so many others, failed to rise to the occasion. Of all the members of the Thirty-Sixth Congress, three or four names only can be picked out, of men who *grew* during this winter. Three or four only, when there was the grandest opportunity for development that ever has occurred under the Government! And, of these few, Mr. Douglas was not one.

[1] Johnson spoke on December 18 and 19, 1860.

Rather through the faults and mistakes of their opponents than through their own skill, the Republicans managed to maintain their ground tolerably well. Their first fear had been that the North would again yield to some compromise by which the old state of things would be brought back and a new struggle become necessary. Probably their fears would have been justified if the southern States had not, by withdrawing, thrown the whole power into the hands of the firmer anti-slavery men. But when it became evident that the danger did not now lie on this side, but was rather lest all the slave States should be dragged out and thus involve the whole country in a common ruin, a difference of opinion, as to the policy to be pursued, soon showed itself. One wing of the party declared for a strong policy by which the seceding States should be compelled to submit to the laws. Many of these really underrated the danger and difficulty, or, if they saw it, yet could not conscientiously take any steps to avoid it. Others confounded the conspirators with the slave-holders, placing all on the same footing, which was exactly what the disunionists were straining every nerve to bring about. Thus these practically played into the hands of the traitors by doing all in their power to combine the southern States. Others were perhaps conscientiously not unwilling that all the slave States should secede, believing that to be the shortest and surest way of obtaining the destruction of the slave power, as it was certainly a very sure way of obtaining the destruction of their own, if their policy should lead to civil war and a revulsion of feeling in the North. On the other hand, an influential portion of the party urged temporizing till the height of the fever was over, and were in favor of shaping their policy in such a way as to secure the border States and prevent bloodshed. Mr. Seward declared himself very early in the winter a favorer of conciliation in this way. He felt that something must be done, not only to resist disunion in the South, where it was every day acquiring more strength, but to sustain himself and his party in the North, where they were not strong enough to sustain the odium of a dissolution and civil war. For it is a fact, and it is right that it should be so, that with the people the question of the nation's existence will in the end override all party issues, no matter what they may be, and Mr. Seward foresaw that if the new administration was to prove a success it must shape its course so as to avoid the responsibility of the convulsion, and obtain the confidence of a large majority of the people.

This difference of opinion, as to the policy to be pursued, began first to develop itself in the Committee which the House had appointed to consider the whole question of the national troubles. When that Committee met, there was of course nothing but confusion in their minds. Heaps of different plans were thrown upon them, and for some time nothing was done but listen to what each member had to say on his own account. After all, the great wish was to gain time. Very few persons expected really that the Committee would agree on anything, or would effect any good result, further than that of relieving the House of the whole matter as long as possible. But the more violent of the southern men were determined not to allow this. They went into the Committee in order either to control it or to break it up, and in order to bring matters to a head they pressed on it measures which they knew could not be adopted. Mr. Rust of Arkansas,[1] who, under the pretence of being a Union man, did all he could to help the seceders, and Mr. Reuben Davis of Mississippi, a violent disunionist, took the lead in trying to dragoon the other southern men into retiring from the Committee. They brought forward an ultimatum which they insisted on having considered at once, or else they would withdraw. The Committee refused to leave the regular order of business, whereupon the individuals executed their threat and withdrew in high anger; but, with that methodical madness which seems to be part of the southern character, they withdrew only to the next room, where they sat in solitary dignity and watched the proceedings through the open door till their own measure should come up for discussion.

A few experiments like this soon showed that the disunion element in the Committee was not strong enough to break it up. The only hope of the disunionists became, then, to place the Republicans in such a position as to make reconciliation impossible. Their cry was that the Republicans showed no wish to conciliate; that they intended the forcible emancipation of the slaves, and so on; all which was denied by the Republicans, to be sure, but

[1] Albert Rust.

which still placed the members from the border States in a very hard position. They were honestly Union men. They were, too, in several cases at least, unconditional Union men, but their States were then very doubtful, and the clamor of the seceders might destroy their influence in case the Committee failed to do anything. They urged earnestly and honestly on the Republicans, a retreat from the positions of the campaign, and when that was refused they entreated only some sign of good-will; something, no matter what, with which they could go home and deny the charges of the disunionists. They offered their own measures of conciliation, and when these were refused they asked the Republicans whether they could do nothing in return; whether they were fixed in their determination to drive away the border States and let the spirit of disunion take its course whatever might be the result.

The Republicans hesitated. On one side they felt the weight of these prayers, for prayers they really were; and wished to do what they could for their allies. But that was not all. One by one the meshes of that vast conspiracy were becoming manifest, in which they were entangled. It was every day clearer that the danger was not imagined; that the flood of disunion feeling was advancing at fearful speed towards Washington, and threatened to overwhelm Virginia and even Maryland. And as State after State set up the standard of rebellion, and treason proclaimed itself in the Capitol and White House itself; when crowded galleries broke into violent applause over disunion speeches, and the whole city was expecting an outbreak from day to day; as it became more and more evident that the credit of the Government was tottering; its army and navy useless or nearly so; its whole frame and action hampered, weakened, broken wherever practicable, and the traitors still at its head; as all this gradually forced itself upon the minds of the leading Republicans, and they began to see the danger they ran, and to feel the tangling knots of that great net in which they were snared, they opened their eyes to their hazardous position and began to stretch their hands about them for some firm support.

While the Committee was still in doubt and the chance of a good result was becoming more and more dim, a blow was delivered by one man at the secessionists, which changed the whole face of the battle. Mr. Winter Davis in the House struck out fiercely at disunion like Andrew Johnson in the Senate, and with the same success.[1] But to understand Mr. Davis's position fairly it is necessary to know something of his history, and he is remarkable enough as a politician to make such a parenthesis interesting.

As for the last eight or ten years the opposition to the slave power developed itself, and it became more and more evident that its ultimate success was only a question of time, it was naturally to be expected that men would appear here and there in the southern States who, either out of ambition or from other motives, would ally themselves with the North, and as the Democratic party had become identified with the slave power, it was evident that these men, if they appeared at all, would be found among the southern Whigs. But there is very little boldness in American politicians, and though it was no rare thing for the southern Whigs to act secretly in concert with the Republicans, only one of them ventured in Congress to place himself openly on the record. His course was that of one man in a hundred thousand.

Mr. Henry Winter Davis of Maryland first rose to any prominence in public life by his connection with the Know-Nothing party in 1854, or thereabouts. When the old Whigs lost their power in the North, the southern Whig States began to fall one after another into Democratic hands. But even the riveting influence of slavery and the growing strength of the Republicans were not enough to unite Whigs and Democrats in the southern border States. They were divided by many years of bitter strife and hatred. To an old Whig in Tennessee, or Kentucky, or Maryland, who had grown up to despise a Democrat as the meanest and most despicable of creatures; who had been taught in the semi-barbarous school of southern barbecues and stump harangues, gouging and pistol shooting, to hate and abhor the very word Democrat with a bitterness unknown to the quieter and more law-abiding northerners, the idea of submitting finally and hopelessly to the Democratic rule, was not to be endured. Accordingly, when the Native American party made its appearance, these men rushed into it, in a mass, as a means of bolstering up their waning power, and

[1] Davis delivered his speech on February 7. It will be found in the Congressional Globe, 36th Congress, 2d Session, Appendix 181.

under the prestige of its extraordinary successes and under-hand organization, managed for a time to sweep everything before them. Among the States which they ruled most completely was Maryland, and among the first to avail himself of this new ladder was Mr. Henry Winter Davis of Baltimore.

But the new movement was not without its drawbacks. One great feature of the Know-Nothings was their enmity to Catholics and the Catholic religion; but in Maryland where the old families still retain their Catholicism and rule the tone of society, no gentleman could become with impunity a leader in a party so obnoxious to them. This alone was cause enough for their hating Davis with a bitter hatred. But this was not all. The secret organization of the Native American attracted large numbers of the worst class of rowdies and bullies into the party, and in Baltimore they made use of their power in the wildest and most disgraceful way, electing a Mayor who sympathized with them, and, on the day of election, surrounding the polls in armed bands. With a sort of fantastic humor, they provided themselves with awls, and punched their political opponents with them, when they came up to deposit their votes. An examination of one sufferer by this torture showed no less than twenty-four such wounds. The amusement became a characteristic of the Baltimore "Plug-ugly," and in the Know-Nothing processions a huge wooden awl was carried about, as one of the insignia of the party. It is among the worst of the charges against Mr. Winter Davis that he allowed himself to speak from a platform on which a symbolical awl was conspicuously placed, and that he himself mentioned in one of his speeches this rowdyism as a mere passing exuberance of the spirit of freedom. In the course of these excesses the evil reached such a height that Baltimore, on election day, lay at the mercy of these ruffians, and several murders of peculiarly brutal and revolting nature heralded and accompanied their triumph.

Outraged in this way, polite society turned on the Native Americans and a bitter war was waged. Mr. Winter Davis gained indeed the political victory for a time, but roused against himself the most intense hatred in that circle of society to which he himself belonged. He, a gentleman, educated, polished, refined, was accused of having countenanced these barbarities; of having given encouragement to crime and protection to murder. Society proscribed him. His name was erased from the books of the clubs. He was persecuted in every way that even female ingenuity could invent. Probably no man in this country ever went through more bitter social trials or a more complete series of mortifications than Mr. Winter Davis and his family at Baltimore; but he was not a man to be crushed by such burdens. He fought it through, and marched on his way.

One may or may not endorse Mr. Davis's course, or believe the excuses and justifications which his friends advance in his favor. It may or may not be true that his ambition dragged him beyond honorable bounds into unprincipled action. But at least it is impossible not to admire the energy and skill of the politician, his buoyancy and his inflexible will.

With these antecedents he took his seat as a member of the Thirty-fourth Congress. It has so happened that in both the Thirty-fourth and Thirty-sixth Congresses, the South Americans, or rather the old Whigs, for such they really are, have held the balance of power in their hands, and more than once the vote of Mr. Winter Davis has turned the scale. So early as the election of Mr. Banks as Speaker[1] his vote exercised an influence which held the opposite party in check. It was his vote that brought to an end the long struggle over the Speakership in 1859-60,[2] and it needed no common courage for a southern man at that time to take the responsibility of electing a Republican Speaker. In the five years of his Congressional course he had made his mark on the House. It is very seldom in that noisy, tumultuous body that any member can command silent attention; but when Mr. Davis rose, members dropped their newspapers, put down their pens, stopped their conversation and crowded around him. He regularly conquered their admiration and finally rose to the first rank of Congressional statesmen. His very appearance told to a certain degree in his favor, for the representatives of the Baltimore "Plugs," perhaps the most reckless and lawless ruffians in the country, was among the very few men in the House who appeared like

---

[1] In the 34th Congress.

[2] Resulting in the election, on February 1, 1860, of William Pennington, of New Jersey.

a quiet, educated, well-bred gentleman. Whatever his associations may have been, his private character was above dispute, and even the scrupulous nicety of his dress and the somewhat studied courtesy of his manner are enough alone to make his bitterest enemies doubt the truth of the charges they themselves bring against him. That his strong points are dashed with a touch of vanity and a certain love of admiration, it is not worth while to deny. There are few public men who are not vain, and generally with much less cause. But even his weaknesses are not without their interest, increasing one's surprise as they do at the life of struggle and conflict he has led.

From the first sitting of the Committee of Thirty-three, Mr. Davis took a bold lead in its deliberations. For him everything depended on the faithfulness of Virginia to the Government, and he fought the disunionists with a desperation warranted by what he had at stake. When it at last became evident that Mr. Crittenden's measure in regard to the Territories was the rock on which they were to split, he did not hesitate to throw over all remaining doubts and hesitation, and declare boldly against it. On the 20th of December, after long discussions and vehement pressure from the South, intended either to drive the Republicans from their position or to break up the Committee, and unite the slave States in the secession movement, and when the scales inclined gradually towards the southern side, and little hope remained that further discussion would be of use, Mr. Davis rose from his seat with a proposition which gave an electric shock to the whole Committee. It was the since well-known measure for the admission of New Mexico.[1] No sooner was it proposed than the southern members, starting as if a bomb-shell had fallen among them, began whispering together, retired into the next chamber and held a long consultation, and finally returned to say that the proposition was inadmissible and not to be thought of. The next day the Committee adjourned for a week, unwilling to renounce all hope, but despairing of any agreement.

The step Mr. Davis had taken was, however, too bold and too

[1] The bill was read for the first time on February 1, 1861, and is printed in the Congressional Globe, 36th Congress, 2d Session, 1326.

skilful, and offered too many advantages, to allow the Republicans to let the chance slip from their hands without an effort, at a time when it was of the gravest importance that the Committee should not be broken up. It was the week of the Christmas holidays. On the 24th, Saturday and Sunday having passed since the Committee adjourned, the Republican members met in caucus and discussed all the proposed measures of conciliation at length. On the 25th, Christmas day, they held another meeting, at which Judge Watts,[1] a gentleman from New Mexico, was present, and told at length all that nine years of experience had taught him about that Territory. His testimony, clear and decided, and lasting through several hours of careful questioning into every particular, was thought conclusive by a majority of the members present, and the next day, at still another meeting, the proposition of Mr. Davis was adopted as a Republican measure. With it was adopted the sketch of an Amendment to the Constitution, providing against the complaints of the southern members as to a possible forced abolition of slavery; an Amendment which met at that time little or no opposition, and which was understood to be merely a reassertion of a similar article of the Chicago platform. And as the fittest person to present these measures in order to carry conviction to the South, the members selected Mr. Adams of Massachusetts, whose position on the slavery question had stood unshaken through sixteen years of trial and sacrifice, and to whose support, at the critical moment, the adoption of the measures was probably due.

It was in this way that the policy of conciliation was initiated. It will be a question that History only can decide, which of the two wings of the Republican party were right; whether that one which saw hope only in an exercise of force, or that which saw in the outbreak of a war for which they could be made in any degree responsible, only the cast of a loaded die, by which they could not win and must lose. This was the sum total of the difference of opinion among the Republicans, and those Democrats and members of the rump of the old Whig party in the North, who flattered themselves with the idea that Mr. Seward and his friends were

[1] John S. Watts.

retracing their steps and modifying their principles, were never more mistaken. The difference was wholly one of future policy; not of recorded principle. The policy of the one wing led to a violent destruction of the slave power; perhaps by war, perhaps by a slave insurrection. The policy of the other wing was to prevent a separation in order to keep the slave power more effectually under control, until its power for harm should be gradually exhausted, and its whole fabric gently and peacefully sapped away. The extremists on the one side did not hesitate to assert that the only cure for the evils of the nation must be looked for in a violent convulsion; that the end of slavery, like all other oppression, was in blood: such was the law of God. The followers of Mr. Seward declared that even if such were law, under some divine system of bloody compensation, it was still their duty to do their utmost to prevent the victory of freedom which they had gained, and which should be a blessing to the American people, from becoming even temporarily its curse. They foresaw, too, as the result of such a contest, a fatal and irresistible revulsion of feeling throughout the country, by which the slave power would be restored to its old position, perhaps at the expense of the northern tier of States, whose resistance to such a reaction would very possibly prove fatal only to themselves. But each portion of the party, notwithstanding the temporary division, was equally hostile to the slave power, and each portion held as sacredly as ever to the principles which had always guided its course.

The full Committee met again on the 28th, and on that day the proposed Amendment to the Constitution was offered by Mr. Adams, and adopted almost unanimously. But in the meanwhile the report of the New Mexico proposition, unexpected and misrepresented as it was, created considerable alarm and opposition. The Senators objected to it, and even Governor Seward was in doubt whether the time for such a step had yet arrived. But on that same day a similar proposition made by Mr. Rice of Minnesota[1] in the Senate Committee, received the Republican votes; and, the last obstacle being thus removed, on the 29th December, as it appears by the Journal of the Committee, Mr. Adams introduced the New Mexico proposition, which was at once adopted by a vote

[1] Henry M. Rice.

of thirteen to eleven, Mr. Bristow of Kentucky[1] being the only southern member who voted in its favor.

The effect of this move was immediate; for, though it satisfied very few persons and commanded the energetic support of still fewer, it still prevented the dissolution of the Committee, and cut at once, as with a knife, through the coalition which was on the brink of forming itself between the border and the cotton States. It drove Mr. Taylor of Louisiana[2] and the other extreme southern members out of the Committee at once; but it gave to the members from the border States an opportunity to remain with honor. Mr. Nelson of Tennessee[3] declared afterward, in his speech before the House, that he had gone up to the Committee on that very morning with his mind made up to announce his formal withdrawal from its deliberation on the ground that there was no chance of reaching an agreement. The change of policy that day initiated, alone prevented him from uniting with the other seceders in their attempt to break down this last bridge by which aid could be hoped for.

The crisis in the Committee was passed, and from this time the interest of their deliberations decreased. But meanwhile the first days of January came on, the blackest our country had seen since the adoption of the Constitution. The traitors were one by one leaving the Cabinet where they had for years shown to the world the singular spectacle of a Government trying to destroy itself. General Scott had at last been summoned to Washington, after Mr. Floyd had, with his usual honesty, counteracted all his previous efforts to place the military force of the nation in a serviceable position. The frauds discovered in the Interior Department had begun to assume a vague and astonishing size. Public confidence and courage were shattered. Everything was in confusion and the new officers found a state of affairs, in the Departments committed to their charge, that filled them with alarm and even despair. And there remained yet two months to be bridged over before any solid foundation for a renewal of hope could be reached.

Through all these scenes Mr. Seward, the great leader of the

[1] Francis M. Bristow.
[2] Miles Taylor.
[3] Thomas A. R. Nelson.

Republicans, had kept silence and had worked in quiet to combine and re-organize the broken and wavering columns of his party. From the first outbreak his course had been clear to his own mind; and he was probably the only man in Congress, on the northern side, who went to Washington prepared for what might happen with a definite policy to meet it. Certainly he was the only one who succeeded in carrying out such a policy and balancing himself and the nation upon it. Early in December the offer had been made to him by the President-elect of the first place in his new administration, and after some hesitation had been accepted. Of this the public knew for some time nothing. But by common consent all eyes were turned on him, and he was overwhelmed by entreaties from men in all sections of the country to do something to save the Union. Utterly panic-stricken they came to him with prayers and tears. The people of Washington came to him on the 1st of January in numbers, with positive assertions that they and the whole city would be in the hands of traitors within a month unless he did something to save them. To such appeals his answer was: "Save yourselves; you alone can do it; organize; form military companies; watch your suspected men." Members of the Cabinet came to him in absolute despair and called on him for counsel. The advice that he gave was not thrown away. Letters on letters came to him from the Union men in the border slave States urging immediate action and asking help and advice. He extended his connections far into the slave States, everywhere striving to guide the Union policy and to raise up and unite the Union sentiment. He became virtually the ruler of the country. With that cool wisdom and philosophical self-control, so peculiar to his character, he comprehended at once the true nature of his position and gave all his energies to carrying on the struggle. Foreseeing that the battle was to be fought in the border States, and that they must at all hazards be held back, at least till the 4th of March, he cleared his eyes, without an effort, of the cobwebs that blinded other men, and devoted himself to the labor of effecting a firm alliance with the Unionists of Virginia and Maryland, to check the evil while there was yet time.

Those who saw and followed Mr. Seward during all the anxieties and cares of this long struggle, are little likely to forget the lessons he then taught them. Cheerful where everyone else was in despair; cool and steady where everyone else was panic-struck; clear-sighted where other men were blind; grand in resource where every resource seemed exhausted; guiding by quiet and unseen influences those who seemed to act independently on their own ground; holding the great threads of public policy in his hand without parade or display, and, with his vast power of combination, touching them all with reference only to one clear and definite end; avoiding harsh contact with all men, and steering with a firm and steady grasp between his friends who were ready to denounce him, and his enemies who were eager to destroy him, the ultras of the North and South alike; yielding without obstinacy where resistance was too great, yet striking with fresh energy wherever resistance seemed weak; pertinacious in his attack, and inexhaustible in his armory of weapons, he fought, during these three months of chaos, a fight which might go down to history as one of the wonders of statesmanship.

It was not till nearly half the session was over and the debate in the Senate approached its close, that he declared himself and his policy to the country.[1] Probably no speech in Congress was ever expected with so much eagerness as his, for it had been announced that he was to be the head of the new administration, which in the absence of his chief made him the most important man in the nation, even without the weight of his great reputation. Forming as it did only one part of his base of operations, it was aimed, as was his whole policy, directly at the border States. It gave form and authority to the other efforts he was making to combine and encourage the Union men in those States, and never were efforts more successful or a course of policy better justified by the result. The effect of the speech was instantaneous. From that day the rumors of war began to subside; the Union men in the South took new courage; public confidence began to re-establish itself, the country breathed more freely and hope rapidly rose. Letters poured in on him from the South, and he received as many from Virginia alone, as he did from his own State. With the short time and the comparatively small means in his power, he could

[1] He spoke on January 12, 1861.—Congressional Globe, 36th Congress, 2d Session, 341.

do little more than give the tone, and the organization of the Union party was very incomplete; but it was enough to form a nucleus for something better, and was effective so far as it went. Luckily for the country, Maryland had an honest man at its head. If a secessionist had then been its governor in Mr. Hicks's place, it is more than probable that under the first violent shock, she would have been dragged out of the Union, as was Georgia, by force of fraud. Andrew Johnson and the Whigs took care of Tennessee; and Kentucky showed no wish to move; so the great and decisive struggle rested always in Virginia. There the secessionists did not dare to declare openly for disunion, but with that specious logic and plausible weakness that had marked more or less nearly all their prominent men from early times, they hid themselves behind the flimsy defence of what they called "reconstruction," by which the anti-slavery portion of the Union was to be thrown aside, and the fable of the Phoenix, or of Medea and Pelias, if experience and appearances be true, was to be at last verified. Already before the election in that State, foreseeing a Convention, which, if not absolutely sympathizing with disunion, must yet be sensitive to every evil influence, Mr. Seward had caused another Convention to be summoned at Washington where all the questions of the day might be discussed by distinguished men from every State, and such measures taken as might seem to them expedient, and offered as a recommendation to the Government.

The Virginia election came at last, and with a long breath of relief the country began to wake from its despair. Slowly the great ship seemed to right itself, broken and water-logged it is true, but not wrecked. A most essential point had been gained, and at last it seemed as though firm ground was felt. But it was still necessary to reach the 4th of March in quiet, and it was very evident that the disunionists there would strain every nerve to force action within the three weeks which still remained. It was then that Mr. Seward's dexterous expedient to control them and paralyze their action, showed its efficiency. With an astuteness that completely outgeneraled all his opponents, he kept the Peace Convention at work until the Inauguration was close at hand, while the Union men in Virginia and the other border States insisted that no step should be taken until the result of that Convention was known. Thus the danger was fought off and the way to the Inauguration was cleared.

Thus all winter long the great battle was kept up with varying success, but on the whole to the disadvantage of the disunionists. Their original hope that the Government would fall to pieces under the shock of their treason, proved vain, and all their efforts to draw any but the cotton States into the rebellion had proved futile. They had been driven from the Government with the disgrace that attaches to thieves and traitors, a disgrace which among themselves they might wear upon their sleeves and call a badge of honor, if they chose, but which with men uninflamed by their passions will be none the less disgraceful. They were held in check by the Government on all sides, and it was evident even to their most enthusiastic supporters that they were on the high road to ruin unless some change for the better took place. Their only means for effecting this was by getting the assistance of Virginia, which would settle the fact of disunion and enable them to force on the world as a "fait accompli" that which no one would acknowledge as good or right in itself. In order to counteract their attempts on Virginia, the more moderate of the Republicans in Congress pressed the passage of the measures passed by the Committee of Thirty-three, which were declared by the southern Whigs sufficient to answer all their purposes. On the passage of these measures the final contest took place, and this time not among the southerners but among the Republicans, who hesitated and doubted about a step which could not do them a straw's weight of harm and which might if properly used save them an overwhelming burden of misfortune. One after another all the men of influence threw their weight into the scales which still wavered in doubt. Mr. Seward, Mr. Winter Davis, and the southern Whigs, Mr. Adams, Mr. Sherman and a large share of the best ability of the party, exhausted their influence in advocating these measures, and still the mass of the party hesitated, and turned for the decisive word to the final authority at Springfield. The word did not come. In its stead came doubtful rumors tending to distract public opinion still more. In spite of the assertions of newspapers and to the surprise of the country it became more and more evident that there was no concerted action between the President-elect and the Republicans at

Washington, and that Mr. Seward had acted all winter on his own responsibility. The effect of this discovery was soon evident in the gradual destruction of party discipline in Congress, where every man began to follow an independent course, or commit himself against the measures proposed, from an idea that the President was against them.

Mr. Lincoln arrived in Washington and took up the reins of control. It soon became very evident that, so far as the Republican party is concerned, secession if properly managed is rather a benefit than a misfortune. Anti-slavery was the only ground on which it could act with anything like unanimity. In ordinary times the tariff bill would have broken it down, and even under the tremendous pressure of disunion, the struggle over the Cabinet shook it to its very centre. On all questions except that of slavery it can never act together with any reliable degree of concert, made up as it is of incongruous elements freshly and roughly joined together. Under these circumstances the task of Mr. Lincoln was one which might well have filled with alarm the greatest statesman that ever lived. He had to deal with men and measures that would have taxed the patience of Washington and required the genius of Napoleon. It was therefore not to be expected, nor indeed wished, that on his arrival he would instantly throw himself into the arms of either set of his friends before judging for himself the merits of the case; nor was it possible that all the dangers and pressing necessities of the time should be wholly apparent to him. The matter of the passage of the Corwin measures became one of secondary interest, the result of those measures depending as they did on the influence which was to prevail in the Cabinet. This influence became now the great feature of the day, and the struggle was vehement between the two wings of the party. The mere fact that the Cabinet had not yet been agreed upon was sufficient to prove that Mr. Lincoln, while placing Mr. Seward in the chief place in his councils, did not intend to allow his influence to rule it, and the result of the contest between the friends of Mr. Winter Davis and Mr. Blair[1] soon decided this question beyond a doubt. Mr. Seward's policy had been to go outside of the party in selecting members of the Cabinet from southern States, and to

[1] Montgomery Blair.

choose men whose influence would have strengthened the administration. The fact that Mr. Blair, a strict Republican, was preferred over any other man to represent Maryland and Virginia in the Cabinet, was decisive of the policy of Mr. Seward.

When once this question was settled it was of little consequence what became of the proposed measures of conciliation, which were worth nothing, except as one weak link in the chain by which the border States were to be held to the Union. Still the battle went on no less fiercely in Congress, and the radical wing of the Republicans, not yet conscious that this question was a mere subordinate, lost on other ground than that on which they resisted it, went so far as to threaten to stop the business of the House, defeat the appropriation bills and throw the burden of an immediate new Congress on the administration. Happily no such folly was committed, and the measure so hardly disputed was passed by bare majorities. The New Mexico proposition was defeated by southern Union votes and no one was sorry to see it so ended. It had been proposed and adopted merely as a means of crushing the Crittenden measures and putting an end to the demand for protection to slavery in the Territories. As such it had answered its purpose, and no one regretted that southern men should take the responsibility of defeating it. On the very morning of the 4th of March, the Senate passed the Amendment to the Constitution by exactly the necessary vote; and even then it was said in Washingon that some careful manipulation, as well as the direct influence of the new President, was needed before this measure, so utterly innocent and unobjectionable, could be passed.

It will be a problem that those who are fond of such riddles may pore over, what would have been the end of the matter if Mr. Seward had then carried his point, and the conciliatory policy had become the policy of the Government. No man, probably, except the actors themselves in these scenes, knows what the course of events really was, yet from what is public it is fair to suppose that Mr. Seward contemplated a very cautious and forbearing course. It is known that he wished to open the Cabinet to the southern Unionists irrespective of party. Hence it is reasonable to suppose that he would have strengthened their hands by every means in his power. Mr. Jefferson Davis, whose whole course was directed towards drawing the border States into the secession movement, and who, to effect this, had restrained his followers from all aggression, had caused the old Constitution to be re-enacted with but few changes, and the old tariff to be adopted in spite of all complaints; Mr. Davis was to be checkmated at all hazards. The Virginia Congressional elections which were to come in May would have been the decisive point. In order to enable the Unionists to carry these and force a reaction, Mr. Seward would no doubt have caused Forts Sumter and Pickens to be abandoned as useless to him except for what they would bring. He would have set every engine to work to redeem the border States and place them in the hands of reliable men, and no doubt he would have employed the same policy upon the Unionists of Georgia and Alabama. Yet towards foreign nations we must suppose that his tone would have been the more dignified, as it was gentle and for-bearing at home. No infringement of our laws, whether in relation to duties or otherwise, would have been permitted, and if at-tempted, would have been instantly resented. And if at last all this caution and delicacy were rewarded by the hoped-for revo-lution in the border States and the gradual disintegration of the seceders, it is not improbable that, exchanging finally his caution for boldness, Mr. Seward would with a single blow have shattered their whole fabric in the dust.

Such is probably the policy which the friends of Mr. Seward hoped to see adopted. Whether it would have answered their hopes, it is of little use to inquire. Like all such attempts at wisdom and moderation in times of heated passions and threatening war, it was swallowed up and crushed under the weight of brute force, that final tribunal to which human nature is subjected or subjects herself without appeal. Yet it is right to make the effort even if overruled. Through all the chaos of anxiety and contest which marked Mr. Seward's reign of two months, it was evident that he at least felt the highest confidence in the course he pursued. He declared himself bent on weathering the storm without the loss of a single life. Under all the dangers and trials, the cares and the triumphs of his dictatorship, he maintained always the same self-control and calmness, never parading his importance and never losing his self-command. "You look worn, Mr. Seward," said a friend to him one day towards the end of the winter. "Yes," he replied with his slow, rough and careless manner; "the short session is generally the hardest work." "God damn you, Seward, you've betrayed your principles and the party; we've followed your lead long enough," growled a Senator at him one day, in answer to some interposed advice on business in the Senate Chamber. The insult was gross enough and pointed enough to hurt perhaps, but caused no retort. In his natural calmness of disposition and his self-taught quiet, he was as immovable outwardly under praise as under blame. Only once was it known that he ever felt what was said of him, and then it was not without reason, when he opened the envelope and read the sonnet which the poet Whittier sent to him from Amesbury.[1]

In this short and superficial sketch of the course of events at the Capitol during the last winter, it is not intended to attempt the accuracy of history, nor would it be possible to detail even the bare record of what took place in those three months without writing a volume at least. Yet merely from this sketch one result plainly appears. It is said very generally among our people that our theory of Government is a failure. We know that it has been the subject of long controversy and stands now as an experiment. As with all other governments, so with this, it was to be expected that time would bring its trials, and until they came, and the fact of their having been endured and surmounted was patent to the world, this experiment, founded by men in whose work theory had been too largely mixed with experience to permit even themselves to feel absolute confidence in it, could never be called a complete success. In the event of such a trial the mere individuals, whom accident made the instruments for upholding or overthrowing the Government, are lost in the interest which attaches to the great argument by which a question of such fearful magnitude is to be decided.

For nearly half a century it has been growing clearer and clearer every day whence this trial was to come. By an unfortunate necessity which has grown with its growth, the country contained in itself, at its foundation, the seeds of its future troubles. By the Constitution a great political, social and geographical or sectional

[1] [Probably "To William H. Seward" in *Complete Poetical Works of John Greenleaf Whittier* (Houghton Mifflin Co., 1904), p. 410.]

power within the Government was created; in its nature a monopoly; in its theory contrary to and subversive of the whole spirit of Republican institutions. A monarchy, such as that of England, may contain, though not without danger, such monopolies and social distinctions, though its permanence must always depend on a nice and intricate adjustment of their powers, but such is not the case with a Republic. Its existence depends upon the absence of such distinctions, and all monopolies or corporations that exercise a direct political influence as such, are contrary to the spirit of the Government and hurtful to its integrity. They must be kept down or they will pervert the whole body politic.

The grand corporation known under the name of the slave-power, peculiarly offensive as it was, not only to the spirit of our Government but to that of our religion and whole civilization, did very shortly pervert the whole body politic, and as an inevitable result of its very existence, the nation divided into parties, one of which favored its continuing to control the Government; the other striving to rescue the power from its hands. While maintaining the Constitution and its grants, good or bad as they might be thought, their effort was to reduce the evil results of such grants to their lowest possible standard and to raise the good results to their highest. After a long and bitter contest the slave power was for the first time defeated, and deprived, not of its legitimate power, not of its privileges as originally granted in the Constitution, but of its control of the Government; and suddenly in the fury of its unbridled license, it raised its hand to destroy that Government. The great secession winter of 1860-61 was therefore the first crucial test of our political system.

Has the system stood that test? The answer will be as various as men's educations and turn of mind. And yet where else, in any country over the broad surface of the globe, has there ever existed the Government capable of sustaining so long and so tremendous a pressure as this! What genius has ever yet described, or what nation has ever drawn from the cumulative wisdom of centuries, a system more strong, more elastic, more tenacious, more full of life and instinct with self-consciousness than ours? Where in all history is there to be found an instance of a power such as slavery has shown itself, peaceably ejected from the Government and forced to become rebels or submit? In other countries it would have needed a violent and bloody struggle to drive it from its throne. Where else is or has there ever been that Government which could for five months remain inactive, while so vast a rebellion was developing itself under its very eyes, without breaking down into anarchy under the weight of its very inactivity? There does not exist and never has existed the Government which could maintain itself and the public peace; which could with wise and cautious patience bear and forbear, wait and endure, and stretch its elastic membranes beyond the limits of all credibility as ours has done during the last year. Nor, if strength is wanted, has ever any Government developed more than our own, when, at one stamp of his foot, the President called the whole nation to arms, and the bristling lines of bayonets poured down from every township in the North, to sustain the integrity of the Union.

Captaine John Smith

SOMETIME GOVERNOUR IN VIRGINIA, AND ADMIRAL OF NEW ENGLAND

Charles Francis Adams was appointed Minister to Great Britain by President Lincoln in March, 1861, and once again his son Henry was chosen to accompany him in the unofficial capacity of private secretary. Once again, too, the son engaged himself as a secret correspondent, hoping, through the pages of the New York Times, *to influence American public opinion in such a way as to assist his father's diplomacy. This delicate venture lasted only until January of 1862 when Henry's authorship of a letter published in the Boston* Courier *was tactlessly revealed and he feared that his identity as the London correspondent of the* Times *was in danger of being discovered.*

Looking about him for some new literary undertaking, Henry became interested in the Pocahontas-John Smith legend and the doubt of its authenticity he had once heard expressed by his father's friend, the historian John Gorham Palfrey. During the year 1862 he engaged sporadically in research on the subject, justifying his occupation with this "literary toy" by the reflection that it was "in some sort a flank, or rather a rear attack, on the Virginia aristocracy, who will be utterly gravelled by it if it is successful." A draft of his essay was finished and sent to Palfrey in May, 1863, but apparently Adams considered that his effort had not been successful after all and he declined to think of publication. Three years later, however, encouraged by Palfrey, his interest in "the old pirate," "that ancient liar Smith" revived, and he rewrote the essay in the form of a review of two old texts which had recently been edited by Charles Deane: Smith's A True Relation of Virginia *and Wingfield's* A Discourse of Virginia. *It was his first published article, and his first work of historical scholarship.*

CAPTAINE JOHN SMITH belonged to the extraordinary school of adventurers who gave so much lustre to the reign of Elizabeth, and whose most brilliant leader King James brought to the Tower and the block. Like Raleigh, though on a much lower level, Smith sustained many different characters. He was a soldier or a sailor indifferently, a statesman when circumstances gave him power, and an author when occasion required. Born in Lincolnshire in 1579, of what is supposed to have been a good Lancashire family, at a very early age he became a soldier of fortune in the Low Countries, and drifted into the Austrian service, where he took part in the campaign of 1600 against the Turks. Afterward he reappeared as a soldier of the Prince of Transylvania, who gave him a coat-of-arms, which was registered at the Herald's College in London. His extraordinary adventures during the three or four years of his life in Eastern Europe were related in his Autobiography, or "True Travels," a work published in London in 1630, near the close of his life. Dr. Palfrey's History of New England contains the earliest critical examination of this portion of Smith's story from

Originally printed in the North American Review for January, 1867. [Unsigned. Reprinted and revised in Chapters of Erie, 1871. Reprinted and further revised in Historical Essays, 1891.]

an historical and geographical point of view, with a result not on the whole unfavorable to Smith.[1]

In 1604 Smith was again in England, where he soon began to interest himself in the enterprise of colonizing America.

On the 10th of April, 1606, King James conferred a charter upon certain persons in England, who took the title of the Virginia Company, and who proceeded to fit out an expedition of three small vessels, containing, in addition to their crews, one hundred and five colonists, headed by a Council, of which Edward Maria Wingfield was chosen President, and Captains Bartholomew Gosnold, John Smith, John Ratcliffe, John Martin, and George Kendall were the other members. After various delays this expedition dropped down the Thames December 20 of the same year, but was kept six weeks in sight of England by unfavorable winds. After a long and difficult voyage, and a further delay of three weeks among the West India Islands, the headlands of Chesapeake Bay were passed April 26, 1607. On the 14th of May following, the colonists formally founded Jamestown.

In the mean while trouble had risen between Smith and his colleagues. Smith's story was told in the "Generall Historie" as follows:—

"Now, Captain Smith, who all this time from their departure from the Canaries was restrained as a prisoner upon the scandalous suggestions of some of the chiefe, (envying his repute), who fained he intended to usurpe the Government, murther the Councell, and make himselfe King; that his confederats were dispersed in all the three ships, and that divers of his confederats that revealed it would affirm it. For this he was committed as a prisoner. Thirteen weeks he remained thus suspected, and by that time the ships should returne, they pretended out of their commisserations to refer him to the Councell in England to receive a check, rather then by particulating his designes make him so odious to the world, as to touch his life, or utterly overthrow his reputation."

Captain Newport, who was about to return to England, exerted his influence so strongly in favor of harmony that Smith was allowed to resume his seat among the Council; but he was not liked by the persons in control of the expedition, and some little light on

[1] Palfrey's History of New England, i. pp. 89-92, note.

the causes of their dislike or suspicion may be found in a passage of Wingfield's "Discourse," which said of Smith that "it was proved to his face that he begged in Ireland, like a rogue without a lycence,"—and he adds, "To such I would not my name should be a companyon." If Smith was accused of conspiring to obtain power, the dark events and questionable expedients of his varied and troubled career might well be flung in his face, and produce a considerable influence on the minds of his judges. Harmony was a blessing little known among the unhappy colonists, and before the close of the year, Captain George Kendall, another of the members of the Council, was accused of the same crime with which Smith had been charged, and was tried, convicted, and actually executed.

Newport, who had great influence over the colonists, sailed for England June 22, leaving three months' supplies behind him, and promising to return in seven months with a new company of settlers. His departure was followed by disasters and troubles of every description. The mortality was frightful. More than forty deaths took place before September, some caused by fevers and sickness, some by the Indians, but the larger number by famine. The kindness of the Indians alone, according to the express statement of Percy, who was among the survivors, preserved the remaining colonists from the fate of the lost Roanoke settlement of 1585.

Even this condition of the colony, though during five months together not five able-bodied men could mount the defences, had no effect in quieting the jealousies and dissensions of the leaders. Captain Gosnold died, leaving only Wingfield, Ratcliffe, Smith, and Martin in the Council. The last three combined to depose Wingfield; and this revolution took place September 10, without resistance. Ratcliffe, as the next in order, was chosen President.

"As at this time," said Smith, "were most of our chiefest men either sicke or discontented, the rest being in such dispaire as they would rather starve and rot with idleness then be perswaded to do anything for their owne reliefe without constraint,—our victualles being now within eighteene dayes spent, and the Indians' trade decreasing, I was sent to the mouth of ye river to trade for Corne, and try the River for Fish; but our fishing we could not effect by reason of the stormy weather." Fortunately the Indians were found willing to trade for corn, and by means of their supplies the lives of the settlers were saved. On the 9th of November, Smith made a longer excursion, partially exploring the Chickahominy, and was received with much kindness by the Indians, who supplied him with corn enough to have "laded a ship." Elated by his success and encouraged by the friendly attitude of the savages,—or, according to his own account, eager "to discharge the imputation of malicious tungs, that halfe suspected I durst not, for so long delaying,"—he determined to carry on his exploration of the Chickahominy to its source. On the 10th of December he started in the pinnace, which he left at a place he called Apocant, forty miles above the mouth of the Chickahominy, and continued his journey in a barge. Finally, rather than endanger the barge, he hired a canoe and two Indians to row it, and with two of his own company, named Robinson and Emry, went twenty miles higher. "Though some wise men may condemn this too bould attempt of too much indiscretion, yet if they well consider the friendship of the Indians in conducting me, the desolatenes of the country, the probabilitie of [discovering] some lacke, and the malicious judges of my actions at home, as also to have some matters of worth to incourage our adventurers in England, might well have caused any honest minde to have done the like, as wel for his own discharge as for the publike good."

At length they landed to prepare their dinner, and Smith with one Indian walked on along the course of the river, while Robinson and Emry with the other Indian remained to guard the canoe. Within a quarter of an hour he heard a hallooing of Indians and a loud cry, and fearing treachery, he seized his guide, whose arm he bound fast to his own hand, while he prepared his pistol for immediate use. As they "went discoursing," an arrow struck him on the right thigh, but without harm. He soon found himself attacked by some two hundred savages, against whose arrows he used his guide as a shield, discharging his pistol three or four times. The Indian chief, Opechankanough, then called upon him to surrender, and the savages laid their bows on the ground, ceasing to shoot.

"My hinde treated betwixt them and me of conditions of peace; he discovered me to be the Captaine. My request was to retire to ye boate; they demaunded my armes; the rest they saide were slaine, only me they would reserve; the Indian importuned me not to shoot. In retiring, being in the midst of a low quagmire, and minding them more then my steps, I stept fast into the quagmire, and also the Indian in drawing me forth. Thus surprised, I resolved to trie their mercies; my armes I caste from me, till which none durst approach me. Being ceazed on me, they drew me out and led me to the King."

Thus far, to avoid confusion, the account has followed the "True Relation," written by Smith, and published in London in 1608, the year after the events described.[1] In 1624 Smith published in London his "Generall Historie," which contained a version of the story varying essentially from that of the "True Relation." In continuing the account of his captivity, the two narratives will be placed side by side, for convenience of comparison, and the principal variations will be printed in Italics.

After describing the circumstances of his capture, which took place far up the Chickahominy River, Smith continued in his double narrative:—

A TRUE RELATION 1608

"They drew me out and led me to the King. I presented him with a compasse diall. . . . With kinde speeches and bread he requitted me, conducting me where the Canow lay, and John Robinson slaine, with 20 or 30 arrowes in him. Emry I saw not. I perceived by the aboundance of fires all over the woods, *at each place I expected when they would execute me, yet they used me with what kindness they could.* Approaching their Towne, which was within 6 miles where I was taken, . . . the Captaine conducting me to his lodging, a quarter of venison and some ten

THE GENERALL HISTORIE 1624

"Then according to their composition they drew him forth and led him to the fire where his men were slaine. Diligently they chafed his benumbed limbs. He demanding for their Captaine they showed him Opechankanough king of Pamaunkee, to whom he gave a round ivory double-compass Dyall. Much they marvailed at the playing of the Fly and Needle. . . . *Notwithstanding, within an houre after they tied him to a tree, and as many as could stand about him prepared to shoot him,* but the King holding up the Compass in his hand, they all laid down their bowes and arrowes, and in a triumphant manner led him to Orapaks, where he was after their

[1] *A True Relation of Virginia.* By Captain John Smith. With an Introduction and Notes, by Charles Deane. Boston, 1866.

pound of bread I had for supper; what I left was reserved for me, and sent with me to my lodging. Each morning 3 women presented me three great platters of fine bread; *more venison than ten men could devour I had;* my gowne, points and garters, my compas and a tablet they gave me again; though 8 ordinarily guarded me, I wanted not what they could devise to content me; and still our longer acquaintance increased our better affection. . . . I desired he [the King] would send a messenger to Paspahegh [Jamestown] with a letter I would write, by which they shold understand how kindly they used me, and that I was well, least they should revenge my death; this he granted, and sent three men, in such weather as in reason were unpossible by any naked to be endured. . . . The next day after my letter came a salvage to my lodging with his sword to have slaine me. . . . This was the father of him I had slayne, whose fury to prevent, the King presently conducted me to another Kingdome, upon the top of the next northerly river, called Youghtanan. Having feasted me, he further led me to another branch of the river called Mattapament; to two other hunting townes they led me, and to each of these countries a house of the great Emperor of Pewhakan,

manner kindly feasted and well used. . . . Smith they conducted to a long house where *thirtie or fortie tall fellowes did guard him,* and ere long *more bread and venison was brought him than would have served twentie* men. I think his stomach at that time was not very good; what he left they put in baskets and tyed over his head; about midnight they set the meat again before him. All this time not one of them would eat a bit with him, till the next morning they brought him as much more, and then did they eate all the olde, and reserved the newe as they had done the other; which made him think they would fat him to eate him. Yet in this desperate estate to defend him from the cold, one Maocassater brought him his gowne in requitall of some beads and toyes Smith had given him at his first arrival in Virginia.

"Two dayes after, a man would have slaine him (but that the guard prevented it) for the death of his sonne, to whom they conducted him to recover the poore man then breathing his last. . . . In part of a Table booke he writ his minde to them at the Fort, and . . . the messengers . . . according to his request went to Jamestowne in as bitter weather as could be of frost and snow, and within three dayes returned with an answer.

"Then they led him to the Youthtanunds, the Mattaponients, the Payankatanks, the Nantaughtacunds, and Omawmanients upon the rivers of Rapahannock and *Patawomeck, over all those rivers* and back againe by divers other severall nations to the King's hab-

whom as yet I supposed to bee at the Fals; *to him I told him I must goe, and so returne to Paspahegh*. After this foure or five dayes march, we returned to Rasawrack, the first towne they brought me too, where binding the Mats in bundles, they marched two dayes journey and crossed the river of Youghtanan where it was as broad as Thames; so conducting me to a place called Menapacute in Pamaunke, where ye King inhabited. . . .

"From hence this kind King conducted mee to a place called Topahanocke, a kingdome upon another River northward. The cause of this was, that the yeare before, a shippe had beene in the River of Pamaunke, who having been kindly entertained by Powhatan their Emperour, they returned thence, and discovered the River of Topahanocke, where being received with like kindnesse, yet he slue the King and tooke of his people; and they supposed I were hee, but the people reported him a great man that was Captaine, and using mee kindly, the next day we departed. . . .

"The next night I lodged at a hunting town of Powhatams, and the next day arrived at Waranacomoco upon the river of Pamauncke, where the great king is resident. . . .

"Arriving at Weramocomoco, their Emperour . . . kindly

itation at Pamaunkee, where they entertained him with most strange and fearfull Conjurations. . . .

"At last they brought him to Meronocomoco, where was Powhatan their Emperor. Here more than two hundred of those grim Courtiers stood wondering at him, as he had been a monster; till Powhatan and his trayne had put themselves in their greatest braveries. . . . At his entrance before the King, all the people gave a great shout. The Queene of Appamatuck was appointed to bring him water to wash his hands, and another brought him a bunch of feathers, instead of a Towell to dry them. *Having feasted him after their best barbarous manner they could, a long consultation was held; but the conclusion was, two great stones were brought before Powhatan; then as many as could lay their hands on him dragged him to them, and thereon laid his head; and being ready with their clubs to beate out his braines, Pocahontas the King's dearest daughter, when no intreaty could prevaile, got his head in her armes, and laid her owne upon his to save him from death; whereat the Emperour was contented he should live to make him hatchets, and her bells, beads, and copper*. . . .

"Two dayes after, Powhatan having disguised himselfe in the most fearfullest manner he could . . . more like a devil than a man, with some two hundred more as blacke as himselfe, came unto him and told him now they were friends, and presently he should goe to Jamestowne, to send him two great gunnes and a grynd-

welcomed me with good wordes and great Platters of sundrie Victuals, *assuring mee his friendship, and my libertie within foure dayes.* . . . Hee desired mee to forsake Paspahegh, and to live with him upon his River, —a Countrie called Capa Howasicke; hee promised to give me Corne, Venison, or what I wanted to feede us; Hatchets and Copper wee should make him, and none should disturbe us. This request I promised to performe; and thus having with all the kindness hee could devise, sought to content me, hee sent me home *with 4 men,* one that usually carried my Gowne and Knapsacke after me, two other loded with bread, and one to accompanie me. . . .

"From Weramocomoco is but 12 miles, yet the Indians trifled away that day, and would not goe to our Forte by any perswasions; but in certain olde hunting houses of Paspahegh we lodged all night. The next morning ere Sunne rise, we set forward for our Fort, where we arrived within an houre, where each man with truest signes of joy they could expresse welcomed mee, except M. Archer, and some 2 or 3 of his, who was then in my absence sworne Counsellour, though not with the consent of Captaine Martin. Great blame and imputation was laide upon mee by them for the losse of our two men which the

stone, for which he would give him the Country of Capahowosick, and for ever esteeme him as his sonne Nantaquoud. So to Jamestowne *with 12 guides* Powhatan sent him, *he still expecting (as he had done all this long time of his imprisonment) every houre to be put to one death or other, for all their feasting.* But almightie God (by his divine providence) had mollified the hearts of those sterne Barbarians with compassion. The next morning betimes they came to the Forte. . . .

"*Now in Jamestowne they were all in combustion, the strongest preparing once more to run away with the Pinnace; which with the hazzard of his life, with Sabre, falcon, and musket shot, Smith forced now the third time to stay or sinke.* Some, no better than they should be, had plotted with the President the next day to have put him to death by the Leviticall law, for the lives of Robinson and Emry, pretending the fault was his that had led them to their ends: but *he quickly tooke such order with such lawyers, that he layd them by the heels till he sent some of them prisoners for England.* . . .

"Newport got in and arrived at James Towne not long after the redemption of Captaine Smith. . . .

"Written by Thomas Studley, the first Cape Merchant in Virginia, Robert Fenton, Edward Harrington, and J. S."

Indian slew; insomuch that they purposed to depose me; but *in the midst of my miseries it please God to send Captaine Nuport, who arriving there the same night so tripled our joy as for a while these plots against me were deferred,* though with much malice against me which Captain Newport in a short time did plainly see."

Comparison of the two narratives thus for the first time placed side by side, betrays a tone of exaggeration in the later story. Eight guards, which had been sufficient in 1608, were multiplied into thirty or forty tall fellows in 1624. What was enough for ten men at the earlier time would feed twenty according to the later version. In 1608 four guides were an ample escort to conduct Smith to Jamestown, but they were reinforced to the number of twelve sixteen years afterward. With the best disposition toward Smith, one cannot forget that he belonged to the time when Falstaff and his misbegotten knaves in Kendal Green appeared upon the stage. The execution wrought upon the lawyers who wished to try Smith for his life on his return to Jamestown was prompt and decisive according to the story of 1624, but in 1608 "in the midst of my miseries it pleased God to send" Captain Newport to defer the plots of Smith's enemies. With sabre, falcon, and musket-shot he forced the mutinous crew of the pinnace to stay or sink, according to the "Generall Historie," while the "True Relation" was silent as to any feat of arms, but simply said that Captain Newport arrived the same evening.

The same exaggeration marked the account of Smith's treatment among the savages. According to the story written a few months after the event, a people was described, savage, but neither cruel nor bloodthirsty; reckless perhaps of life in battle, but kind and even magnanimous toward their captive. The "True Relation" implied that no demonstration was made against Smith's life, such as he described in 1624 as occurring within an hour after his capture. Only a few days after he was taken prisoner, he directed Opechankanough to take him to Powhatan, and even then he knew that he was to be allowed to return to Jamestown. "To him I told him I must go, and so return to Paspahegh." Powhatan received him with cordiality, and having sought to content him with all the kindness he could devise, sent him with a guard of honor back to his friends. In the "True Relation," the behavior of the Indians toward Smith was more humane than he would have received at the hands of civilized peoples. He found no cause to fear for his life, except from a savage whose son he had killed, and from whom Opechankanough protected him. One line indeed alluded to a fear that they fed him so fat as to make him much doubt they meant to sacrifice him; but this evidence of the kindness of the Indians implied that he believed himself to have been mistaken in having entertained the suspicion. Yet in 1624, throughout his long imprisonment, he was still expecting every hour to be put to one death or another.

These variations would not concern the ordinary reader of colonial history, if they stopped at trifling inconsistencies. They would merely prove the earlier narrative to be the safer authority for historians to follow, which is an established law of historical criticism. The serious divergence occurred in Smith's account of his visit to Powhatan, which in 1608 was free from the suspicion of danger to his life, but in 1624 introduced Pocahontas as his savior from a cruel execution. The absence of Pocahontas, and of any allusion to her interference, or of reference to the occasion on which she interfered, makes the chief characteristic of the earlier story, and if the law of evidence is sound, requires the rejection of the latter version as spurious.

Smith's silence in 1608 about his intended execution and his preservation by Pocahontas was the more remarkable, because the "True Relation" elsewhere mentioned Pocahontas, with every appearance of telling the whole share she had in Smith's affairs. Smith's captivity occurred in December. In the following month of May, Smith imprisoned at Jamestown some Indians whom he suspected of treachery. The "True Relation" continued:—

"Powhatan, understanding we detained certaine Salvages, sent his daughter, a child of tenne yeares old, which not only for feature, countenance, and proportion much exceedeth any of the rest of his people, but for wit and spirit the only Nonpareil of his Country:

this he sent by his most trustie messenger, called Rawhunt, as much exceeding in deformitie of person, but of a subtill wit and crafty understanding. He with a long circumstance told me how well Powhatan loved and respected mee, and in that I should not doubt any way of his kindnesse he had sent his child, which he most esteemed, to see me: . . . his little daughter he had taught this lesson also."

Smith regarded Pocahontas as a person so much worth winning to his interests that he surrendered the prisoners to her.

"We guarded them as before to the Church, and after prayer gave them to Pocahontas, the King's daughter, in regard of her father's kindnesse in sending her. . . . Pocahontas also we requited, with such trifles as contented her, to tel that we had used the Paspaheyans very kindly in so releasing them."

Had Pocahontas saved Smith's life four months before, Smith would have been likely to surrender the prisoners out of gratitude to her, rather than "in regard of her father's kindnesse in sending" his favorite child to ask a return for his own hospitality.

No American needs to learn that Pocahontas is the most romantic character in the history of his country. Her name and story are familiar to every schoolboy, and families of the highest claim to merit trace their descent from the Emperor's daughter that saved the life of Captain John Smith. In the general enthusiasm, language and perhaps common-sense have been strained to describe her attributes. Her beauty and wild grace, her compassion and disinterestedness, her Christian life and pure character, have been dwelt upon with warmth the more natural as the childhood of the nation furnished little latitude to imagination. One after another, American historians have contented themselves with repeating the words of the "Generall Historie," heaping praises which no critics were cynical enough to gainsay, now on the virtues of Pocahontas, and now on the courage and constancy of Smith.

The exclusive share of the later narrative in shaping popular impressions was well shown by the standard authority for American history. In the early editions of Bancroft's "History of the United States," the following version of Smith's adventure was given:—

"The gentle feelings of humanity are the same in every race, and in every period of life; they bloom, though unconsciously, even in the bosom of a child. Smith had easily won the confiding fondness of the Indian maiden; and now, the impulse of mercy awakened within her breast, she clung firmly to his neck, as his head was bowed to receive the strokes of the tomahawk. Did the childlike superstition of her kindred reverence her interference as a token from a superior power? Her fearlessness and entreaties persuaded the council to spare the agreeable stranger, who might make hatchets for her father, and rattles and strings of beads for herself, the favorite child. The barbarians, whose decision had long been held in suspense by the mysterious awe which Smith had inspired, now resolved to receive him as a friend, and to make him a partner of their councils. They tempted him to join their bands, and lend assistance in an attack upon the white men at Jamestown; and when his decision of character succeeded in changing the current of their thoughts, they dismissed him with mutual promises of friendship and benevolence."

In a note appended to these paragraphs the author quoted:—

"Smith, I. 158-162, and II. 29-33. The account is fully contained in the oldest book printed on Virginia in our Cambridge library. It is a thin quarto, in black-letter, by John Smith, printed in 1608,— A True Relation, etc."

The story, in passing through the medium of Mr. Bancroft's mind, gained something which did not belong to the original, or belonged to it only in a modified degree. The spirit of Smith infused itself into the modern historian, as it had already infused itself into the works of his predecessors. The lights were intensified; the shadows deepened; the gradations softened. The copy surpassed its model. This tendency went so far that the author quoted the "True Relation" as the full authority for what was to be found only in the "Generall Historie," if indeed it was all to be found even there. When Mr. Bancroft collated his version of the story with the black-letter pamphlet in the Cambridge library, the popular reputation of Smith had already created an illusion in his mind resembling the optical effect of refracted light. He saw something which did not exist,—the exaggerated image of a figure beyond.

The labors of Charles Deane have made necessary a thorough examination into the evidence bearing on Smith's story; and Deane's notes make such an inquiry less laborious than the mass of material seemed to threaten. With that aid, an analysis of the evidence can be brought within narrow compass.

The first President of the colony was Edward Maria Wingfield, who in September, 1607, was deprived of his office, and placed in confinement by Smith and the other members of the Council. When Newport—who with a new company of settlers arrived at Jamestown Jan. 8, 1608, immediately after Smith's release—began his second return voyage to London, he took the deposed President Wingfield with him, and they arrived safely at Blackwall on the 21st of May. Wingfield kept a diary during his stay in Virginia, and after his return he wrote with its assistance a defence of himself and his administration, privately circulated in manuscript, and at a later period used by Purchas, but afterward forgotten and hidden in the dust of the Lambeth Library. From this obscurity it was drawn by Mr. Deane, who published it with notes in the fourth volume of the Archæologia Americana in 1860.[1] Excepting a few papers of little consequence, this is the earliest known writing which came directly from the colony. The manuscript of Smith's "True Relation," its only possible rival, could not have reached England before the month of July, while Wingfield's manuscript was intended for immediate circulation in May or June. Wingfield's work, which was called "A Discourse of Virginia," is therefore new authority on the early history of the colony, and has peculiar value as a test for the correctness of the "True Relation." Its account of Smith's captivity could only have been gained from his own mouth, or from those to whom he told the story, and its accuracy can be tested by the degree of its coincidence with the "True Relation."

A number of passages in this short pamphlet would be worth extracting; but the inquiry had best be narrowed to the evidence in regard to Pocahontas. The passage from Wingfield, telling of Smith's adventures among the Indians, ran as follows:—

"*Dec.* The 10th of December Mr. Smith went up the ryver of the Chechohomynies to trade for corne. He was desirous to see the

[1] *A Discourse of Virginia.* By Edward Maria Wingfield, the First President of the Colony. Edited by Charles Deane, Member of the American Antiquarian Society, and of the Massachusetts Historical Society. Boston: Privately printed. 1860.

heade of that river; and when it was not passible with the shallop, he hired a cannow and an Indian to carry him up further. The river the higher grew worse and worse. Then he went on shoare with his guide, and left Robinson and Emmery, twoe of our men in the cannow, which were presently slaine by the Indians, Pamoanke's men, and he himself taken prysoner; and by the means of his guide his lief was saved. And Pamaonche haveing him prisoner, carryed him to his neybors wyroances to see if any of them knewe him for one of those which had bene, some two or three yeres before us, in a river amongst them Northward, and taken awaie some Indians from them by force. At last he brought him to the great Powatan (of whome before wee had no knowledg), who sent him home to our towne the viiith of Januarie. . . .

"Mr. Archer sought how to call Mr. Smith's lief in question, and had indited him upon a chapter in Leviticus for the death of his twoe men. He had had his tryall the same daie of his retorne, and I believe his hanging the same or the next daie, so speedie is our law there; but it pleased God to send Captn. Newport unto us the same evening to our unspeakable comfort, whose arrivall saved Mr. Smyth's life and mine."

Deane, in editing Wingfield in 1860, furnished a note upon this passage, in which for the first time a doubt was thrown upon the story of Pocahontas's intervention. Yet the discovery of Wingfield's narrative added little to the evidence contained in the "True Relation,"—always a well-known work. The "Discourse" supplied precise dates, fixing Smith's departure on the 10th of December, and his return on the 8th of January, his absence being exactly four weeks in length; it said that Smith's guide saved his life, which might be a variation from the story of the "True Relation;" it dwelt on the danger Smith ran, from the enmity of Archer, which might be only the result of Wingfield's dislike of that person. In general, this new evidence, though clearly independent of the "True Relation," confirmed it in essentials, and especially in the omission of reference to Pocahontas. So remarkable an incident as her protection of Smith, if known to Wingfield, would scarcely have been omitted in this narrative, which must have contained the version of Smith's adventures current among the colonists after his return to Jamestown.

These two works are the only contemporaneous authority for the first year of the colonial history. A wide gap intervenes between them and the next work; and the strength of Deane's case rests so largely on the negative evidence offered by the "True Relation" and the "Discourse," that for his purpose further search was useless. Every one, whether believing or disbelieving the "Generall Historie," must agree that Pocahontas was not mentioned, either by name or by implication, as the preserver of Smith's life either by Smith in the "True Relation" or by Wingfield in his "Discourse." The inquiry might stop here, and each reader might be left to form his own opinion as to the relative value of the conflicting narratives; but the growth of a legend is as interesting as the question of its truth.

Newport returned to England April 10, 1608, carrying Wingfield with him, and leaving Ratcliffe President of the Colony, with Martin, Smith, and Archer in the Council, together with a new member, Matthew Scrivener, who had arrived with Newport. Smith in June explored successfully a part of Chesapeake Bay, and returning July 21, found, according to the "Generall Historie," the colonists in a miserable condition, unable to do anything but complain of Ratcliffe, whose principal offence appears to have been his obliging the colonists to build him "an unnecessary building for his pleasure in the woods." Ratcliffe, whose real name was Sicklemore, was a poor creature, if the evidence in regard to him can be believed. He was deposed, and Scrivener, Smith's "deare friend," though then exceedingly ill, succeeded him as President. This revolution was rapidly effected; for three days later, July 24, Smith again set out with twelve men, to finish his explorations, and made a complete tour round the bay, which supplied his materials for the map published at Oxford in 1612. He did not return to Jamestown till the 7th of September, and on the 10th he assumed the Presidency, "by the Election of the Councell and request of the Company." Scrivener appears merely to have held the office during Smith's pleasure, and voluntarily resigned it into his hands.

The history of Smith's administration of the colony from Sept. 10, 1608, till the end of September, 1609, is given in the "Generall Historie," and may be studied with advantage as an example of Smith's style. Whatever may have been the merits of his government, he had no better success than his predecessors, and he not only failed to command obedience, but was left almost or quite without a friend. He was ultimately deposed and sent to England under articles of complaint. The precise tenor of these articles is unknown; but Mr. Deane has found in the Colonial Office a letter of Ratcliffe, alias Sicklemore, dated October 4, 1609, in which he announced to the Lord Treasurer that "this man [Smith] is sent home to answere some misdemeanors whereof I perswade me he can scarcely clear himselfe from great imputation of blame." Beyond a doubt the difficulties of the situation were very great, and the men Smith had to control were originally poor material, and were made desperate by their trials; but certainly his career in Virginia terminated disastrously, both for himself and for the settlement. The Virginia Company, notwithstanding his applications, never employed him again.

The colony went from bad to worse. George Percy, a brother of the Earl of Northumberland, succeeded Smith in the Presidency. The condition of the colonists between Smith's departure in October, 1609, and the arrival of Sir Thomas Gates in May, 1610, was terrible. Percy was so "sicke hee could neither goe nor stand." Ratcliffe, with a number of others, was killed by Indians. The remainder fed on roots, acorns, fish, and actually on the savages whom they killed, and on each other,—one man murdering his wife and eating her. Out of the whole number, said to have been five hundred, not more than sixty were living when Gates arrived; and he immediately took them on board ship, and abandoning Jamestown, set sail for England. Only by accident they met a new expedition under Lord Delaware, at the mouth of the river, which brought a year's provisions, and restored the fortunes of the settlement. In spite of the discouragement produced in England by these disasters, the Company renewed its efforts, and again sent out Sir Thomas Gates with six vessels and three hundred men, who arrived in August, 1611. The government was then in the hands of Sir Thomas Dale, who assumed it in May, 1611, and retained it till 1616. If the ultimate success of the colony was due to any single man, the merit appears to belong to Dale; for his severe and despotic rule crushed the insubordination that had been the curse of the State, compelled the idle to work, and maintained order between the colonists and the Indians.

In the mean while Smith, who had taken final leave of the colony, appears to have led a quiet life in London during several years. Lost from sight during the years 1610 and 1611, he appeared again in 1612 busied in the same direction as before. In that year he published at Oxford a short work called "A Map of Virginia. With a Description of the Countrey, the Commodities, People, Government, and Religion. Written by Captain Smith, sometimes Governour of the Countrey. Whereunto is annexed the proceedings of those Colonies, &c., by W. S." The latter part of the publication, which purported to be drawn from the writings of certain colonists, was afterward reprinted, with alterations, as the Third Book of the "Generall Historie," from the title of which it appears that "W. S." stood for the initials of William Simons, Doctor of Divinity.

In this tract only one passage bore upon Smith's story of Pocahontas. Among the customs described as peculiar to the Indians was the form of execution practised against criminals. Their heads, Smith said, were placed upon an altar, or sacrificing-stone, while "one with clubbes beates out their braines." During his captivity Smith added, not indeed that he had actually seen this mode of execution, but that an Indian had been beaten in his presence till he fell senseless, without a cry or complaint. The passage is remarkable for more than one reason. In the first place, the mode of execution there described was uncommon, if not unknown, among the Indians of the sea-coast; in the second place, the passage contained the germ of Smith's later story. Practised lawyers may decide whether, under the ordinary rules of evidence, this passage implies that Smith had himself not been placed in the position described, and future students may explain why Smith should have suppressed his own story, supposing it to have been true. The inference is strong that if anything of the sort had occurred, it would have been mentioned here; and this argument is strengthened by a short narration of his imprisonment given in the second part of the pamphlet, for which Dr. Simons was the nominal authority. This version ran as follows:—

"A month those barbarians kept him prisoner. Many strange triumphs and conjurations they made of him; yet he so demeened himself amongst them as he not only diverted them from surprising the fort, but procured his own liberty, and got himself and his company such estimation among them that those savages admired him as a Demi God. So returning safe to the Fort, once more stayed the pinnace her flight for England."

This work was, as above mentioned, afterward reprinted, under the author's name, as the Third Book of the "Generall Historie." The passage just quoted was there reproduced with the evidently intentional substitution of "six or seven weekes" for "a month," as in the original. In the "Generall Historie" the concluding paragraph was omitted, and in its place stood, "The manner how they used and delivered him is as followeth." Then, breaking abruptly into the middle of the old narrative, the story which has been quoted was interpolated.

The narrative in the second part of the "Map of Virginia," of which the above extract forms a part, was signed by the name of Thomas Studley alone, while in the "Generall Historie" the enlarged account bore also the signatures of Edward Harrington, Robert Fenton, and Smith himself. A question may arise as to the extent to which these persons should be considered as dividing with Smith the responsibility for the story. Thomas Studley died on the 28th of August, 1607. Both he and Edward Harrington had lain four months in their graves before Smith ever heard of Powhatan or Pocahontas. The date of Robert Fenton's death is not so clear, but there is no reason to suppose that he had any share in the narration of events which Smith alone witnessed.

The argument so far as the Oxford tract is concerned would be strong enough, if it went no further; but it becomes irresistible when this tract not only mentions Pocahontas, but introduces her as the savior of Smith's life, although it says no word of her most famous act in this character. The allusion occurred toward the end of the pamphlet, where the assumed writer took occasion to defend Smith against certain charges, one of them being an alleged scheme on his part of marrying Powhatan's daughter Pocahontas in order to acquire a claim to the throne. The writer denied the charge, and added:—

"It is true she was the very nonparell of his kingdome, and at most not past 13 or 14 yeares of age. Very often shee came to our fort with what shee could get for Captaine Smith, that ever loved and used all the countrie well, but her especially he ever much respected; and she so well requited it that when her father intended to have surprised him, shee, by stealth in the darke night, came through the wild woods and told him of it."

The Oxford tract of 1612 may be considered decisive that down to that date the story of Pocahontas had not been made public. Here we take leave of Smith as an authority for a period of some ten years, during which he published but one work, not relating to the present subject. An entirely new class of colonists had in 1610-1611 taken the place of the first settlers, almost exterminated by the disasters of 1609-1610. Among the new-comers in the train of Lord Delaware, in 1610, was William Strachey, who held the office of Secretary of the Colony. Little is known of Strachey, except that after his return to England he compiled a work called the "Historie of Travaile into Virginia," never completed in its original plan, but still extant in two neatly written manuscripts, printed by the Hakluyt Society in 1849. The date of its composition was probably about the year 1615. It consisted largely of extracts from Smith's previous works, though without acknowledgement of their origin; it also contained original matter, and especially some curious references to Pocahontas,[1] but no reference, direct or indirect, to her agency in saving Smith's life, and no trace of the high esteem which such an act would have won for her.

Next in order after Strachey's manuscript comes a work which is quite original, and gives perhaps the best account of the colony ever made public by an eye-witness. This is a small volume in quarto, printed in London in 1615, and called "A True Discourse of the Present Estate of Virginia . . . till the 18th of June, 1614, together with . . . the Christening of Powhatan's daughter and her Marriage with an Englishman. Written by Raphe Hamor, late Secretarie in the Colonie." It contains a minute and graphic story how "Pocahuntas, King Powhatan's daughter, whose fame has spread even to England, under the name of Non Parella," while staying with some tribe, subject to her father, on the Potomac, was seized and carried away by Captain Argol, who had sailed up that

[1] See Deane's edition of the True Relation, p. 72.

river on a trading expedition. Her imprisonment as a hostage at
Jamestown, her visit to her father's residence with Sir Thomas Dale
and a strong force of English, Powhatan's failure to redeem her, and
her subsequent marriage to John Rolfe April 5, 1613, are all circum-
stantially narrated; and finally an extremely interesting account is
given of a visit which Hamor made to Powhatan, and of the conversation he had with that extraordinary savage. Besides this work
of Hamor, the volume also contains several letters from persons in
Virginia, one of which is by John Rolfe, written with the object of
justifying his marriage. Afterward, when the arrival of Pocahontas
in England had excited an interest throughout Europe in her story,
Hamor's book was translated and published in Germany.

Although repeated allusions to Pocahontas occur in the works already mentioned, in Hamor she makes, for the first time, her appearance as a person of political importance. In the "True Relation"
Smith represented her as a pretty and clever child ten years old,
once sent with a trusted messenger by Powhatan to the fort to en-
treat the liberation of some Indians whom Smith had seized. The
Oxford tract mentioned her as a friend of Smith, but a mere child.
Strachey gave a curious description of her intimate relations with
the colony during his residence there:—

"Pocahuntas, a well featured but wanton yong girle, Powhatan's
daughter, sometymes resorting to our fort, of the age then of eleven
or twelve yeares, would get the boyes forth with her into the mar-
kett place, and make them wheele, falling on their hands, turning
up their heeles upwards, whome she would followe and wheele
so her self, naked as she was, all the fort over."

Pocahontas was then apparently considered as a child like any
other; but from the time when Argol treacherously seized her she
took an important position,—in the first place, as the guaranty of
a peace which Powhatan promised, and preserved during the remainder of her life and of his own; in the second place, as a person
calculated to excite interest in England in behalf of the colony; and
finally, as an eminent convert to the English Church, through whom
a religious influence might be exercised among her father's subjects.
Hamor's book was filled with her history, and Rolfe's letter showed
much anxiety to prove the propriety of his course in marrying her.
Both writers were interested in exciting as much sympathy for her

as could be roused. Yet neither the one nor the other alluded to the act which has since become her first claim to praise, and which has almost thrown the rest of her story out of sight. There is no reason to suppose that in Virginia in 1614 the persons best informed were yet aware that Pocahontas had saved Smith's life.

In the month of June, 1616, Sir Thomas Dale arrived at Plymouth on his return home, bringing with him among his suite the baptized Pocahontas, then called Rebecca Rolfe, who with her husband and child came at the charge of the Company to visit England, and to prove to the world the success of the colony. She became at once the object of extraordinary attention, and in the following winter she was the most distinguished person in society. Her portrait taken at that time still exists, and shows a somewhat hard-featured figure, with a tall hat and ruff, appearing ill at ease in the stiff and ungraceful fashions of the day. Gentlemen of the court sent the engraving, as the curiosity of the season, in their letters to correspondents abroad. The Church received her with great honor, and the Bishop of London gave her an entertainment, celebrated in enthusiastic terms by Purchas. At the court masque in January, 1617, Pocahontas was among the most conspicuous guests. The King and Queen received her in special audiences; and to crown all, tradition reports, with reasonable foundation, that King James, in his zeal for the high principles of divine right and the sacred character of royalty, expressed his serious displeasure that Rolfe, who was at best a simple gentleman, should have ventured so far beyond his position as to ally himself with one who was of imperial blood.

Just at that time, when the influence of London society had set its stamp of fashion on the name of the Indian girl, and when King James had adopted her as rightfully belonging within the pale of the divinity that hedges a king, Samuel Purchas, "Parson of St. Martin's by Ludgate," published the third edition of his "Pilgrimage." Purchas, although not himself an explorer, was an enthusiast on the subject of travels and adventures; and in compiling the collection now so eagerly sought and so highly valued by collectors of books, he had, so far as related to Virginia, the direct assistance of personal witnesses, and also of manuscripts now unhappily lost except for his extracts. He was well acquainted with Smith, who "gently communicated" his notes to him, and who was in London, and visited Pocahontas at Brentford. Purchas himself saw Pocahontas. He was present when "my Honble. and Rev^d. Patron the Lord Bishop of London, D^r. King, entertained her with festivall state and pompe beyond what I have seen in his great hospitalitie afforded to other ladies," in his "hopeful zeale by her to advance Christianitie." He knew Tomocomo, an Indian of Powhatan's tribe, who came with her to England. "With this savage I have often conversed at my goods friend's Master Doctor Goldstone, where he was a frequent guest; and where I have both seen him sing and dance his diabolicall measures, and heard him discourse of his countrey and religion, Sir Thomas Dale's man being the interpretour." He knew Rolfe also, who lent him his manuscript Discourse on Virginia. Yet Purchas's book contained no allusion to the heroic intervention on behalf of Smith, the story of whose captivity is simply copied from Simon's quarto of 1612; the diffuse comments on men and manners in Virginia contain no trace of what would have been correctly regarded as the most extraordinary incident in colonial history.

Silence in a single instance, as in Wingfield or in Strachey, might be accounted for, or at all events might be overlooked; but silence during a long period of years and under the most improbable circumstances, cannot be ignored. Wingfield, Smith himself, Simons, Strachey, Hamor, Rolfe, and Purchas, all the authorities without exception known to exist, are equally dumb when questioned as to a circumstance which since 1624 has become the most famous part of colonial history. The field is exhausted. No other sources exist from which to draw authentic information. Nothing remains but to return to Smith, and to inquire when it was that this extraordinary story first made its appearance, and how it obtained authority.

The blaze of fashionable success that surrounded Pocahontas in London lighted the closing scene of her life. She was obliged, against her will as was believed, to set out on her return to Virginia, but she never actually left the shores of England. Detained in the Thames by several weeks of contrary winds, her failing strength altogether gave way; and in March, 1617, in the word-play of Purchas, "she came at Gravesend to her end and grave." Her father, Powhatan, survived her less than a year.

Smith in the mean while was busied with projects in regard to New England and the fisheries. His efforts to form a colony there and to create a regular system of trade had little success; but to spread a knowledge of the new country among the people of England, he printed, in 1616, a small quarto, called "A Description of New England," and in 1620 he published another pamphlet, entitled "New England's Trials," a second and enlarged edition of which appeared in 1622. There at last, in 1622, the long-sought allusion to his captivity occurred in the following words:—

"For wronging a soldier but the value of a penny I have caused Powhatan send his own men to Jamestowne to receive their punishment at my discretion. It is true in our greatest extremitie they shot me, slue three of my men, and by the folly of them that fled took me prisoner; yet God made Pocahontas the King's daughter the means to deliver me; and thereby taught me to know their treacheries to preserve the rest."

The first appearance of this famous story can therefore be fixed within five years,—between 1617 and 1622,—although the complete account is only to be found in the "Generall Historie," printed in 1624, from which copious extracts have already been quoted. Only one point of difficulty still requires attention.

Smith there said (pp. 121-123) that when Pocahontas came to England he wrote for her a sort of letter of introduction to the Queen, or, in his own words, "a little booke to this effect to the Queen, an abstract whereof followeth."

"Some ten yeeres agoe, being in Virginia and taken prisoner by the power of Powhatan their chiefe King, . . . I cannot say I felt the least occasion of want that was in the power of those my mortall foes to prevent, notwithstanding all their threats. After some six weeks fatting amongst those Salvage Courtiers, at the minute of my execution, she hazarded the beating out of her owne braines to save mine, and not onely that, but so prevailed with her father that I was safely conducted to Jamestowne."

This letter rests on the authority of the "Generall Historie," and has neither more nor less weight than that work gives it. Smith's "abstract of the effect" of the little book was as liable to interpola- tions as the text of the "Generall Historie" elsewhere. At the time it was published, in 1624, not only had Pocahontas long been dead, but Queen Anne herself had in 1619 followed her to the grave, and Smith remained alone to vouch for his own accuracy. The Virginia Company had no interest in denying the truth of a story so well calculated to draw popular sympathy toward the colony.

Smith's character was always a matter of doubt. Thomas Fuller, one of Smith's contemporaries, published the "Worthies of Eng- land" some thirty years after Smith's death, when the civil wars had intervened to obliterate the recollection of personal jealousies, and when Smith must have been little remembered. Fuller devoted a page to Smith's history in the following vein:—

"From the Turks in Europe he passed to the Pagans in America, where, towards the latter end of the reign of Queen Elizabeth, such his perils, preservations, dangers, deliverances, they seem to most men above belief, to some beyond truth. Yet have we two witnesses to attest them, the prose and the pictures, both in his own book; and it soundeth much to the diminution of his deeds that he alone is the herald to publish and proclaim them."

The essential evidence on each side of this curious question has now been exhausted, although it would be easy to argue indefi- nitely in regard to Smith's general character. This must be done by the first historian who attempts again to deal with the history of the Virginia Colony. The argument may be left for future and final judgment, but some reasonable theory is still required to explain the existence of the story assumed to be false. Deane, like Palfrey, hints that Smith in the latter part of his life fell into the hands of hack-writers, who adapted his story for popular effect. Perhaps the truth may be somewhat as follows.

The examination of Smith's works has shown that his final nar- rative was the result of gradual additions. The influence exercised by Pocahontas on the affairs of the colony, according to the account given in 1608, was slight. In 1612 she first appeared in her heroic character. Her capture and her marriage to Rolfe gave her impor- tance. Her visit to England made her the most conspicuous figure in Virginia, and romantic incidents in her life were likely to be created, if they did not already exist, by the exercise of the popular imagination, attracted by a wild and vigorous picture of savage life.

The history of the emperor's daughter became, as Smith implied, a subject for the stage. Nothing was more natural or more probable. It is not even necessary to assume that Smith invented the additions to his own story. He may have merely accepted them after they had obtained a hold on the minds of his contemporaries.

In the mean while Smith's own career had failed, and his ventures ended disastrously, while in most cases he did not obtain the employment which he continued to seek with unrelaxed energy. In 1622 a disaster occurred in Virginia which roused the greatest interest and sympathy in England, and gave occasion for renewed efforts in behalf of the colony. The Indians rose against the English, and in the month of May a massacre took place around Jamestown. The opportunity was one not to be lost by a man who like Smith, while burning to act, was still smarting under what he considered undeserved neglect, and he hastened to offer his services to the Company, with a plan for restoring peace; but his plan and his offer of services were again declined. Still, the resource which he had frequently used remained, and by publishing the "Generall Historie" he made a more ambitious appeal to the public than any he had yet attempted. In this work he embodied everything that could tend to the increase of his own reputation, and drew material from every source that could illustrate the history of English colonization. Pocahontas was made to appear in it on every possible occasion, and his own share in the affairs of the colony was magnified at the expense of his companions. None of those whose reputations he treated with harshness appeared to vindicate their own characters, far less to assert their knowledge in regard to Pocahontas. The effort indeed failed of its object, for he remained unemployed and without mark of distinction. "He led his old age in London, where his having a Prince's mind imprisoned in a poor man's purse rendered him to the contempt of such who were not ingenuous. Yet he efforted his spirits with the remembrance and relation of what formerly he had been and what he had done." So Fuller wrote, who might have known him in his later years. Smith died quietly in his bed, in London, in June, 1631. His will has been published by

Deane, but furnishes little new information. In the absence of criticism, his book survived to become the standard authority on Virginian history. The readiness with which it was received is scarcely so remarkable as the credulity which has left it unquestioned almost to the present day.

The Session

Perhaps the scope of Henry Adams' youthful ambitions is best revealed in his project for a series of articles to be called "The Session," which were to appear annually in the North American Review. Modelled after Lord Robert Cecil's influential "review of politics" in the London Quarterly, the "Session" articles were to bring events in Washington into the perspectives of history and philosophical statesmanship. Only two were actually published—in 1869 and 1870—but they contain some of the young Adams' best writing.

The first "Session" received more attention in the press and elsewhere than anything its author had yet done, and he was elated. "For once I have smashed things generally," he wrote to a friend in England, "and really exercised a distinct influence on public opinion by acting on the limited number of cultivated minds." The prospect of continuing his series and building it into a vehicle of real authority seemed immensely attractive. "If the future goes straight," he said, "I will make my annual 'Session' an institution and a power in the land."

THERE is much reason to regret that every voter in the United States cannot be compelled, at some period of his life, to visit Washington, for the purpose of obtaining the passage, through the various stages of legislation, of some little bill, interesting only to himself, and perhaps having "a little money in it." The lesson would be a useful one. As the visitor cast from the lobby a momentary glance through the swinging doors of the House, and was bewildered by the crash and war of jealous and hostile interests within,—as he felt how his own just and proper request was the sport of a thousand accidents,—as he appreciated the difficulties in the way of getting a committee to report his bill at all, and the still greater difficulty of putting it on its passage, and as he then watched it float here and there in the eddying current of legislation, he would be better able for the future to understand one of the greatest difficulties of Government. Within the walls of two rooms are forced together in close contact the jealousies of thirty-five millions of people,—jealousies between individuals, between cliques, between industries, between parties, between branches of the Government, between sections of the country, between the nation and its neighbors. As years pass on, the noise and confusion, the vehemence of this scramble for power or for plunder, the shouting of reckless adventurers, of wearied partisans, and of red-hot zealots in new issues,—the boiling and bub-

[From the North American Review, CVIII (April 1869), 610-640.]

bling of this witches' caldron, into which we have thrown eye of newt and toe of frog and all the venomous ingredients of corruption, and from which is expected to issue the future and more perfect republic,—in short, the conflict and riot of interests, grow more and more overwhelming; the power of obstructionists grows more and more decisive in the same proportion as the business to be done increases in volume; the effort required to accomplish necessary legislation becomes more and more serious; the machine groans and labors under the burden, and its action becomes spasmodic and inefficient. The capacity of our Government to reconcile these jarring interests, to control refractory dissentients, and to preserve an appearance of governing, is already tested to its utmost, and one can, while watching the embarrassments of Congress, scarcely think without alarm of the day, already so near, when the country will have to support, first fifty, then one hundred millions of people, their passions sharpened by the increasing energy of the struggle for existence. Even this prospect, however, is comparatively bright, so long as the population remains tolerably homogeneous; but with the absorption into our system of Canada, Mexico, and the West Indies, on which it would be a great mistake to suppose that popular feeling is less firmly bent now than formerly, one can scarcely conceive a method by which the mere duties of necessary legislation could be performed at all.

A curious example of the manner in which public business is now done was drawn out very recently in the Dyer court-martial in Washington. The joint committee of Congress had made a report filled with charges against General Dyer,[1] of which General Dyer complained, and upon which he demanded a court of inquiry. The Government did not itself prosecute the charge, but left this duty to Mr. Clifford Arrick and other interested parties. By dexterous management, General Dyer's counsel, Mr. Dudley Field, enticed

[1] [General Alexander B. Dyer, who had been appointed chief of ordnance of the U. S. army in September, 1864, was accused of awarding contracts for rifle projectiles to favored manufacturers from whom he received kickbacks. It was also charged that he ordered the manufacture of his own invention, the Dyer projectile, despite its alleged inferiority to other shells, again for reasons of private gain. The joint committee recommended the removal of General Dyer from office, but he was fully exonerated by the court of inquiry and retained his post until his death in 1874.]

Mr. Arrick upon the witness-stand, and there elicited the fact that Mr. Arrick was himself the author of the Congressional Report of the joint committee which had impeached General Dyer. We do not wish to anticipate the decision of General Thomas, General Hancock, and the other members of the Commission of Inquiry; but General Dyer has been injured in reputation and put to anxiety and to expense he could ill afford, the Government has been attacked and obliged to institute a most costly inquiry, and Congress has placed itself in a most unfortunate and mortifying position, all because the joint committee had not the time to do its work properly, and employed an unfit person, without due caution.

The late Session has shown more clearly than ever the necessity of finding some means of improving our legislative machinery. Underneath a thousand personal matters, which, like so many mosquitoes, annoy and distract the attention of legislators, there are always a few great questions in which all public interests have their root, and from which all important legislation must take its start. When Congress met in December last, action was required on certain points: Reconstruction, Re-establishment of the Executive in its Privileges and Proper Functions, Revenue Reform, Monetary Reform, Administrative Reform, Internal Improvements, Foreign Policy. We believe it is simple truth to say that not one of these subjects received anything but superficial attention; and yet we have no intention of charging Congress with any wilful neglect of duty. That there was great waste of valuable time no one can deny; but that Congress could, by the strictest possible economy of its means, have given proper study and attention to all these subjects, scarcely any one would venture to assert. If, therefore, in calling attention to the short-comings of the Session, we seem to criticise more sharply than is just, it is not that we wish to throw undeserved blame on Congress, but that the system itself is at fault, and has failed to expand with the expansion of the country. On this subject we shall have more to say in the sequel. Leaving aside for the present the question of what has not been done by Congress, let us examine the merits of the actual work of the Session.

Reconstruction natually comes first in the list of subjects claiming public attention, although Reconstruction, thanks to the general acquiescence of the country in the result of the November elections, and thanks also to the increasing prosperity which has drawn the attention of the Rebel States to more profitable matters, has lost much of its old prominence in politics. Nevertheless, the point of negro-suffrage was thought to require attention, and even to need acknowledgment as part of the fundamental law of the land. Like most of the measures adopted by Congress, the Constitutional Amendment is more remarkable for what it does not than for what it does contain. Beau Brummell's valet was one day met on his master's stairs with a bundle of crumpled neck-cloths on his arm, and being asked what on earth he had there, answered, with a modesty tinged with becoming pride: "These are our failures." Congress, too, has had its failures, and the neck-tie with which it proposes at last to adorn the statue of American Liberty is the result of many efforts. Apart from the general doubt whether it is advisable to insert in the Constitution such special provisions, there is little in this Fifteenth Amendment to which we can fairly object. The dogma that suffrage is a natural right, and not a trust, is by implication denied. The "right" to hold office, as well as to vote, is not asserted. Educational and even property qualifications are not excluded. We know little of legal ingenuity, if it is not found that this Amendment is of small practical value. Its sting and its danger rest in the possible abuse of the power granted to Congress by the second section, to enforce the article by such legislation as it may deem appropriate.

As Congress postponed action in regard to the status of Georgia, we are relieved from the necessity of discussing this difficult question.[1] The responsibility of deciding it must now rest on the present Congress, whose action we do not care to anticipate. At the same time we can scarcely think that inaction in regard to so serious a legal difficulty was a satisfactory mode of dealing with it. It is true that Georgia is not likely to run away in the mean while; but it is also true that inaction is equivalent to a confession of incompetency, and that of such confessions we have far too many.

[1] [It was in doubt at this time whether Georgia had satisfied Congressional requirements for readmission to the Union. She had no members in the U. S. Senate and her representatives in the House were excluded after March, 1869. The issue was not settled by Congress until July, 1870, when Georgia's statehood was recognized and her right to representation in Congress established.]

Passing on to the second great subject of public anxiety, the restoration to the Executive of its proper control, we touch already upon very dangerous ground, where a battle is unavoidable and imminent. General Butler,[1] in pressing with so much earnestness the repeal of the Tenure-of-Office Bill,[2] scarcely took the trouble to conceal his opinion that sooner or later a struggle for power must arise between the Senate and the House, with or without the aid of the President. The Senate gave countenance to this opinion by its conduct in regard to the repeal. To allege as a cause of inaction its fear of a triumphant lecture from President Johnson had not only more the appearance of giving a pretext than a reason, but was an implied rebuff to the House, which was, or might have been supposed to be, as good a judge as the Senate of what their combined dignity should fear. This jealousy broke out again in the joint convention for counting the electoral votes; and if General Butler's manner had not put him in the wrong, he would have won far more sympathy than showed itself.[3] In whatever light the Senate may be consid-

[1] [Representative from Massachusetts.]

[2] [The Tenure-of-Office Act of 1867 grew out of the struggle between Congress and President Johnson. It was designed primarily to give the Senate a check on executive removals from office. President Johnson's refusal to recognize the rights of the Senate under the act in his dismissal of Secretary of War Stanton was the immediate cause of his impeachment. The act was repealed by Congress in December, 1886.]

[3] [At the joint convention (February 11, 1869) of House and Senate for the counting of the electoral votes, objections were raised against the legality of the votes from Louisiana and Georgia. In separate ballots the two houses decided to accept the votes of Louisiana, but split over those of Georgia, the Senate voting to accept, the House to reject Georgia's electoral votes. Senator Benjamin F. Wade of Ohio, President of the Senate *pro tempore* and presiding officer of the joint convention, ordered Georgia's votes to be counted, whereupon General Butler, who had originally raised the objection to them, protested so vigorously this implied assumption of authority by the Senate over the House that the proceedings of the convention were reduced almost to chaos. The threatened intervention of the Sergeant-at-Arms finally restored order and the votes of Georgia were counted. When the Senate had retired from the House chamber, General Butler offered the following resolution: "Resolved, That the House protests that the counting of the vote of Georgia by the order of the Vice President *pro tempore* was a gross act of oppression, and an invasion of the rights and privileges of the House." This resolution was soon toned down by Butler, and tabled by the House.]

ered, it is not a popular body, and can command popular support
only in consequence of the mistakes of its rivals. For this reason the
whole country waited with extreme anxiety, after the Senate's refusal to act on the Tenure-of-Office Bill until General Grant should
announce his Cabinet; and if politicians became more and more un-
easy as the delay was prolonged, it was because they felt that any
mistake made by General Grant at the outset of his career would
result in strengthening the hold which the Senate had acquired
upon political patronage and power. The idea now so popular, that
politicians are bad counsellors, is one of the most unfortunate mistakes of our day. There are politicians of all sorts, and the dishonest
class no doubt would be bad advisers; but to exclude politicians
would imply also the exclusion of statesmen, and to conduct the
Government without the aid of trained statesmen is as dangerous
as to conduct a war without the aid of trained generals. When Congress saw that General Grant placed himself in isolation, the annoyance was extreme, and was entirely justified by the event. It is
to be hoped that no future President will repeat the experiment,
least of all in critical times.

We do not mean by this to express any unfavorable opinion of
General Grant's Cabinet, to which this Review has only good wishes
and support to offer; but it is obvious, that, if the balance of our
government is to be restored, there must be no more mistakes in
administration, and no hazardous experiments, whose failure may
shake public confidence. We shall have something to say presently
of the reforms which the Executive should attempt; but its immediate policy is one of caution and conciliation, not one of heroism.
The mere repeal of the Tenure-of-Office Bill cannot at once restore
its prestige, or wrest from Congress the initiative which Congress
is now accustomed to exercise. The Senate has no idea of abandoning its control of power, either with or without the Tenure-of-Office
Bill; and the people alone, acting upon the Lower House, after a
fair trial of the new Administration, can re-establish the Presidency
in spite of the Senate, and restore harmony to the political system.
General Grant and his Cabinet, no matter whether they are men of
metal or men of straw, must accept the fact that our system of government has practically suffered a modification, from which no
power but that of patient wisdom can retrieve it; and if the influ-

ence of General Grant himself, or of his Cabinet, is exerted in the direction of isolated action, however brilliant, the chances are that our system will be permanently fixed on a new and not an improved basis. On the question, therefore, of restoring its powers to the Executive, Congress failed to take action, as it had failed to take action in regard to Georgia.

The case was no better in regard to reform in the revenue system. Mr. Schenck,[1] it is true, did his utmost for the passage of the improved internal-revenue law, consolidating all the previous revenue acts, but without success. Meanwhile, Mr. Wells,[2] in his annual Report, had, for the first time, called public attention to the character of the Tariff. His Report was a simple and business-like document, avoiding carefully all theoretical flightiness, containing no praises of free-trade, advocating no extreme legislation, but merely pointing out, in a way so clear that no one could misunderstand the evidence, his reasons for thinking that our present customs-duties are mischievous and need reform. Mr. Wells has by no means exhausted the subject; on the contrary, he has yet done little more than to open discussion. He has rigidly abstained, with a care that does him great credit, from the wide and philosophical treatment of this question, which he was perfectly able to give, but for which neither President, Congress, press, nor people are as yet prepared. He has no party to serve, no interest to enrich, nor any "ring" to work for. We need scarcely say that we give to him and to the principles of his Report, as we should give to every liberal and honest movement, a hearty support. There is still less necessity for adding that in Congress Mr. Wells is not strong, and that no action was suggested in the sense of his recommendations.

No sooner had Mr. Wells's Report been published than a cry of rage arose from Pennsylvania. A swarm of stinging insects darted out from that mass of protected interests, and, what was more significant, they were met by another body, equally active, which came spontaneously from the working classes to defend and affirm the

[1] [Representative from Ohio.]
[2] [David A. Wells, Special Commissioner of the Revenue. "The four Reports of Mr. Wells," Adams wrote in *American Finance, 1865-1869*, ". . . are the most useful documents—we had almost said the only useful documents—which have been published in regard to the United States Revenue system."]

statements of Mr. Wells. The controversy in the Middle States has raged all winter with fury. We confess that our interest in its result would be less lively, if we looked at it merely from an economical point of view; but in this respect we are not obliged to follow Mr. Wells, and prefer to go beyond him. The Tariff, as it stands, is indeed grossly extravagant and partial, but its direct economical result is only to neutralize a certain amount of labor, to throw away so many days' work in every year without any return of any kind. The nation is young and overflowing with animal strength, and the mere pecuniary loss could be borne. But unfortunately this is not all; nor is the story finished, when Mr. Wells adds, that the rich are daily becoming richer, and the poor poorer. Behind this there is a political result of far greater moment, in the debauching effect of the system upon parties, public men, and the morals of the State.

Few men who are accustomed to watch the course of Washington politics will be at a loss to understand the difficulty of Mr. Wells's position, or the reason why his efforts have found so little co-operation in Congress. We are touching here upon a delicate subject, but we have no office to ask of any generous constituency, and can afford to say what every one already knows. The condition of parties precludes the chance of reform. The "rings" which control legislation—those iron, or whiskey, or Pacific Railway, or other interests, which have their Congressional representatives, who vote themselves the public money—do not obtain their power for nothing. Congressmen themselves, as a class, are not venal, it is true. Perhaps not more than one member in ten of the late Congress ever accepted money. But though Congress itself has still a sense of honor, party organizations have no decency and no shame. The "rings" obtain their control of legislation by paying liberally towards the support of these party organizations, Republican or Democratic, as the case may be; and the distiller or iron-founder who pays his five or ten thousand dollars towards the expenses of his party has as fair a claim upon it as Judge Pierrepont, or any other honest man, and is more certain to force his claim against opposition. Parties cannot escape the obligations thus incurred; and the result is, that these interests combine in Congress for mutual protection, and members who are by their tastes well disposed towards reform dare not move a finger. A network of rings controls Congress, and forms a hedge which marks the limit within which argument and reason may prevail. When the President sent in his veto to the Copper Bill,[1]—a veto which was certainly not his own composition, if one may judge from its form,—all the iniquity of the law could not win over the two votes necessary to sustain the veto, although members in plenty approved it, and would have voted for it, had the vote been taken by count, and not by yeas and nays. The rings whipped into line the recalcitrant members. Perhaps the most creditable vote given this winter was that of Mr. Senator Sumner, who, on this sole occasion, sustained President Johnson.

Mr. Wells, therefore, can do nothing, except to place his arguments before the people, and wait until some party finds its interest involved in supporting him. We are unable to say whether General Grant himself, or his Cabinet, will be disposed to undertake the superhuman task of reforming party organizations and purifying Congress. The simpler task of economy, or what the French call *économie de bouts de chandelles,* has thus far seemed to satisfy them. To follow out the path indicated by Mr. Wells, to clean and purify the national legislature, and to break down by main force one of the strongest supports of party corruption, can be done only by reforming the revenue system, and placing stringent restrictions upon all grants of the public money. Not merely, therefore, as a matter of political economy, but as one of political reform, the policy of Mr. Wells demands the support of the Administration. At this moment everything tends to increase the dictatorial power of parties. Even the new Constitutional Amendment seems to have this inevitable result, of swelling the blind, unreasoning vote which follows mechanically a party standard, and thus encourages and protects party corruption. We submit that Government is wrong in plundering the people in order to support party organizations, and that the system of protecting special interests should be reformed.

If the public waits for Congress to move in this direction, it will wait long, and it will wait in vain. And in the same way we can expect little or nothing from Congress towards administrative reform. Suddenly, in the middle of the Session, the new whiskey-tax broke down. New York was no longer the favorite haunt of dis-

[1] [This bill raised the duty on copper ore and finished copper goods imported into the United States.]

tillers. They had retired to the West, and there they again succeeded in cheating the Government,—necessarily by collusion with
Government officials. Mr. Jenckes's Civil-Service Bill lay untouched
on the Clerk's table.[1] We are not enthusiastic admirers of Mr.
Jenckes's bill, but we do insist that a decent self-respect should
oblige Congress to show or feign some disposition to purge the civil
service from the taint of political corruption. The country, after an
experience which for a time brought it literally within sight of disorganization, has at last nearly escaped its dangers, not by reform,
but by prosperity and good luck. The Government, under a war-
pressure, instituted a system of internal revenue, and in the attempt
to enforce its laws was utterly defeated by private interests. The
taxes were therefore reduced, and will ultimately be abandoned.
But the time must come, and may come sooner than is commonly
supposed, when a foreign war will force us back to the internal
revenue system as our only source of income, and there is no risk
in predicting that a few more years of the old system of internal
revenue would leave little sound material in our Government. So
virulent a source of corruption was never known in our national
experience. For this reason we are inclined to think that such national prosperity as would allow our Government to escape, without
obliging it to meet and overcome its difficulties, would in the end
prove a national disaster. The people of the United States already
have become too much accustomed to the idea that they can violate
with impunity every fundamental principle of good government.

The dependence of civil offices upon political influence is a support even more essential to party organizations than are the protected interests which Mr. Wells has attacked. There is little disposition in Congress, and there is still less in either party organization,
to introduce such a separation between politics and the civil service
as would purify both. The evil is rooted in popular habit; it springs
from the people; it was created by the people; it is maintained for

[1] [Thomas A. Jenckes, Representative from Rhode Island. The bill would have
created a civil service examination board to be appointed by the President with
the advice and consent of the Senate, and a system of competitive examinations
for most Federal civil service offices. It would further have regulated promotions
and removals from office. Its most unusual feature was a provision creating a
Department of the Civil Service to be headed by the Vice-President.]

the people; and yet we venture to assert that the mere fact of bringing this temptation into party strife will ultimately, if continued long enough, break down the Government. The Democratic party, if wrong otherwise, is yet perfectly right in asserting that corruption is no peculiar fault of its own; for the fault lies, not in the party, but in the system, which for both parties is the same. So long as party organizations remain what they are, honesty in the long run is impossible; corruption must be the rule, and not the exception. General Grant may, indeed, purify the revenue service, but his successor will with much less effort corrupt it again, unless the public takes its stand upon some solid principle which shall remove the Government patronage from the shifting influence of politics. This is a matter which has nothing to do with law; it is custom that should rule; and until the natural good sense of the people, acting over the heads of all party organizations, shall decide the point that no officer of the Government shall be removed from his post for merely political reasons, except in a few specified cases, honesty is not likely to prevail, nor are parties likely to be pure.

We have ventured to dwell a little on these two points of reform,—the abolition of Government grants to favored interests, and the withdrawal of Government patronage, so far as practicable, from party organizations,—not so much because they were mentioned during the late Session, as because the House, and even General Grant, seemed to be carried away by the idea that economy and proper care in selecting persons for appointments would cure all our national ills. Economy is in itself not a policy; it is, or should be, a condition of existence, and no government should boast of it any more than a gentleman should boast of sobriety. A government that understands its duties is economical always, even in its extravagance. We see a healthy and useful reaction in this tendency to pare cheese-rinds, but we protest against the idea that this is a policy of reform, or that General Grant should be considered as a sort of presidential terrier chosen to snap at vermin in the public offices. What the country needs is not a narrow and pinching economy, nor even a merely honest administration, that during its term of office will heal over the running sores of our body politic, with a certainty that they will again break out at the first change of circumstances,—but a wise and careful correction of the system itself.

We can see no reason why a democracy should be necessarily corrupt. We believe that a timely reform may long postpone the day when corruption will become intolerable, but we should augur the worst of the effect that another great shock to the country in its present loose condition would produce upon our whole system of government, and we maintain that the first and last duty of Congress and the President is to draw from the experience of the last ten years a lesson as to the PRINCIPLES OF REFORM. The country is not permanently aided by piecemeal legislation to stop abuses which spring from radical difficulties; nor can the nation in the long run respect a Government which announces, that, as Pacific Railways and other great national works breed corruption, therefore they cannot be constructed. So far as we understand the object of creating governments, it is that they may do the work of governing; and we should like to know for what earthly purpose Presidents and Congressmen are elected, except to perform this duty, and to see at their peril that no corruption follows. It is their duty to prevent or to cure corruption; but it is also their duty to do the work, to collect the revenue, to build, or cause to be built, whatever public works it comes within their province to provide for, to employ officers, and to see that they are efficient and faithful. A more extraordinary claim to popular respect than that advanced in defence of the late Session, on the ground that it stopped many extravagant schemes, could scarcely be imagined. The schemes were no doubt extravagant, but their objects were in many cases proper and necessary, and the public has a right to insist that Congress shall do the work it was sent to do, and do it properly, or ask such reforms as will enable it to be done. Instead of this, popular wrath is met by an intolerably calm confession that there are certainly corrupt officials, but General Grant will detect them and turn them out, and never again in our national history shall corrupt officials be appointed; that it is true the revenue system has been evaded and nullified by fraud, but that it will, please God, soon be—not reformed, but—abolished; that Pacific Railways are very apt to produce corruption, and therefore it is best not to meddle with them; that political organizations are selfish and unscrupulous, but that General Grant is not a party man; that, in short, they who are charged with the Government are the most senseless and fit men for the constables of the watch, and if any man refuses to obey their orders, they are to come together and thank God they are rid of a knave. We are bound to call attention to the fact, which seems to have been forgotten, that these incessant confessions of ignorance, or of impotence, or even—pardon us the word—of imbecility, cannot, even with the best will, be considered as a performance of duty.

One administrative measure—the bill for amending the judicial system—was, however, passed in this Session, and failed only by accident, we believe, to receive President Johnson's signature. There was also one very important measure which we may class under the head of monetary reform, and which also failed to become law. Mr. Schenck's bill for the improvement of the public credit was a simple recognition of the financial principle established in the November election.[1] The Supreme Court had already forestalled this measure so far as regarded the legalizing of coin contracts, and indeed it may perhaps be said that the whole bill tended rather to affirm a principle which ought never to have been brought in question than to effect any real progress in finance. Nevertheless, the measure was highly creditable to Congress and to the country, and, unless foreign complications arise, it may be considered as having brought our finances to a point where one may see a clear path to the settlement of all our financial difficulties. It is true that Mr. Schenck's bill left untouched the serious problem of a return to specie payments, or, if it indicated anything in this respect, indicated a leaning towards that favorite doctrine of "growing up to the situation," which is merely another example of what we have already so strongly criticised as the fashionable custom of confessing impotence and abnegating governmental functions. The West could not be induced to join in any settled and effective action for a re-establishment of the currency on a sound basis. But with a large surplus revenue, a rapid diminution of taxes, a reduction of interest on the debt, and a decrease in its volume, sooner or later the time must come when return to specie payments will be unavoidable. Whenever and however it comes, the process must be the same, if the national credit is to be maintained; but if the difficulty were boldly

[1] [This bill provided for the legalization of gold contracts and the redemption and payment of interest on all bonds in gold, except for those expressly made payable in legal tender.]

faced at present, it might, perhaps, be possible to devise some means by which the debtor class would be more equitably dealt with, and business less exposed to annoyance, than if the whole subject were left to the action of time and chance.

Yet, if it must be allowed that no progress was made during the late Session towards sound monetary principles, it is equally true that the unsound theorists gained no ground. The eloquent denunciation of gold and silver by General Butler failed to make the slightest impression on Congress, or even to provoke notice, although it was strikingly original, and in Mr. Butler's best style. "It is now admitted by all political economists," said he, "that finely engraved printing upon paper, fixing its value, is the best of all possible substitutes for coined money. Not until the people of Greece and Rome became deteriorated by vices and luxury, yielding their liberties to tyrants, did gold and silver, the ever-ready adjuncts of despotic power in all its forms and degrees, obtain place and scope to do their appropriate and never-failing work,—the enslavement of the labor of the masses. . . . Coined gold and silver has ever been the handmaid of despotism, the prop of monarchical power, the supporter of thrones, the upholder of nobilities and priesthoods, the engine by which the privileges and pretensions of aristocrats have always been sustained in trampling down the rights, devouring the substance, and absorbing the unrequited labors of the masses. Through all time the possession of money has given power to the few to enslave the labor of the many for the benefit of princes and nobles, and its use has been the badge of servitude of all peoples to some king or tyrant. To deny this at one time was treason."

Both as regards originality of conception and elegance of style, this passage deserved more notice than the sullen, and no doubt envious, silence with which it was received. General Garfield and his friends,[1] in fact, asserted that the speech was contemptible and ridiculous, and that to answer it would be almost as great folly as to make it, and thus General Butler's argument was stifled by a conspiracy of silence. Silence, indeed, on the whole subject of the currency, was an understood rule of the Session. No agreement on a common principle was possible, and Congress had, apart from

---

[1] [James A. Garfield, at this time Representative from Ohio, and later twentieth President of the United States. Adams was one of his friends.]

monetary affairs, far more work on its hands than could possibly be attended to. Monetary reform, therefore, like administrative reform, like revenue reform, like the re-establishment of the Executive, and like the reconstruction of Georgia and the development of the national resources, was postponed.

What, then, was accomplished by this expiring Congress, besides the Constitutional Amendment and Mr. Schenck's gold bill? In reply to this question, we might fairly say, as a sufficient answer, that the business of the Government has been carried on. To do even this as it should be done, to prepare and to pass the Appropriation Bill alone, is a prodigious effort, and especially difficult in the short session at the close of an Administration. We may add, that economical, and even parsimonious, principles have received surprising support at the hands of the Committee on Appropriations, and that the clerks have been taught what it is to have an economical Government. But much as we admire economy, we cannot think that Molière's Harpagon is the best model of a finance minister, nor that it is good policy for a government to pay its clerks meanly. Let us starve the Cabinet, if we like, and reduce our Supreme Court to the wages of country lawyers; there remains still the honor of the position, which would tempt distinguished ability, even though there were no salary whatever to be earned. But with the subordinate posts there is no dignity, but rather degradation involved, as the service is now organized. The precarious tenure of a Government office drives away the better class of applicants. Nor is there common sense in the idea that a government which every year votes tens and hundreds of millions into the hands of favored classes, and supports a revenue and currency system far more burdensome than the national debt, should claim merit from the country for grinding a few thousand dollars from its clerks.

But we are obliged to return at last to the proposition with which we began,—that one principal reason why the public business is neglected, or inefficiently performed, is to be found in the inevitable waste of time under the present legislative system. So necessary has it proved to provide some check to this evil, that debate has, under the rules of the House, been to a great extent stopped, and measures are habitually hurried through in spite of every remonstrance, without allowing an opportunity for amendment or discussion. So long as the dominant party has sufficient strength to override opposition in this way, the expedient may answer its purpose in economizing time, but in the long run parties must be more evenly balanced, and some other expedient must be invented. One such expedient might, perhaps, be, that members should better understand their work; but as the House does not elect its own members, it can do little towards producing this result. Nor does popular feeling tend in this direction. The oldest members of the House and the Senate have had but eighteen years' service, and this is so unusual as to be thought surprising. Yet the lessons of statesmanship, or even of statecraft, are not easily learned, especially in their higher branches; principles of political economy, or of international law, and, above all, the limits of legislation, are matters to which trained statesmen themselves come with a humiliating confession of doubt or ignorance. As Congress is at present constituted, the trained statesmen have more than they can accomplish merely in stopping mischievous legislation. In this respect, Reconstruction has had anything but a good influence on Congress. Setting aside entirely all question as to the merits or demerits of Reconstruction in the Rebel States, there is no doubt whatever that it has brought into Congress a class of men whose influence has not been favorable, and who have increased the power of the lobby rather than the dignity of either House. Let us instance the case of Collector Smythe, who was lately appointed by President Johnson Minister to Russia, with the idea that he would be acceptable to the Senate. Senator Sumner and the Committee on Foreign Relations thought the appointment unsuitable, and we believe they were right, although Mr. Smythe could scarcely have been so unfit for the post as its present occupant. Mr. Smythe, however, laughed at the Committee. He had, as he thought, already won a majority of the Senate. He had been among the obstructionists and carpet-baggers, and secured their votes, and he hoped to march with their assistance over the prostrate bodies of Senator Sumner and his Committee. We will not pretend to say what influences he had used. We do not know. But, at all events, he had, as Collector of New York, gained influence enough with the Senate to be able to say in so many words, that, if the Senate did not confirm him, it should confirm no one; and he did in fact succeed in stopping confirmations.

Public business was kept at a stand-still in order that a ring largely composed of reconstructed Senators might force Mr. Smythe into a position for which he was unfit. Here is an example of the probable working of Senatorial government; but it is also an illustration of the growing power of the lobby and of obstructionists in our legislature, and of the difficulties which threaten sooner or later to bring the whole machinery of our Government to a stand-still.

Let us now turn to the Department of Foreign Affairs, or, as the Senate prefers to style it, of Foreign Relations. Congress has postponed action on points of foreign policy, as well as on most domestic matters, but their importance and the tone in which they have been discussed warrant us in going into a somewhat detailed statement of the situation. Various treaties were under consideration in the Senate, but we shall undertake to examine only those negotiated with Denmark and Great Britain.

The public, always curiously ill-informed in regard to its foreign relations, had flattered itself that the affair of St. Thomas was quietly disposed of, and even the Senate labored for a time under the delusion that the treaty would be allowed to expire without scandal or dispute.[1] The Danish Government, however, was in a position which did not admit of withdrawal. The very weakness of Denmark, and her helpless situation as regards Germany, obliges her to struggle against humiliation, and in this matter her national pride was involved. During our war, she had behaved extremely well. The proposition to part with St. Thomas had not come from her, but had been suggested by our Government at a time when the possession of the island was a matter of great interest to the United States. She had declined at first to negotiate on any terms. The settled policy of the western European powers has always been to exclude the United States from the West Indies, since they well know that their colonial possessions in that neighborhood would be placed in great peril, if our Government once obtained a foothold among them. Denmark naturally hesitated to take a step which placed her

[1] [In October, 1867, Secretary of State Seward had signed a treaty with Denmark for the purchase of the Danish West Indies (Virgin Islands) of which St. Thomas is the principal island. The Senate, however, refused to ratify the treaty, and persisted in this course until 1917 when the purchase was finally accomplished.]

in direct antagonism to the traditional policy of Great Britain and France, the two countries on whose sympathy she is compelled to rely. Nevertheless, after long doubt, she yielded, not merely on account of the money to be gained, (for Denmark is one of the few states in the world which do not stand in need of money,) but on the distinct principle that it was expedient to change her foreign policy and to attach herself more closely to the United States by abandoning to them her colonial possessions in our seas, and, as a consequence, the ultimate control of the Antilles and of Central America. The treaty was signed, and sent to the Senate. After a sufficient lapse of time, Denmark took a vote of the people of St. Thomas on the subject, and, the result being favorable, the island was formally transferred to an authorized agent of our Government. The Senate had the treaty in its hands, but did not interfere. When the period within which ratification was required had passed without bringing any movement from the Senate, the time was by further agreement extended to October, 1869. Still the Senate made no sign. Then at last the Danish Government sent over General Raaslof, its Secretary of War, to Washington, and this gentleman, who had already been Minister here, who understood our people and was highly popular with them, who had, moreover, been principally responsible for the new policy which Denmark had adopted towards us, and whose official position, as well as that of his colleagues in the Ministry, depended upon the ratification of this treaty, undertook to disturb the serene repose of the Senate, and to insist that action should be taken.

We have little sympathy with the policy which prompted Mr. Lincoln and his Cabinet to purchases of new territory. There is a peculiar brilliancy and seductiveness in that vast scheme which, without war or ill-feeling or unnecessary expense, grasped in succession three such commanding points as Russian America, St. Thomas, and the Isthmus of Darien; the imagination is dazzled by it; and yet we should be heartily glad to discover any honorable mode of release from the obligations of the St. Thomas Treaty. We cannot in honor listen to the suggestion of General Butler, that Denmark having abandoned the island, in pursuance of a popular vote, we are now at liberty to take it without paying for it at all. The only argument which has any show of weight is, that the Senate has a constitutional right to reject the treaty,—that Denmark was perfectly aware, in fact was formally notified, of this limitation on the President's power,—and that she is therefore debarred from complaint.

The internal difficulties of a government are often most immediately felt in its foreign relations, and this is the case here. Undoubtedly the Senate has the right to reject any treaty, this among the rest; but the condition of holding any friendly relations whatever with the outside world requires that this right of rejection should be kept in reserve for extraordinary occasions. If the treaty betrays the national honor, if it sacrifices national territory or the rights of citizens, if it was obtained by disgraceful means, if it is untrue to a national pledge, by all means let the Senate interpose and reject it. But a proper respect for the countries with which we deal, and for international comity, which we are bound to observe, requires that in rejecting a treaty we should give strong and solid reasons for the act. We cannot conceive what strong or solid reasons the Senate can give for refusing to ratify this treaty. *Stat pro ratione voluntas.* Say it is our humor,—is Denmark answered, or is our national credit redeemed in the world's eyes? Seven years ago our whole nation wanted St. Thomas; now we need it no longer; a few years hence we may again require it; and the world must learn submission to these passing whims!

If the United States through the President had negotiated a treaty with Denmark, requiring that within a certain time she should declare war against Prussia, and our Government had bound itself to pay her seven million dollars in consideration thereof,— if this treaty were duly sent to the Senate, if Denmark thereupon did declare war in pursuance of the agreement, and if our Government then refused to perform its part of the compact, we are inclined to think that the world, without stopping long to study constitutional theories, would hold that our behavior was scurvy; and we ourselves, as a nation, would hold and express the same opinion in regard to any foreign government that placed itself in a similar situation.

We repeat, that a sound and sufficient reason for rejecting this treaty is much to be desired; but there is something to be desired still more earnestly, and this is, that the Senate may not assume the absolute and irresponsible control of our international affairs. There is a perfectly clear line here which it is dangerous to overstep. The confusion which such a conflict of authority would create in our foreign relations cannot be overestimated; for abroad, even more than at home, division of responsibility lowers the national character and destroys all faith in national pledges. As regards foreign nations, the President, and not the Senate, is the representative and the spokesman of the United States; and if the Senate intervenes without so sound a reason as must convince the world that intervention is right and necessary, the only result must be to degrade the Presidential authority, and with it the national dignity, in the eyes of other governments. Hitherto there has been so seldom any occasion for appealing to this principle, that it has sometimes in practice been overlooked; but the present occasion is a grave one; in spite of our own wishes, we are compelled to say, that the rejection of this treaty would be an unwarrantable and mischievous act.

The position in regard to the English treaties is somewhat different; since in the first place, there is no special reason for being civil to England; and in the second place, no action was stipulated, or has been taken under these treaties, by which any one has been compromised. The treaties, therefore, are a fair subject for rejection, if there is reason to reject them. We will even go so far as to say that they ought to be rejected by the Senate, unless they fully accord every demand our Government has ever made on Great Britain. We frankly confess that Great Britain is not entitled at our hands to any delicacy of treatment whatever. There are still a few persons in America who have reason to remember Lord Palmerston, and the happy manner of that nobleman did much to keep his memory fresh in this country.

There have been three grave difficulties existing between England and the United States during the last few years,—difficulties partly of long standing, dating back to the foundation of our Government, and partly resulting from the war. Mr. Seward, who was seldom satisfied with a small policy, as we have already noticed in the cases of Alaska, St. Thomas, and Darien, undertook to combine the three subjects of dispute with England and produce a comprehensive scheme of settlement, which should, perhaps, (although this is a mere inference on our part,) establish such friendly relations between the two countries as would in time lead England to the same point to which Denmark had been led. The foreign policy of Mr. Seward was, in principle, simple enough, although his expedients were innumerable. His intention was always to avoid war, but always to gain his objects; and he achieved astonishing success.

The San Juan affair offered no serious difficulty.[1] It was readily referred to arbitration. The naturalization controversy threatened for a long time to prove a serious obstacle, and accordingly Mr. Seward, spurred on no doubt by the President and Congress, gave precedence to this subject, and pressed earnestly for a settlement. Lord Stanley made no opposition, and a protocol was accordingly signed, by which the British Government abandoned all its old theories of citizenship, and conceded all, and more than all, that had ever been asked by the United States.

There remained the serious question of claims, arising out of violations of English neutrality by the Rebels during our late war: a difficult subject, involving new principles of international law, binding England now, but binding us also for all future time; a subject which ought not to be made the football of party warfare, or even of national antipathies; a subject, too, in regard to which the United States Government ought to be peculiarly cautious in establishing precedents. No strong nation has an interest in restricting the limits of its own action, least of all when it will inevitably be the first to overthrow the very law it has established.

Early in our national history, the United States occupied, as regarded Great Britain, a position similar in some respects to that which Great Britain now occupies as regards the United States. In the year 1793, the French Republic, acting, as it claimed, under treaty stipulations, caused cruisers to be fitted out in our ports, which captured British vessels even within our territorial jurisdiction, and caused the British Minister to address energetic remonstrances and claims of indemnity to our Secretary of State. Mr. Jefferson acknowledged the justice of these claims. Such of the captured vessels as our Government could reach were taken by force

---

[1] [Ownership of the San Juan islands, at the head of Puget Sound, was a subject of dispute and negotiation between the United States and Great Britain from 1856 on. The Treaty of Washington of 1871 submitted the question to the arbitration of the German emperor who decided in favor of the United States.]

from the captors, and restored to their owners. In the face of great difficulties, the United States faithfully performed all its duties as a neutral towards Great Britain. Nevertheless, claims for the value of such captured vessels as had not been recovered were made by the British Government, and by the treaty of 1794 the justice of these claims was conceded, and they were referred, together with other pecuniary demands made by citizens of both nations, to a commission of five persons, two to be appointed by the British King, two by the President, subject to confirmation by the Senate, and one by the unanimous choice of the other four, or, in case of disagreement, by lot between two persons named by either party. The decision of three of these commissioners was to be final, provided one on each side and the fifth were present. The commission was to meet in Philadelphia, and to decide all claims and receive all evidence which the commissioners might think consistent with equity and justice.

The last paragraph of the seventh article of this treaty runs as follows:—

"And whereas certain merchants and others, His Majesty's subjects, complain that in the course of the war they have sustained loss and damage by reason of the capture of their vessels and merchandise, taken within the limits and jurisdiction of the States, and brought into the ports of the same, or taken by vessels originally armed in ports of the said States, it is agreed that in all such cases, where restitution shall not have been made agreeably to the tenor of the letter from Mr. Jefferson to Mr. Hammond, dated at Philadelphia, September 5, 1793, a copy of which is annexed to this treaty, the complaints of the parties shall be, and hereby are, referred to the commissioners to be appointed by virtue of this article, who are hereby authorized and required to proceed in the like manner relative to these as to the other cases committed to them; and the United States undertake to pay to the complainants or claimants, in specie, without deduction, the amount of such sums as shall be awarded to them respectively by the said commissioners, and at the times and places which in such awards shall be specified, and on condition of such releases or assignments to be given by the claimants as in the said awards may be directed; and it is further agreed, that not only the now existing cases of both descriptions, but also all such as shall exist at the time of exchanging the ratifications of this treaty, shall be considered as being within the provisions, intent, and meaning of this article."

There is this difference between the British claims of 1794 and the *Alabama* claims of 1869,—that in the latter case there had been no capture of vessels within neutral jurisdiction, nor any actual arming of cruisers in British ports. The arming was constructive. Nor was the British Government directly responsible for the escape of all these unarmed, unmanned, and unequipped vessels from British ports. Except in the case of the *Alabama*, and, perhaps, the *Florida*, the British Government had acted, or tried to act, and had done what was required by its laws for the fulfilment of its international obligations. In establishing a claim for the depredations of the *Florida*, the *Shenandoah*, and so forth, our Government took the ground that the British Government ought to have amended its laws, and that these vessels, after escaping, ought to have been seized wherever they had come within British jurisdiction. Again, that our whole claim might be covered, even this argument needed to be supported by the general principle that the premature declaration of belligerency by the British Government had given these cruisers the only status they ever had, and therefore had made Great Britain responsible for all damages that ensued.

This argument, though satisfactory as a ground of war, has its disadvantages as the basis of a pecuniary claim. It is loose; it is susceptible of gross abuse in the hands of a strong nation against a weak one; it appears to apply no more to England than to France and Spain since their action was simultaneous, and Rebel cruisers received the same treatment from each of these powers; nor can we understand how England can be required to pay, for example, for the mischief done by the *Sumter*, and Spain be excused; finally, its gravest objection is, that it establishes a new rule of international law, restricting our own sovereignty and hampering our right of action in a manner which the nation will never admit it its own practice.

Our Government knew these objections, and, though fixed in its determination to force England into a settlement, did not undertake to insist upon a settlement on these terms. From the beginning it considered the subject as a proper one for argument and arbitration, although no formal offer of arbitration was ever made on its part. All that was done was to present the claim. Mr. Adams's note to Lord Russell, of May 20th, 1865, stated nine distinct points in the argument; the first and ninth ran as follows:—

"1. That the act of recognition by Her Majesty's Government of insurgents as belligerents on the high seas, before they had a single vessel afloat, was precipitate and unprecedented."

"9. That the injuries thus received by a country which has meanwhile sedulously endeavored to perform all its obligations, owing to the imperfection of the legal means at hand to prevent them, as well as the unwillingness to seek for more stringent powers, are of so grave a nature as in reason and justice to constitute a valid claim for reparation and indemnification."—*Mr. Adams to Lord Russell,* May 20th, 1865.

Lord Russell, for some reason of his own, waited until the 30th of August, and then responded as follows:—

"It appears to Her Majesty's Government that there are but two questions by which the claim of compensation could be tested. The one is: Have the British Government acted with due diligence, or, in other words, with good faith and honesty, in the maintenance of the neutrality they proclaimed? The other is: Have the law officers of the Crown properly understood the Foreign Enlistment Act, when they declined, in June, 1862, to advise the detention and seizure of the *Alabama,* and on other occasions when they were asked to detain other ships building or fitting in British ports? It appears to her Majesty's Government that neither of these questions could be put to a foreign government with any regard to the dignity and character of the British Crown and the British nation. Her Majesty's Government are the sole guardians of their own honor. They cannot admit that they may have acted with bad faith in maintaining the neutrality they professed. The law officers of the Crown must be held to be better interpreters of a British statute than any foreign government can be presumed to be. Her Majesty's Government must therefore decline either to make reparation and compensation for the captures made by the *Alabama,* or to refer the question to any foreign State."—*Lord Russell to Mr. Adams,* August 30th, 1865.

By this note the British Government declined an offer of arbitration which had never been made, and absolutely refused to admit the possibility of entertaining the idea of indemnity. The United

States Government contented itself with quietly insisting, and for a time the discussion ceased. Lord Palmerston died. Lord Clarendon succeeded Earl Russell in the Foreign Office, but no advance was made. In June, 1866, Lord Stanley and a Conservative ministry came into power, and justified the old maxim of our diplomatic service that a Conservative ministry is always the easiest for America to deal with. On the 27th of August, Mr. Seward sent to him a list of our claims, with an invitation to enter into a comprehensive settlement. Lord Stanley was well disposed to do so, but was fettered by the acts of Earl Russell and Earl Clarendon; nevertheless, he responded, on the 30th of November, 1866, by an offer of limited arbitration:—

"It is impossible for Her Majesty's present advisers to abandon the ground which has been taken by former governments so far as to admit the liability of this country for the claims then and now put forward. They do not think that such liability has been established according to international law or usage; and though sincerely and earnestly desiring a good understanding with the United States, they cannot consent to purchase even the advantage of that good understanding by concessions which would at once involve a censure on their predecessors in power, and be an acknowledgment, in their view uncalled for and unfounded, of wrong-doing on the part of the British Executive and Legislature. But, on the other hand, they are fully alive to the inconvenience which arises from the existence of unsettled claims of this character between two powerful and friendly governments. They would be glad to settle this question, if they can do so consistently with justice and national respect; and with this view they will not be disinclined to adopt the principle of arbitration, provided that a fitting arbitrator can be found, and that an agreement can be come to as to the points to which arbitration shall apply. Of these two conditions, the former need not at present be discussed; the latter is at once the more important and the more pressing. With regard to the ground of complaint on which most stress is laid in Mr. Seward's despatch, viz.: the alleged premature recognition of the Confederate States as a belligerent power, it is clear that no reference to arbitration is possible. The act complained of, while it bears very remotely on the claims now in question, is one as to which every State must be held to be the sole judge of its duty; and there is, so far as I am aware, no precedent for any government consenting to submit to the judgment of a foreign power, or of an international commission, the question whether its policy has or has not been suitable to the circumstances in which it was placed."—*Lord Stanley to Sir F. Bruce,* November 30th, 1866.

Before taking this ground, Lord Stanley had sounded leading Liberals, and had ascertained that they were in sympathy with him in rejecting unlimited arbitration. He had therefore succeeded for the first time in uniting all parties in England on his American policy. Our diplomatic correspondence shows that Mr. Bright remonstrated earnestly against the ground taken by Mr. Seward, whom he suspected of acting in bad faith, with the hidden purpose of preventing a settlement. Mr. Seward only replied, that he knew the American people better than Mr. Bright did.

Mr. Seward replied to Lord Stanley on the 12th of January, 1867:—

"The United States think it not only easier and more desirable that Great Britain should acknowledge and satisfy the claims for indemnity which we have submitted than it would be to find an equal and wise arbitrator who would consent to adjudicate them. If, however, Her Majesty's Government, for reasons satisfactory to them, should prefer the remedy of arbitration, the United States would not object. The United States, in that case, would expect to refer the whole controversy, just as it is found in the correspondence which has taken place between the two governments, with such further evidence and arguments as either party may desire, without imposing restrictions, conditions, or limitations upon the umpire, and without waiving any principle or argument on either side. They cannot consent to waive any question upon the consideration that it involves a point of national honor; and, on the other hand, they will not require that any question of national pride or honor shall be expressly ruled and determined as such."—*Mr. Seward to Mr. Adams,* January 12, 1867.

Lord Stanley then wrote to Sir Frederick Bruce on the 9th of March:—

"To such an extensive and unlimited reference Her Majesty's Government cannot consent, for this reason among others, that it would admit of, and indeed compel, the submission to the arbiter of the very question which I have already said they cannot agree to submit."—*Lord Stanley to Sir F. Bruce,* March 9th, 1867.

On the 16th of April, Mr. Seward took his old position again:—

"While we agree that all mutual claims which arose during the civil war between the citizens and subjects of the two countries ought to be amicably adjusted, and adjusted soon, we must nevertheless insist that they be adjusted by one and the same form of tribunal, with like or the same forms, and upon principles common to all of them. The proposal of Her Majesty's Government is therefore respectfully declined by the President of the United States."—*Mr. Seward to Mr. Adams,* April 16, 1867.

The second effort, therefore, resulted in moving the British Government so far as to concede the general principle that the claims were a proper subject for negotiation, and to offer of its own accord a reference to arbitration, if the question as to the declaration of belligerency were omitted. The United States accepted the principle of arbitration, but refused to omit any part of the argument. Mr. Seward now subsided again into silence, and left the British Government to reflect upon the situation. Sir Frederick Bruce died. Mr. Adams retired. Mr. Seward's own retirement was near at hand, and Lord Stanley had but a slender hold on his post. One more effort was felt to be necessary, in view of the hazards involved in leaving the question open.

A new expedient now occurred to our Government. On examination of the Claims Convention of 1853, it was found to contain the following general expression in regard to evidence offered to the Commission:—

"The Commissioners . . . shall be bound to receive and peruse all written documents or statements which may be presented to them by or on behalf of their respective governments in support of or in answer to any claim." The arbitrator was under the same obligation.

This form of convention, if adopted without any change, would satisfy all the requirements of the situation. The argument as to premature recognition would be admitted, and the British Government was at liberty to excuse its concession on the ground that it was merely re-adopting the Convention of 1853, which had proved so successful. Mr. Reverdy Johnson was accordingly despatched with the Convention of 1853 in his hand. He found Lord Stanley anxious to effect a settlement, and he negotiated a convention which was, as he supposed, conformable to his instructions. Lord

Stanley abandoned his own ground as completely as he had abandoned the ground taken by his predecessors. But this was not enough. When the treaty arrived in Washington in November last, it was found that Mr. Johnson had departed more widely than was approved from the text of 1853. Mr. Seward sent word that more concessions were required. Our Government actually dictated the treaty in its own words, and, as though to complete the revenge, Lord Stanley, the signer of the November treaty, represented the Conservative party, and Lord Clarendon, representing Earl Russell and the memory of Lord Palmerston, put his name to the final treaty of December.

Our national history furnishes no other example of such diplomatic triumph. Within three years, England yielded in rapid succession every point we had ever claimed. Well may the "Times" say that she had gone to the verge of humiliation! Had she in 1862 foreseen any such result, she would have followed the suggestion of France, and there would have been combined interference of the great powers in our affairs. This end was what Lord Palmerston feared, when he hesitated so long as to the policy to be pursued, and was outvoted, it is said, in the Cabinet.

The Senate has decided to reject this treaty for reasons of its own. We have no intention of criticising the Senate's action, and if, in rejecting this treaty, any better form of settlement is suggested, if the difficulty is merely one of form and not of substance, the new Administration will be able to carry on the negotiation as before. But if the objection to the treaty is essential and absolute, the implication is that our Government has conceded too much. Our Government has conceded nothing, however, except the principle of arbitration. How, then, after the Senate's absolute rejection of the treaty, can any President again propose or accept arbitration on these claims?

To reject arbitration in regard to a matter like this, which is peculiarly suitable for arbitration, and requires disinterested judgment, is equivalent to saying that we intend to take the law into our own hands. We declare ourselves in the right, and we require this fact to be acknowledged as a preliminary to further negotiation. When we say that the principles of adjudication must be established before creating a commission to adjudicate upon the claims, we mean that *our* principles must be established; otherwise we have no cause for refusing arbitration.

Now let us for a moment suppose a foreign minister in Washington meditating upon this problem: "What object has the United States Government in refusing arbitration on the *Alabama* claims?" He would dismiss at once the idea that this action was due to a mere passing ebullition of spite against the late Cabinet. The determination to reject is not restricted to the opponents of Mr. Seward. He might perhaps ask himself for a moment, whether it were not due to a wish to conciliate President Grant; but why should General Grant himself desire to hamper his whole administration by so serious a complication? The mere gratification of a long-nursed wrath against England might explain the action of some Senators, but not of all. We regret to add, that the diplomatist would not entertain the idea that the Senate was influenced by any virtuous devotion to the improvement of international law; for he would feel confident, and with reason, that, if England offered to cede Canada to the United States, on condition of being relieved of these claims, the Senate would immediately assent, without giving a second thought to international law or establishing any new principle whatever. In fact, the more he considered and reconsidered all other motives for an absolute rejection of the treaty, the more confident would his conclusion be, that the idea of territorial aggrandizement lay at the bottom of Senators' minds, —or, in other words, that these claims were to be reserved and used to lead or force England into a cession of territory.

We do not mean to say that this is to be the policy of the new Administration, but we do say that this is the policy which foreign nations will attribute to it. We do not know what are the opinions of President Grant, but there is little doubt that they belong more to the camp than to the cabinet. The Secretary of State can scarcely lay down in terms the doctrine, that, as the young dace is bait to the old pike, so Canada, Cuba, and Mexico are good food for the United States; but foreign nations are quick to catch an idea, and they will spare him the trouble.

The absolute rejection of this treaty must make itself felt in the whole future policy of the new Administration towards foreign nations, causing distrust, anxiety, possible derangement of commerce, and disturbance of credit. Our securities will be affected in value. Our politics will be confused by a new element. The situation cannot be indefinitely prolonged, and war is always within sight. The Senate practically forces this complication upon the President and the Cabinet. We have no idea of depreciating the foreign policy of the Senate,—if, indeed, the Senate is to dictate to the Secretary of State. We are confident that Mr. Sumner, as Chairman of the Committee on Foreign Relations, would have, and would deserve, entire confidence; but as it has already become a diplomatic maxim in Washington that it is worse than useless to negotiate with a President who is powerless to redeem his pledges, so it has become a recognized fact in Congress that the report of a regular committee cannot prevail against the lobby, backed by obstructionists and carpet-baggers.

Persons whose tastes lead them to useless speculations may amuse themselves by peering into the future as well as they can, in order to distinguish the dim outlines of the result, so far as our foreign relations are concerned. That the whole continent of North America and all its adjacent islands must at last fall under the control of the United States is a conviction absolutely ingrained in our people. Granting this result, against which, if we struggle at all, we shall struggle in vain, there are two ways of reaching it. Whether two democracies of England and America will dislike each other more or less cordially than did the United States republic and the British crown we will not decide; but if there comes an appeal to arms, no great effort of the imagination is needed to foresee a political conspiracy, which will have for its object to throw British America into the arms of the United States and British India upon the bayonets of a Russian army. This is the kind of speculation which Russia would naturally dwell upon, and which implies universal war. We prefer to think that there is a better alternative. In the darkest days of our national trials, the winter of 1861-62, when in England public opinion had been artificially roused to fever heat against our country, a few Englishmen still stood by us with a courage and a confidence which only those are likely to appreciate who had personal occasion to feel their value. Even then, when there seemed to be no light in any quarter, we clung to the idea that there would come a day when

America would have conquered all her difficulties, when her few constant friends in England should under the spur of her success have climbed to power, and when our Government and theirs should act in harmony on large and liberal principles. These men are now in the English Ministry, and have sent us our own selected treaty, which we have refused to accept.[1] Our Government seems to threaten to use its pecuniary claims for driving a good bargain for land. We will not discuss the respectability of this policy, which is a point that every one can decide for himself. We prefer to look for the grounds of a wider settlement. We know the strength and weakness of Great Britain. Her political interests do not lie in America, but in Asia; and no principle is now more firmly established than that her American possessions are a source of weakness, not of strength, while a wise policy requires the concentration of all her military and naval power on her Indian possessions, and on her ways of communication with them. She must ultimately of her own accord effect this concentration, for her existence as a great nation depends upon it. On the other hand, we need not require her to cede territory, but should induce her to abandon it to itself: so it will be safer from violence than if it were a part of the British Empire. Thus she might be separated absolutely, completely, and of her own free will from all political power or interference whatever in this quarter of the globe. We believe that our foreign policy, if properly managed, can peacefully effect this result; and we shall look with extreme interest to see whether the administration of General Grant is disposed to use with patience the slow, but, as we believe, the sure, means of diplomacy and conciliation to work out this large and permanent settlement of our English relations.

[1] [The Senate eventually ratified a new agreement, the Treaty of Washington, in May, 1871, which set the terms for the arbitration of the *Alabama* claims and related matters.]

Civil Service Reform

One of the recurring issues of post-Civil War politics, and one that particularly exercised the minds of Henry Adams and his friends, was civil service reform. The war had occasioned an immense increase in the power of Congress relative to the presidency, and the spoils system, inaugurated by an ambitious president, had become a means of controlling the executive power, since Congress had, in effect, usurped the president's right of appointment. The balance of powers, which had been John Adams' leading constitutional idea, was therefore threatened, and the character of the American government seemed in danger of being permanently revised. Thus Henry Adams' demand for reform of the civil service was based not on the usual "arguments drawn from finance or from administrative convenience" but on an appeal to "the fundamental principles of the Constitution." He exhibits very clearly in this appeal the family-inherited conservatism that was so large a part of his early political attitude. It is a species of conservatism, to be sure, which has characteristically been a moving force in American reform.

Civil Service Reform

"In the government of this Commonwealth, the legislative department shall never exercise the executive and judicial powers, or either of them; the executive shall never exercise the legislative and judicial powers, or either of them; the judicial shall never exercise the legislative and executive powers, or either of them: *to the end it may be a government of laws and not of men.*" The Massachusetts Bill of Rights, which contains this article, inimitable for grasp and conciseness, adds elsewhere the warning that among the precautions absolutely necessary for the maintenance of a free government is a frequent recurrence to the fundamental principles of the Constitution. Laying aside, therefore, the usual arguments in favor of civil-service reform,—arguments drawn from finance or from administrative convenience,—this essay will attempt to show that the soundness and vigor, nay, even the purpose of the reform movement, must depend upon its recurrence to the fundamental principles of the Constitution.

When President Grant took the oath of office, he held in his hands a greater power than any President chosen for many years past or likely to be chosen for many years to come. Turn which way he liked, it was supposed that a majority of the people was ready to lend him its support. Whatever might have been said of his abilities or character as a whole, it was still universally believed

[From the *North American Review*, CIX (October 1869), 443-475.]

that in the two essential qualities of honesty and obstinacy he enjoyed a considerable superiority over any candidate that the country could hope to see pass the ordeal of a political caucus. If there was one quality expressed in General Grant's face, it was that of dogged resolution. If there was any moral in his career, it was to be found in the example of silent perseverance. The most careful search could not have produced out of the whole population of the United States a single man who had offered more proofs of a stubborn will, nor one from whom the public might expect a more resolute adherence to a purpose once fixed.

It was commonly supposed that the new President had determined, even before the inauguration, on his course in regard to the civil service. His non-partisan character, his military training, his inheritance of an administrative system in which the two great parties divided the patronage, and, above all, his open and frank expressions of opinion, publicly reported and undenied, all seemed to point towards a very moderate exercise of executive power. The public, outside the ranks of the trifling proportion of citizens who are directly engaged in managing party machinery, accepted this foregone conclusion with a sense of relief and almost of joy. The press was resigned to it, and as a body was ready if not actively to support, at any rate to abstain from actively opposing the conservative tendencies of the President. A stranger who looked at the national institutions with the old assumption that the voice of the people guides the course of the government, would have thought nothing more easy than for the President to lift his administration, by a single touch, out of the mire of political corruption.

Perhaps the President himself shared in this belief. At all events, the most natural explanation of his first proceedings is to be found in some such idea. He selected a Cabinet which seemed to have but one bond of sympathy, and this one bond the common freedom from political entanglement. The wish to escape party dictation was more evident than the means of doing so were well chosen. The attempt failed, and the President yielded to political pressure so far as to make a new selection; but even after this partial check, the Cabinet contained only one member who was distinctly a representative rather of the Republican party than of the Republican sentiment of the country.

The Cabinet once formed, it became necessary to establish a rule in regard to inferior appointments. Here too the popular expectation turned out to be well founded. Instructions were duly given to the effect that there should be no sweeping and partisan changes. Removals from office might indeed be made in cases of incompetence or misbehavior, or for reasons of economy, or even where extreme partisanship had compromised the loyalty due to the government, but no general proscription on account of political opinions was to be authorized. This was the principle laid down by the President to the members of his Cabinet for the rule of the departments,—a principle sound, just, and popular, which deserved and in the end would probably have received universal applause.

How was it that this rule was not carried into effect? Upon whom does the blame rest that this opportunity, which was so rare and so promising, was thrown away? That the President's intentions were defeated here even more decisively than in the arrangement of the Cabinet, is only too evident, but that the blame for this defeat rests on him or on his advisers is an assumption that the public is not justified in making. However strongly one may be prejudiced against General Grant's final capitulation, it is only his due to say that he did not surrender with a good grace. No distant observer can judge fairly of the difficulties to which a President is subjected when he attempts to maintain such a position in face of the party organization which supports him. Nothing could be easier than to announce that faithful and competent servants of the government should not be disturbed, but nothing was more difficult than to maintain the promise. In the struggle which followed, the President stood alone. The great mass of his friends, who cared nothing for office or patronage, could neither see what was going forward, nor could they lend him encouragement or support. They only knew that General Grant, penned up in the White House, was surrounded by a hungry army of political adventurers whose trade was an object of popular odium or contempt.

Had the army of office-seekers marched alone against the White House, General Grant would probably have routed it, large as it was, with the utmost ease. Such men might fret him, but they would have found him a difficult instrument to play upon. They came, therefore, supported on one side by all the personal influence, on the other by all the political power, they could control, and day after day the whole phalanx flung itself upon the President. Escape was impossible. There are many things that a President cannot evade, and among the first of these is the duty of listening with patience and replying with courtesy to the leading men of his party. A senator may be tedious, ill-mannered, and a notorious rogue, but the double majesty of State and Senate speaks from his lips and commands a hearing.

Nor was it possible for the President to say that the remonstrances and the complaints of office-seekers were without foundation. The practice of removing officials, in order to appoint political or personal friends to their vacant posts, was one which custom had firmly established. Whether good or bad, it existed, and President Grant had been nominated and elected without having given any public warning that this custom was to be changed. To act upon the new rule without suitable notice was unfair to his friends; for however just the reform might be in the abstract, in practice it would be considered a refusal of confidence to individuals, and would tend to discredit them in the eyes of their constituents. A friendly appeal of this sort was difficult to resist. The applicant was perhaps a soldier, a comrade of the President, a man who had suffered in the national cause. His spokesman might be a member of Congress, a consistent Republican, and a cordial supporter of General Grant in days when his supporters were few; as a member of Congress his value might be all the greater because he came from a district which no other Republican could control, and where even he thought the executive patronage essential for his re-election. He would urge that the principle of rotation in office was a necessary element in the organization of parties; it held them together, stimulated their activity, and could not be suddenly abandoned without a shock, the only possible result of which would be that the President must lose a devoted friend in Congress in order to substitute a Democrat in his place, and this for the mere purpose of retaining Andrew Johnson's officials. Or if the President held firm against reasoning, there remained the earnest appeal to personal friendship, far more difficult to resist or evade than any weapon in the whole armory of logic. Even when this had failed to affect a muscle of the President's dogged and imperturbable features, there were expedients in reserve which might smooth away every difficulty. There are few things to which politicians will not descend, and one favorite method by which to rid themselves of their enemies, as it is the most dishonest and the most insidious, is generally the most successful. The duties of a government officer are such as very commonly make trouble between him and the persons with whom he is obliged to come in contact, and it frequently happens that men who imagine themselves ill-treated are ready to believe, and active in spreading, any charges against a government officer whose only fault is perhaps too great activity or too sharp a tongue. To put these charges on paper is an easy task, and to obtain a list of signatures extensive enough to call for attention is not very difficult, if the affair is carefully managed. If the treasury could tell the secret history of the many attempts made, not only by the famous whiskey ring, but by the more dangerous and powerful political ring, to drive old and tried servants from the public service, no one could fail to see that even in the best times the department is often deceived and with difficulty maintains its ground against outside pressure. There seems to be no limit to the elasticity of respectable men's consciences when their interests and their pride are involved. Thus the provision that government officers shall not be removed except for cause may be practically evaded, and the President or the Secretary, wearied out by incessant annoyance, is happy at last to yield the point and to cover his conscience by the "charges" which he has never investigated.

All this, however, is but child's play. The President might perhaps have yielded to these incessant personal appeals or to the small intrigues which backed them, but he would have yielded in this case to individual influence, not to political combinations; he would have lowered his personal authority, but he would not have deserted his official trust. To show that the heart of the evil is here, and that, until reform can reach this height, reform must be imperfect and may be mischievous, it will be necessary to look back for an instant on the past history of the government.

The early administrations, from the time of Washington to the time of Jackson, were, in spite of all political differences, practically one continuous government; that is, the President, whoever he might be, stood as regarded the legislature and the political parties as merely the temporary head of a permanent executive system, which was meant to furnish, and did in fact furnish, the necessary solidity and continuity without which no government can last. The President represented, not a party, nor even the people either in a mass or in any of its innumerable divisions, but an essential part of the frame of government; that part which was neither legislature nor judiciary; a part which in the nature of society must of necessity exist,—which in the United States was intentionally and wisely made a system by itself, in order to balance the other portions of the structure. The President might die, but the office could not be vacant. He might be sent back to private life, but his successor took up the instruments which he laid down. He might be incompetent as a British king, but the permanent system of which he represented the power and the wisdom would save him from contempt. He might be unprincipled as a French emperor, but the established courses of administration, more powerful than mere law, would hold his hand. The five early Presidents accepted and maintained this position, to their own advantage and to that of the country. Nor did President Jackson essentially change it. He introduced, it is true, the rule of punishing officials whose only duty was to the government for holding opinions which were hurtful only to himself, if they were hurtful at all; but his very attitude towards the Senate implied a high sense of his official duty, and so long as his strong hand guided the executive system it was maintained in all its power, if not in all its dignity. When he passed away, however, and a succession of weaker men assumed his place, the effects of his example were little by little drawn into service to break down this bulwark of the executive. By an unwritten law of the Constitution, which has seldom been found at fault, the nervous system of the great extra-constitutional party organizations finds its centre in the United States Senate. As the party organizations grew in development and strength, the Senate became more and more the seat of their intrigues; and when the party organizations discovered that their power would be greatly increased by controlling the executive patronage, the Senate lent all its overruling influence to effect this result, and soon became through its individual members the largest dispenser of this patronage.

This was, however, only the first step. Mr. Marcy's celebrated declaration, drawn from the sink of New York politics, "To the victors belong the spoils," was mischievous, but it was not fatal. The President had always been in the habit of consulting friendly senators and representatives in regard to special appointments, and when he now broke down the permanence and dignity of that administrative system of which he ought to have been the champion, he only admitted individual members of the legislature to a wider influence in executive patronage than they had hitherto enjoyed. But the movement could not stop here. When it was that Congress first began to claim as a right the nominating power which it had until then held as a favor, is a question difficult to answer with exactness, but at all events the concession has been made within the last ten years. It may be safe to say, on the authority of a person well informed as to the history of times in which he has acted a great part, that the assumption by members of Congress of local patronage as a right was first conceded in principle by the first administration of Mr. Lincoln, in 1861. The earlier and notorious instance of Mr. Douglas, in his Illinois campaign, was probably exceptional, and considered as such by the President. By this concession, the executive, the great, permanent constitutional power, which Washington and Jefferson represented, and which the wisdom of our own times aims to suppress, delivered over to the legislature its independence as a co-ordinate branch of the government. Its moral weight, and its individual character as a permanent influence in the government, ruled by administrative principles and guided by conservative maxims drawn from its own history, were rudely shaken by the first blow, but its absolute power was reduced only by the second.

"If the executive power, or any considerable part of it, is left in the hands either of an aristocratical or a democratical assembly, it will corrupt the legislature as necessarily as rust corrupts iron, or as arsenic poisons the human body; and when the legislature is corrupted the people are undone." [1] This principle, laid down by an American writer upon government before the Constitution

[1] [John Adams, preface to *A Defence of the Constitutions of Government of the United States of America*, 1787. *Works of John Adams*, ed. Charles Francis Adams (Boston, 1850-1856), IV, 290.]

was framed, received a striking illustration in the result of that revolution which threw the executive patronage into the hands of the legislature. Mr. Lincoln's death was the accidental cause of bringing the evil to a head, and if any one is curious to follow the exact process by which this poison of executive power works in corrupting a legislature and a people, it is only necessary to watch what has since occurred. Since the foundation of the government there has been no scandal and no corruption which could be compared in its mischievous effects to the disgraceful bargaining for office which took place between President Johnson and the Senate. Even the men who shared in it were ashamed. No one has a word of defence for it. This attempt on the part of the legislature to exercise the executive power, has produced in Congress and in the country an indifference to strict rules of wrong and right, a contempt for personal dignity, a cynical assumption of official dishonesty, and a patient assent to the supposed necessity of corruption, which nothing but a great popular reaction can overcome.

There is no room here for moderate language or for half-way modes of thought. Men must strip from the subject all imaginary distinctions, and confront face to face the bald and disgusting fact that members of Congress cannot be honest with such a power in their hands. Even the best will consult his own interests in distributing patronage, and this means that he will convert a sacred public trust into a private property,—an act which by every known code is stigmatized as the highest of crimes. The senator who buys outright with his own money his seat in the national legislature is guilty of an act not more dishonorable to himself and far less hurtful to the public interests than that which he commits in paying for the same dignity out of the nation's means, at the expense of the nation's future good, by an appointment to office. Intrigue and venality are the necessary accompaniments of such an adjustment of powers, and unfortunately, under the American system, political corruption cannot be confined to a class. An aristocracy may indeed be corrupt without infecting the great mass of people beneath it; these may remain sound to the core, and ready to apply the remedy when the evil becomes intolerable. Such has again and again been the case in England when she seemed tottering on the verge of fall. But in America there is no such reserved force. The inevitable effect of opening a permanent and copious source of corruption in the legislature must be that the people are undone.

Thus, when General Grant came into power, the executive which had originally been organized as a permanent system with a permanent and independent existence, and a temporary head, was wholly changed in its nature. While the first five Presidents had in fact formed a continuous government, protected from encroachments by its continuous character, the last five have been the representatives of so many violent revolutions. At first it had been supposed that these revolutions were only the results of party triumphs ("I never said that the victors should plunder their own camp," is the commentary of Mr. Marcy on his own previous declaration). As such, they were excused. But this is no longer pretended. The whole executive system has become the avowed plaything of the legislature. Whatever happens, Congress has established the right to seize and overthrow the whole administration once in every four years forever. It is folly to suppose that the executive can maintain itself while such a right is conceded or even theoretically acknowledged. It is equal folly to imagine that the government itself can endure under a strain which would have broken the Roman Empire into fragments.

General Grant, therefore, whether he knew it or not, was attempting a far more serious reform than any mere improvement of the civil service implies, a reform in comparison with which the proposed saving of $100,000,000 a year to the treasury was but a trifle. The question was not whether he as an individual would make or refuse to make certain appointments, but whether he had the power to wrest the executive authority from the hands of Congress; whether he could obey or understand the meaning of his oath; whether the President was to remain where the Constitution placed him, or whether the Senate was to snatch more and more of the functions of administration, until corruption had taken so deep a root that the people in their disgust would cheer on some modern Gracchus to attempt by sedition a reform which could no longer be accomplished by law. What might have been the result of President Grant's experiment, had he persevered, is a problem that for the present must remain unsolved. Before a week had passed it had become clear that the President's perseverance in his attempt would provoke a personal rupture with so many members of the legislature, and secret hostility in so many more, as to endanger the success of the administration.

The President gave way. Then began those cruel scenes which for months reduced the city of Washington to such a condition as is caused by an ordinary pestilence or famine. Private suffering is of small consequence where the nation is the chief sufferer. It matters little how many miserable women and worn-out men, the discarded servants of the Republic, are to be ground to death under the wheels of this slow-moving idol of faction, since their tears or agony are as little likely to save others as they are to help these in their supplications to the inexorable appointment-clerk. Therefore, if it is any consolation to the public to doubt or to hope that the private injustice done and misery caused were exaggerated,— although few persons who had occasion to be near will share their trust,—let them have the benefit of the doubt and rejoice in it. The argument can well afford to spare this poor appeal to human sympathy.

To a certain extent General Grant's administration did only what had been done by its predecessors, and what has long been familiar to the public mind. Although much has been said against the President for his selection of personal friends and relatives for office, so far as this choice had any political meaning it was rather deserving of praise and support, as the last remnant of the President's defeated purpose of rescuing the public service from the taint of political corruption. If a similar process of selection had been carried, with proper care and a wider acquaintance with men, through all the public service, one principal source of corruption, the low intrigues of partisan politicians, would have been greatly checked. In this particular, on the contrary, it was reserved for the administration of President Grant to descend lower than the worst of its predecessors in the scale of self-degradation.

The Grand Army of the Republic was not perhaps organized as a political association. Its nominal object was rather one of charity, and it is believed to have proved useful in lending its protection or assistance to soldiers and soldiers' families in distress. As a charitable and useful society, it contains many members of the highest character, and its chief, General Logan, has done good service to the country, and deserves respect for it. But whether the original organization was intended to be political or not, it certainly plunged into politics very soon after its existence began, and by the time General Grant entered office it had already reached the lowest level of political activity. Under the pretence of clearing Rebels from the public service, it organized within the departments an elaborate system of espionage, such as the American government had never yet been degraded enough to cover with its protection. The history of every clerk, from the highest to the lowest, was ransacked to obtain evidence of his political opinions; and every one who fell under suspicion was watched, his words taken down, even his looks carefully noted. The evidence thus collected was duly reported to the proper authorities of the organization, and the officers of the Grand Army of the Republic, on the strength of this testimony, secretly acquired by means which were once thought disgraceful, then made a formal demand upon the United States government, through the heads of departments, denouncing, like Jacobins of the reign of terror, the criminals thus condemned without a hearing, and demanding their removal for the benefit of soldiers of the Grand Army.

If there is anything in the most liberal view of this action that can be made to palliate or excuse the outrage, it would be well to make it known. The government owes it to its own dignity, if not to decency, to repel the idea that it could ever have tolerated any approach to such interference with its duties, while the mere suggestion that its action could have been affected by such means is in itself so near an insult that it would not be fitting for the pages of this Review. But in order that there may be no danger of incurring the charge of exaggerating the importance of the subject, it will be well to insert here the actual form of address used by the Grand Army in communicating with the administration.

"To the Hon. . . . . . .
      "Secretary of . . . . .
   "Sir:—We, the undersigned, a committee of the G.A.R. appointed for the purpose of examining into the political status of the employees of the . . . . . Department, have the honor to present to the Honorable Secretary the accompanying lists, and respectfully ask the removal of

these persons and the appointment, to fill the vacancies, of soldiers and sailors.

"Very respectfully,

"· · · · · ·"

Then follows the list of names, with the accompanying annotations:—

"1. Those strongly suspected of having been Rebel sympathizers.

"2. Those who made it their duty to rigidly enforce 'my policy' in word and deed.

"Those having no mark against their names are or have been recognized as Democrats until recently.

"Those marked 'doubtful' left open for further examination."

The extraordinary nature of this performance becomes doubly striking when it is remembered that "we, the undersigned," who were thus acting as a committee for "examining into the political status of the employees of the departments," and who assumed to dictate to the Secretary as to who was to be removed and who appointed, were of necessity the Secretary's own clerks!

The Treasury was the richest field for rewarding the labor of these disinterested men. Mr. Boutwell, fresh from Congress and trained in a partisan school, was the only member of the Cabinet who had thoroughly mastered the practice and principles of that species of political science which is peculiarly American, and who believed in its wisdom and necessity with all the earnestness of the New England mind. He alone, or with but one companion, turned to the work with zeal; but it would be unfair to suppose that he could lower himself so far as to lend direct support to a system so odious and so disreputable as that pursued by the Grand Army. Mr. Boutwell did not act directly upon the information furnished by the Grand Army. Instead of this, he inaugurated another inquisition of his own, by which he might test the political fidelity of his subordinates. It is surely impossible that these two tribunals can have carried on their investigations side by side and hand in hand within the walls of the Treasury. *Non tali auxilio!* Without such an additional humiliation, it is enough to know that under this double terror the whole moral tone of the department gave way. Every clerk distrusted his neighbor, and the air of the Treasury, which in ordinary times is not altogether pure, now seemed heavy with the whispers of delators. The new administration began its career by creating or encouraging in its service the same system of spies and secret denunciation which is usually charged as the crowning disgrace of an absolute despotism. To palliate it by alleging its narrow field of action is absurd. It not only existed, but its single fault was found to be its too great efficiency. In more than one case the denounced and removed official proved to have been as good and true a Republican as the Secretary himself, no matter how narrow the creed; and before the work was completed, it was commonly understood at Washington that both Mr. Boutwell and his appointment-clerk had expressed themselves as profoundly disappointed and disgusted with the mistakes which they had made.

While these events were taking place in the Treasury building, the city of Washington was filled with adventurers in search of office. Senators and members stood aghast at the work they were expected to do; but they did it. Almost every department of the executive patronage was swept clean; and although there may be a question whether the new appointments were as a whole better or worse than the old, there can be no doubt that they were not made for any purpose of improving the service, but were for the most part the same gross political jobs that have for so many years stamped the character of American politics. Yet although the Treasury with its vast power was entirely in the hands of the plunderers, and the Post-Office seemed to follow the Treasury, the resistance to political dictation was still vigorously maintained in other departments of the government, where men of another temper were in control. Several of the Secretaries preserved their trust with courage and dignity, but among all the members of the Cabinet the most remarkable contrast to the pliability of Mr. Boutwell was furnished by the dogged obstinacy of the Attorney-General. Accident had brought side by side in President Grant's Cabinet two men who might naturally have been supposed to hold the same political ideas. They both came from the same Congressional district; they had for years belonged to the same political party; there was no jealousy to divide them; both were sincere, honest, and capable. Yet one was the type of that narrow political morality which has obtained so general a control of America,—the product of caucuses and party promotion; the other was by birth and by training a representative of the best New England school, holding his moral rules on the sole authority of his own conscience, indifferent to opposition whether in or out of his party, obstinate to excess, and keenly alive to the weaknesses in which he did not share. Judge Hoar belonged in fact to a class of men who had been gradually driven from politics, but whom it is the hope of reformers to restore. Mr. Boutwell belonged to the class which has excluded its rival, but which has failed to fill with equal dignity the place it has usurped. At the outset of the administration the essential difference in the characters of these two men was brought out in lively contrast. While Mr. Boutwell distributed his offices with liberal hands to senators and representatives, Grand Armies and State delegations, the Attorney-General sat silently at his desk, and glared through his spectacles with a sort of grim humor at the man who dared ask him to perpetrate a political job. While Mr. Boutwell, buttonholed in corners, was listening with approval to the account of some assessor's entire unfitness for the Republicans of Ohio or Minnesota, Judge Hoar had reached the somewhat absurd determination that not even his bedridden messenger should be removed, although the Attorney-General should be reduced to running his own errands. The men who attempted to lead the Attorney-General came away from his office with a low opinion of his intelligence, which they expressed with somewhat excusable intemperance both in public and private. They complained that he did not "see things," where his real offence was in seeing far too much; and they added that his temper was unpleasantly irritable, and his obstinacy that of a mule. Much allowance is to be made for politicians in such a position, and it is possibly true that the Attorney-General may have occasionally allowed his wit or his temper to express his thoughts with impolitic freedom. He had not been placed in that office in order to provide for politicians, and he certainly carried out this negative purpose. The removals and appointments which a proper regard for the public service required were made with little reference to personal preferences. Among other posts, the New York marshalship, usually considered as an important item in senatorial patronage, was for once given unsought and unexpected to a man who was by no means calculated to serve the ordinary ends of New York politicians. Such reckless indifference to the claims of party managers was naturally followed by a liberal distribution of personal abuse, which must be the inevitable lot of any public man who holds that his duty to the government is higher than his duty to factions among the people or in the legislature; and the public may confidently expect that the persevering attempts to drive Judge Hoar from the Cabinet, from which his approaching retirement is so regularly announced by the officious agents of the press, will end only when their object is accomplished.

Notwithstanding the resistance of this portion of the Cabinet, it is still true that the administration of President Grant as a whole will be considered as having carried the principle of rotation in office and submission to external interference in executive powers to a point beyond anything that had been reached before. The claim of members of the legislature to control the local and even the general appointments for which the President and the President alone ought to be held responsible has not been met by any sufficient assertion of the executive dignity, and is now so deeply rooted in custom that few members of the legislature can at once succeed in grasping the idea that no corresponding right exists. One of the characteristic stories told of the Attorney-General represents him as bewildering some delegation that recommended a certain appointment by the simple reply that he did not think the public service required a change of the incumbent. The bewilderment of the gentlemen was due to the fact that this recommendation happened to be the unanimous act of an entire State delegation in Congress, and it seemed impossible that the executive could assert a higher duty to itself than it owed to an entire State delegation. But even the partial independence which the executive is still allowed, an independence commonly gained by balancing one congressional influence against another, works evil rather than good. It is one of the unfortunate but inevitable results of the situation that the better class of politicians on whom a President ought to rely, men of dignity and self-respect, will not lower themselves to this struggle for patronage. Their suggestions or wishes once expressed and met by refusal or neglect, they retire, offended and mortified, but too proud to beg for favors. Not so with the baser type of professional politicians. These are never wearied and never absent. Day and night they weave their web round the President and his advisers. Some intriguer, who has made his way to eminence by means of the skill with which he has managed the tools of political corruption in a State where even before his time political corruption had become an art that few could master; who by the meanness of his policy and the pliancy of his character had fairly broken the back of his party, which at its last gasp made itself a stepping-stone to pass him safely into the Senate, and then sank into hopeless impotence; some such man, thus sent to Washington to pursue there the same grovelling and selfish policy which had already brought a great party into contempt on the narrower field of State politics, allows few things to stand in the way of his determination to control the tremendous patronage which the government holds in his constituency. One repulse does not affect him. The government may at first disregard his remonstrances and scarcely conceal its contempt for his opinions; but sooner or later his persistence and his skill conquer a foothold, and he stands before the country the dispenser of Federal patronage, while, just as surely "as rust corrupts iron or as arsenic poisons the human body," his advice and his presence enfeeble and pervert the tone and energy of the administration.

This difficulty of dividing responsibility between the executive and the legislature is one which is too serious to exist long. The country has now arrived at a point where it must either go back or go forward. The great executive authority established by the Constitution as the counterpoise of the great legislative authority has gradually abandoned, first, that character as a permanent and regular system which served as the defence of weak Presidents; secondly, the right of nomination to executive offices which belong within the constituencies of members of the legislature; and finally, it only remains to adopt a measure formally urged in the last session of Congress, by which the entire patronage of the executive may be allotted between the several States in *pro rata* proportions, and then the legislature will have grasped the whole executive power, leaving in its place only the empty honor of a name.

The experience of the present government has shown that even a President so determined in character and so strong in popular support as General Grant shrank from the attempt to reform the civil service as one which was beyond his powers. Not only has this opportunity been lost,—an opportunity which may never occur again,—but the Republican party by its action in this case seems to have shut the door to reform. Had General Grant succeeded in carrying out his original purpose, public opinion might have been roused to enforce the precedent on future administrations; but it is difficult to understand how any Republican member of Congress can now propose a measure of reform, which, if worth consideration at all, must, by securing the permanence of present office-holders, practically jockey any future administration out of its power; and it is equally difficult to see why any future Democratic President should consider himself bound by such a law. Nothing remains but to act outside of all party organizations, and to appeal with all the earnestness that the emergency requires, not to Congress nor to the President, but to the people, to return to the first principles of the government, and to shut off forever this source of corruption in the state.

If there were any reason to suppose that a deep-laid scheme existed on the part of any member or members of the legislature to usurp the government, there might indeed be some reason to despair, but in fact the danger is at present due rather to the indifference of the better senators and to their natural and proper spirit of common pride in the dignity of their House, than to any far-sighted policy. It is not Congress that has betrayed the executive, but a long line of Presidents who have failed to respect their trust. And as the evil is due, not so much to Congress as to the Presidents, so the remedy must be sought, not in any arbitrary legislation, but in the creation of such a sound public opinion as will hold future Presidents more closely to their charge. Supported by such an aroused public feeling, the President will certainly act with success. It is not merely his right, but his duty, to originate any reform in the civil service which may seem to him useful or necessary; and if he understands the meaning of an oath, he is bound to carry out such a reform in spite of all resistance. Every President, even though steeped from his cradle in an atmosphere of county politics, must still feel, on assuming his office, some part of that permanent responsibility which weighs upon the executive chair no matter who may be its occupant. The outward forms of royalty, the symbols of that dignity which attaches not to the person but to the office, are not allowed to republican rulers, but the great administrative system over which the accident of a birth has placed one man, and the still greater accident of a popular caucus has placed another, demands of both the same submission and sacrifice of selfish purposes, and gives to both the same sense of deep responsibility. No ruler will intentionally betray this trust. The system is too vast for one weak man to overthrow. He may indeed betray the people who have trusted him, but he will do his best to defend or increase the powers of his office. He cannot entirely pervert the great system behind him into a personal property. He must be controlled and guided by it, even more than it can be controlled by him. If its machinery is clogged, he is the sufferer; if mistakes are committed, he is responsible; if violence is at hand, his life is the forfeit. Of the thirty-six million people in the United States, the President is the one most interested in the regular working of the administrative system.

The President therefore, be he who he may, must be expected to prefer for his service the old and educated servants of the government, and to exericse, or at least wish to exercise, some discretion in his appointments. Arguing from general principles, it is safe to assume that the President does as a rule attempt, though of late years more and more feebly, to resist the dictation of politicians within the range of his official duties. With a sympathetic public behind him, the President may commonly be depended upon to institute and to maintain such reforms as experience has proved to be necessary. Even of late years the executive has shown examples of its capacity for originating, and of its persistence in urging, its ideas of reform, such as only need application on a wider field in order to carry every measure that reformers demand.

The history of the struggle made by the State Department to improve its consular service throws a flood of light, not only upon the difficulties that stand in the way of reform, but upon the manner in which alone they can be properly met. There are probably few persons in the United States who are aware that any such attempt has ever been made by the government, or who have the least idea whether it has succeeded or whether it has failed. It will therefore be interesting to tell the story, so far as it can be disinterred from congressional debates and executive documents.

In 1853, Mr. Everett, when Secretary of State to President Fillmore, negotiated with the government of France a consular convention, which was then thought to be the most successful model for that especial class of treaty that had yet been framed. Among the articles of the convention was one by which the existence of consular pupils was formally recognized as a part of the system in both countries. No such office, however, existed in the American service, and the department appears to have framed or accepted the article only with the intention of availing itself at some future time of this expedient for quietly improving its foreign corps of officers. Mr. Everett, having signed the treaty, almost immediately quitted office, and was succeeded by Mr. Marcy under the presidency of Mr. Pierce.

Nothing was done by Mr. Marcy either in 1853 or in the following year, nor even when in 1855 the necessity of revising the entire consular system had compelled Congress to pass a very elaborate act for the purpose. But in 1856 it was found that this act of 1855 was itself incomplete, and required a supplementary law, which was duly prepared in committee after much consultation with the department, and the original draft, furnished by the department to the committee, contained a clause authorizing the President to appoint twenty-five consular pupils with salaries of $1,000 a year, first having subjected them to a proper examination to secure their fitness for the post. Mr. Marcy had asked for seventy-five, but the committee cut the number down by two thirds, and the department acquiesced, having by its urgency succeeded in convincing the committee of the material advantages to be gained by the new agents thus created. Late in the session the bill was introduced into Congress and passed without debate by common agreement, probably no member outside of the committee ever having taken the trouble to read it.

Mr. Marcy instantly issued elaborate instructions regulating the standard of qualification, and the process to be followed in examining candidates, and he promised somewhat too hastily that deserving pupils should be recommended to the President from time to time for promotion to vacant consulates. Unfortunately Congress had made no special appropriation for these pupils, and before Mr. Marcy could make any actual appointment it was necessary to wait for the appropriations of the following year. Accordingly, when Congress met in December, the Appropriation Bill contained the little item: "For consular pupils, $25,000." No sooner had the House in committee reached this paragraph than it burst into a fit of temper. The Committee of Ways and Means attempted feebly to defend it, but General Quitman, of Mississippi, after stating that consuls were diplomats, and that the best diplomacy was the diplomacy of the backwoods, the honest diplomacy of republican freemen, not that which was taught in the diplomatic schools of Europe, threatened to propose by way of amendment an appropriation for establishing a professorship of diplomacy in the Department of State. This idea, in itself not altogether unworthy of consideration, seemed to settle the doubts of the House. The appropriation was struck out with scarcely a dissentient vote, and the Republican majority for once congratulated itself and its Democratic friends upon an agreement of opinion.

The bill next went to the Senate Committee on Finance, of which Mr. R. M. T. Hunter, of Virginia, was chairman. In the mean while Mr. Marcy had heard of the action taken by the House, and was not prepared to abandon his scheme so easily. He wrote a long letter to Mr. Hunter, urging him to restore the appropriation, and stating with much force the arguments in its favor. Mr. Hunter acceded to his wish, and the bill was reported to the Senate with the item replaced. Debate instantly rose on this point, and continued at some length. Curiously enough, Mr. Fessenden took the lead in opposition, on the ground, first, that the project was impracticable, owing to the want of permanence in our system of government; and, secondly, that it would merely enable the President to cause his friends' sons to be educated abroad. Mr. Collamer suggested—and his suggestion was met by the laughter of the Senate—that the next step might be to educate a President; a notion which might perhaps please the public better than it would suit the ambition of senators. But it was reserved for Mr. Hale, of

New Hampshire,[1] to state the true ground of objection in a manner which admits of no response.

"I am opposed to this policy entirely," said Mr. Hale. "I am opposed to it, not because I think our consuls are educated too highly as a general fact, but I dislike this way of doing it. If we begin here, where is it to stop? We shall have then to appoint pupils for ambassadors, and, when you begin that, there is no ending."

There is little satisfaction in striking at a fallen man, and Mr. Hale is now fallen so low that an assailant must stoop far to reach him. It would be pleasanter now to pass him by and abstain from pointing a moral at his expense; but in this case Mr. Hale was the representative of a class which must be struck wherever it can be reached, by every legitimate weapon, until it is beaten into insignificance, or the hope of reform may be abandoned at the outset. In the light of subsequent history there is a bitterness of satire in these words of Mr. Hale, that Juvenal might have envied. What was it to Mr. Hale whether ambassadors were to be educated or not? Was it that such a condition would shut the door to him and his like? If by any such provision the country could have been spared the degradation which has been inflicted upon it by the conduct of men like Mr. Hale as its representatives, there can be no stronger arguments for its instant adoption.

Mr. Rusk, of Texas, was of the opinion that the President already had patronage enough, and that this appropriation was made in the interest of politicians to increase it. This objection was ingenious, but it showed either that Mr. Rusk was deeply skilled in the least straightforward practices of European diplomacy, or that his political knowledge was not such as to fit him for the high office of senator. The true secret of opposition to this measure, and to all similar measures which aim at restoring permanence to the

[1] [John P. Hale, Senator from New Hampshire 1847-1853, 1855-1865; candidate for the presidency on the Free-Soil ticket in 1852; minister to Spain 1865-1869. In the Senate Hale was one of the earliest and most prominent opponents of the extension of slave territory. His reputation first suffered publicly in 1863 when an investigation revealed that he had, for a fee, interceded with the Secretary of War on behalf of one J. M. Hunt who had been convicted of defrauding the government. Early in 1869 he was recalled from the Spanish mission after having been charged with abusing his import license privileges.]

public service, is the fear indicated by Mr. Hale that the President
will then have fewer offices to divide among members of Congress.
The political purity of Mr. Rusk and Mr. Hale stood out in brilliant
relief on these two conflicting backgrounds.

In spite of the exertions of the two Virginia senators, when the
vote was taken twenty-five senators recorded themselves against
the measure, while only eleven could be found to support it. Side
by side in the majority stand the names of Brown of Mississippi
and Collamer of Vermont, of Fessenden of Maine and Fitzpatrick
of Alabama, of Foot of Vermont and Iverson of Georgia, of Hale
and of Mallory, of Toombs and of Trumbull, of Wade, of Wilson,
and of Yulee. The list alone shows that no common principle could
have directed the vote, and the result will show whether the
honest men or the rogues had reason to be best pleased with such
a coalition. Among the minority were Messrs. Bayard, Hunter,
Mason, Pugh, Toucey, and—most significant of all—Cass.

Not yet satisfied with his triumph, Mr. Rusk immediately offered
an amendment repealing the clause in the bill of 1856, by which
the President was authorized to appoint the consular pupils whose
pay had so quickly been stopped. It was indeed unusual to introduce such legislation in an appropriation bill, but Mr. Brown justified this step on the ground that "this lubberly Congress," as he
was pleased to call the body in which he took a somewhat prominent part, would not stop to pass an independent measure; and
all the Republicans present supported the amendment, which was
intended to put an end forever to the obstinate attempt of the
government to provide the nation with a better service. The clause
was accordingly repealed by a vote of twenty-one to fourteen.

According to modern theories of the United States government,
this signal discomfiture should have stopped further discussion,
and the executive should have rested content with such a consular service as Congress was disposed to maintain. The President,
it is true, has sworn faithfully to execute the laws, but he never
meant in earnest to fulfil his pledge. Congress makes and Congress
executes the laws. The President is but the instrument of the legislature. Mr. Marcy, whose name has sheltered from contempt the
political maxim which has brought the executive so low, made in
this instance an attempt to repair in part the injury he had helped

to inflict, and found that it was easier to degrade than to elevate. With one hand he had overthrown the government; with the other he attempted only to restore an insignificant corner of it, and he failed so utterly as to leave the matter in a worse condition than if he had attempted nothing at all. Fifty years ago the whole administrative service was permanent; yet in 1856 even such a man as Mr. Fessenden could say that the permanence of twenty-five consular clerks was contrary to the spirit of the government, and the public would have believed him if it had cared enough about the subject ever to read the debate. Nevertheless, though Congress had in effect sharply reproved the executive, though Mr. Marcy was compelled to abandon forever his hope of undoing some slight portion of the mischief he had helped to cause, and though Mr. Fessenden sneered at the notion of permanence and technical education in the civil service, yet the Department of State, vindicating its rights as a permanent executive power which was intended to guide the President as well as to be guided by him, and thus by its experience and knowledge to give character and solidity to the government, refused to accept the result as final, and persevered in its project of reform.

Mr. Marcy retired from office in March, 1857, and was succeeded by Secretary Cass. Within less than twelve months, Mr. Cass renewed the effort to obtain these consular pupils. A question of salary was involved in the matter, and complicated it to some extent. This formed a side-issue which had nothing to do with the principle involved. It was perhaps easier both for the Secretary to press, and for Congress to resist, the proposed change when it was presented merely as an increase of salary to a half-starved race of officials who in most cases were incompetent to do their work, than when it came in the form of a direct question of educating public servants. In every point of view, however, the department continued to urge the reform. One letter of Secretary Cass bears date the 25th January, 1858, another the 11th May of the same year, and the correspondence forms an executive document printed for the use of the House in 1859. Yet Secretary Cass went out of office in 1861, and the department had not then succeeded in gaining the slightest concession from Congress.

Mr. Seward next appeared upon the stage. He took possession of the department in March, 1861, and during the next year was probably not less busied with his duties than Mr. Cass and Mr. Marcy had been with theirs. It was not likely that a small administrative matter such as this would seem to Mr. Seward to require attention at a time when the national existence depended on his success. Yet, before the year 1862 was over, Congress again received the inevitable document urging the creation of consular pupils. Ten years had now passed since Mr. Everett's first step, and the department had thus far, in spite of all its obstinacy, failed to make the smallest progress; nor was it more successful in 1862. Congress paid no more attention to Mr. Seward than it had paid to Mr. Cass, and the year 1863 passed by without a sign.

In those days, however, Mr. Seward had power, and knew how to overcome an obstacle. By the close of 1863 the department had discovered the way to work with effect. Instead of wasting argument on the House of Representatives, Mr. Seward turned his efforts to the Senate, and when the usual recommendation on behalf of the consular pupils was made by the department to the committees, the Senate Committee had been so thoroughly canvassed that it at last adopted an amendment to the Appropriation Bill as sent up from the House, and, by restoring the old law of 1856, again brought the whole subject up for discussion in Congress. The debate that followed was in a somewhat different tone from that of 1856. Either senators had made a stride in advance, or they had given place to new men. Mr. Hunter, Mr. Mason, and Mr. Pugh, the supporters of Secretary Marcy, had vanished, as well as Mr. Rusk, Mr. Hale, Mr. Brown, and the rest, his opponents. Nevertheless, Mr. Fessenden and Mr. Collamer, Mr. Trumbull, Mr. Wade, and Mr. Wilson, were still there, allowing ample means for determining whether it was the time that had changed, or only the men.

In point of fact only one man seems to have changed, but by good fortune this one man was Senator Fessenden. His committee had reported the amendment; and when the amendment came on for debate, he met the attack of Mr. Collamer with a frank avowal which was likely to carry sympathy wherever it was read. He spoke at once of the old bill of 1856, and of the opposition which compelled its repeal: "The great and leading consideration for its repeal was that Congress did not believe the thing would be of a permanent character. . . . Upon deliberation I have changed my views, and I am willing to admit that I have changed my views. . . . I have a hope that the intelligence of the country will bring it and is fast bringing it to the conclusion that, if we can find men who are competent and educated to the business of attending to our commercial affairs abroad without being politicians and partisans, their services will be recognized by any administration that may come into power, for the benefit of the government itself, and that where they have distinguished themselves they will take in these important places the places themselves, and be able to render us vastly better services than we have as yet received from any quarter." To this appeal, Mr. Sumner added the most energetic support, and between them, these two Senators and their committees made successful head against the attacks of Mr. Collamer and Mr. Reverdy Johnson, Mr. John Sherman and Mr. Grimes. The consular pupils were restored by a vote of twenty to sixteen,—Messrs. Trumbull and Wilson following Mr. Fessenden, while Mr. Wade remained true to his old vote.

The amended bill then went back to the House, where an earnest attempt was made to procure its passage, but the House again took the bit in its teeth and kicked viciously at the consular pupils. The most characteristic argument against them was made by Mr. Brooks of New York. "True," said he, "there are but twenty-five consular pupils named in this bill, but these twenty-five are but a nest-egg of a vast system which in the end will be imposed upon the whole diplomatic system of this country. . . . I should look upon it as a great calamity, a great misfortune to this country, if we should be represented abroad in high places by consular pupils, by men who have been twenty or thirty years from their country. It is necessary for every young man to come home within five or ten years and free himself of the courtly associations and despotic modes of European thinking, to breathe once more the spirit of our free institutions." This argument was probably suited to a certain class of congressmen, although personally Mr. Brooks is much too clever to allow his own eyes to be blinded by the dust which he throws in the faces of honest countrymen. Even he allowed, however, that after the short vacation, or purge, of the republican consul, his country might again employ him to advantage. But this argument of Mr. Brooks, even though he never believed a word of it, is certainly one of the most curious instances of the want of self-respect in American society that has ever been displayed. The utter contempt and hatred for European governments which is the common stock-in-trade of American demagogues would logically result in the conclusion that, if the American government is not a humbug, the citizen who remained longest abroad would be the truest to his own land. It is the foreign despot who should fear the spirit of free institutions, not the free institutions which should be harmed by the odious spectacle of foreign despotism; yet it has never been alleged that Napoleon or his brother emperors have feared the contact of free American opinion on their consuls and diplomats, or would have cared what the result might be, so long as their service was improved. The argument made by Mr. Brooks was a cowardly acknowledgment of distrust of democratic society. Had he said in so many words that the American citizen had no love of country and could not be trusted with the charge of himself without running a great risk of learning to hate freedom, he would not have expressed the idea in clearer language. This indeed would be the only possible logical ground for retaining the present consular system; but even this would scarcely apply to consuls and diplomats in countries like the South American republics, unless the citizen of the United States in his misery loves any foreign soil better than his own.

The House, however, sustained Mr. Brooks and non-concurred in the amendment. The Senate insisted; a committee of conference was appointed, and a compromise was reached,—a compromise of so curious a nature that it is calculated to make its authors somewhat ridiculous. On the one hand, a certain number of men opposed the consular pupils because they were to be made a means of improving the service by promotion, and to gratify these opponents the bill was changed in such a manner as to authorize "clerks," but on no account to admit the notion of "pupils." In order to diminish still further the dangers which this formidable array of twenty-five clerks threatened to the national liberties, their number was reduced to thirteen. On the other hand, a certain amount of opposition had been roused by the precisely opposite idea that perhaps, after all, these clerks might not be permanent, and to conciliate this class of members a clause was added providing against removal except for cause. Thus improved, the bill was passed,[1] and the department, after eleven years' perseverance, obtained as a result thirteen consular clerks.

Nevertheless, to the department consular pupils they were, and such they were sure to remain. Nothing is more curious, in this long contest, than to notice how incessantly the department returned to this idea of pupils,—an idea to which it seemed to cling with a kind of dogged and hopeless desperation,—and how persistently Congress set it aside. Mr. Everett, Mr. Marcy, Mr. Cass, Mr. Seward, one after another, in their vain efforts to benefit the national service begged and implored for pupils. Congress declared in reply that it would create what other offices it saw fit, but pupils they should not have. With the exception of Mr. Sumner and a few others, no members of the legislature dared even to argue in favor of pupils. The argument whenever possible was pressed on different ground. Thus it resulted that when Congress, fairly wearied out, flung its dozen clerks to the department, the department caught at them with great satisfaction, but at once proceeded to make them pupils after its own heart. Mr. Marcy's instructions for pupils were at once revived. Mr. Seward had indeed reminded the Senate in a long and very interesting letter, written to affect the result, that the foreign service still boasted of men who had served for twenty, thirty, and forty years, and whom the department had always succeeded in protecting against all political influence. He avowed his wish to educate new men to take their places, and he intended to effect his object in the best way he might. The consular clerks therefore were,

[1] "The President is hereby authorized . . . to appoint consular clerks, not exceeding thirteen in number at any one time, who shall be citizens of the United States, and over eighteen years of age at the time of their appointment, and shall be entitled to compensation for their services respectively at a rate, not exceeding one thousand dollars per annum, to be determined by the President; and to assign such clerks, from time to time, to such consulates and with such duties as he shall direct; and before the appointment of any such clerk shall be made, it shall be satisfactorily shown to the Secretary of State, after due examination and report by an examining board, that the applicant is qualified and fit for the duties to which he shall be assigned; and such report shall be laid before the President. And no clerk so appointed shall be removed from office, except for cause stated in writing, which shall be submitted to Congress at the session first following such removal."

now as before, not clerks, but pupils, in the view of the department, the act of Congress to the contrary notwithstanding.

This expedient answered its purpose admirably so long as it was only necessary for the department to act for itself. The appropriation was this time secured. One by one, candidates appeared at considerable intervals, were formally examined, passed, commissioned, and assigned to consuls abroad. The system worked eminently well. The pupils, so-called clerks, were useful, and their usefulness grew continually greater. Some of them were young men of parts and promise. One in particular passed a highly creditable examination, which attracted the attention of the department. He was assigned to an important consulate, and his reports were marked by so much ability that the President soon sent in his name to the Senate for promotion to the consulship itself. It is perhaps best not to attempt to penetrate the mysteries of an executive session, nor to seek any further explanation for the Senate's action on appointments than such as the long story just told may be thought to indicate. In the language of the Massachusetts Bill of Rights, the legislative department has learned to exercise executive powers, and the government is one of men and not of laws. No senator would protect the consular clerk, and the Senate rejected the nomination.

Whatever may have been the immediate cause of this rejection, it was not such as to discourage the department. Within a short time another consular clerk was nominated to a vacant consulate, and to him the Senate appears to have offered no opposition. He was confirmed, and the department was so well pleased with its success that it quickly sent in a third and a fourth nomination of the same nature, both of which were duly confirmed by the Senate. Thus, at the close of the last administration, the department had actually made a considerable advance towards its darling object, the improvement of the service. Eleven permanent consular clerks were distributed over the world, and three more had already been promoted to consulates. The experiment had fully answered every expectation, and the system was at last firmly established.

Nevertheless, the department was not yet destined to pass beyond the range of disappointments. Another trial of its patience and endurance was now at hand,—a contingency foreseen by Mr. Fessenden, and strangely pressed by many persons as a ground for discouraging any attempt at reform. A new administration came into power, welcomed by the public as a vindictive enemy of all political jobbery and corruption. The story of this disastrous time has already been told. Few disinterested spectators of the outrages then committed under cover of blind power are ever likely to look back upon that experience without a certain warmth of indignation and contempt which seems to require some personal object to vent itself upon; but in this instance there seems to be no reason for accusing any individual of intentional wrong-doing; or if any one was to blame the secret is hid in official places, where it cannot be reached. All that the Register shows is that the department succeeded in protecting only one of its promoted pupils; the other two, although no complaint appears to have been made either against their efficiency or their loyalty, were removed, and their places filled in the old manner. If these were not corrupt political jobs, the department may consider itself as more than usually fortunate.

After more than fifteen years of perseverance, however, which has hitherto proved successful, it is unlikely that the department will be discouraged by any ordinary chance. Unless it is crushed outright by the legislature, it will still do its best to serve the public honestly and efficiently, and in this attempt it will receive the support of the best senators. Nor is this statement true of only one department. The story of these consular pupils has been told to show that the executive as a governing influence must and does feel the burden of its responsibility, and that no President, even though he is selected by politicians to act as their tool, can ever entirely forget or betray the trust which a power far beyond the politicians has placed in his hands. If the President is weak, it is merely because public opinion is silent and support is not to be found. Arouse this, and there will then be no danger that the President will prove indifferent to the duty of protecting the purity of his administration, or that politicians within Congress or elsewhere will assume an authority which belongs not to a man nor to any body of men, but to the laws alone.

The final propositions which must stand as the basis of any permanent reform may now be gathered together, and summed up in a single sentence: The system of government in the United States has suffered a radical change; the executive, held by weak hands, has thrown away first its shield and then its sword, first its permanence and then its power, until it has been reduced so low that even General Grant, the most resolute and the most popular of Presidents, has recoiled from the task of raising it. As a necessary consequence of a weakened executive, Congress has seized and now claims as its right the most important executive powers. In exercising these powers, the legislature has, in obedience to a principle well understood by students of the science of government, converted a high public trust into an instrument of private gain,—a crime which, in morals if not in law, deserves the punishment attached to a felony, and justly causes, and has already brought about, a forfeiture of public confidence. As a necessary result of a weakened executive and a corrupted legislature, party organizations have become the tools of personal intrigue; public offices serving as the bribes by which a few men purchase personal support at the nation's expense. Even the remotest local politics have been perverted by this curse, and beyond the limit of political activity the evil extends ultimately to the relations of man to man, degrading and corrupting society itself.

If the conclusions insisted on in these pages are in any way correct, the whole subject of civil-service reform is reduced to a single principle,—the same which is asserted in the thirtieth article of the Massachusetts Bill of Rights. Tested by this touchstone, all mere experiment, all novel legislation like that suggested by Mr. Jenckes, however excellent in purpose, must be held wrong both in principle and in detail, calculated to aggravate rather than to check the evil. So far as the legislature is concerned, there is but one rule to follow. Let Congress keep its hands off executive powers. Let it not undertake to interfere by any mandatory legislation in matters which are beyond its sphere, unless indeed it is disposed to make solicitation for office, either directly or indirectly, a penal offence. Let it imitate the example of the British Parliament, which, omnipotent as it is, respects the principles of government so far that it wisely contents itself with advising or approving competition in the civil service, but has never ventured to legislate upon it. The President already possesses all the law he needs, all the law which Jefferson or Madison required. The executive system should not depend on the legislature for the character of its service. Two separate powers should not be blindly confused. If Congress can give, Congress can take away, and as a necessary result an act of Congress may forbid the President to exercise powers which are essential to the executive office, and confer them upon a creature of the legislature. The executive cannot with safety lean on this treacherous staff of legislative enactments.

No doubt a great burden of responsibility is thus thrown upon the President; and if Presidents betray the trust which the people repose in them, and, knowing what should be done, refuse to do it; if they consider their great office as merely that of a servant to the legislature, and not that of a guardian to the public interests; if they find their arms too weak to hold up the authority they have sworn to maintain, or if they decide to place their own ease before their official duty,—reform will indeed become more difficult, although still not desperate. With a President equal to his post, who understood and accepted his responsibilities and trusted to the deep public sympathy which seldom fails a bold and honest leader, the struggle would be comparatively short. Such a President might restore the executive to its early dignity, might elevate the tone and morals of the legislature, might redeem the character of party organizations, might purify even local politics; he might, if competitive examinations are the panacea for every evil, extend a network of them over every office, down to the Treasury porters, and establish his reforms so firmly in the minds of the people that the Republic would never again be in danger on this score; finally, he might revive the fainting hopes of honest men, giving to the government many years of renewed life, and, what is better still, a few years of high example; but such a President is to be prayed for rather than expected.

Be this as it may, the true policy of reformers is to trust neither to Presidents nor to senators, but appeal directly to the people. Whatever troubles distract the state, public opinion is first responsible either for creating or tolerating them. Whenever public opinion has once declared itself in favor of civil-service reform, and against the corrupt use of patronage by politicians, the evil will cease; nor need any anxiety be thrown away in regard to resistance by the Senate, since such factious opposition would only give to the people the opportunity of striking at the agents of corruption, an opportunity which may one day be used with effect so soon as old political issues can be finally disposed of. But before this time arrives, the public must be convinced that reform is a vital question, that the evils and dangers are real, and not mere inventions of a lively fancy. To effect this there is no way but to attack corruption in all its holes, to drag it before the public eye, to dissect it and hold the diseased members up to popular disgust, to give the nation's conscience no rest nor peace until mere vehemence of passion overcomes the sluggish self-complacency of the public mind.

To build by slow degrees this deep foundation of moral conviction, to erect upon it a comprehensive and solid structure of reform, and to bequeath the result to posterity as a work not inferior in quality to that of the Republic's founders, is an aim high enough to satisfy the ambition of one generation. Such a movement must necessarily be slow. It is scarcely worth while even to pretend a hope that anything can be at once accomplished, least of all in Congress. The few members of the legislature who are conscious of their own shortcomings, and the still smaller number who would honestly aid in restoring a better tone to the government and to politics, are united by no common bond of sympathy, and have neither a name nor even a power of combination. Time alone, and the steady increase of corruption, can bring them so close together as to act with any purpose or vigor. Yet if there is one of them who feels in earnest the evils for which many are ready enough to profess a theoretical antipathy, he may by a comparatively simple expedient effect everything that can or need be effected by legislative action. Without in any way interfering with Mr. Jenckes's bill,—a measure too cumbrous for the weak reforming influence in Congress to put in motion,—let him move, and press to a debate and a vote, two concise resolutions: one, recommending the President to extend the principle of competitive examinations to all branches of the service in which it might in his opinion be usefully applied; the other, declaring the opinion of Congress that, in respect to removals from office, the executive should return to the early practice of the government. Whenever Congress can be brought to assert these two principles, it will be time enough for the public to discuss the details of reform.

The Legal-Tender Act

After a year in Washington, Henry Adams was evidently well pleased with his manner of life—which he thought of as "Bohemian"—and with the results of his activity. "Though I have no power whatever," he wrote, "and am held up solely by social position and a sharp tongue, yet I float"—and he did not float inconspicuously. Among his friends were cabinet members and congressmen; he was a prominent contributor to E. L. Godkin's Nation; and his articles in the North American Review were gaining more and more attention. He could now and then put aside his habitual self-doubt so far as to admit that "I come on and the people here are beginning to acknowledge me as someone to be considered."

Furthermore, he found the violence of political controversy exhilarating; his letters of this time are filled with expressions of a joyous ferocity that is utterly without bitterness. When "The Legal-Tender Act" appeared, he told a friend, "I have brought all the respectable old fools of the country down on me by a mighty impudent article published in the April North American. . . . Well! it certainly was savage!"

After its first publication, Adams scrupulously credited Francis A. Walker with a share in the authorship of "The Legal-Tender Act." Walker was one of the group of Washington reformers; he had been Chief of the Bureau of Statistics and was appointed Superintendent of the Ninth Census on the very day the Supreme Court

129

found the Legal Tender Act unconstitutional in certain of its applications. Out of prudence, or perhaps merely because the job no longer seemed so urgent, Walker gave his notes to Adams who is entirely responsible for the article as it stands. That the combative Adams was pleased with it is more than suggested by the analogy it brought to his mind: "I . . . have written a piece of intolerably impudent political abuse for the North American . . . where I . . . say that never since the days of Cleon and Aristophanes was a great nation managed by such incompetent men as our leaders in Congress during the rebellion—bien entendu *that I am Aristophanes.*"

Dᴜʀɪɴɢ the Rebellion the United States armies suffered many disasters in the field, which for the moment were felt as personal misfortunes by every loyal citizen. So strong was the public feeling of anger and astonishment, that Congress appointed committees of investigation to examine into the causes of these military failures, and subjected the conduct of the war to a searching and sometimes a severe criticism. In finance the nation suffered only one great disaster, but its effects have extended far beyond the period of the war, and are likely to be felt for an indefinite time to come. The causes of this catastrophe have not been investigated by Congress; but as the day may probably arrive when the national government will admit that the act of national bankruptcy was a calamity involving the credit of every man in whose charge the people then placed the common interests, it may be useful to point out the path which any future Congressional committee on the Conduct of the Finances will be obliged to follow in investigating the causes which led to that miscarriage, the results of which have exceeded in importance any defeat of the national armies or the failure of any campaign.

An article by Francis A. Walker and Henry Adams, in the *North American Review* for April, 1870. [Originally printed over Adams' signature alone. Reprinted and revised in *Chapters of Erie*, 1871. Reprinted and further revised in *Historical Essays*, 1891.]

The timid and hesitating criticism with which the subject has been commonly treated speaks ill for the sound sense of the community. The public has adopted the idea that it is itself the responsible governing power, and its representatives only delegates to enroll its orders, until the healthy process of criticising a policy once adopted seems to it almost an attack on its own authority. The confusion involved in this assumption of responsibility is peculiarly unfortunate. The task of citizens who are selected to govern is one thing. They bear the burden of leaders, and they enjoy the honor; they are at liberty to excuse or palliate their mistakes, their ignorance, or their crimes by whatever arguments they can make to answer their purpose. The task of the public is wholly different. It is that of insisting, without favor or prejudice, on the observance of truth in legislation and in the execution of the laws. To apply the principles of truth is the first duty of every writer for the press and every speaker on the hustings. Whatever seems harsh in criticism or vehement in temper may be excused in the citizen who clings to the logic of fundamental principles, and leaves to those whose public conduct fails to reach his standard the labor of justifying themselves in the best way they can.

Critics of American finance commonly begin with the assumption that the Legal-Tender Act was necessary and inevitable. As a matter of criticism, nothing can be less sensible than such a beginning; and as a matter of intelligence, nothing can be feebler. Congress and the country permitted no such assumption to be made in excuse for the beaten generals at Fredericksburg and Chancellorsville. No satisfactory conclusion can be reached from such a premise. No sound result can be obtained except by assuming at the outset that the Legal-Tender Act was not necessary; that the public was not responsible for it; that the men who made it law were answerable to the people for their act, and are bound to show that so extraordinary and so grave a misfortune could by no means have been avoided. If they fail to prove their case, they are condemned.

The law of legal tender, passed by Congress in February, 1862, cannot be assumed to have been necessary, and its supporters are bound to prove that they had no alternative. To this task Mr. Spaulding, the principal author of the measure, has applied himself; while, on the other hand, Mr. Chase, without whose assent the law could not have passed, has assumed the contrary ground.[1] At the outset, a strong presumption against the law is raised by the unquestionable fact that the men who in 1862 were charged with the conduct of the finances, and were responsible for this law in particular, had no claim to confidence on the ground of their financial knowledge or experience. Something better might have been expected among a people devoted to commerce and habituated to self-government. Military disasters were to be looked for, seeing that the nation had no training or taste for war; but though war or art or philosophy or abstract knowledge were beyond the range of public or popular interest, an experience of two hundred years ought to have insured the country against mistakes in practical politics. Such was far from the truth. Among the leading statesmen then charged with responsibility, not one was by training well fitted to perform the duties of finance minister, or to guide the financial opinions of Congress.

The Secretary of the Treasury, certainly the most capable of the men then connected with finance, suffered under the disadvantage of inexperience. In the Senate, finance, like every other subject, was treated rather as though it were a branch of the common or constitutional law, than as though it were a system with established principles and processes of its own; but in the House of Representatives the want of education was most apparent and most mischievous, while by a significant coincidence the law of legal tender, more than almost any other great financial measure of the Rebellion, was peculiarly the work of this House. Of the members who originated and whose activity carried through all opposition the Act of February, 1862, it is difficult to speak in language which will not seem unduly and unreasonably severe. Yet it may honestly be doubted whether since Kleon, the leather-seller, was sent by the people of Athens to command its armies at Sphacteria and Amphipolis, and since Aristophanes on the public stage covered the powerful popu-

[1] History of the Legal-Tender Paper Money issued during the Great Rebellion, being a Loan without Interest, and National Currency. Prepared by Hon. E. G. SPAULDING, Chairman of the Sub-Committee of Ways and Means at the time the Act was passed. Buffalo. 1869.

Opinion delivered in the Supreme Court of the United States by CHIEF-JUSTICE CHASE, on the 7th of February, 1870, in Regard to the Construction of the Legal-Tender Act.

lar leader with an immortal ridicule which surely reflected most severely on the Athenian people itself,—it may honestly be doubted whether history records an occasion when the interests of a great country in an extreme emergency have been committed to hands more eminently disqualified for the trust.

In February, 1862, Thaddeus Stevens was chairman of the Committee of Ways and Means, from which emanates the ordinary financial legislation of Congress. That Mr. Stevens was as little suited to direct the economical policy of the country at a critical moment as a naked Indian from the plains to plan the architecture of St. Peter's or to direct the construction of the Capitol, expresses in no extreme language the degree of his unfitness. That Stevens was grossly ignorant upon all economical subjects and principles was the least of his deficiencies. A dogmatic mind, a high temper, and an overbearing will are three serious disqualifications for financial success, especially when combined with contempt for financial knowledge. It is no exaggeration to say that every quality of his nature and every incident of his life which gave Stevens power in the House, where he was almost omnipotent in the legislation which belonged to the war and to reconstruction, conspired to unfit him for the deliberate and difficult discussions of finance. Yet the principal burden of blame or praise for the financial legislation of that momentous year is not to be awarded to Stevens. In the press of business upon the committee, when in the brief space of a few months the whole system of loans, of taxation, and of currency demanded by a war of tremendous proportions had to be created, so to speak, out of nothing, two sub-committees were formed to divide the duties which fell upon the committee. One of these, under the lead of Morrill of Vermont, undertook to enlarge and adjust the scheme of taxation to the new necessities of the government. The other, under the chairmanship of the Hon. Elbridge G. Spaulding of New York, assumed the care of the national currency, the raising of loans, and the issue of Treasury notes or bonds. Stevens remained chairman of the whole committee, charging himself particularly with the matter of appropriations, and lending his powerful voice to both sections below him, as either by turn encountered opposition in carrying its measure through the House.

The intellect of a Congressman, gifted with no more than the ordinary abilities of his class, is scarcely an interesting or instructive subject of study; nor are the discussions that arise among such men likely to be rich in stores of knowledge or experience; but when an accidental representative carries "over the Administration and through Congress," [1] as Spaulding is claimed to have done, and he clearly did, a measure of such far-reaching consequences as the Legal-Tender Act of 1862, the character of that person's mind and the facts of his life cease to be matters of insignificance. One may well inquire who it was that could lead a nation so far astray, and what the condition of things that made it possible for him to effect results of such magnitude. Financiers who make an addition of hundreds of millions of dollars to the debts of their countries, representing not a penny of value enjoyed, are entitled to a place in history whether they boast the intellectual capacity of Pitt or of Spaulding.

Unlike Stevens, Spaulding had the advantage or disadvantage of a certain sort of financial experience. He had been for a time treasurer of the State of New York. By profession he was, in 1862, president of a joint-stock bank at Buffalo, and on this circumstance he based his chief claim to speak as an expert in finance. At the conference on the 11th of January, 1862, at the Treasury, between the Secretary, the committees of Congress, and the representatives of the principal Northern banks,—a conference whose momentous importance will require close attention,—Spaulding expressed his convictions both "as a banker and legislator." The association of functions was not unimportant, and Spaulding was right in laying stress upon it. Had he not been a banker as well as a legislator, the Legal-Tender Act might never have been enacted. Being a provincial banker, and at the same time chairman of a sub-committee dealing with the nominally financial but really universal interests of thirty millions or more of citizens, and dealing too with the whole future of a nation whose development no bounds seem to limit, Spaulding naturally applied to the situation the principles of finance he had learned in shaving notes at a country bank.

The situation was unquestionably serious; but few persons now

[1] Spaulding's share in the passage of the Act is described in these words by his colleague, Hon. T. M. Pomeroy, in a speech delivered in the House of Representatives Feb. 19, 1862, reprinted in Spaulding's book, p. 132.

retain any distinct recollection of its actual shape. To the minds of men living in 1870 the events of 1862 appear bound in close connection with the long series of events that have intervened. The necessity of the Legal-Tender Act is now assumed, not on account of what had happened before the law was passed, or on account of anything that was foreseen by its authors, but because of what afterward occurred,—the exigencies of a situation far more difficult and alarming than existed at that earlier time. Against such a confusion of ideas every candid man should be on his guard. The vague notion that sooner or later legal-tender paper was inevitable, is part of the loose and slovenly popular criticism with which the subject has been habitually treated, and is scarcely worth comment; but the actual circumstances under which Congress declared the measure to be necessary are a matter of fact, and with these law, history, and political science have first to deal.

Congress met Dec. 2, 1861, and Secretary Chase immediately set before it an account of the financial situation, and his own scheme for supplying the wants of the Treasury. He required about $200,-000,000, in addition to resources already provided, in order to meet the demands of the next half-year. His immediate necessity was for $100,000,000 within three months. He estimated that the debt would reach $517,000,000 on the 1st of July, 1862, and that a year later it would probably become $900,000,000. In fact it rose to $1,100,000,000. A part of the heavy government expenses was to be met by taxation; a part by the sale of bonds; and for the rest Secretary Chase proposed the assumption by the government of the bank circulation, amounting to some $200,000,000, with a view not only of obtaining the money, but of providing a sound currency on which to conduct the war. The secretary did not, in this connection, overlook the possibility of resorting to a forced paper circulation, but "the immeasurable evils of dishonored public faith and national bankruptcy" deterred him from recommending the measure, or rather obliged him to reject it as dangerous and unnecessary.

Thus, on the 1st of December, 1861, according to the Secretary of the Treasury, no occasion existed for resorting to the moderate measure of issuing government paper, except so far as concerned a possible guaranty to a new bank circulation. The idea of legal tender was expressly rejected. The government believed itself able to meet its demands on the basis of the bank circulation, provided Congress would place the bank circulation on an available footing. Nothing was done by Congress toward supplying the wants of the Treasury until, toward the end of December, Spaulding began to draft a bill for establishing a national banking currency. While preparing this draft, Spaulding, "upon mature reflection, came to the conclusion that the bill could not be passed and made available quick enough to meet the crisis then pressing upon the government for money to sustain the army and navy. He therefore drafted a legal-tender Treasury-note section." This was done about December 30; and this was the origin of the measure destined to have a vast influence on the American people. The "mature reflection" of Mr. Spaulding could discover no other or better method of supplying a temporary want of $100,000,000 than a resort to the last expedient known to finance,—what he himself calls a forced loan, made in the first year of the war by means equivalent to a debasement of the standard of value and a bankruptcy of the government. Any reader in the least familiar with financial history must appreciate the extravagance of Spaulding's assumption. That he acted with honesty and good intention no one will think it worth while to dispute; but that he had a conception of the consequences of what he was doing, or that he grasped in any degree the principles of statesmanship, no unprejudiced or cool observer could imagine. Like all ignorant men impatient of resistance or restraint, the moment he saw an obstacle he knew but one resource,—an appeal to force.

Spaulding then, "upon more mature consideration," converted this section into a separate bill, and laid it before his committee. The committee was by no means unanimous in accepting Spaulding's views of necessity. It is true that the only doubt entertained by Thaddeus Stevens regarded the constitutionality of the law; and one is at loss whether most to wonder at the ignorance thus betrayed or at the Constitutional scruples which suggested themselves to this veteran expunger of Constitutions. Stevens and one half the committee approved the bill, but the other half stood out firmly against it, and only as a matter of courtesy allowed it to be reported to the House.

The bill, reported Jan. 7, 1862, authorized the issue of $100,000,-000 in Treasury notes, to be a legal tender, and exchangeable on demand for six per cent bonds. Public opinion at once became sharply divided on the merits of the measure. Delegates from the Boards of Trade and banks of the principal Northern cities appeared in Washington to oppose the bill; and on the 11th of January these gentlemen met the Secretary of the Treasury and the finance committees of the Senate and House, at Secretary Chase's office in the Department. There the whole financial policy of the government was made a subject of discussion, and the two paths between which the country was still at liberty to choose were marked out with precision. Spaulding, on the one hand, insisted not only that his measure was the best, but that it was the only means of raising the money required, and he demanded to know what alternative could be suggested. On the part of the bank committees, James Gallatin of New York submitted a complete financial scheme, and replied to Spaulding's inquiry by the simple remark that the government should sell its bonds in the open market for what they would bring, without limitation of price. To this suggestion Spaulding made the following response:—

"The Sub-Committee of Ways and Means, through Mr. Spaulding, objected to any and every form of 'shinning' by government through Wall or State streets to begin with; objected to the knocking down of government stocks to seventy-five or sixty cents on the dollar, the inevitable result of throwing a new and large loan on the market without limitation as to price; claimed for Treasury notes as much virtue of par value as the notes of banks which have suspended specie payments, but which yet circulate in the trade of the North; *and finished with firmly refusing to assent to any scheme which should permit a speculation by brokers, bankers, and others in the government securities, and particularly any scheme which should double the public debt of the country, and double the expenses of the war, by damaging the credit of the government* to the extent of sending it to 'shin' through the shaving shops of New York, Boston, and Philadelphia. He affirmed his conviction as a banker and legislator, that it was the lawful policy as well as the manifest duty of the government, in the present exigency, to legalize as tender its fifty millions issue of demand Treasury notes, authorized at the extra session in July last, and to add to this stock of legal tender, immediately, one hundred millions more. *He thought that this financial measure would carry the country through the war, and save its credit and dignity.* At the same time we should insist upon taxation abundantly ample to pay the expenses of the government on a peace footing, and interest of every dollar of the public obligation, and to give this generation a clear show of a speedy liquidation of the public debt."

Before further comment on this speech, the fact must be noticed that throughout the legal-tender contests in 1862 no question was involved but one of *resource*. The sum of one hundred million dollars was wanted to carry on the government, and Spaulding closed every mouth by asking how else the money could be raised, since the banks could provide no more coin, and their paper would not properly answer the purpose. At that time no one thought of any ulterior process of "floating the bonds," which became the ultimate function of the legal-tender paper; and indeed this argument, which implied an intentional depreciation of the paper, would in 1862 have scarcely worked in favor of the bill. How little weight was put on the idea of "making money easy" is evident from the whole debate; but as far as Spaulding is concerned, the following letter, written Jan. 8, 1862, is sufficient:—

DEAR SIR,—In reply to yours of the 4th instant, I would say that the Treasury Note Bill for $100,000,000 agreed upon in committee yesterday is a measure of *necessity* and not one of *choice*. You criticise matters very freely, and very likely you may be right in what you say. We will be out of means to pay the daily expenses in *about thirty days,* and the committee do not see any other way to get along till we can get the tax-bills ready, except to issue temporarily Treasury notes. Perhaps you can suggest some other mode of carrying on the government for the next one hundred days. . . . It is much easier to *find fault* than it is to suggest *practicable means or measures*. We must have at least $100,000,000 of paying means during the next three months, or the government must stop payment. . . . I will thank you to suggest a better *practicable* mode of getting $100,000,000 of paying means during the next three months. I would be glad to adopt it, and the committee would be glad to adopt it. Let us have *your specific plan* for this purpose, one that will produce the money, and we will be very much obliged to you.

This curious letter, which Spaulding has published, italics and all, as a valuable document, tells the story of the legal tender in its origin. As a specimen of American finance and Congressional ability it will live in history. It presents the view on which, then as now, the adherents of this measure have always wished to place it before the public,—as the only alternative to the immediate stoppage of government. Not as a means of supplying currency, or of easing the money market, or of "floating" bonds, was the legal-tender paper first created, but solely to supply a temporary want of $100,000,000, without which the Treasury must stop payments. Spaulding flung into the face of every doubter his contemptuous request to suggest some better mode of raising the money, or in future to keep silence.

Three days after this letter was written, James Gallatin, on the part of the New York banks, replied to Spaulding's entreaties by the remark of a man who knew what he was talking about, that Secretary Chase need only sell his bonds at their market value, and obtain what money he wanted. To this suggestion Spaulding was called upon for a rejoinder. Obviously he was bound to show that Gallatin was mistaken; that no such alternative existed; and that, for some reason or other, government bonds could not be sold in the way proposed. In the speech just quoted Spaulding did undertake to answer Gallatin, but he took no such ground as this; he did not deny the efficacy of the proposed measure. He did not even question that the resource suggested was simple and easy. He appealed to the dignity of the government.

It appears, therefore, that there was an alternative to legal tender, in spite of Spaulding's assertions that there was none. The existence of this alternative was acknowledged by the supporters of the bill almost in the same breath with which they declared legal tender to be a necessity. In his speech of January 28, on introducing the bill in the House of Representatives, Spaulding said:—

"The bill before us is a war measure,—a measure of *necessity*, and not of choice. . . . *We have the alternative* either to go into the market and sell our bonds for what they will command, or to pass this bill. . . . If you offer to the people and put upon the market $300,000,000 to the highest bidder in the present state of affairs, they would not be taken except at ruinous rates of discount. . . . I fear the twenty years six per cent bonds would under the pressure fall to 75, 70, 60, and even 50 cents. . . . Why, then, go into the streets at all to borrow money? I prefer to assert the power and dignity of the government by the issue of its own notes."

Samuel Hooper, who was second on Mr. Spaulding's committee, said:—

"The propositions of committees from Boards of Trade and banks, which recently visited Washington, differed from the theory of this bill so far as to require that . . . the government bonds must first be disposed of, and the money received for them paid to the contractors. . . . The obvious effect of such an arrangement would be to put the reins of our national finances in the hands of the banks. . . . *To render the government financially more independent,* it is necesary to make the United States notes a legal tender. *It is possible that they would become a practical tender without providing for them to be a legal tender.*"

The alternative, therefore, as seen by Hooper, was not between legal tender and a stoppage of payments, but between legal tender and dependence on the banks. John A. Bingham's idea of necessity was only a little more ridiculous.

"Great names," said Bingham, "have been invoked [against legal tender] in this debate. For what purpose? For the purpose of laying at the feet and at the mercy of brokers and hawkers on 'Change the power of the people over their monetary interests in this hour of their national exigency."

Thaddeus Stevens, again, had views of his own in regard to the meaning of the word "necessity."

"This bill," said he, "is a measure of necessity, not of choice. . . . *Here, then, in a few words lies your* CHOICE. Throw bonds at six or seven per cent on the market between this and December enough to raise at least $600,000,000, or issue United States notes. . . . I maintain that the highest sum you could sell your bonds at would be seventy-five per cent, payable in currency itself at a discount. That would produce a loss which no nation or individual doing a large business could stand a year."

John Sherman also used the word "necessity" in a sense which would have been ludicrous if the subject had concerned the metaphysical doctrine of fate and free-will: "We must no longer hesitate as to the necessity of this measure. That necessity does exist, and now presses upon us. I rest my vote upon the proposition that this is a necessary and proper measure *to furnish a currency.*" A better example of anti-climax is seldom seen in rhetoric.

It would be pleasant to linger over this subject, and enjoy among these apparently tedious speeches the touches of involuntary humor which a critic finds so difficult to resist, but evidence is not needed on a point that is self-evident; and unquestionably even the strongest supporters of the bill did not in any true and absolute sense maintain that legal tender was necessary, but only that it was preferable to the process of selling bonds at a discount and retaining the old bank currency.

Finance is a subject which the liveliest writer may despair of making popular, since the sight or suspicion of it is alone enough to cause every reader, except the dullest, to close the most promising volume. A writer can have no hope of gaining a general hearing on such a topic. Rarely can he expect sympathy even among business men, unless he adopts the views they hold. Yet notwithstanding this, it is and will remain true, and not only true but interesting, that in the large experience of modern nations some solid principles in finance have been established too firmly to be shaken; and whether or no busy politicians or local bankers choose to believe them, and whether or no the ordinary reader choose to listen to them, the principles are sound, and will hold.

Hitherto in human history the mind of man has succeeded in conceiving of but two means by which governments can obtain money. One of these is, to take. The other is, to borrow. The hybrid and self-contradictory notion of a forced loan resolves ultimately into one or the other of these conceptions, and as a permanent policy is impossible. In practice, where a government does not take, it must borrow.

Almost all modern nations are, to a greater or less extent, habitual borrowers so far as their governments are concerned, and during two hundred years of experience the principles which regulate loans have been studied with some care, and simplified in some degree into a science. After innumerable costly experiments and elaborate study of the interests and motives of lenders and borrowers, the effect of complicated financial schemes and special pledges and conditions, it seems to be now acknowledged by the shrewdest governments that the simplest bargain is the best for the public, and that all financial tricks and devices, all attempts to coax or deceive capitalists into better conditions than they are ready to offer, in the end injure only the government and the people. Simplicity has of late years been carried by the great borrowing nations to a degree of perfection beyond which there seems to be no possibility of passing. According to this principle, governments sell their own credit without stipulation, reserve, or condition. They sell, for example, their promise to pay a thousand dollars a year so long as it is demanded. To this promise no condition, expressed or implied, is attached, except that the payment of a nominal principal may at any time discharge the debt. For this promise they obtain whatever they can; and experience has proved that in the competition of the world the bargain thus struck is for both parties the fairest.

Another simple law has also been established: and this is that lenders will always prefer, and pay most for, a security on which there is a certainty of permanence or a chance of profit, other things being equal: that is to say, that a security is relatively less valuable as it approaches its par and its redemption than it should be, judging from the price paid for an exactly similar security which has a better chance of permanence or a wider limit of possible profit. The English 3 per cents at eighty would commonly have a marked advantage in the markets over 3½ per cents,—in the first place, because the margin of possible profit would be greater; and in the second place, because there would be no prospect of disturbance in the one case, while in the other redemption would be near at hand. Experience shows that governments as a rule obtain relatively a low price for a security which they insist upon selling at par.

Most governments adapt their offer to the market in such a way as to combine these inducements. If the market rate of interest is at 4 per cent, they commonly offer 3½ or 3 per cent, and thus dispose of their credit at a discount on better terms than if they attempted to outbid the market rate. The American government has commonly pursued a different course. While insisting that it will borrow only at the market rate, that is, at par, it has found itself compelled to concede something in order to borrow at all. In the first place it has conceded a high rate of interest; but this is not enough. Lenders require permanence. It accepts, therefore, the condition that it shall not attempt to redeem its bonds until after the lapse of a term of years,—five or ten, or whatever may be agreed upon. The expedient is clumsy; but the prejudice against usury compels its adoption, although, like all such devices, it works in practice only against the public interest and in favor of the capitalist.

Every established principle of finance indicated that government credit could be sold to more advantage at a certain nominal discount than if a higher interest or any equivalent condition were insisted upon in order to "float" it at par. If the government had chosen to authorize the sale of six per cent bonds at their market price, as it did in the War of 1812, omitting from the contract all restriction on its own free control over them, it would have done what all established financial rules enjoin; and for such bonds it would have obtained the best terms then to be had, while at the present day the nation would have owed a homogeneous debt, with which it would have been free to deal as it chose. Congress declined to do this. Spaulding apparently wished to discover some principle in finance by which the government might raise money through a process which should be neither taxation nor loan. Before three years had passed, the government was selling its six per cent bonds at a rate equivalent to very nearly thirty-five cents on the dollar; but in 1861 the idea of its credit selling at a discount of twenty or thirty or forty per cent was so revolting as not to be entertained. Gallatin talked in vain. Nor were members of Congress alone extravagant on this theme. At least one gentleman who should have known better,—Moses H. Grinnell, of New York,—encouraged the same delusion. "As for G[allatin] and a few egotistical gentlemen that act with him, they should be driven out of Washington, as they only embarrass the government. There are not eight bank presidents that side with G[allatin]. He is an odd fish,—has very little influence here." These were the terms used by Grinnell in a letter dated Jan. 30, 1862; and it was a curious sign of the times that the son of Albert Gallatin—the only man who seems to have had a knowledge of what the occasion required—should have been "an odd fish."

The idea about "shinning" through Wall Street was absurd, seeing that every government always does and always must borrow on the best terms it can get, or not borrow at all, in which case it can have no resource but to tax. The event soon showed that the men who treated so contemptuously the idea of the nation's credit being sold at a discount were the first to convert their legal-tender paper into the instrument by which the government was to "shin," not only through Wall Street during the short emergency of the war, but through every lane and alley of the land during a period that now seems interminable. Congress and the Government followed Spaulding's doctrine, that the nation's credit must not be sold at a discount; and as the laws of society are inflexible, while the laws of Congress are not omnipotent, a period of "shinning" ensued which has seldom had a parallel. The dollar which Congress set up was "shaved" through Wall Street at twenty, thirty, forty, fifty, and sixty cents discount. Europe bought United States six per cents at about thirty-five cents on the dollar, notwithstanding Stevens's asseverations that no nation could afford to borrow at seventy without being ruined in a year. If Spaulding and his friends could have foreseen not only that the government would be compelled to perform this process of "shinning" during four long years, but that, thanks to them and to them alone, the government credit and its broken promises-to-pay would for years longer be hawked about Wall Street at whatever price they could command, and would become the support by which Jay Gould and James Fisk, Jr., and their like, would succeed in bolstering up their scandalous schemes against the pressure of sound economical laws,—the statesmen of 1862 might perhaps have gained more sensible ideas in regard to the treatment of government credit.

In justice to the Secretary of the Treasury it must be said that on the day of the conference he showed no symptom of yielding to Spaulding's influence. He remained then as before hostile to the principle of legal tender, and before the bank delegates left Washington he succeeded in agreeing with them upon a new financial arrangement which rejected the resort to legal tender, and adopted his own policy in regard to the bank currency. Spaulding and his committee deemed the scheme inadequate, and withheld their assent; but a different reason caused the compromise between Chase and the banks to fail. The gentleman who represented the Boston banks on that occasion found on his return to Massachusetts that the arrangement he had made was not satisfactory to them, and at once telegraphed this information to the secretary. Then for the first time Chase yielded his better judgment, and relying on his own power and will to control the issues, accepted the policy of legal tender, for which Boston influence thus became immediately answerable. Having once made his determination to adopt the policy, the secretary was not a man to hesitate in carrying it out. He had been drawn into it against his most deeply rooted convictions and his better judgment; but no sooner was the decision made, than he threw his whole weight in favor of the bill.

Thus, in spite of the Treasury and the banks and the active remonstrances of a great part of the community, the bill came before the House of Representatives as a government measure. Two months of delay and confusion had seriously complicated the difficulties of the case, but even yet no necessity existed which could in any just sense be considered to require the adoption of legal tender. The cry of necessity was indeed raised, and prolonged without a pause, but it was raised merely because no solid argument could be found. The ablest members of Congress denied the necessity without qualification, and, as has already been shown, the ideas of necessity held by the different supporters of the bill were almost as various as the speeches.

The debate began January 28 by a speech from Spaulding, in which he explained at considerable length his reasons for forcing on the country a measure so generally obnoxious. Spaulding was at the moment in a position of vast responsibility. His activity and persistence had carried the bill "over the Administration," and were to carry it through the House. However open to criticism his opinions may have been, Spaulding has a right to claim that they were little if at all inferior in merit to those expressed by the other friends of the bill. The good sense and high moral standard of a few men served only to make more conspicuous the cloud of ignorance against which their efforts were thrown away. This language is strong, but it is true. With difficulty could any human being compress within the same limited space a greater number of mistaken ideas than are contained in the following extract from Spaulding's speech of January 28:—

"The bill before us is a war measure,—a measure of necessity, not of choice. . . . Congress may judge of the necessity in the present exigency. It may decide whether it will authorize the Secretary of the Treasury to issue demand Treasury notes, and make them a legal tender in payment of debts; or whether it will put its six or seven per cent bonds on the market, at ruinous rates of discount, and raise the money at any sacrifice the money-lenders may require, to meet the pressing demands upon the Treasury. In the one case the government will be able to pay its debts at fair rates of interest; in the other, it must go into the streets *shinning* for the means, like an individual in failing circumstances, and sure of being used up in the end by the avarice of those who may exact unreasonable terms. But, sir, knowing the power of money, and the disposition there is among men to use it for the acquisition of greater gain, I am unwilling that this government, with all its immense power and resources, should be left in the hands of any class of men, bankers or money-lenders, however respectable or patriotic they may be. The government is much stronger than any of them. Its capital is much greater. It has control of all the bankers' money and all the brokers' money, and all the property of the thirty millions of people under its jurisdiction. Why then should it go into Wall Street, State Street, Chestnut Street, or any other street, begging for money? Their money is not as secure as government money. All the gold they possess would not carry on the government for ninety days. They issue only promises to pay, which, if Congress does its duty, are not half so secure as United States Treasury notes based on adequate taxation of all the property of the country. *Why, then, go into the streets at all to borrow money?* I am opposed in our present extremities to all shifts of this kind. I prefer to assert the power and dignity of the government by the issue of its own notes."

He would be a bold man who should undertake to say that these remarks can be made intelligible, but the conclusion is clear enough, and is worth attention. Had Mr. Spaulding's studies ever led him to read Goethe's Faust, he might at this point have recalled the scene where Mephistopheles, in the character of court-jester, invents for the empire a legal-tender currency based on the firm foundation of old treasures which in past ages might have been hidden underground, and applauds his own creation as better than coin, because if the bankers refused to give coin for it, the holder would at worst have only the trouble of digging. The great satirist with all his genius was not so great a satirist as Mr. Spaulding. He never thought of carrying his sarcasm so far as to invoke the *dignity* of the empire as the chief glory of paper money, and yet Mephistopheles closed the scene with the exulting exclamation,—

"Wer zweifelt noch an unsers Narren Witz!"

Yet one thing remains to be said before quitting Spaulding. If he sincerely believed that the government need not go into the streets to borrow money, and that a simple assertion of its own dignity would place it in command of indefinite resources,—in other words, if he thought that the dignity of the government forbade its borrowing except on its own terms, and that there was no necessity for it to borrow at all, he was bound to explain his consent that the government should pay six per cent or even one per cent for money, or should promise to repay any money whatever.

The argument of Samuel Hooper was less extravagant. He avoided committing himself beyond a cautious opinion that the paper issue would make the government financially more independent, and that if Secretary Chase were discreet, the quality of legal tender would help him to keep the notes at par. The latter opinion might perhaps be questioned, and indeed the chief-justice has himself questioned it in his late judgment; but at least it was not absurd.

Bingham rivalled Spaulding, though in a different way. His speech was necessarily made without reference to financial principles, since Bingham made no pretence to acquaintance with that subject. He assumed at the outset that the bill was necessary, because it was said to be necessary, and then burst into a denunciation of all persons who refused to believe in the necessity. Roscoe Conkling was the victim first immolated.

"Sir," said Bingham, "as a representative of the people I cannot keep silent when I see efforts made upon this side of the House and upon that, to lay the power of the American people to control the currency at the feet of brokers and of city bankers, who have not a tittle of authority, save by the assent or forbearance of the people, to deal in their paper issued as money. I am here to-day to assert the rightful authority of the American people as a nationality, sovereignty, under and by virtue of their Constitution."

Such legal finance would not call for notice except that it came from a leader in Congress, who in order to protect the sovereignty of the American people from bankers and brokers insisted upon creating a legal-tender paper currency, which has always been and always will be the most efficient instrument ever discovered for the purposes of this very class of men. Bingham denounced his opponents for acting with the purpose of sacrificing the public interest to the interest of bankers and brokers. It was mortifying to observe the ignorance and vulgar prejudice with which the bankers and brokers of the country were always mentioned in these debates. Perhaps no other single characteristic offered so much instruction in regard to the temper and the range of thought exhibited in this momentous discussion. Stevens, with his usual discrimination, characterized the dealers in money as "sharks and brokers," to which he afterward added "harpies." Shellabarger of Ohio, after appropriating bodily and almost literally several pages of Macaulay's most luminous and most familiar writing, in the effort to maintain himself on Macaulay's level without Macaulay's aid could discover no more original idea for his peroration than to denounce the outside opposition to this bill as coming from interested persons, in the expectation "that out of the blood of their sinking country they may be enabled to coin the gains of their infamy." Even Henry Wilson announced that the practical question lay between "brokers and jobbers and money-changers on the one side, and the people of the United States on the other."

Invective like this properly belonged only to a debating-club of boys; but if invective were to be used, and if these bankers had been represented in Congress by any person capable of using it, he might have retaliated in a manner which would have left little opportunity for an effective rejoinder. He might have replied that men who claimed to be trusted in regard to a financial exigency; who asserted in one breath that a necessity existed which in the next breath they acknowledged did not exist; who presumed on this unwarrantable plea of necessity to exculpate themselves from what, without exculpation, was the wickedest vote the representatives of the people could ever give,—a vote which delivered labor to the mercy of capital; a vote which forced upon the people that as money which in no just sense was money; a vote which established as law one of the most abominable frauds which law could be prostituted to enforce,—that such persons were not qualified to judge of other men's patriotism, honesty, or good sense.

A very large part of the debate turned on the technical construction of the Constitution; and many members of the Legislature who hesitated about nothing else found an insurmountable obstacle there. The Constitutional argument, whatever its weight may be, is one on which only lawyers will be likely to insist. Whether under a strict interpretation of Constitutional powers the law of legal tender is justified or not, can make but little difference to persons who look for their principles of action beneath the letter of the Constitution, —to the principles upon which all government and all society must ultimately rest. The law of legal tender was an attempt by artificial legislation to make something true which was false. This is the sum-total of the argument against legal tender; and this argument rests on the maxim that the foundation of law is truth. If the rhetoric of Congressional orators or the ingenuity of professional lawyers can reduce the principle involved to simpler elements than this, at all events neither the debates at the Capitol nor the arguments at the bar, however brilliant or elaborate they may have been, have as yet shown any probability of success.

It would be pleasant to extract from the speeches delivered in favor of this bill such portions as show depths of knowledge, elevation of morals, or breadth of mind. Nothing of the sort exists. Almost all the soundest minds in the house declared themselves against legal tender and denied its necessity. Judge Thomas of Massachusetts and Roscoe Conkling of New York, Morrill of Vermont, from the Committee of Ways and Means, Horton of Ohio, also of the Ways and Means, all the Democratic members, and others who contented themselves with a silent vote, opposed the legal-tender clause. The speech of Owen Lovejoy of Illinois was in its short space as clear, as vigorous, and from a rhetorical point of view as perfect, as the oldest statesman or the most exacting critic or the deepest student of finance could have hoped or wished to make. The opponents of the measure were far superior in intellect to its supporters; their arguments were essentially sound, and under ordinary circumstances would probably have proved successful; but they could not deal with the authority of the Executive, which Chase used with all his energy in favor of the bill. On the 6th of February Spaulding pressed his measure to a vote, and it passed the House by a majority of ninety-three to fifty-nine.

One can scarcely resist the conclusion that had the bill originated in the Senate, and been discussed without the prejudice arising from the responsibility of rejecting what was approved by the

House and urged by the Executive, and had it been acted upon before so much valuable time was lost, the country would probably for the time have been spared the great misfortune of its adoption. This opinion is rendered probable by the higher and more statesmanlike spirit in which the Senate discussed the proposed measure. If a word of unqualified admiration could please the ear or help to soothe the rest of a statesman whose loss the nation has regretted but has never fairly appreciated, one would take a personal pleasure in repeating the language of William Pitt Fessenden of Maine, who reported this bill to the Senate:—

"The question after all returns, Is this measure absolutely indispensable to procure means? If so, as I said before, necessity knows no law. What are the objections to it? I will state them as briefly as I can. The first is a negative objection. A measure of this kind certainly cannot increase confidence in the ability or integrity of the country. . . .

"Next, in my judgment, it is a confession of bankruptcy. . . .

"Again, say what you will, nobody can deny that it is bad faith, . . . and encourages bad morality both in public and private. . . .

"Again, it encourages bad morals, because if the currency falls (*as it is supposed it must, else why defend it by a legal enactment*), what is the result? It is that every man who desires to pay off his debts at a discount, no matter what the circumstances are, is able to avail himself of it against the will of his neighbor who honestly contracted to receive something better.

"Again, sir, necessarily as a result, in my judgment, it must inflict a stain upon the national honor. . . .

"Again, sir, it necessarily changes the value of all property. . . .

"Again, sir, a stronger objection than all that I have to this proposition is that the loss must fall most heavily upon the poor by reason of the inflation."

Fessenden concluded by declaring that in his opinion the legal-tender clause was not necessary, and he reported several amendments. One of these, the second, he described in these terms: "The committee . . . give to the secretary the power to sell the bonds of the government at any time that it may be necessary, at the market price, in order to raise coin. *That can always be done.*" This amendment was ultimately adopted and became part of the bill; but the secretary preferred reaching the same result by a different policy, and the old system was therefore retained.

Collamer of Vermont took yet stronger and more uncompromising ground. "Even if it was a *necessity*," said he, "I would not vote for this measure." Fidelity to a trust is not so universal but that one might sympathize with a man who when placed between the alternative of destruction on the one hand and what he thinks a breach of trust on the other, in spite of necessity still maintains the standard of honor; but there was in reality no such bravado in this declaration of Judge Collamer. No mere impracticability prompted his resistance, but a superior discernment that the evidence of necessity which imposes on a legislative body in times of panic is not to be trusted. Even on a calculation of chances, it is always more likely that other resources are available than that so desperate an expedient should offer the only hope of salvation. Collamer's speech was an energetic expression of his resolution, not that he would refuse to obey necessity, but that he would refuse to believe it.

The position taken by Charles Sumner wanted only the same defiant confidence in the laws of truth to make it more impressive than any of the others. Unhappily, by the side of Fessenden and Collamer, his conclusions seemed tinged with irresolution:—

"And now, as I close, I will not cease to be frank. Is it necessary to incur all the unquestionable evils of inconvertible paper, forced into circulation by act of Congress; to suffer the stain upon our national faith; to bear the stigma of a seeming repudiation; to lose for the present that credit which in itself is a treasury; and to teach debtors everywhere that contracts may be varied at the will of the stronger? Surely, there is much in these inquiries which may make us pause. . . . It is hard, very hard, to think that such a country, so powerful, so rich, and so beloved, should be compelled to adopt a policy of even questionable propriety. . . . Surely we must all be against paper money,—we must all insist on maintaining the integrity of the government; and we must all set our faces against any proposition like the present, except as a temporary expedient rendered imperative by the exigency of the hour. . . . Others may doubt if the exigency is sufficiently imperative, *but the Secretary of the Treasury does not doubt.* . . . Reluctantly, painfully, I consent that the process should issue."

The authority of the Secretary of the Treasury overruled the scruples of the Senate, and the bill passed by a majority of five votes on the legal-tender clause. It is scarcely worth while to carry the scene back to the House, in order to ascertain the fate of the Senate amendments, or to cull from the second debate new subjects for quotation. Spaulding at least did strongly and invariably insist upon the difference between legal-tender notes that were fundable and the later issue of greenbacks which were not so. In point of fact the difference was slight. There was nothing in the condition of fundability which made legal tender anything but legal tender; nor would the principle of legal tender have been any sounder, even though attached to the bonds themselves. As the later issues of legal tender were made, and the depreciation became excessive, Spaulding by similar steps became virtuous, until at last his virtue grew intense. He attributed the failure of his favorite financial scheme to the mistakes of others, and he proposed as an infallible cure a restoration of his funding proviso. He never succeeded in gaining a higher stand-point than this, or looking over a wider horizon where he could measure the uncontrollable power of the elements which he, like the unlucky companions of Ulysses, ignorantly set free.

Such was the history of the Legal-Tender Bill. So far as any evidence of its necessity can be drawn from the action of the Executive at the time, the late decision of Chief-Justice Chase has left no doubt as to the facts. That Chase should as Secretary of the Treasury have adopted the course he did was doubly unfortunate,—in the first place, because he created legal tender; and in the second place, because when the delusion was over, and his mind reverted to its first sound principles, the action he had taken as Secretary of the Treasury remained in the public memory to reduce the authority of the opinions he was bound to express as chief-justice. Into the legal correctness or political propriety of these opinions it is no purpose of this essay to enter. No one who holds strong convictions against legal tender as a measure of finance is likely to trouble his mind with the question whether such a power has or has not been conferred by the Constitution upon Congress. Though it were conferred in the most explicit terms language is capable of supplying, there could be no excuse on that account for changing an opinion as to its financial merits; and its financial merits are not a subject for lawyers, or even for judges, as such, to decide. These happily rest on principles deeper than statute or than Constitutional law. They appeal to no written code; and whenever the public attempts to overrule them, the public does so at its own peril.

One more point remains. The common impression is that even though there were no actual necessity for a law of legal tender so early as February, 1862, yet at some subsequent time the enactment of such a law would have proved inevitable. This opinion should properly form the subject of a separate paper. If it be acknowledged that the law of February, 1862, was unnecessary and passed by a practical deception, the condition of the argument is changed. Whenever the public has reached this point, it can enter upon the wider field of discussion into which so vague and general a proposition must lead. Without venturing at present on a denial of the theory, since this would require much explanation and reasoning, it is fair to say that although the subject is scarcely capable of positive demonstration, absolutely no evidence proves that the government might not have carried the war to a successful conclusion without the issue of legal-tender paper. Such appears to be the opinion of the chief-justice, as it is undoubtedly the inference from economical principles.

After the first issues of the paper money, its original purpose and importance as a resource against a temporary exigency—that purpose which had been used in forcing the bill through Congress—was lost from sight, and the paper assumed new functions as a financial instrument.

The government, adhering to the policy of selling its bonds only at par, was obliged to consider its paper as the par standard, and to issue enough paper to "float" the successive loans. This was equivalent to selling its credit at the market price, with the addition of voluntarily degrading its own standard of value. In order to protect the nation's credit from degradation in the hands of bankers and brokers, the government dishonored it of its own free will. As a financial policy, this tortuous and disreputable expedient will not bear examination; but one incidental function of the paper, closely connected with this, claims more attention. The issue of paper money in large quantities does produce a temporary and feverish excitement, which during a certain length of time may facilitate borrowing, though at a frightful ultimate cost. If the object of legal tender were to cause this temporary stimulus, and if this stimulus can be proved to have been essential to financial success, the management of the nation's financial affairs during the war may admit of excuse if not of praise. Neither of these conditions can be established.

[This essay aims at no advocacy of any financial nostrum, nor at any cure of present difficulties. In the popular humor of the moment, it is more than ever doubtful whether any advice that is wise would be listened to, or whether any advice that has a chance of being listened to could possibly be wise. Mere knowledge has no hold upon political power in its treatment of this subject. Other considerations are supreme both in Congress and in the public mind. But although knowledge, and the application of simple truth in politics, are for the present divorced from power and no longer control the course of current events, yet at least the past belongs to them as their exclusive property, and no one can prevent the past from receiving, sooner or later, the judgment which historical criticism must inevitably exact for the betrayal of principles to which it pretended allegiance.] [1]

[1] [The concluding paragraph, deleted from the last published version of the essay, is reprinted from the original version in the *North American Review*.]

The New York
Gold Conspiracy

*Not long after he came to Washington, Henry Adams had expressed
interest in doing an article that would show "the practical expedients by which traders make a profit out of the currency. These fields
are gloriously rich and stink like hell, if we were only of the force
to distil their flowers." A perfect opportunity to try his force arose
when Adams' friend, Representative James A. Garfield, conducted
an investigation of the famous plot of Jay Gould and Jim Fisk to
corner the gold market in September, 1869. The incident epitomized
the new business spirit that had emerged in the country since the
beginning of the Civil War, a spirit of unscrupulous and irresponsible devotion to the sole end of making money. In writing the history
of the gold market scandal, Henry Adams for the first time seems
to have clearly identified this spirit and its peculiar embodiment,
the corporation—first mentioned with distrust in the article on
"American Finance" published over a year earlier in the* Edinburgh
Review—*as far realer enemies of the "moral laws of society" than
any governmental imbalance of powers or partisan spoliation of the
civil service. Having access to the Garfield committee's findings, he
immediately projected an article—"such an article!"—for the* Edinburgh Review. *But the outspoken and potentially libellous nature
of what he had to say evidently terrified even English editors.
Henry Reeve wrote that he wanted "nothing controversial about currency;" the* London Quarterly *was equally reluctant; and the essay
finally appeared, somewhat anti-climactically for its author, in the
liberal* Westminster Review.

157

THE Civil War in America, with its enormous issues of depreciating currency and its reckless waste of money and credit by the government, created a speculative mania such as the United States, with all its experience in this respect, had never before known. Not only in Broad Street, the centre of New York speculation, but far and wide throughout the Northern States, almost every man who had money employed a part of his capital in the purchase of stocks or of gold, of copper, of petroleum, or of domestic produce, in the hope of a rise in prices, or staked money on the expectation of a fall. To use the jargon of the street, every farmer and every shopkeeper in the country seemed to be engaged in "carrying" some favorite security "on a margin." Whoever could obtain a hundred dollars sent it to a broker with orders to buy whatever amount of stocks the broker would consent to purchase. If the stock rose, the speculator prospered; if it fell until the deposit or margin was lost, the broker demanded a new deposit, or sold the stock to protect himself. By means of this simple and smooth machinery, which differs in no essential respect from the processes of *roulette* or *rouge-et-noir*, the nation flung itself into the Stock Exchange, until the "outsiders" as they were called, in opposition to the regular brokers

From the *Westminster Review*, for October, 1870. [Reprinted and revised in *Chapters of Erie*, 1871. Reprinted and further revised in *Historical Essays*, 1891.]

of Broad Street, represented the entire population of the American Republic. Every one speculated, and for a time successfully.

The inevitable reaction began when the government, about a year after the close of the war, stopped its issues and ceased borrowing. The greenback currency had for a moment sunk to a value of only 37 cents to the dollar. On the worst day of all, the 11th of July, 1864, one sale of $100,000 in gold was actually made at 310, equivalent to about 33 cents in the dollar.[1] At that point depreciation stopped, and the paper which had come so near falling into entire discredit steadily rose in value, first to 50 cents, then to 60 and 70, until in the summer of 1869 it stood at about 73½ cents.

So soon as the industrious part of the public felt the touch of solid values, the fabric of fictitious wealth began to melt away under their eyes. Before long the so-called "outsiders," the men who speculated on their own account, and could not act in agreement or combination, began to suffer. One by one, or in masses, they were made the prey of larger operators; their last margins were consumed, and they dropped to the solid level of slow, productive industry. Some lost everything; many lost still more than they had; and few families of ordinary connection and standing in the United States cannot tell, if they choose, some story of embezzlement or breach of trust committed in those days. Some men who had courage and a sense of honor, found life too heavy for them; others went mad. The greater part turned in silence to their regular pursuits, and accepted their losses as they could. Almost every rich American could produce from some pigeon-hole a bundle of worthless securities, and could show checkbooks representing the only remaining trace of margin after margin consumed in attempts to satisfy the insatiable broker. A year or two of incessant losses swept the weaker gamblers from the street.

Even those who continued to speculate found it necessary to change their mode of operations. Chance no longer ruled over the Stock Exchange and the gold market. The fate of a battle, the capture of a city, or the murder of a President had hitherto broken the plans of the strongest combinations, and put all speculators, whether great or small, on fairly even ground; but as the period of sudden and uncontrollable disturbing elements passed away, the

[1] See *Men and Mysteries of Wall Street*, by James K. Medbery, pp. 250, 251.

market fell more and more completely into the hands of cliques which found a point of adhesion in some great mass of incorporated capital. Three distinct railways, with their enormous resources, became the property of Cornelius Vanderbilt, who by means of their credit and capital again and again swept millions of dollars into his pocket by a process curiously similar to gambling with loaded dice. Vanderbilt was one of the most respectable of these great operators. The Erie Railway was controlled by Daniel Drew, and while Vanderbilt at least acted in the interest of his corporations, Drew cheated equally his corporation and the public. Between these two men and the immense incorporated power they swayed, smaller operators one after another were crushed, until the survivors learned to seek shelter within some clique sufficiently strong to afford protection. Speculation in this manner began to consume itself, and the largest combination of capital was destined to swallow every weaker combination which ventured to appear in the market.

Between the inevitable effect of a healthy currency and the omnipotence of capital in the stock market, a sounder state of society began. The public, which had been robbed with cynical indifference by Drew and Vanderbilt, could feel no sincere regret when they saw these two cormorants reduced to tearing each other. In the year 1867 Vanderbilt undertook to gain possession of the Erie Road, as he had already obtained possession of the New York Central, the second trunk-line between New York and the West. Vanderbilt was supposed to own property to the value of some $50,000,-000, which might all be made directly available for stock operations. He bought the greater part of the Erie stock. Drew sold him all he could take, and then issued as much more as was required to defeat Vanderbilt's purpose. After a violent struggle, which overthrew the guaranties of social order, Drew triumphed, and Vanderbilt abandoned the contest. The Erie corporation paid him a large sum to reimburse his alleged losses. At the same time it agreed that Drew's accounts should be passed, and he obtained a release in full, and retired from the direction. The Erie Road, almost exhausted by such systematic plundering, was left in the undisturbed, if not peaceful, control of Mr. Jay Gould and Mr. James Fisk, Jr., whose reign began in the month of July, 1868.

Jay Gould was a partner in the firm of Smith, Gould, & Martin,

brokers in Wall Street. He had been engaged in railway enter-
prises, and his operations had not been of a nature likely to encourage public confidence in his ideas of fiduciary relations. He was
a broker, and a broker is almost by nature a gambler,—perhaps the
last profession suitable for a railway manager. In character he was
marked by a disposition for silent intrigue. He preferred to operate
on his own account, without admitting other persons into his confidence. His nature suggested survival from the family of spiders:
he spun webs, in corners and in the dark. His disposition to subtlety
and elaboration of intrigue was irresistible. He had not a conception
of a moral principle. The class of men to whom he belonged understood no distinction between right and wrong in matters of speculation, so long as the daily settlements were punctually effected.
In this respect Gould was probably as honest as the mass of his
fellows, according to the moral standard of the street; but he was
an uncommonly fine and unscrupulous intriguer, skilled in the processes of stockgambling, and passably indifferent to the praise or
censure of society.

James Fisk, Jr., was still more original in character. He was not
yet forty years of age, and had the instincts of fourteen. He came
originally from Vermont, probably the most respectable and correct
State in the Union, and his father had been a pedler who sold goods
from town to town in his native valley of the Connecticut. The son
followed his father's calling with boldness and success. He drove his
huge wagon, made resplendent with paint and varnish, with four
or six horses, through the towns of Vermont and Western Massachusetts; and when his father remonstrated at his reckless management, the young man, with his usual bravado, took his father into
his service at a fixed salary, with the warning that he was not to
put on airs on the strength of his new dignity. A large Boston firm
which had supplied young Fisk with goods on credit, attracted by
his energy, took him into the house. The war broke out; his influence drew the firm into some bold speculations which were successful. In a few years he retired with some $100,000, which he subse-
quently lost. He formed a connection with Daniel Drew in New
York, and a new sign, ominous of future trouble, was raised in Wall
Street, bearing the names of Fisk & Belden, brokers.

Personally Fisk was coarse, noisy, boastful, ignorant, the type of a young butcher in appearance and mind. Nothing could be more striking than the contrast between him and his future associate Gould. One was small and slight in person, dark, sallow, reticent, and stealthy, with a trace of Jewish origin; the other was large, florid, gross, talkative, and obstreperous. Fisk's redeeming point was his humor, which had a flavor of American nationality. His mind was extraordinarily fertile in ideas and expedients, while his conversation was filled with unusual images and strange forms of speech, quickly caught up and made popular by the New York press. In respect to honesty as between Gould and Fisk, the latter was perhaps, if possible, less deserving of trust than the former. A story not without a stroke of satirical wit was told by him to illustrate his estimate of abstract truth. An old woman who had bought of the elder Fisk a handkerchief which cost ninepence in the New England currency, where six shillings are reckoned to the dollar, complained to Mr. Fisk, Jr., that his father had cheated her. Mr. Fisk considered the case maturely, and gave a decision based on *a priori* principles. "No!" said he, "the old man wouldn't have told a lie for ninepence;" and then, as if this assertion needed some reasonable qualification, he added, "though he would have told eight of them for a dollar!" The distinction as regarded the father may have been just, since the father held old-fashioned ideas as to wholesale and retail trade; but in regard to the son this relative degree of truth cannot be predicated with confidence, since, if the investigating committee of Congress and its evidence are to be believed, Mr. Fisk seldom or never speaks truth at all.[1]

An intrigue equally successful and disreputable brought these two men into the Erie board of directors, whence they speedily drove their more timid predecessor Drew. In July, 1868, Gould made himself president and treasurer of the corporation. Fisk became comptroller. A young lawyer named Lane became counsel. These three directors made a majority of the executive committee, and were masters of Erie. The board of directors held no meetings.

[1] House of Representatives. Report, No. 31. Forty-first Congress, Second Session. Report of the Committee on Banking and Currency, in response to a Resolution of the House of Representatives, passed Dec. 13, 1869, directing the Committee "to investigate the causes that led to the unusual and extraordinary fluctuations of Gold in the City of New York, from the 21st to the 27th of September, 1869;" accompanied by the testimony collected by the Committee.

The executive committee was never called together, and the three men—Fisk, Gould, and Lane—became from that time the absolute, irresponsible owners of the Erie Railway, not less than if it had been their personal property and plaything.

This property was in effect, like all the great railway corporations, an empire within a republic. It consisted of a trunk-line of road four hundred and fifty-nine miles in length, with branches three hundred and fourteen miles in extent, or seven hundred and seventy-three miles of road in all. Its capital stock amounted to about $35,000,000. Its gross receipts exceeded $15,000,000 per annum. It employed not less than fifteen thousand men, and supported their families. Over this wealth and influence,—greater than that directly swayed by any private citizen, greater than is absolutely and personally controlled by most kings, and far too great for public safety either in a democracy or in any other form of society,— the vicissitudes of a troubled time placed two men in irresponsible authority; and both these men belonged to a low moral and social type. Such an elevation has been rarely seen in modern history. The most dramatic of modern authors, Balzac himself, who loved to deal with similar violent alternations of fortune, or Alexandre Dumas, with all his extravagance of imagination, never reached a conception bolder or more melodramatic than this, or conceived a plot so enormous, or a catastrophe so original, as was to be developed.

One of the earliest acts of the new rulers was such as Balzac or Dumas might have predicted and delighted in. They established themselves in a palace. The old offices of the Erie Railway were in the lower part of the city, among the wharves and warehouses,— a situation no doubt convenient for business, but not agreeable as a residence; and the new proprietors naturally wished to reside on their property. Mr. Fisk and Mr. Gould accordingly bought a building of white marble, not unlike a European palace, situated about two miles from the business quarter, and containing a large theatre, or opera-house. They also purchased several smaller houses adjoining it. The opera-house cost about $700,000, and a large part of the building was at once leased by the two purchasers to themselves as the Erie corporation, to serve as offices. This suite of apartments was then furnished by themselves, as representing the corporation, at an expense of some $300,000, and in a style which, though called vulgar, was not more vulgar than that of almost any palace in Europe. The adjoining houses were connected with the main building; and in one of these Mr. Fisk had his private apartments, with a private passage to his opera-box. He also assumed direction of the theatre, of which he became manager-in-chief. To these royal arrangements he brought tastes commonly charged as the worst results of royal license. The atmosphere of the Erie offices was not disturbed with moral prejudices; and as the opera supplied Mr. Fisk's mind with amusement, so the opera *troupe* supplied him with a permanent harem. Whatever Mr. Fisk did was done on an extraordinary scale.

These arrangements regarded only the pleasures of the American Aladdin. In the conduct of their interests, the new directors showed a capacity for large conceptions and a vigor in the execution of their schemes that alarmed the entire community. At the annual election in 1868, when Gould, Fisk, and Lane, having borrowed or bought proxies for the greater part of the stock, caused themselves to be elected for the ensuing year, the respectable portion of the public throughout the country was astonished and shocked to learn that the new board of directors contained two names peculiarly notorious and obnoxious to honest men,—William M. Tweed and Peter B. Sweeney. To every honest American they conveyed a peculiar sense of terror and disgust. The State of New York in its politics was much influenced, if not controlled, by the city of New York. The city politics were so entirely in the hands of the Democratic party as to preclude even the existence of a strong minority. The party organization centred in a political club, held together by its patronage and by a system of jobbery unequalled elsewhere in the world. The Tammany Club, thus swaying the power of a small nation of several million souls, was itself ruled by William M. Tweed and Peter B. Sweeney, absolute masters of this system of theft and fraud, and to American eyes the incarnation of political immorality.

The effect of this alliance was felt in the ensuing winter in the passage of a bill through the State legislature, and its signature by the governor, abolishing the former system of annual elections of the entire board of Erie directors, and authorizing the board to classify itself in such a manner that only a portion should be changed each year. The principle of the bill was correct; but its practical effect enabled Gould and Fisk to make themselves directors for five years in spite of any attempt on the part of the stockholders to remove them. The formality of annual re-election was spared them; and so far as the stockholders were concerned, there was no great injustice in the act. The Erie Road was in the peculiar position of being without an owner. There was no *cestui que trust*, unless the English stockholders could be called such. In America the stock was almost exclusively held for speculation, not for investment; and in the morals of Wall Street, speculation had almost come to mean disregard of intrinsic value. In this case society at large was the injured party, and society knew its risk.

This step was only a beginning. The Tammany ring exercised a power beyond politics. Under the existing Constitution of the State, the judges of the State courts are elected by the people. Thirty-three such judges formed the State judiciary, and each of the thirty-three was clothed with equity powers running through the whole State. Of these judges Tammany Hall elected several, and the Erie Railway controlled others in country districts. Each of these judges might forbid proceedings before any and all the other judges, or stay proceedings in suits already commenced. Thus the lives and the property of the public were in the power of the new combination; and two of the city judges, Barnard and Cardozo, had already acquired a peculiarly infamous reputation as so-called "slaves to the ring," which left no question as to the depths to which their prostitution of justice would descend.

The alliance between Tammany and Erie was thus equivalent to investing Gould and Fisk with the attributes of sovereignty; but in order to avail themselves to the utmost of their judicial powers, they also required the ablest legal assistance. The degradation of the bench had been rapidly followed by the degradation of the bar. Prominent and learned lawyers were already accustomed to avail themselves of social or business relations with judges to forward private purposes. One whose partner might be elevated to the bench was certain to be generally retained in cases brought before this special judge; and litigants were taught by experience that a retainer in such cases was profitably bestowed. Others found a similar advantage resulting from known social relations with the court. The debasement of tone was not confined to the lower ranks of advocates; and probably this steady demoralization of the bar made it possible for the Erie ring to obtain the services of Mr. David Dudley Field as its legal adviser. Mr. Field, a gentleman of European reputation, in regard to which he was understood to be peculiarly solicitous, was an eminent law reformer, author of the New York Code, delegate of the American Social Science Association to the European International Congress, and asserted by his partner, Mr. Shearman, in evidence before a committee of the New York legislature, to be a man of quixotic sense of honor. Mr. Shearman himself, a gentleman of English parentage, had earned public gratitude by arraigning and deploring with unsurpassed courage and point the condition of the New York judiciary, in an admirable essay in the "North American Review" for July, 1867. The value of Mr. Field's services to Messrs. Fisk and Gould was not to be measured even by the enormous fees their generosity paid him. His power over certain judges became so absolute as to impress the popular imagination; and the gossip of Wall Street insisted that he had a silken halter round the neck of Judge Barnard and a hempen one round that of Cardozo. He who had a year before threatened Barnard on his own bench with impeachment next appeared in the character of Barnard's master, and issued as a matter of course the edicts of his court.

One other combination was made by the Erie managers to extend their power. They bought a joint-stock bank in New York city, with a capital of $1,000,000. The assistance thus gained was purchased at a moderate price, since it was by no means represented by the capital. The great cliques and so-called "operators" of Wall Street and Broad Street carry on their transactions by a system of credits and clearing-houses with little use of money. The banks certify their checks, and the certified checks settle balances. Nominally and by law the banks only certified to the extent of bona fide deposits, but in reality the custom of disregarding the strict letter of the law was not unknown; and in case of the bank in question, the Comptroller of the Currency, an officer of the national Treasury, testified that on an examination of its affairs in April, 1869, out of fifteen checks deposited in its hands as security for certifications made by it, selected at hazard for inquiry, and representing a nominal value of $1,500,000, three only were good. The rest represented accommodation extended to brokers and speculators without security. This bank on Thursday, Sept. 24, 1869, certified checks to the amount of nearly $7,500,000 for Gould alone. What sound security Gould deposited against this mass of credit may be left to the imagination. His operations were not confined to this bank alone, although this was the only one owned by the ring.

Thus Gould and Fisk created a combination more powerful than any that has been controlled by mere private citizens in America or in Europe since society for self-protection established the supreme authority of the judicial name. They exercised the legislative and the judicial powers of the State; they possessed almost unlimited credit, and society was at their mercy. One authority alone stood above them, beyond their control; and this was the distant but threatening figure of the national government.

Powerful as they were, the Erie managers were seldom in funds. The marble palace in which they lived, the theatre they supported, the bribery and profusion of management by which they could alone maintain their defiance of public opinion, the enormous schemes for extending their operations into which they rushed, all required greater resources than could be furnished even by the wholesale plunder of the Erie Road. They were obliged from time to time to issue from their castle, and harry the industrious public or their brother freebooters. The process was different from that known to the dark ages, but the objects and the results were the same. At one time Fisk is said to have ordered heavy speculative sales of stock in an express company which held a contract with the Erie Railway. The sales being effected, the contract was declared annulled. The stock naturally fell, and Fisk realized the difference. He then ordered heavy purchases, and having renewed the contract the stock rose again, and Fisk a second time swept the street.[1] In the summer and autumn of 1869 the two managers issued and sold two hundred and thirty-five thousand new shares of Erie stock, or nearly as much as its entire capital when they assumed power in July, 1868. With the aid of the money thus obtained, they succeeded in withdrawing about $12,500,000 in currency from circulation at the very moment of the year when currency was most in demand in order to harvest the crops. For weeks the nation writhed and quiv-

[1] *Men and Mysteries of Wall Street*, p. 168.

ered under the torture of this modern rack, until the national government itself was obliged to interfere and threaten a sudden opening of the Treasury. Whether the Erie speculators operated for a rise or for a fall, whether they bought or sold, and whether they were engaged in manipulating stocks or locking up currency or cornering gold, they were always a nuisance and scandal.

In order to understand a so-called corner in gold, readers must bear in mind that the supply of gold immediately available for transfers was limited within distinct bounds. New York and the country behind it contained an amount usually estimated at about $20,000,000 to $100,000,000, which might be thrown bodily on the market if the President ordered it. To obtain gold from Europe or other sources required time.

In the second place, gold was a commodity bought and sold like stocks, in a special market or gold-room situated next the Stock Exchange in Broad Street and practically a part of it. In gold as in stocks, the transactions were both real and speculative. The real transactions were mostly purchases or loans made by importers who required coin to pay customs-duties on their imports. This legitimate business was supposed to require from $5,000,000 to $7,500,-000 per day. The speculative transactions were wagers on the rise or fall of price, and neither required any transfer of gold nor implied its existence, although in times of excitement hundreds of millions were nominally bought, sold, and loaned.

Under the late Administration, Mr. McCulloch, then Secretary of the Treasury, had thought it his duty to guarantee a stable currency, although Congress forbade him to restore the gold standard. During four years gold had fluctuated little, and principally from natural causes, and the danger of attempting to create an artificial scarcity had prevented the operators from trying an experiment sure to irritate the government. The financial policy of the new Administration was not so definitely fixed, and the success of a speculation would depend on the action of Mr. Boutwell, the new secretary, whose direction was understood to have begun by a marked censure on the course pursued by his predecessor.

Of all financial operations, cornering gold is the most brilliant and the most dangerous, and possibly the hazard and splendor of the attempt were the reasons of its fascination to Jay Gould's fancy.

He dwelt upon it for months, and played with it like a pet toy. His fertile mind discovered that it would prove a blessing to the community; and on this theory, half honest and half fraudulent, he stretched the widely extended fabric of the web in which mankind was to be caught. The theory was partially sound. Starting from the principle that the price of grain in New York was regulated by the price in London, and was not affected by currency fluctuations, Gould argued that if the premium on gold could be raised from thirty to forty cents at harvest-time, the farmers' grain would be worth $1.40 instead of $1.30; and as a consequence the farmer would hasten to send his crop to New York over the Erie Railway, which was sorely in need of freights. With the assistance of another gentleman, Gould calculated the exact premium at which the Western farmer would consent to dispose of his grain, and thus distance the three hundred sail then hastening from the Danube to supply the English market. Gold, which was then heavy at 134, must be raised to 145.

This clever idea, like the other ideas of the gentlemen of Erie, had the single fault of requiring that some one somewhere should be swindled. The scheme was probably feasible; but sooner or later the reaction from such an artificial stimulant must have come, and whenever it came some one must suffer. Nevertheless, Gould probably argued that so long as the farmer got his money, the Erie Railway its freights, and he his small profits on the gold he bought, he need not ask who else might be injured; and indeed by the time the reaction came and gold was ready to fall as he expected, Gould would probably have been ready to assist the process by speculative sales in order to enable the Western farmer to buy his spring goods cheap as he had sold his autumn crops dear. Gould was equally ready to buy gold cheap and sell it dear on his private account; and as he proposed to bleed New York merchants for the benefit of the Western farmer, so he was willing to bleed Broad Street for his own. The patriotic object was the one which for obvious reasons Gould preferred to put forward, and on which he hoped to rest his ambitious structure.

The operation of raising the price of gold from 133 to 145 offered no great difficulty to men who controlled the resources of the Erie Railway. Credit alone was needed, and of credit Gould had an un-

limited supply. The only serious danger lay in the possible action of
the national government, which had not taken the philanthropic
view of the public good peculiar to the managers of Erie. Secretary
Boutwell, who should have assisted Gould in "bulling" gold, was
gravely suspected of being a bear, and of wishing to depress the
premium to nothing. If the Secretary of the Treasury were determined to stand in Gould's path, even the combined forces of Erie
and Tammany dared not jostle against him; and therefore Gould
must control the government, whether by fair means or foul, by
persuasion or by purchase. He undertook the task; and after his
proceedings in both directions have been thoroughly drawn into
light, the public can see how dramatic and artistic a conspiracy in
real life may be when slowly elaborated from the subtle mind of
a clever intriguer, and carried into execution by a band of unshrink-
ing scoundrels.

The first requisite for Gould's purpose was a channel of direct
communication with the President; and here he was peculiarly favored by chance. Mr. Abel Rathbone Corbin, formerly lawyer, editor, speculator, lobby-agent, familiar, as he claims, with everything,
had succeeded during his varied career in accumulating from one
or another of his hazardous pursuits a comfortable fortune, and
had crowned his success, at the age of sixty-seven or thereabout,
by contracting a marriage with General Grant's sister at the moment when General Grant was on the point of reaching the highest
eminence possible to an American citizen. To say that Corbin's
moral dignity had passed absolutely pure through the somewhat
tainted atmosphere in which his life had been spent would be flattering him too highly; but at least he was no longer engaged in active occupation, and he lived quietly in New York watching the
course of public affairs, and remarkable for respectability becoming to a President's brother-in-law. Gould enjoyed a slight acquaintance with Corbin, and proceeded to improve it. He assumed and
asserts that he felt a respect for Corbin's shrewdness and sagacity.
Corbin claims to have first impressed the crop theory on Gould's
mind; while Gould testifies that he indoctrinated Corbin with this
idea, which became a sort of monomania with the President's
brother-in-law, who soon began to preach it to the President himself. On the 15th of June, 1869, the President came to New York,

and was there the guest of Corbin, who urged Gould to call and
pay his respects to the Chief Magistrate. Gould had probably aimed
at this result. He called; and the President of the United States not
only listened to the president of Erie, but accepted an invitation to
Fisk's theatre, sat in Fisk's private box, and the next evening became the guest of these two gentlemen on their Newport steamer,—
while Fisk, arrayed, as the newspapers reported, "in a blue uniform,
with a broad gilt cap-band, three silver stars on his coat-sleeve,
lavender gloves, and a diamond breast-pin as large as a cherry,
stood at the gangway, surrounded by his aids, bestarred and be-
striped like himself," and welcomed his distinguished friend.

The Erie managers had already arranged that the President
should on this occasion be sounded in regard to his financial policy;
and when the selected guests—among whom were Gould, Fisk, and
others—sat down at nine o'clock to supper, the conversation was
directed to the subject of finance. "Some one," says Gould, "asked
the President what his view was." The "some one" in question was
of course Fisk, who alone had the impudence to put such an inquiry. The President bluntly replied that there was a certain amount
of fictitiousness about the prosperity of the country, and that the
bubble might as well be tapped in one way as another. The remark
was fatal to Gould's plans, and he felt it, in his own words, as "a
wet blanket."

Meanwhile the post of assistant-treasurer at New York had become vacant, and it was a matter of interest to Gould that some
person friendly to himself should occupy this position, which in its
relations to the public is second in importance only to the Secre-
taryship of the Treasury itself. Gould consulted Corbin, and Corbin
suggested the name of General Butterfield,—a former officer in the
volunteer army. The appointment was not a wise one; nor does it
appear in evidence by what means Corbin succeeded in bringing it
about. He was supposed to have used A. T. Stewart, the wealthy
importer, as his instrument for the purpose; but whatever the influence may have been, Corbin appears to have set it in action, and
General Butterfield entered upon his duties toward the 1st of July.

The preparations thus made show that some large scheme was
never absent from Gould's mind, although between the months of

May and August he made no attempt to act upon the markets. Between August 20 and September 1, in company with Messrs. Woodward and Kimber, two large speculators, he made what is known as a pool or combination to raise the premium on gold, and some ten or fifteen millions were bought, but with very little effect on the price. The tendency of the market was downward, and was not easily counteracted. Perhaps under ordinary circumstances he might have abandoned his project; but an incident suddenly occurred which drew him headlong into the operation.

Whether the appointment of General Butterfield strengthened Gould's faith in Corbin's secret powers does not appear in evidence, though it may readily be assumed as probable; but the next event seemed to authorize an unlimited faith in Corbin, as well as to justify the implicit belief of an Erie treasurer in the corruptibility of all mankind. The unsuspicious President again passed through New York, and came to breakfast at Corbin's house on the 2d of September. He saw no one but Corbin while there, and the same evening at ten o'clock departed for Saratoga. Gould was immediately informed by Corbin that the President, in discussing the financial situation, had shown himself a convert to the Erie theory about marketing the crops, and had "stopped in the middle of a conversation in which he had expressed his views and written a letter" to Secretary Boutwell. This letter was not produced before the investigating committee; but Secretary Boutwell testified as follows in regard to it:—

"I think on the evening of the 4th of September I received a letter from the President dated at New York, as I recollect it; I am not sure where it is dated. I have not seen the letter since the night I received it. I think it is now in my residence in Groton. In that letter he expressed an opinion that it was undesirable to force down the price of gold. He spoke of the importance to the West of being able to move their crops. His idea was that if gold should fall, the West would suffer and the movement of the crops would be retarded. The impression made on my mind by the letter was that he had rather a strong opinion to that effect. . . . Upon the receipt of the President's letter on the evening of the 4th of September, I telegraphed to Judge Richardson [Assistant Secretary at Washington] this despatch: 'Send no order to Butterfield as to sales of gold until you hear from me.'"

Gould had succeeded in reversing the policy of the national government; but this was not all. He knew what the government would do before any officer of the government knew it. Gould was at Corbin's house on the 2d of September; and although the evidence of both these gentlemen was very confused on the point, the inference is inevitable that Gould saw Corbin privately within an hour or two after the letter to Boutwell was written; and that at this interview, while the President was still in the house, Corbin gave information to Gould about the President's letter,—perhaps showed him the letter itself. Then followed a transaction worthy of the French stage. Corbin's evidence gives his own account of it:—

"On the 2d of September (referring to memoranda) Mr. Gould offered to let me have some of the gold he then possessed. . . . He spoke to me, as he had repeatedly done before, about taking a certain amount of gold owned by him. I finally told Mr. Gould that for the sake of a lady, my wife, I would accept $500,000 of gold for her benefit, as I shared his confidence that gold would rise. . . . He afterward insisted that I should take a million more, and I did so on the same condition for my wife. He then sent me this paper."

The paper in question was as follows:—

SMITH, GOULD, MARTIN, & Co., Bankers.

11 BROAD STREET, NEW YORK, Sept. 2, 1869.

Mr.———

DEAR SIR,—We have bought for your account and risk,—
500,000, gold, 132, R.
1,000,000, gold, 133⅜, R.
which we will carry on demand with the right to use.

SMITH, GOULD, MARTIN, & Co.

The memorandum meant that for every rise of one per cent in the price of gold Corbin was to receive $15,000, and his name nowhere to appear. If Gould saw Corbin in the morning and learned from him what the President had written, he must have made his bargain on the spot, and then going directly to the city he must in one breath have ordered this memorandum to be made out and large quantities of gold to be purchased before the President's letter left Corbin's house.

No time was lost. The same afternoon Gould's brokers bought large amounts in gold. One testifies to buying $1,315,000 at 134⅛. September 3 the premium was forced up to 36; September 4, when Boutwell received his letter, it had risen to 37. There Gould met a check, as he described his position in nervous Americanisms:—

"I did not want to buy so much gold. In the spring I put gold up from 32 to 38 and 40, with only about seven millions. But all these fellows went in and sold short, so that in order to keep it up I had to buy or else to back down and show the white feather. They would sell it to you all the time. I never intended to buy more than four or five millions of gold, but these fellows kept purchasing it on, and I made up my mind that I would put it up to 40 at one time. . . . We went into it as a commercial transaction, and did not intend to buy such an amount of gold. I was forced into it by the bears selling out. They were bound to put it down. I got into the contest. All these others fellows deserted me like rats from a ship. Kimber sold out and got short. . . . He sold out at 37. He got short of it, and went up" (or, in English, he failed).

The bears would not consent to lie still and be flayed. They had the great operators for once at a disadvantage, and were bent on revenge. Gould's position was hazardous. When Kimber sold out at 37, which was probably on the 7th of September, the market broke; and on the 8th the price fell back to 35. At the same moment, when the "pool" was ended by Kimber's desertion, Corbin, with his eminent shrewdness and respectability, told Gould "that gold had gone up to 37," and that he "should like to have this matter realized,"— which was equivalent to saying that he wished to be paid something on account. This was said September 6; and Gould was obliged the same day to bring him a check for $25,000, drawn to the order of Jay Gould, and indorsed in blank by him with a proper regard for Corbin's modest desire not to have his name appear. The transaction did credit to Corbin's sagacity, and showed at least that he was acquainted with the men he dealt with. Uudoubtedly it placed Gould in a difficult position; but as Gould already held some fifteen millions of gold and needed Corbin's support, he preferred to pay $25,000 outright rather than allow Corbin to throw his gold on the market. Yet the fabric of Gould's web had been so seriously injured that for a week—from the 8th to the 15th of September— he was unable to advance and equally unable to retreat without severe losses. He sat at his desk in the opera-house, silent as usual, tearing little slips of paper which he threw on the floor in his abstraction, while he revolved new combinations in his mind.

Down to this moment James Fisk, Jr., had not appeared in the affair. Gould had not taken him into his confidence; and not until after September 10 did Gould decide that nothing else could be done. Fisk was not a safe ally in so delicate an affair; but apparently no other aid offered itself. Gould approached him; and as usual Gould's touch was like magic. Fisk's evidence begins here, and may be believed when very strongly corroborated:—

"Gold having settled down to 35, and I not having cared to touch it, he was a little sensitive on the subject, feeling as if he would rather take his losses without saying anything about it. . . . One day he said to me, 'Don't you think gold has got to the bottom?' I replied that I did not see the profit in buying gold unless you have got into a position where you can command the market. He then said he had bought quite a large amount of gold, and I judged from his conversation that he wanted me to go into the movement and help strengthen the market. Upon that I went into the market and bought. I should say that was about the 15th or 16th of September. I bought at that time about seven or eight millions, I think."

The market responded slowly to these enormous purchases; and on the 16th the clique was still struggling to recover its lost ground.

Meanwhile Gould placed a million and a half of gold to the account of General Butterfield, as he had done to the account of Corbin, and notified him of the purchase; so Gould swears, in spite of General Butterfield's denial. The date of this purchase is not fixed. Through Corbin a notice was also sent by Gould about the middle of September to the President's private secretary, General Porter, informing him that half a million was placed to his credit. Porter repudiated the purchase, but Butterfield took no apparent notice of Gould's transaction on his account. On the 10th of September the President again came to New York, where he remained his brother-in-law's guest till the 13th; and during this visit Gould again saw him, although Corbin avers that the President then intimated his wish to the servant that this should be the last time Gould obtained admission. "Gould was always trying to get something out of him," he said; and if he had known how much Gould had succeeded in getting out of him, he would have admired the man's genius, even while shutting the door in his face.

On the morning of September 13 the President set out on a journey to the little town of Washington, situated among the mountains of western Pennsylvania, where he was to remain a few days. Gould, who consulted Corbin regularly every morning and evening, was still extremely nervous in regard to the President's policy; and as the crisis approached, his nervousness led him into the blunder of doing too much. Probably the bribe offered to Porter was a mistake, but a greater mistake was made by pressing Corbin's influence too far. Gould induced Corbin to write an official article for the New York press on the financial policy of the government,—an article afterward inserted in the "New York Times" through the kind offices of Mr. James McHenry; and he also persuaded or encouraged Corbin to write a letter directly to the President. This letter, written September 17 under the influence of Gould's anxiety, was instantly sent by a special messenger of Fisk to reach the President before he returned to the capital. The messenger carried also a letter of introduction to General Porter, the private secretary, in order to secure the personal delivery of this important despatch.

On Monday, September 20, gold again rose. Throughout Tuesday and Wednesday Fisk continued to purchase without limit, and forced the price up to 40. At that time Gould's firm of Smith, Gould, & Martin, through which the operation was conducted, had purchased some $50,000,000; yet the bears went on selling, although they could continue the contest only borrowing Gould's own gold. Gould, on the other hand, could no longer sell and clear himself, for the reason that the sale of $50,000,000 would have broken the market. The struggle became intense. The whole country watched with astonishment the battle between the bulls and the bears. Business was deranged, and values were unsettled. There were indications of a panic in the stock market; and the bears in their emergency vehemently pressed the government to intervene. Gould wrote to Boutwell a letter so impudent as to indicate desperation and loss of his ordinary coolness. He began:—

SIR,—There is a panic in Wall Street, engineered by a bear combination. They have withdrawn currency to such an extent that it is impossible to do ordinary business. The Erie Company requires eight

hundred thousand dollars to disburse,— . . . much of it in Ohio, where
an exciting political contest is going on, and where we have about ten
thousand employed; and the trouble is charged on the Administration
. . . Cannot you, consistently, increase your line of currency?"

From a friend such a letter would have been an outrage; but from
a member of the Tammany ring, the principal object of detestation
to the government, such a threat or bribe—whichever it may be
called—was incredible. Gould was, in fact, at his wits' end. He
dreaded a panic, and he felt that it could no longer be avoided.

The scene next shifts for a moment to the distant town of Washington, among the hills of western Pennsylvania. On the morning of
September 19, President Grant and his private secretary General
Porter were playing croquet on the lawn, when Fisk's messenger,
after twenty-four hours of travel by rail and carriage, arrived at the
house, and sent in to ask for General Porter. When the President's
game was ended, Porter came, received his own letter from Corbin,
and called the President, who entered the room and took his
brother-in-law's despatch. He then left the room, and after some
ten or fifteen minutes' absence returned. The messenger, tired of
waiting, then asked, "Is it all right?" "All right," replied the President; and the messenger hastened to the nearest telegraph station,
and sent word to Fisk, "Delivered; all right."

The messenger was altogether mistaken. Not only was all not
right, but all was going hopelessly wrong. The President had at the
outset supposed the man to be an ordinary post-office agent, and
the letter an ordinary letter which had arrived through the post-
office. Not until Porter asked some curious question as to the man,
did the President learn that he had been sent by Corbin merely to
carry this apparently unimportant letter of advice. The President's
suspicions were excited; and the same evening, at his request, Mrs.
Grant wrote a hurried note to Mrs. Corbin, telling her how greatly
the President was distressed at the rumor that Mr. Corbin was
speculating in Wall Street, and how much he hoped that Mr. Corbin would "instantly disconnect himself with anything of that sort."

This letter, subsequently destroyed—or said to have been destroyed—by Mrs. Corbin, arrived in New York on the morning of
Wednesday, September 22, the day when Gould and his enemies
the bears were making simultaneous appeals to Secretary Boutwell.

Mrs. Corbin was greatly excited and distressed by her sister-in-law's language. She carried the letter to her husband, and insisted that he should instantly abandon his interest in the gold speculation. Corbin, although considering the scruples of his wife and her family highly absurd, assented to her wish; and when Gould came that evening as usual, with $50,000,000 of gold on his hands and extreme anxiety on his mind, Corbin read to him two letters,—the first, written by Mrs. Grant to Mrs. Corbin; the second, written by Mr. Corbin to President Grant, assuring him that he had not a dollar of interest in gold. The assurance of this second letter was, at any sacrifice, to be made good.

Corbin proposed that Gould should give him a check for $100,-000, and take his $1,500,000 off his hands. A proposition more impudent than this could scarcely be imagined. Gould had already paid Corbin $25,000, and Corbin asked for $100,000 more at the moment when it was clear that the $25,000 he had received had been given him under a misunderstanding of his services. He even represented himself as doing Gould a favor by letting him have a million and a half more gold at the highest market price, at a time when Gould had fifty millions which he must sell or be ruined. What Gould might under ordinary circumstances have replied, may be imagined; but for the moment he could say nothing. Corbin had but to show this note to a single broker in Wall Street, and the fabric of Gould's speculation would fall to pieces. Gould asked for time, and went away. He consulted no one; he gave Fisk no hint of what had happened. The next morning he returned to Corbin, and made him the following offer:—

" 'Mr. Corbin, I cannot give you anything if you will go out. If you will remain in, and take the chances of the market, I will give you my check [for $100,000].' 'And then,' says Corbin, 'I did what I think it would have troubled almost any other business man to consent to do,— refuse one hundred thousand dollars on a rising market. If I had not been an old man married to a middle-aged woman, I should have done it (of course with her consent) just as sure as the offer was made. I said, "Mr. Gould, my wife says *no!* Ulysses thinks it wrong, and that it ought to end." So I gave it up. . . . He looked at me with an air of severe distrust, as if he was afraid of treachery in the camp. He remarked, "Mr. Corbin, I am undone if that letter gets out." . . . He stood there for a little while looking very thoughtful, exceedingly thoughtful. He then left and went into Wall Street; . . . and my impression is that he it was, and not the government, that broke that market.' "

Corbin was right; throughout all these transactions his insight into Gould's character was marvellous.

It was the morning of Thursday, September 23. Gould and Fisk went to Broad Street together; but as usual Gould was silent and secret, while Fisk was noisy and communicative. Their movements were completely separate. Gould acted through his own firm of Smith, Gould, & Martin, while Fisk operated principally through his old partner, Belden. One of Smith's principal brokers testifies:—

" 'Fisk never could do business with Smith, Gould, & Martin very comfortably. They would not do business for him. It was a very uncertain thing of course where Fisk might be. He is an erratic sort of genius. I don't think anybody would want to follow him very long. I am satisfied that Smith, Gould, & Martin controlled their own gold, and were ready to do as they pleased with it without consulting Fisk. I do not think there was any general agreement. . . . None of us who knew him cared to do business with him. I would not have taken an order from him nor had anything to do with him.' " Belden was considered a very low fellow. " 'I never had anything to do with him or his party,' said one broker employed by Gould. 'They were men I had a perfect detestation of; they were no company for me. I should not have spoken to them at all under any ordinary circumstances.' " Another says, " 'Belden is a man in whom I never had any confidence in any way. For months before that, I would not have taken him for a gold transaction.' "

Yet Belden bought millions upon millions of gold. He himself swore that he had bought twenty millions by Thursday evening, without capital or credit except that of his brokers. Meanwhile Gould, on reaching the city, had at once given secret orders to sell. From the moment he left Corbin he had but one idea, which was to get rid of his gold as quietly as possible. "I purchased merely enough to make believe I was a bull," says Gould. This double process continued all that afternoon. Fisk's wild purchases carried the price to 144, and the panic in the street became more and more serious as the bears realized the extremity of their danger. No one can tell how much gold which did not exist they had contracted to deliver or pay the difference in price. One of the clique brokers swears that by Thursday evening the street had sold the clique one hundred and eighteen millions of gold; and every rise of one per cent of this sum implied a loss of more than $1,000,000 to the bears. Naturally the terror was extreme, for half Broad Street and thousands of speculators would have been ruined if compelled to settle gold at 150 which they had sold at 140. By that time nothing more was heard in regard to philanthropic theories of benefit to the Western farmer.

Gould's feelings may easily be imagined. He knew that Fisk's reckless management would bring the government upon his shoulders, and he knew that unless he could sell his gold before the order came from Washington he would be a ruined man. He knew, too, that Fisk's contracts must inevitably be repudiated. This Thursday evening he sat at his desk in the Erie offices at the opera-house, while Fisk and Fisk's brokers chattered about him.

"I was transacting my railroad business. I had my own views about the market, and my own fish to fry. I was all alone, so to speak, in what I did, and I did not let any of those people know exactly how I stood. I got no ideas from anything that was said there. I had been selling gold from 35 up all the time, and I did not know till the next morning that there would probably come an order about twelve o'clock to sell gold."

Gould had not told Fisk of Corbin's retreat, or of his own orders to sell.

Friday morning Gould and Fisk went together to Broad Street and took possession of the private back-office of a principal broker, "without asking the privilege of doing so," as the broker observes in his evidence. The first news brought to Gould was a disaster. The government had sent three men from Washington to examine the bank which Gould owned; and the bank sent word to Gould that it feared to certify for him as usual, and was itself in danger of a panic, caused by the presence of officers, which created distrust of the bank. It barely managed to save itself. Gould took the information silently, and his firm redoubled sales of gold. His partner, Smith, gave the orders to one broker after another,—"Sell ten millions!" "The order was given as quick as a flash, and away he went," says one of these men. "I sold only eight millions." "Sell, sell, sell! do nothing but sell! only don't sell to Fisk's brokers," were the orders which Smith himself acknowledges. In the gold-room Fisk's brokers were shouting their rising bids, and the packed crowd grew frantic with terror and rage as each successive rise showed their increasing losses. The wide streets outside were thronged with excited people; the telegraph offices were overwhelmed with messages ordering sales or purchases of gold or stocks; and the whole nation was watching eagerly to see what the result of this convulsion was to be. Trade was stopped, and even the President felt that it was time to raise his hand. No one who has not seen the New York gold-room can understand the spectacle it presented,—now a pandemonium, now silent as the grave. Fisk, in his dark back-office across the street, with his coat off, swaggered up and down, "a big cane in his hand," and called himself the Napoleon of Wall Street. He believed that he directed the movement, and while the street outside imagined that he and Gould were one family, and that his purchases were made for the clique, Gould was silently flinging away his gold at any price he could get for it.

Whether Fisk expected to carry out his contract and force the bears to settle, or not, is doubtful; but the evidence seems to show that he was in earnest, and felt sure of success. His orders were unlimited. "Put it up to 150!" was one which he sent to the gold-room. Gold rose to 150. At length the bid was made, "160 for any part of five millions!" and no one any longer dared take it. "161 for five millions!" "162 for five millions!" No answer was made, and the offer was repeated, "162 for any part of five millions!" A voice replied, "Sold one million at 62!" The bubble suddenly burst; and within fifteen minutes amid an excitement without parallel even in the wildest excitements of the war, the clique brokers were literally swept away and left struggling by themselves, bidding still 160 for gold in millions which no one would any longer take their word for, while the premium sank rapidly to 135. A moment later the telegraph brought from Washington the government order to sell, and the result was no longer possible to dispute. Fisk had gone too far, while Gould had secretly weakened the ground under his feet.

Gould was saved. His fifty millions were sold; and although no one knows what his gains or losses may have been, his firm was able to meet its contracts and protect its brokers. Fisk was in a very different situation. So soon as it became evident that his brokers would be unable to carry out their contracts, every one who had sold gold to them turned in wrath to Fisk's office. Fortunately for him it was protected by armed men whom he had brought with him from his castle of Erie; but the excitement was so great that both Fisk and Gould thought best to retire as rapidly as possible by a back entrance leading into another street, and to seek the protection of the opera-house. There nothing but an army could disturb them; no civil madate was likely to be served without their permission within those walls, and few men cared to face Fisk's ruffians in order to force an entrance.

The winding up of this famous conspiracy may be told in few words; but no account could be complete which failed to reproduce in full the story of Fisk's last interview with Corbin, as told by Fisk himself:—

"I went down to the neighborhood of Wall Street Friday morning, and the history of that morning you know. When I got back to our office, you can imagine I was in no enviable state of mind, and the moment I got up street that afternoon I started right round to old Corbin's to rake him out. I went into the room, and sent word that Mr. Fisk wanted to see him in the dining-room. I was too mad to say anything civil, and when he came into the room, said I, 'You damned old scoundrel, do you know what you have done here, you and your people?' He began to wring his hands, and, 'Oh,' he says 'this is a horrible position! Are you ruined?' I said I didn't know whether I was or not; and I asked him again if he knew what had happened. He had been crying, and said he had just heard; that he had been sure everything was all right; but that something had occurred entirely different from what he had anticipated. Said I, 'That don't amount to anything; we know that gold ought not to be at 31, and that it would not be but for such performances as you have had this last week; you know damned well it would not if you had not failed.' I knew that somebody had run a saw right into us, and said I, 'This whole damned thing has turned out just as I told you it would.' I considered the whole party a pack of cowards, and I expected that when we came to clear our hands they would sock it right into us. I said to him, 'I don't know whether you have lied or not, and I don't know what ought to be done with you.' He was on the other side of the table, weeping and wailing, and I was gnashing my teeth. 'Now,' he says, 'you must quiet yourself.' I told him I didn't want to be quiet. I had no desire to ever be quiet again, and probably never should be quiet again. He says, 'But, my dear sir, you will lose your reason.' Says I, 'Speyers [a broker employed by him that day] has already lost his reason; reason has gone out of everybody but me.' I continued, 'Now, what are you going to do? You have got us into this thing, and what are you going to do to get us out of it?' He says, 'I don't know. I will go and get my wife.' I said, 'Get her down here!' The soft talk was all over. He went upstairs, and they returned tottling into the room, looking older than Stephen Hopkins. His wife and he both looked like death. He was tottling just like that. [Illustrated by a trembling movement of his body.] I have never seen him from that day to this."

This is sworn evidence before a committee of Congress; and its humor is the more conspicuous, because the story probably contained from beginning to end not a word of truth. No such interview ever occurred, except in the unconfined apartments of Fisk's imagination. His own previous statements make it certain that he was not at Corbin's house at all that day, and that Corbin did come to the Erie offices that evening, and again the next morning. Corbin denies the truth of the account without limitation; and adds that when he entered the Erie offices the next morning, Fisk was there. "I asked him how Mr. Gould felt after the great calamity of the day before." He remarked, "Oh, he has no courage at all. He has sunk right down. There is nothing left of him but a heap of clothes and a pair of eyes." The internal evidence of truth in this anecdote would support Mr. Corbin against the world.[1]

[1] Mr. Fisk to the Editor of the Sun:—

ERIE RAILWAY COMPANY, COMPTROLLER'S OFFICE
NEW YORK, Oct. 4, 1869.

To the Editor of the Sun.

DEAR SIR,—. . . Mr. Corbin has constantly associated with me; . . . *he spent more than an hour with me in the Erie Railway Office on the afternoon of Saturday, September 25, the day after the gold panic.* . . . I enclose you a few affidavits which will give you further information concerning this matter.

I remain your obedient servant,

JAMES FISK, JR.

Affidavit of Charles W. Pollard.
State of New York, City and County of New York, ss.

C. W. Pollard being duly sworn, says: "I have frequently been the bearer of messages between Mr. James Fisk, Jr. and Mr. Abel R. Corbin, brother-in-law

In regard to Gould, Fisk's graphic description was probably again inaccurate. Undoubtedly the noise and scandal of the moment were extremely unpleasant to this silent and impenetrable intriguer. The city was in a ferment, and the whole country pointing at him with wrath. The machinery of the gold exchange had broken down, and he alone could extricate the business community from the pressing danger of a general panic. He had saved himself, but in a manner that could not have been to his taste. Yet his course from this point must have been almost self-evident to his mind, and there is no reason to suppose that he hesitated.

Gould's contracts were all fulfilled. Fisk's contracts, all except one, in respect to which the broker was able to compel a settlement, were repudiated. Gould probably suggested to Fisk that it was better to let Belden fail, and to settle a handsome fortune on him, than to sacrifice something more than $5,000,000 in sustaining him. Fisk therefore threw Belden over, and swore that he had acted only under Belden's order; in support of which statement he produced a paper to the following effect:—

September 24.

DEAR SIR,—I hereby authorize you to order the purchase and sale of gold on my account during this day to the extent you may deem advisable, and to report the same to me as early as possible. It is to

---

of President Grant. . . . Mr. Corbin called on me at the Erie building on Thursday, 23d September, 1869, telling me he came to see how Messrs. Fisk and Gould were getting along. . . . He called again on Friday, the following day, at about noon; appeared to be greatly excited, and said he feared *we* should lose a great deal of money. The following morning, Saturday, September 25, Mr. Fisk told me to take his carriage and call upon Mr. Corbin and say to him that he and Mr. Gould would like to see him (Corbin) at their office. I called and saw Mr. Corbin. He remarked upon greeting me: 'How does Mr. Fisk bear his losses?' and added, '*It is terrible for us.*' He then asked me to bring Mr. Fisk up to his house immediately, as he was indisposed, and did not feel able to go down to his (Fisk's) office. I went after Mr. Fisk, who returned immediately with me to Mr. Corbin's residence, but shortly after came out with Mr. Corbin, who accompanied him to Mr. Fisk's office, where he was closeted with him and Mr. Gould for about two hours. . . ."

There are obvious inconsistencies among these different accounts, which it is useless to attempt to explain. The fact of Saturday's interview appears to be beyond dispute.

be understood that the profits of such order are to belong entirely to me, and I will, of course, bear any losses resulting.

Yours,

WILLIAM BELDEN.

JAMES FISK, JR.

This document was not produced in the original, and certainly never existed. Belden himself could not be induced to acknowledge the order; and no one would have believed him had he done so. Meanwhile the matter is before the national courts, and Fisk may probably be held to his contracts; but it will be difficult to execute judgment upon him, or to discover his assets.

One of the first acts of the Erie gentlemen after the crisis was to summon their lawyers and set in action their judicial powers. The object was to prevent the panic-stricken brokers from using legal process to force settlements, and so render the entanglement inextricable. Messrs. Field and Shearman came, and instantly prepared a considerable number of injunctions, which were sent to their judges, signed at once, and immediately served. Gould then was able to dictate the terms of settlement; and after a week of paralysis, Broad Street began to show signs of returning life. As a legal curiosity, one of these documents issued three months after the crisis may be reproduced in order to show the powers wielded by the Erie managers:—

SUPREME COURT

H. N. SMITH, JAY GOULD, H. H. MARTIN,
and J. B. BACH, Plaintiffs,

against

JOHN BONNER and ARTHUR L. SEWELL,
Defendants.

} Injunction by order.

It appearing satisfactorily to me by the complaint duly verified by the plaintiffs that sufficient grounds for an order of injunction exist, I do hereby order and enjoin . . . that the defendants, John Bonner and Arthur L. Sewell, their agents, attorneys, and servants, refrain from pressing their pretended claims against the plaintiffs, or either of them, before the Arbitration Committee of the New York Stock Exchange, or from taking any proceedings thereon, or in relation thereto, except in this action.

GEORGE G. BARNARD, J.S.C.

NEW YORK, Dec. 29, 1869.

Bonner had practically been robbed with violence by Gould, and instead of his being able to bring the robber into court as the criminal, the robber brought him into court as criminal, and the judge forbade him to appear in any other character. Of all Mr. Field's distinguished legal reforms and philanthropic projects, this injunction is beyond a doubt the most brilliant and the most successful.[1]

---

[1] These remarks on Mr. Field's professional conduct as counsel of the Erie Railway excited a somewhat intemperate controversy, and Mr. Field's partisans in the press made against the authors of the "Chapters of Erie" a charge that these writers "indelicately interfered in a matter alien to them in every way,"— the administration of justice in New York being, in this point of view, a matter in which Mr. Field and the Erie Railway were alone concerned. Mr. Field himself published a letter in the "Westminster Review" for April, 1871, in which, after the general assertion that the passages in the "New York Gold Conspiracy" which related to him "cover about as much untruth as could be crowded into so many lines," he made the following corrections:

First, he denied, what was never suggested, that he was in any way a party to the origin or progress of the Gold Conspiracy, until (secondly) he was consulted on the 28th of September, when (thirdly) he gave an opinion as to the powers of the members of the Gold and Stock Exchanges. Fourthly, he denied that he had relations of any sort with any judge in New York, or any power over these judges, other than such as English counsel have in respect to English judges. Fifthly, he asserted that among twenty-eight injunctions growing out of the gold transactions his partners obtained only ten, and only one of these ten, the one quoted above, from Justice Barnard. Sixthly, that this injunction was proper to be sought and granted. Seventhly, that Mr. Bonner was not himself the person who had been "robbed with violence," but the assignee of the parties.

On the other hand, Mr. Field did not deny that the injunction as quoted was genuine, or that he was responsible for it, or that it did, as asserted, shut the defendants out of the courts as well as out of the Gold Exchange Arbitration Committee, or that it compelled them to appear only as defendants in a case where they were the injured parties.

In regard to the power which Mr. Field, whether as a private individual or as Erie counsel, exercised over the New York bench, his correction affected the story but little. In regard to Mr. Bonner, the fact of his being principal or representative scarcely altered the character of Mr. Field's injunction. Finally, so far as the text is concerned, after allowing full weight to all Mr. Field's corrections, the public can decide for itself how many untruths it contained. The sub-

The fate of the conspirators was not severe. Corbin went to Washington, where he was snubbed by the President, and disappeared from public view, only coming to light again before the Congressional committee. General Butterfield, whose share in the transaction is least understood, was permitted to resign his office without an investigation. Speculation for the next six months was at an end. Every person involved in the affair seemed to have lost money, and dozens of brokers were swept from the street. But Jay Gould and James Fisk, Jr., continued to reign over Erie, and no one can say that their power or their credit was sensibly diminished by a shock which for the time prostrated the interests of the country.

Nevertheless, sooner or later the last traces of the disturbing influence of war and paper money will disappear in America, as they have sooner or later disappeared in every other country which has passed through the same evils. The result of this convulsion itself has been in the main good. It indicates the approaching end of a troubled time. Messrs. Gould and Fisk will at last be obliged to yield to the force of moral and economical laws. The Erie Railway will be rescued, and its history will perhaps rival that of the great speculative manias of the last century. The United States will restore a sound basis to its currency, and will learn to deal with the political reforms it requires. Yet though the regular process of development may be depended upon, in its ordinary and established

---

ject ceased to be one of consequence even to Mr. Field after the subsequent violent controversy which arose in March, 1871, in regard to other points of Mr. Field's professional conduct. [In March, 1871, Francis C. Barlow, formerly United States marshal of the southern district of New York and subsequently attorney-general of the state of New York, published a series of letters in the New York *Tribune* denouncing Field's conduct as lawyer for Fisk and Gould in their attempt of 1869 to take over the Albany and Susquehanna Railroad. (For an account of this affair, see Charles F. Adams, Jr., "An Erie Raid" in *Chapters of Erie*.) Barlow exposed the connivings of the Erie managers and charged that Field "conducts their litigations in defiance of all rules of professional honor and common honesty." As a result of his agitation, and that of other members of the New York bar, Judge Barnard was impeached in 1872, found guilty, and removed from office, and Field was severely censured by a report of the Committee on Grievances of the Association of the Bar of the City of New York. The committee's recommendations with respect to Field, which were reported to have been of a "serious character," were tabled by the Association.]

course, to purge American society of the worst agents of an exceptionally corrupt time, the history of the Erie corporation offers one point in regard to which modern society everywhere is directly interested. For the first time since the creation of these enormous corporate bodies, one of them has shown its power for mischief, and has proved itself able to override and trample on law, custom, decency, and every restraint known to society, without scruple, and as yet without check. The belief is common in America that the day is at hand when corporations far greater than the Erie— swaying power such as has never in the world's history been trusted in the hands of private citizens, controlled by single men like Vanderbilt, or by combinations of men like Fisk, Gould, and Lane, after having created a system of quiet but irresistible corruption—will ultimately succeed in directing government itself. Under the American form of society no authority exists capable of effective resistance. The national government, in order to deal with the corporations, must assume powers refused to it by its fundamental law,— and even then is exposed to the chance of forming an absolute central government which sooner or later is likely to fall into the hands it is struggling to escape, and thus destroy the limits of its power only in order to make corruption omnipotent. Nor is this danger confined to America alone. The corporation is in its nature a threat against the popular institutions spreading so rapidly over the whole world. Wherever a popular and limited government exists this difficulty will be found in its path; and unless some satisfactory solution of the problem can be reached, popular institutions may yet find their existence endangered.

The Session. 1869-1870

The second "Session" was written at white heat early in June, 1870, immediately after Adams finished "The New York Gold Conspiracy." Unexpectedly enough, it was the last product of his brief career as a free-lance journalist, for within a few months he had left Washington and begun a new life as professor of medieval history at Harvard. The article was in many ways a fitting culmination of Adams' two years in the capital. With a perfect lack of moderation, it vented in one fierce assault all his accumulated disgust with the Grant administration. The new era of governmental "normalcy" inaugurated by the soldier-president seemed to him, both as a moralist and a politician, a betrayal of all those standards by which government was made meaningful. The very pointlessness and drift of Grantism was perhaps most infuriating to him as a negation of intelligence in practical affairs. The "Session" of 1870, therefore, declared Adams publicly in opposition, and began the task of formulating a rationale for the emerging Independent Republican movement.

The article was undoubtedly Adams' most widely read and influential piece of early writing. In 1872 it was reprinted and distributed by the Democratic Party as a campaign document under the title: The Administration—A Radical Indictment! Its Shortcomings. Its Weakness, Stolidity. Thorough Analysis of Grant's and Boutwell's Mental Calibre. No Policy. No Ability. *When Senator*

Timothy Howe of Wisconsin replied to it with no little violence in the Wisconsin State Journal, *Adams commented loftily, "To be abused by a Senator is my highest ambition, and I am now quite happy. My only regret is that I cannot afford to hire a Senator to abuse me permanently. That, however, might pall in time. . . ."*

THAT the government of the United States is passing through a period of transition is one of the common-places of politics. This transition, which few persons deny, illustrates in a scientific point of view the manner in which principles are established. The generation that framed the American form of government meant it to be, not only in mechanism but in theory, a contradiction to opinions commonly accepted in Europe. The men who made the Constitution intended to make by its means an issue with antiquity; and they had a clear conception of the issue itself, and of their own purposes in raising it. These purposes were perhaps chimerical; the hopes then felt were almost certainly delusive. Yet persons who grant the probable failure of the scheme, and expect the recurrence of the great problems in government which were then thought to be solved, cannot but look with satisfaction at the history of the Federal Constitution as the most convincing and the most interesting experiment ever made in the laboratory of political science, even if it demonstrates the impossibility of success through its means.

The great object of terror and suspicion to the people of the thirteen provinces was *power;* not merely power in the hands of a president or a prince, of one assembly or of several, of many citizens

From the *North American Review* for July, 1870, [Reprinted and revised in *Historical Essays*, 1891.]

or of few, but power in the abstract, wherever it existed and under whatever name it was known. "There is and must be," said Blackstone, "in all forms of government, however they began or by what right soever they exist, a supreme, irresistible, absolute, uncontrolled authority, in which the *jura summi imperii*, or the rights of sovereignty, reside;" and Parliament is the place "where that absolute despotic power which must in all governments reside somewhere is intrusted by the Constitution of the British kingdoms." Supreme, irresistible authority must exist somewhere in every government—was the European political belief; and England solved her problem by intrusting it to a representative assembly to be used according to the best judgment of the nation. America, on the other hand, asserted that the principle was not true; that no such supreme power need exist in a government; that in the American government none such should be allowed to exist, because absolute power in any form was inconsistent with freedom, and that the new government should start from the idea that the public liberties depended upon denying uncontrolled authority to the political system in its parts or in its whole.

Every one knows with what logic this theory was worked out in the mechanism of the new republic. Not only were rights reserved to the people never to be parted with, but rights of great extent were reserved to the States as a sacred deposit to be jealously guarded. Even in the central government, the three great depositories of power were made independent of each other, checks on each other's assumption of authority, separately responsible to the people, that each might be a protection and not a danger to the public liberties. The framers of the Constitution did not indeed presume to prescribe or limit the powers a nation might exercise if its existence were at stake. They knew that under such an emergency paper limitations must yield; but they still hoped that the lesson they had taught would sink so deep into the popular mind as to cause a re-establishment of the system after the emergency had passed. The hope was scarcely supported by the experience of history, but, like M. Necker in France, they were obliged to trust somewhat to the "virtues of the human heart."

The two theories of government stood face to face during three quarters of a century. Europe still maintained that supreme power must be trusted to every government, democratic or not; and America still maintained that such a principle was inconsistent with freedom. The civil war broke out in the United States, and of course for the time obliterated the Constitution. Peace came, and with it came the moment for the settlement of this long scientific dispute. If the Constitutional system restored itself, America was right, and the oldest problem in political science was successfully solved.

Every one knows the concurrence of accidents, if anything in social sequence can be called accident, which seemed to prevent a fair working of the tendency to restoration during the four years that followed the close of actual war. With the year 1869 a new and peculiarly favorable change took place. Many good and true Americans then believed that the time had come, and that the old foundation on which American liberties had been planted would be fully and firmly restored. A brilliant opportunity occurred for the new Administration, not perhaps to change the ultimate results, but to delay some decades yet the demonstration of failure. The new President had unbounded popular confidence. He was tied to no party. He was under no pledges. He had the inestimable advantage of a military training, which, unlike a political training, was calculated to encourage the moral distinction between right and wrong.

No one could fail to see the mingled feelings of alarm and defiance with which senators and politicians waited President Grant's first move. Not they alone, but almost the entire public, expected to see him at once grasp with a firm hand the helm of government, and give the vessel of state a steady and determined course. The example of President Washington offered an obvious standard for the ambition of Grant. It was long before the conservative class of citizens, who had no partisan prejudices, could convince themselves that in this respect they had not perhaps overrated so much as misconceived the character of Grant, and that they must learn to look at him in a light unlike any they had been hitherto accustomed to associate with him. This misconception or misunderstanding was not matter for surprise, since even to the President's oldest and most intimate associates his character is still in some respects a riddle, and the secret of his uniform and extraordinary success a matter of dispute. Indeed, if he ever fell into the mischievous habit of analyzing his own mind, he could answer his own questions in no manner that would satisfy curiosity. Nothing could be more interesting to any person who has been perplexed with the doubts which President Grant's character never fails to raise in every one who approaches him, than to have these doubts met and explained by some competent authority,—by some old associate like General Sherman, with an active mind ever eager to grapple with puzzles; by some civil subordinate such as a civil subordinate ought to be, quick at measuring influences and at unravelling the tangled skein of ideas which runs through the brains of an Administration. Yet as a rule, the reply to every inquiry comes in the form of confessed ignorance: "We do not know why Grant is successful; we only know that he succeeds."

Without attempting to explain so complicated an enigma, one might still predict General Grant's probable civil career from facts open to all the world. Grant's mind rarely acts from any habit of wide generalization. As a rule, the ideas executed with so much energy appear to come to him one by one, without close logical sequence; and as a person may see and calculate the effect of a drop of acid on an organic substance, so one may sometimes almost seem to see the mechanical process by which a new idea eats its way into Grant's unconscious mind,—where its action begins, and where its force is exhausted. Hence arise both advantages and misfortunes. This faculty for assimilation of ideas, this nature which the Germans would call objective, under ordinary circumstances and when not used by selfish men for corrupt purposes gives elasticity, freedom from inveterate prejudices, and capacity for progress. It would be likely to produce a course of action not perhaps strictly logical, or perfectly steady, or capable of standing the sharper tests of hostile criticism, but in the main practical, sensible, and in intention honest. When used by Jay Gould and Abel Rathbone Corbin with the skill of New York stock-brokers for illegitimate objects, the result is the more distastrous in proportion to the energy of execution for which the President is remarkable.

Most persons, and especially those who had formed their ideas of the President from his Vicksburg campaign, entertained a different notion of his intellectual qualities. The Vicksburg campaign puzzled equally the enemies and the friends of General Grant. General Sherman's frank expression of surprise found its way into print in the form of a sincere tribute of admiration spoken by a man conscious of having underrated his superior officer. The public, on the strength of this brilliant campaign, assumed with reason that a general capable of planning and executing a military scheme such as Napoleon might have envied, must possess an aptitude for elaboration of idea and careful adaptation of means to ends such as would in civil administration produce a large and vigorous political policy. Yet no such refinement of conception was in Grant's nature; no such ambition entered his head,—he neither encouraged it nor believed in its advantages. His own idea of his duties as President was openly and consistently expressed, and is best described as that of the commander of an army in time of peace. He was to watch over the faithful administration of the government; to see that the taxes were honestly collected, that the disbursements were honestly made, that economy was strictly enforced, that the laws were everywhere obeyed, good and bad alike; and as it was the duty of every military commander to obey the civil authority without question, so it was the duty of the President to follow without hesitation the wishes of the people as expressed by Congress.

This is not the range of duties prescribed to an American President either by the Constitution or by custom, although it may be that which Congress desires and to which the system tends. The President may indeed in one respect resemble the commander of an army in peace, but in another and more essential sense he resembles the commander of a ship at sea. He must have a helm to grasp, a course to steer, a port to seek; he must sooner or later be convinced that a perpetual calm is as little to his purpose as a perpetual hurricane, and that without headway the ship can arrive nowhere. President Grant assumed at the outset that it was not his duty to steer; that his were only duties of discipline.

Under these circumstances, with a President who while disbelieving in the propriety of having a general policy must yet inevitably assume responsibility,—with one to whose mind, if not imaginative or highly cultivated, was still sensitive to surrounding influences,—the necessity was all the greater that the gentlemen on whose advice and assistance he would be compelled to lean should be calculated to supplement his natural gifts. From him the public had not required high civil education. Rulers have always the right to command and appropriate the education and the intelligence of their people. Knowledge somewhere, either in himself or in his servants, is essential even to an American President,— perhaps to him most of all rulers; and thus, though it was a matter of comparatively little importance that the President's personal notions of civil government were crude, and his ideas of political economy those of a feudal monarch a thousand years ago, it was of the highest consequence that his advisers should supply the knowledge that he could not have been expected to possess, and should develop the ideas which his growing experience would give him. Questions of finance having assumed overruling importance, a responsibility of the most serious character would evidently rest on the Secretary of the Treasury.

The official importance of the Secretary of the Treasury can hardly be over-estimated. Not only is his political power in the exercise of patronage greater than that of any other Cabinet officer, but in matters of policy almost every proposition of foreign or domestic interest sooner or later involves financial considerations and requires an opinion from a financial stand-point. Hence in the English system the head of administration commonly occupies the post of premier lord of the Treasury. In the American form of government the head of the Treasury is also the post of real authority, rivalling that of the President, and almost too powerful for harmony or subordination. The secretary's voice ought to have more weight with the President than that of any other adviser. The secretary's financial policy ought to be the point on which each member of the Administration is united with every other. At a time like the summer of 1869, when old issues were passing away and a new condition of things was at hand, when the public was waiting to be led or kneeling to take up its master, it was more than ever important that the President should have in the Treasury a man who could command and compel respect.

Secretary Boutwell was not a person to make good the needs of the President. General Grant wanted civil education, but in return was open to new ideas, and had the capacity to learn from any one who had the faculty to teach. Mr. Boutwell had no faculty for teaching, and little respect for knowledge that was not practical. He believed in knowledge so far as was convenient to justify his theory that knowledge was a deception. He believed in common schools, and not in political science; in ledgers and cash-books, but not in Adam Smith or J. S. Mill,—as one might believe in the multiplication-table, but not in Laplace or Newton. By a natural logic he made of his disbelief in the higher branches of political science a basis for his political practice; and thus grounding action on ignorance, he carried out his principle to its conclusions. He too, like the President, announced that he had no policy; and even more persistently than the President he attempted to govern on the theory that government was no concern of his. Other persons in a similar position would commonly have leaned either to the theorists on one side, or to so-called practical men on the other; but Mr. Boutwell treated both with the same indifference. He had all the theorists in Europe and America to choose from, but he did not listen to their teachings; he had all the practical men in the country at his service, but he did not follow their advice; he had all the best members of the Legislature to depend upon, but he did not desire their assistance; he had a costly and elaborate machinery maintained by the country to furnish him with any information he might require, but Mr. Boutwell never required information. Nay, sitting twice a week in consultation with his colleagues in the Cabinet, Mr. Boutwell cannot have controlled their measures or even discussed his own. The President himself at the time of his Message could hardly have been consulted by the secretary.

To analyze a policy which does not exist, to trace the adaptation of means to ends where no adaptation was intended, is a waste of time and ingenuity. Yet no man can succeed in obliterating all ideas from his mind, or can prevent his acts from showing traces of intelligence. This relation between ideas and acts, commonly known as a policy, was visible in Mr. Boutwell's course, although it was visible only within a narrow range. Of most political leaders it might have been foretold with certainty that they would expend their energy on a restoration of the currency, or on a reduction of the taxes, confident that if these were once settled the financial situation would be secure. Mr. Boutwell's passion was different.

He had only one object of great ambition, but this was to redeem the national debt. To do this from day to day; to collect more and more millions from the people; to cut down the expenses to their lowest point; to accumulate the surplus in the Treasury; to buy with it, month by month, more and more of the government's own debts, and thus to see the huge mass of indebtedness slowly dwindle and diminish in his hands,—this was a tangible, self-evident proof of success, which appealed directly to the lowest order of intelligence, and struck with the greatest possible force the mind of the voting public. To this idea Mr. Boutwell sacrificed currency reform, revenue reform, and every hope of relief from taxation; and to this idea he subordinated even his own next ambition, that of lowering the rate of interest on the debt. Beyond this he abnegated ideas. He did nothing, said nothing, heard nothing, except when necessity compelled.

Although the policy thus embraced by Mr. Boutwell was neither broad nor deep, and certainly not that of a great statesman, yet in pursuing this easy and simple course Mr. Boutwell may have taken the most direct path to an apparently brilliant success,—a success far better calculated for his purposes than though he had strayed aside into the vast and comprehensive reforms which would have dazzled the imaginations of Turgot, of Pitt, or of Hamilton. But the success which is gained by so meagre and sterile a conception is of little permanent value, even when compared with a bold and generous failure. If a critic were called upon to name the most unfortunate of all the financiers who have ever controlled the resources of France, he might, from Mr. Boutwell's point of view, find difficulty in discovering a more conspicuous failure than the administration of Turgot. If he applied the same process to British finance, he might probably be compelled at last to fix upon no less illustrious a career than that of William Pitt. But if he were to test his theory by the opposite experiment of selecting from English history the nearest approach to Mr. Boutwell's ideal of financial success, he would certainly be compelled to pass in silence over the names of Montagu and of Walpole, of Pitt, of Peel, and of Gladstone, in order to draw from its almost forgotten resting-place the memory of some third-rate Chancellor of the Exchequer, some Nicholas Vansittart, whose very name is a blank even to the students of biographical cyclopaedias. Vansittart, indeed, would in most respects, except for his curious financial knowledge and his reverence for the financial teachings of his great master Pitt, serve well as the ideal of Mr. Boutwell. A Chancellor of the Exchequer who coming into office in 1812, at almost the darkest moment of England's struggle with the world, remained at the head of the finances through the war; met and triumphantly stood the shock of the return from Elba, and of Waterloo; carried England back to specie payments after twenty years of paper money; at a single operation reduced the interest on a capital of nearly $800,000,000, at that time the largest sum ever dealt with in a mass; and who, to crown all, arrived at the height of his ambition in 1823 by raising the surplus, applicable to the reduction of debt, to the unprecedented point of $25,000,000 in spite of the opposition of the whole body of liberal and educated politicians,—a Chancellor of the Exchequer with twelve years of such triumphs as these could scarcely be denied the credit of supreme and unrivalled success. Yet such is the perverseness of history, and so unreasonable is human prejudice, that not only the contemporaries of Mr. Vansittart, although attached to him by his genial and good-natured manners, but also posterity, to which his name is so little familiar, have combined in agreeing that as a financial minister he was a conspicuous example of incompetence, who for years hung like a clog on the progress of England.

So far as finance was concerned, Mr. Boutwell's policy might have been poorer even than it was, and yet the vigor of the country would have made it a success. The greatest responsibilities of a Secretary of the Treasury are not financial, and an administration framed upon the narrow basis of mere departmental activity must be always, except under the strongest of Presidents, an invitation to failure. The stormiest of Cabinets, the most venturesome of advisers, the boldest of political rivals for power, are likely to produce in combination a better result than that unorganized and disjointed harmony, that dead unanimity, which springs from divided responsibility. Mr. Boutwell had neither the wish nor the scope to assume the functions or to wield the power of his office; and instead of stamping upon the President and his administration the impress of a controlling mind, he drew himself back into a corner of his own, and encouraged and set the example of isolation at a time when concentrated action was essential to the Executive.

Even in the quietest of times and under the most despotic chief such a departmental government is a doubtful experiment, but in the summer and autumn of 1869 it was peculiarly ill-timed. Every politician felt that the first year of the new Administration would probably fix the future character of the government. The steady process by which power was tending to centralization in defiance of the theory of the political system; the equally steady tendency of this power to accumulate in the hands of the Legislature at the expense of the Executive and the Judiciary; the ever-increasing encroachments of the Senate, the ever-diminishing efficiency of the House; all the different parts and processes of the general movement which indicated a certain abandonment of the original theory of the American system, and a no less certain substitution of a method of government that promised to be both corrupt and inefficient,— all these were either to be fixed upon the country beyond recall, or were to be met by a prompt and energetic resistance. To evade the contest was to accept the revolution. To resist with success, the President must have built up his authority upon every side until the vigor of his Administration overawed the Senate, and carried away the House by the sheer strength of popular applause. That such a result was possible no one can doubt who had occasion to see how much it was dreaded by the Washington politicians of the winter and spring of 1869, and how rapidly they resumed confidence on discovering that the President had no such schemes.

By the time Congress came together, in December, 1869, the warm hopes which illumined the election of November, 1868, had faded from the public mind. Clearly, the Administration was marked by no distinctive character. No purpose of peculiar elevation, no broad policy, no commanding dignity indicated the beginning of a new era. The old type of politician was no less powerful than under other Presidents. The old type of idea was not improved by the personal changes between 1861 and 1870. The Administration was not prepared for a contest with Congress, and at the last moment it was still without a purpose, without followers, and without a head.

Under these circumstances the President's Message was sent to the Capitol. It was studied with the more curiosity because it was supposed to reflect the internal condition of the government. Nothing could have presented a less reassuring prospect. The want of plan and unity of idea was so obvious that no one needed to be assured of the harmony of the Administration. An Administration that did not care enough for its own opinions to quarrel about them was naturally harmonious. The President and the Secretary of the Treasury were discovered expressing opinions and offering recommendations diametrically opposed to each other, apparently unconscious that under ordinary theories of government a head is required. Nor was this all. The absence of a strong mind in the Treasury was as conspicuous in what was omitted as in what was said. Not only was the political economy, both of the Message and of Mr. Boutwell's Report, a subject into which the ridicule of the press cut with easy facility, to the mortification of every friend of the Government, but even where simpler declarations, not requiring previous knowledge of principles, would have satisfied every purpose, their absence was almost as marked as was the presence of Mr. Boutwell's famous barrels of flour.[1] In regard to the currency alone was the President in advance of public opinion, and in regard to the currency his secretary offered him no active support. Other reforms shared a worse fate. The reduction of taxes was discouraged, the civil service was not noticed, and tariff reform was distinctly opposed. Had it not been for the good sense of the remarks on reconstruction and foreign affairs, the President's

[1] [Boutwell's Treasury Report of 1869 urged the nation to develop its merchant marine as a way of earning more foreign currency and hence enabling the resumption of specie payments. The example he gave was as follows: "If . . . an American citizen purchase in New York a thousand barrels of flour for six thousand dollars, and export it to Liverpool in an American vessel, and it is there sold for seven thousand dollars, a bill of exchange may be drawn against the proceeds, and an invoice of goods of the value of seven thousand dollars purchased in England entirely liquidated, although at the custom-house at New York there would be an apparent balance against the country of one thousand dollars. But if, on the other hand, the thousand barrels of flour are exported in a British vessel, the proceeds of the flour realized in New York, and which can be applied to the payment of goods bought in England, will be only six thousand dollars, and there will remain an actual balance against the country of a thousand dollars. This familiar example shows the importance of re-establishing our commercial supremacy upon the ocean."]

first appearance before Congress would have hazarded the reproach of absurdity.

The result, already a foregone conclusion, became apparent when Congress took up its work. So far as initiative was concerned, the President and his cabinet might equally well have departed separately or together to distant lands. Their recommendations were uniformly disregarded. Mr. Sumner, at the head of the Senate, rode rough-shod over their reconstruction policy, and utterly overthrew it in spite of the feeble resistance of the House. Senator Conkling then ousted Sumner from his saddle, and headed the Senate in an attack upon the Executive as represented by Judge Hoar, the avowed *casus belli* being that the attorney-general's manners were unsatisfactory to the Senate. Then Conkling attacked the Census Bill, where he had a three-fold victory; and it would be hard to say which of the three afforded him the keenest gratification. Single-handed he assailed Sumner, the House, and the Executive, and routed them all in disastrous confusion. Never was factiousness more alluring or more successful than under Conkling's lead. Then again Sumner came to the front, and obtained a splendid triumph over the President in the struggle over San Domingo. Senator Sherman was less vigorous and less fortunate in regard to the currency and funding measures, but Boutwell asked so little it was difficult for Sherman to do more than ignore him; and even in the House, Mr. Dawes, the official spokesman of the Government, if the Government has an official spokesman, startled the country by a sudden and dashing volunteer attack on the only point of General Grant's lines on the security of which he had prided himself,—his economy; and to this day no man understands how Dawes's foray was neutralized or evaded, or whether he was right or wrong.

The principal subjects of the session within the scope of the present review have been Reconstruction, Finance, and Foreign Affairs.

On the subject of Reconstruction little need be said. The merits or demerits of the system adopted are no longer a subject worth discussion. The resistance to these measures rested primarily on their violation of the letter and spirit of the Constitution as regarded the rights of States, and the justification rested not on a denial of the violation, but in overruling necessity. The measures were adopted with reluctance by a majority of Congressmen, they were approved with equal reluctance by a majority of the people; but they have become law, and whatever harm may ultimately come from them is beyond recall and must be left for the coming generation, to which the subject henceforth belongs, to regulate according to its circumstances and judgment. The present generation must rest content with knowing that so far as legal principles are involved, the process of reconstruction has reached its limits in the legislation of 1869. The powers originally reserved by the Constitution to the States are in future to be held by them only on good behavior and at the sufferance of Congress; they may be suspended or assumed by Congress; their original basis and sanction no longer exist; and if they ever offered any real protection against the assumption of supreme and uncontrolled power by the central government, that protection is at an end. How far Congress will at any future day care to press its authority, or how far the States themselves may succeed in resisting the power of Congress, are questions which must be answered by a reference to the general course of events. Something may be judged of the rate of progress from the theory so energetically pressed during the past season by Senator Sumner, that the New England system of common schools is a part of the republican form of government as understood by the framers of the Constitution,—an idea that would have seemed to the last generation as strange as though it had been announced that the electric telegraph was an essential article of faith in the early Christian Church. Something also may be judged from the condition of New York city and the evident failure of the system of self-government in great municipalities. Something more may be guessed from the rapid progress of corruption in shaking public confidence in State legislatures. Finally, something may be inferred from the enormous development of corporate power, requiring still greater political power to control it. Under any circumstances the first decisive, irrevocable step toward substituting a new form of government in the place of that on which American liberties have heretofore rested has been taken, and by it the American people must stand.

Finance, if not so important as Reconstruction, had at least the advantage of novelty. Reduction of taxation was the popular cry. Reform of taxation was equally essential. Secretary Boutwell, and with him though less positively the President, resisted at the outset either reduction or reform. The process of bond-buying supplied in Boutwell's mind the want of any more difficult conception, while in regard to free-trade ideas the secretary, like all political New England, sympathized with the President in cold indifference. The revenue reformers had not expected such a result; they were not prepared for the hostility they met from the Administration, and were thus placed in a position of great difficulty.

Whatever was the reason that the President leaned to high protectionist ideas, no one was more surprised or less gratified than many of his warmest friends when they found the fact announced in his Message. Undoubtedly the reformers had hoped and expected to have his sympathy in their efforts for revenue reform, as they had hoped it in regard to civil-service reform, and as they received it in the case of the currency; nor was there reason to suppose that the President, even on this important subject, acted from firm conviction, or considered the matter in reference to any general class of political ideas. The responsibility for the President's course could not be thrown upon his Secretary of the Treasury, since Secretary Boutwell on this subject as on all others, except one, abnegated influence. The difficulty was that the Administration without active hostility blocked the path of the reformers. It would consent to no absolute war upon them, but its practical influence was more mischievous than the bitterest warfare. To break down the monopolies which the central government had created and was engaged in supporting, and whose corrupt influence was felt at every step, seemed the first and most pressing necessity to those who believed that a purer political and moral atmosphere was only to be found by freeing the country from them; but to do this by disjointed, unorganized effort, without support from the Administration and in face of a large party majority, against the sneers and contempt of every Republican Congressman from New England, without a voice of open or secret encouragement and at the same time to meet and overcome Pennsylvania and her organized body of allies,—to do it all by means of the Republican party when the Republican party in Congress dreaded nothing so much as the necessity of meeting this issue, seemed a project of hopeless temerity.

The small body of men in and out of Congress who were determined to force the issue of reform began the winter under every influence of discouragement. Not only had the President abandoned them, but Congress was in the hands of their opponents; and the Committee of Ways and Means, controlled by protectionist influence, prepared an ingenious bill, calculated to reduce taxation and to check popular complaint, but still more carefully constructed to maintain and increase the protecting duties wherever special interests asked it. The Forty-first Congress was considered as more thoroughly devoted to protectionist ideas than any of its predecessors, and about fifty Democratic votes were all that could be classed as determined for free-trade, with the exception of three or four Western Republicans. Tariff reform, as advocated by David A. Wells, commanded a certain amount of sympathy; but its friends in the House were few and timid, while the charge of free-trade sounded to their ears as terrible as that of having worn a rebel uniform or having been out with the Ku-klux Klan. To convert such a body of men by such small means as the reformers could command was a desperate undertaking. The friends of reform in 1869, quitting in despair the President and his Cabinet with their inertia and cold neutrality, and Congress with its bristling hostility, turned to ask counsel of the popular masses. They worked throughout the summer and autumn with all the energy they possessed, and they continued to work throughout the winter, not in the lobbies of the Capitol or in the ante-chambers of the departments, but directly and earnestly upon popular opinion. As spring approached they began to resume confidence. Their leaders in Washington, whose interest was sharpened by the anxiety to maintain control of their constituencies, received from every quarter beyond the Alleghanies, with few exceptions, assurances of popular support, so vigorous and so universal that their tone began to change from depression to boldness, and they felt themselves strong enough to do without the Administration if the Administration could do without them. From every great organ of public opinion in the Western country they poured out a volume of argument and appeal that no popular influence could resist. Party lines were broken under their incessant attrition. Members of Congress began to hesitate, to consult, and to seek information. The formal opening debate upon the new tariff developed the existence of a feeling such as no one had expected; and when the bill went into committee to be taken up in detail, it is hard to say who were more astonished, protectionists or reformers, to learn that in the first division the reformers carried the reduction on sugar by a majority of two.

Then ensued a struggle which dumfounded the friends of the tariff, who at first refused to credit their defeat, and insisted on considering it an accident due to the absence of their allies. When the same result occurred again and again, while the resistance to the bill became more and more general instead of diminishing, they began to comprehend their danger. General Schenck, who made every effort to force his measures through the House, with more success than any other member could have obtained, soon lost his temper, having at best no very considerable supply of temper to lose, and described his difficulties in graphic language.

"There is nobody in this House," said he, "upon either side, there is nobody anywhere that has watched the progress of the Tariff Bill through the Committee of the Whole, who does not know that peculiarly, and beyond perhaps the manifestation of hostility and attack upon any other measure in this or almost any former Congress, it has been fought inch by inch, step by step, line by line, persistently, with heavy attacks and with light attacks,—and most frequently light. I defy a denial of that."

The fact was not one which the reformers proposed to deny. Not only did they intend to resist all increase of protective duties, but they meant to lower the duties wherever they could. They urged their amendments to every line and word with a persistency which astonished themselves; and, what was still more surprising, the House in Committee of the Whole supported their efforts, and drove the Committee of Ways and Means to amend its own bill. Nor did their success end there. The whole subject was forced before the public attention, and the political issue for the coming elections was marked out beyond evasion.

Meanwhile Secretary Boutwell yielded so far to the popular outcry that he unwillingly accepted the necessity of reducing, if not of reforming, taxation, and the President showed signs of yielding to both demands. Their acceptance of the principle of reform, though too late to give aid to reformers, might perhaps have served to save a few Republican Congressmen from defeat in the autumn elections; but it was a sign of weakness rather than of strength, and indicated a want of stability which had scarcely been expected. As for Secretary Boutwell's persistent efforts to obtain authority to fund a portion of the debt, the subject is somewhat too technical for ordinary readers, and is fortunately subordinate in importance. Whatever respect Boutwell's policy deserved, it received extremely little, and may be dismissed without further comment. In regard to the currency, where reform ought properly to have begun, no approach to agreement could be made. The subject was amply discussed, both formally and informally. Every method of contraction, both direct and indirect; every process of acting on the national greenback circulation through the national banking currency, or on the banking currency through the greenback circulation, on either separately or on both at once; every theory, no matter how new or how old; every objection, no matter how frivolous,—all in turn were argued and laid aside, because public opinion was not yet ripe for action. As usual, nothing could be done by the government, which invariably failed to govern.

In the midst of this universal dead-lock on every issue except reconstruction, the Supreme Court on the 7th of February pronounced its decision that the Legal-Tender Act, so far as it applied to debts contracted before its passage, exceeded the authority of Congress, and assumed powers forbidden by the Constitution.

To any one on the stand-point assumed at the outset of these remarks, the decision of the Supreme Court must obviously have appeared not only sound in itself, but the single step which had been taken by any department of the government since the close of the war toward the restoration either of a solid basis to the currency or of a solid foundation to the republic. It was a moderate and cautious reassertion of the fundamental principle on which the private liberties of the American citizen had been originally based. It was the only indication yet seen that Hamilton and Madison might have been right in hoping that their system of checks and balances would operate to restore an equilibrium once disturbed by the exigencies of a troubled time. As such it received popular acquiescence. Hardly a murmur was raised against it by the press. Only in Congress, where opposition might naturally have been expected, was hostility shown to a movement threatening the usurped power of Congress alone; and only in the Senate, which has always been, as it always must be, the furnace of intrigue and aggression, was actual attack upon the Court expected.

The public naturally assumed that the Administration would be glad to accept and support this decision, not only because the interests of the Executive and the Supreme Court are identical, or because this special decision tended to check the arrogant and domineering Congressional power, which had been felt in a manner humiliating to the Cabinet, but because the decision strengthened the declared policy of the President in regard to the currency, and partially withdrew the government from the false position into which it had confessedly been forced by the exigencies of war. Hence, although senators instantly declared that the decision should be reversed, and that no candidate favorable to the decision should be confirmed to either of the seats on the Supreme bench then vacated by the deaths of Justices Grier and Stanton, a strong feeling of surprise and astonishment was perceptible when gentlemen supposed to be thoroughly well informed asserted that the President, the Secretary of the Treasury, and Attorney-General E. R. Hoar were agreed in considering the decision as an attack upon the policy of the war, a denial of necessary powers to Congress, and a Democratic electioneering trick. The incredulity was great when authority above ordinary doubt further asserted, on direct information from the White House, that neither Judge Bradley nor Judge Strong would have been nominated to the bench, had it been supposed that either of them favored the legal-tender decision. These nominations, whether influenced by such a consideration or not, removed all doubt from senators' minds in regard to this particular difficulty; while at the same time little doubt could remain in the public mind that a reversal obtained by introducing on the bench two gentlemen occupying the position of Messrs. Strong and Bradley would establish beyond dispute a precedent for packing the Court whenever it suited Congress to do so, and destroying the independence of the Judiciary as a co-ordinate branch of the American government.

Judge Strong took his seat on the 14th of March. Judge Bradley was confirmed by the Senate a week later, and summoned by telegraph to Washington. He took his seat on the 23d of March. Two days later, at the earliest possible moment, the attorney-general surprised the Court by moving to take up and argue two cases formerly passed over, which involved the principle of the legal-tender decision.

In the course of the attorney-general's remarks he said:—

"This Court, at a time when by law it consisted of nine judges, did by a majority of four to three enter its judgment, with two vacancies upon the bench; and it stands therefore, reducing it to its essence, that upon the judicial opinion of a single man, whose voice turned the majority, that great question is adjudicated. And if (which is a supposable case) it turned out that it was an opinion about which even the deciding judge of the Court had entertained a different opinion at some other time, it would come down to the point that on the differing opinions at different times of his life of a single man, the whole Constitutional power of Congress . . . was to be subverted."

What answer this personal attack on the chief-justice would have received had it been made by an attorney-general of Massachusetts before the Supreme Bench of that State, with Hoar, C. J., presiding, must be matter of opinion, only to be decided by an appeal to that tribunal under these conditions. He would have been a rash attorney-general who attempted to browbeat a court so constituted. Whether the opinions of the Secretary of the Treasury in 1861 were the same as those of the chief-justice in 1870, was a question not worth discussing unless the attorney-general meant to impute dishonest and culpable motives as the cause of change; and if this was in fact the intention, the chief-justice might probably have been satisfied with pointing out, not to the attorney-general but to the Court, the passage in the secretary's official Report of 1862, the next expression of opinion made by him to Congress after the adoption of legal tender, where he took occasion to avow his opinion that "gold and silver are the only permanent basis, standard, and measure of values recognized by the Constitution."

These points were rather matters of taste than of reasoning; but in some other respects the assertions of Mr. Hoar went to the verge of fair dealing, especially from an attorney-general appealing to two new judges selected by himself, and asking them to overthrow existing law. Strictly speaking, he was correct in saying that judgment was "entered" while there were two vacancies on the bench, and by a majority of four to three. Judgment was entered on the 7th of February. Yet the attorney-general must have been aware that the decisions in the case of Hepburn *vs.* Griswold was settled as long before as November 27, 1869, and that the decision itself was read and adopted by the Court on the 29th of January, by a majority of five to three, at a time when the Court by law consisted of eight judges, and no vacancy existed on the bench. If the actual entry was postponed another week, it was probably only because the minority opinion of Justice Miller was not yet fully prepared; so that the attorney-general, by using this argument, incurred danger on the one hand of subjecting Justice Miller to the suspicion of having purposely delayed the entry in order to lay the Court open to this attack, and on the other hand of subjecting himself to the charge of acting in collusion with Justice Miller.

What occurred when the Court retired for consultation might be guessed from the subsequent scene in open Court April 11 with clearness enough to leave little doubt as to the suspicions the public, with or without reason, would certainly entertain if the attorney-general carried his purpose. Chief-Justice Chase, and Justices Nelson, Grier, and Field appear to have agreed in the statement that the two cases referred to by the attorney-general had been passed over by the Court with the understanding that they should abide the result in the case of Hepburn *vs.* Griswold, and that counsel had been so ordered. No reasonable doubt of the fact existed; and both Mr. Carlisle, counsel for the appellants in these cases, and Mr. Norton, the solicitor for the Court of Claims from which the appeal had been taken, subsequently informed the Court that they had so understood, and had received the order as stated. The ground taken by Justices Miller, Swayne, and Davis is not clearly explained; but these judges must have either rested on the fact that the order was not recorded, or they must have pleaded want of memory. The new judges held power to decide the dispute, and they did accordingly decide that the order had not been given. As the public might probably put the issue, the two new judges decided that the understanding of the Court, made long before they came upon the bench, was the reverse of what it had undoubtedly been.

The Court therefore determined, by a majority of five to four, that the cases should be argued; and already, on the motion for further delay, a scene was presented to the public such as had rarely if ever before been offered by this dignified tribunal. The four dissenting judges, the late majority, felt that they were to be tried by their own colleagues at the order of the Executive and the Senate, and they made up their minds to resist the attack with all their energy. The most memorable example in American history of partisan attack on the Judiciary was the impeachment of a judge whose name and family suggested an ominous precedent for a similar proceeding at the present day.[1]

Whether the Administration as a whole would have allowed itself to be drawn into such a struggle may be doubted; but the determined character of the attorney-general leaves no doubt that he would have begun nothing which he did not feel it his duty to press to the extremest logical conclusions, and he had for the moment the Senate behind him. The Administration might have broken to pieces, but could not have stopped a struggle once begun. Hence many persons began to watch the course of events with uneasiness; and although little was known of the personal feelings of the contending parties, yet it was obvious that the Executive was pressing with extreme severity on the Court, and the Court was already split into two hostile parties. Even among the people the struggle had begun to rouse deep interest. Perhaps the only point on which all men and all parties agreed was that the independence of the Judiciary ought to be preserved, and the dominant political party was on the point of giving this cry to its antagonist.

Fortunately for the Court, for the Administration, and for the

[1] [Adams' reference is to the impeachment of Justice Samuel Chase of Baltimore who was tried and acquitted by the U. S. Senate in February, 1805. A complete account of this incident is contained in Adams' *History of the United States . . . during the Administrations of Thomas Jefferson and James Madison*, II, chaps. 7, 10.]

country, the danger, which for a moment seemed inevitable, was evaded. On the morning of April 20, the day fixed for the hearing, the judges and the counsel went to the Capitol ready to face the issue. It was an occasion of extraordinary interest, a struggle between the dignity of the Court and the power of Congress,—an unequal match, in which public sympathy could not but cluster about the four arraigned judges. Ordinary observers could think only with terror of the irreparable harm that would result if these four judges, dragged into a political contest, should be held up by popular enthusiasm as the noble objects of a miserable persecution, while the two new justices became the mark of popular hatred, and the Court itself, torn by party passions, became the centre of political strife. At that moment such a result was almost reached. There seemed to be no hesitation on any side, either among the three dissenting judges, or the two new judges, or the four judges of the old majority, and least of all in the attorney-general, whose mind appeared to be bent with the peculiar intensity which is the historical or traditional ideal of New England character, on converting, as he would say—or as others might think, on crushing—the obnoxious Court.

All these separate actors, their internal anxieties or passions concealed as well as might be under the calm exterior belonging to the presence of justice, arrived at the Capitol only to be confronted by what had the appearance of a practical joke. The appellants had that morning withdrawn their appeal, and the cases were no longer before the Court. Probably every man of the party breathed freer after his first moment of surprise, yet the effect of the sudden change was to cover the proceeding with ridicule. The attorney-general struggled against defeat, and pressed another motion to reopen the case of Hepburn *vs.* Griswold; but the point seemed to have been reached beyond which none of the judges were willing to go in straining the rules of the Court, and as neither of the four who made the decision desired it to be reopened, the attorney-general's motion was without dissent refused.

Thus this peril was by a mere trick happily escaped, and the Court was saved; but its rescue was due to no strength of its own, to no aid from the Executive, to no mercy from either branch of

Congress. It was a momentary relief from a pressing danger; but nothing indicated that the danger had passed away, and whenever the Court should be again placed under the necessity of asserting the law as declared in the Constitution, it was little likely to be again preserved by such means.

If from the confused arena of internal politics the reader turns to the region of Foreign Affairs, he can find only a repetition of the same class of phenomena, offering little evidence of political progress, but pointing to some political change in a not distant future.

Foreign Affairs, so far as they have had immediate importance during the last year, may be divided under two heads. In regard to each of these divisions the single controlling interest has been found in the extension of the national territory. No other real point was at issue in the foreign relations of the United States, and the two heads into which the general subject of territorial enlargement divides itself are distinct only so far as one embraces extension to the north; the other, movement toward the tropics.

Of the departments of the government, that of foreign affairs has been, on the whole, most steady since the earliest days of the republic. It has acted upon a single general principle, which has slowly developed with the national progress until now it approaches its possible limits,—the absorption of neighboring territory. The policy of Secretary Seward was based upon this idea, which, under his direction, assumed a development somewhat too rapid for the public; and in consequence, although President Grant was in general sympathy with Seward, yet the new Administration came into power under influences that amounted to a reaction.

Little need be said of the questions in dispute with England, except that the only essential obstacle to a settlement is the English occupation of Canada. The effort of Seward to settle the *Alabama* claims by arbitration, and to leave the Canadian question to seek a settlement in the natural course of events, was rejected by the Senate mainly because the Senate meant that the first issue should be retained as an instrument to force the solution of the last. Without commenting upon the dignity or elevation of this policy, or upon the manner and spirit in which it has been carried into practice, it is enough to say that the new Administration on assuming office found the policy already determined by the Senate, and accepted it as a matter in regard to which the Executive was not consulted and had no voice. The subject may be here dismissed with the general remark, which time may be trusted to verify, that every separate item of American relations with England or her colonies, large or small,—whether it was a question of treaties, of claims, of boundaries, of neutrality, of Fenians, or of coal and lumber; whether treated by the Executive, by the Senate, by the House, or by individual members of the government,—under every form and every disguise, has been primarily and principally considered, subject to the rules of international custom, in its separate bearing on the subject of annexation.[1]

The Northern policy was therefore simple enough, and Secretary Fish, not responsible for its creation, carried out his share of it with a tact and good temper which gained for him and for the Administration general credit. But the issues involved on the side of the tropics were more difficult, and the variance of opinion was more strongly marked. From the outset of the new Administration the policy of interference in the Antilles was forced upon its attention in a manner leaving no chance of escape. The St. Thomas treaty, under which a popular vote had already been taken and the island formally transferred to an authorized agent of the United States government, had for some six months reposed on the table of the Senate Committee of Foreign Relations. If the government meant to pursue a policy of annexation in the Antilles, it was peculiarly bound, by every obligation of international decency and of common self-respect, to begin with the ratification of this treaty. Indeed, one may doubt whether the obligation to ratify was not absolute and irrespective of conditions; but in any case the refusal to ratify this treaty was only to be excused on the understanding that it implied a reversal of the policy of annexation. Whether this excuse was ever actually offered to the Danish government as a bar to its remonstrances could be ascertained only by reference to the Danish government, nor is it a question of real importance. The essential point was that government should act with self-respect and honest intentions. The refusal to ratify the St. Thomas

[1] See Bancroft Davis's Letter to the N. Y. *Herald* of Jan. 4, 1878. Sumner's Memorandum of Jan. 17, 1871.

treaty was a strong measure which gravely compromised the dignity of the government, and found its only excuse in the conviction that annexation to the southward of the continent was a danger and a mistake. That on such a subject the Senate could have one policy and the Executive another was equivalent to rendering the government ridiculous. For the policy that prevails the whole government must be held responsible.

If a new tendency to check the national extension was brought to light by this treatment of the St. Thomas treaty, it was made more conspicuous by the voluntary action of the Executive in regard to Cuba. The President personally leaned toward interference in Cuban affairs, and his Secretary of War, General Rawlins, was earnest in support of the Cuban insurgents. The influence of Secretary Fish succeeded in checking this bent of the Executive. Further, it was understood that in order to obviate the want of a harbor in the West Indies, the St. Thomas treaty being practically rejected, the Bay of Samana would be permanently leased and occupied as a naval station. These movements indicated that a new policy had been adopted by the government, and that after mature deliberation the present Administration would assume as its rule of action in the Antilles the principle which was soon to find utterance in the concise formula: "No annexation within the tropics."

Suddenly the San Domingo treaty made its appearance.[1] Whence it came, why it was made, what influences supported it, were not explained. One point alone was clear,—that the San Domingo treaty stood in flat opposition to the entire policy pursued till then by the Administration toward the West Indies, and that neither Fish nor his colleagues as a body could have sympathized in the proposed annexation, which was contrary to their modes of thought and to their political education. No one would have believed them had they asserted their approval. No one did believe in Fish's earnestness, though he loyally and energetically supported the treaty. The obvious inference was one which the public had a

[1] [A treaty for the annexation of the Dominican Republic, negotiated and signed for General Grant by his private secretary, Orville E. Babcock, in December, 1869. Neither this treaty nor an alternative one signed at the same time for the lease of the Bay of Samana was ratified by the Senate.]

right to draw,—that as heretofore Fish and his colleagues had succeeded in bringing the President to their point of view in regard to Cuba and St. Thomas, so the President had broken through the restraint and overruled Fish in regard to San Domingo.

A foreign policy so unsteady could scarcely command respect, although respect was what the Cabinet most needed to command. Whatever the Administration might choose to do, the Senate was unlikely to follow its changes of opinion, and for once the Senate had the strength of argument as well as of power on its side, while the Administration put itself in a position where success or failure was almost equally disastrous. Senator Sumner again stood forward to assume the control and direction of foreign affairs. He again wielded the power of the Senate and declared the policy of the government. The President and the Secretary of State struggled in vain against this omnipotent senatorial authority, although the President made the issue personal, and condescended to do the work of a lobbyist almost on the floor of the Senate chamber, using his personal influence to an extent scarcely known in American experience, and offering a curious commentary on his own theory of Executive duties. Senator Sumner flung them both aside, and issued his orders with almost the authority of a Roman triumvir.

The ultimate result of this contest, so far as regards foreign policy, is a subject which may be left for future annual Reviews to discuss, as the situation of affairs becomes more clearly determined. There is room for more than a doubt whether the growth of the country can be stopped by the adoption of any arbitrary law for the tropics; and the resistance now made to annexation of countries little fitted to enter into the duties of American States may ultimately yield to the growing public indifference to the States themselves. From another point of view the affair has still deeper significance, as showing an unsteadiness and a spasmodic irregularity of action in the Executive, which, contrasted with the opposite qualities displayed by the Senate, indicates that the regular diminution of Executive authority first clearly marked under Andrew Johnson has not been checked, but on the contrary has been aggravated by the appearance of some internal weakness never before known in the history of American administrations.

The success of any Executive measure must now be bought by the use of public patronage in influencing the action of legislators. The Executive has yielded without a protest to this necessity, which it has helped to establish. Senators already claim special Executive offices as their private property, and their claim is conceded. A senator from Michigan claims a consulate in India; a senator from Maine claims a consulate in England; a senator from Kansas claims the mission to the Hague, and as proof of his right of property nominates the clerk of his committee to the post. A senator who desires the removal of an excellent officer does not scruple to accuse a member of the Cabinet of interference with his patronage if his request is denied. Senators do not hesitate to insult the President by rejecting one nomination to the Supreme Court because the candidate as member of the Cabinet has failed to reach their own standard of polished manners, nor to intimate their intention of rejecting any required number of others unless the candidates are prepared to reverse, as judges of the Supreme Court, the established Constitutional law which limits the powers of Congress. Notwithstanding the exceptional case of San Domingo, the Executive has practically abandoned to the Senate the treaty-making power. The Executive has joined with Congress in assuming the powers reserved to the States, and in attacking the authority of the Supreme Court, while the precedent of the legal-tender action appears to warrant the belief that Congress and the Executive have also established the principle that they hold between them the power to suspend private rights, not merely during war, but during will.

Not only has the internal fabric of the government been wrenched from its original balance until Congress has assumed authority which it was never intended to hold, but as the country grows and the pressure of business increases, the efficiency of the machine grows steadily less. New powers, new duties, new responsibilities, new burdens of every sort are incessantly crowding upon the government at the moment when it has become unequal to managing the limited powers it is accustomed to wield. Responsibility no longer exists at Washington. Every department of the Executive says with truth that it cannot deal with the questions before it because Congress neglects legislation. If members of

Congress are charged with the responsibility for the neglect, they reply that the fault is not theirs; that the action of Congress is wholly in the hands of committees which constitute small, independent, executive councils; that some of these committees are arbitrary, some timid; some overpoweringly strong, some ridiculously weak; some factious, some corrupt. The House has little or no control over the course of business. The rules have become so complicated as to throw independent members entirely into the background. The amount of business has become so enormous as to choke the channels provided for it. In the Senate greater power, less confusion, and more efficiency exist, but on the other hand more personal jealousy and factiousness. In both Houses all trace of responsibility is lost; and while the Executive fumes with impatience or resigns itself with the significant consolation that it is not to blame, that this is the people's government and the people must accept the responsibility, the members of the lower House are equally ready with the excuse that they are not responsible for the action of senators; and senators, being responsible to no power under heaven except their party organizations, which they control, are able to obtain what legislation answers their personal objects or their individual conceptions of the public good.

Under the conditions of fifty years ago, when the United States was a child among nations, and before railways and telegraphs had concentrated the social and economical forces of the country into a power never imagined by past generations, a loose and separately responsible division of government suited the stage of national growth, and was sufficiently strong to answer the requirements of the public. All indications point to the conclusion that this system is outgrown. The government does not govern. Congress is inefficient, and becomes every year more and more incompetent, as at present constituted, to wield the enormous powers forced upon it; while the Executive, in enjoyment of theoretical independence, is practically deprived of its necessary strength by the jealousy of the Legislature. Without responsibility, direct, incessant, and continuous, no government is practicable over forty millions of people and an entire continent; but no responsibility exists at Washington. Every one in the least acquainted with the process of

American government knows that the public business is not performed.

Meanwhile reformers are straining every nerve to carry such a reform in the tariff as may make the system, not indeed good,— they cannot even hope this,—but a shade less absurd, less mediaeval, less dishonest than it now is. Perhaps, as the result of unremitted labor extended over a period of years, they may ultimately succeed in carrying their point. The national government may at last be obliged to drop the unhealthy children whose precocious birth and growth it has stimulated by drugs and drams, and their political influence may vanish from the Capitol. Yet while the whole reforming strength is laboriously concentrated on the people, with no further object than to obtain force to contest the possession of the national government with a single creature of the government's own creation, the government all the while continues to call into being other creatures more fatal to its integrity than those that already control it. While the reformers in Congress rejoice at carrying a small reduction on pig-iron, or regret the omnipotence of the steel lobbyists, they turn about in their seats and create by a single stroke of special legislation a new Pacific railway,—an imperishable corporation with its own territory, an empire within a republic, more powerful than a sovereign State, and inconsistent with the purity of Republican institutions or with the safety of any government, whether democratic or autocratic. While one monopoly is attacked, two are created; while old and true believers in republican purity and simplicity are engaged in resisting a single corruption, they are with their own hands stimulating the growth of many more. The people require it, and even if the people were opposed, yet with the prodigious development of corporate and private wealth resistance must be vain.

Two points, distinct to outward appearance, but closely connected in reality, have received the whole attention of this Review. The first has consisted in general evidence that the original basis of reserved powers on which the Constitution was framed has yielded and is yielding to natural pressure, and the gradual concession of power to the central government has already gone so far as to leave little doubt that the great political problem of all ages cannot, at least in a community like that of the future America, be solved by the theory of the American Constitution. The second has depended on correlative evidence that the system of separate responsibility realized in the mechanism of the American government as a consequence of its jealous restriction of substantial powers will inevitably yield, as its foundation has yielded, to the pressure of necessity. The result is not pleasant to contemplate. It is not one which the country is prepared to accept or will be soon in a temper to discuss. It will not be announced by professional politicians, who are not fond of telling unpleasant truths. Nor is it here intended to suggest principles of reform. The discussion of so large a subject is matter for a lifetime, and will occupy generations. The American statesman or philosopher who enters upon this debate must make his appeal, not to the public opinion of a day or of a nation, however large or intelligent, but to the minds of those persons who in every age and in all countries attach their chief interest to working out the problems of human society.

Harvard College

1786-1787

*The fall of 1870 marked an important transition in Henry Adams'
career from journalist and politician to professional historian. On
his return from a vacation in Europe, the offer of a professorship
at Harvard, which had already been made once and refused, was
"sprung upon" him again and this time accepted. At odds with
himself over his decision—"I hate Boston and am very fond of
Washington"—he was nevertheless amused and intrigued by his
new position. "Now," he announced, "I am, I believe, assistant
professor of history at Harvard College with a salary of £400 a
year, and two hundred students, the oldest in the college, to whom
I am to teach mediæval history, of which, as you are aware, I am
utterly and grossly ignorant. Do you imagine I am appalled at this
prospect? Not a bit of it!"*

*"Utterly and grossly ignorant" as he was, Henry Adams brought
his Washington pugnacity with him to Boston. Almost immediately he cast himself in the role of reformer: "the devil is strong in
me, and my rage for reform is leading me into an open war with
the whole system of teaching. Rebellion is in the blood, somehow
or other. I can't get on without a fight." The attitude of rebellion
naturally led to a greater sense of kinship with the students than
the faculty. Only thirty-two himself, he felt out of place among his
colleagues, yet, as a man of the world, contemptuous of them. At
meetings of the college faculty, for example, he wrote letters*

"while," he informed his correspondent, *"some thirty twaddlers are discussing questions of discipline around me."*

To reform the system of education so as to *"make the scholar its chief object of interest"—this* was his aim. One had to know, therefore, something of the scholar's point of view. In order to shed light on this subject, Adams went back to his grandfather's college diary and deduced from an era of Harvard's past the contemporary moral that social equality among students and instructors was a necessary preliminary of learning, and hence that the *"duty of giving instruction, and the duty of judging offences and inflicting punishment, [can] never be intrusted to the same hands without injury to the usefulness of the instructor."*

FOR the large and increasing class of instructors, or persons interested in the improvement of instruction in this country, few more entertaining and suggestive books could be written than a history of instruction at Harvard College,—an account, not of the numbers of students, or the gifts of donors, but of the processes tried, the experiments that failed, the discipline enforced, the customs observed, and, above all, the improvement in scholarship. One wishes to know with what standard the college started, and to what extent the standard has been raised or lowered. Since its foundation the college has greatly altered its character, and will continue to experiment with new methods and in new directions as rapidly as is safe. Its history is of no small importance to illustrate the growth of American society. Both as a social and as an educational question, the matter has interest.

Such a story to be well told should come directly from first sources,—and, with the exception of the college records, first sources are not easily reached. The college records have the disadvantage of telling a formal tale of boys' experiences and discipline, without entering into boys' feelings. One wishes to know what the student thought of himself, of his studies, and of his instructors; what his studies and his habits were; how much he

From the *North American Review* for January, 1872. [Revised and reprinted in *Historical Essays*, 1891.]

knew and how thoroughly; with what spirit he met his work, and what amount of active aid and sympathy he received from his instructors in his work or his amusements. The past left traditions of solid learning and careful training in the branches of study it assumed to deal with. One would like to know whether the present generation, in making what it calls its progress, has sacrificed anything once useful to its predecessors, aside from the further question whether such a sacrifice, if ever made, was a matter of necessity.

Unfortunately the means are wanting; but this is not all. Attempts without number have been made to use college life as a groundwork for fiction, and the result has commonly been failure, for the reason that the field of interest is too narrow, and the attempt to enlarge it by introducing forced situations is more fatal to success than the narrowness of the field. The same difficulty would be found in a practical treatment of the subject. The details are numerous and fatiguing, the possible combinations few and simple. The treatment must make atonement for the want of incident; and such treatment could come only from a critic who could employ his labor to more effect in matters of wider and deeper interest. The student must remain content to have no history of education written from his stand-point.

Yet the family records of more than one household in New England contain papers that might be of service in following out this path of inquiry. One such manuscript record at least offers a curious and characteristic picture of the education given at Cambridge toward the close of the last century. The record is a student's diary for fifteen months in the years 1786-1787,[1]—years of great depression in America, immediately following the peace with Great Britain, but preceding the establishment of a responsible national government. The winter was famous for the outbreak and forcible repression of Shays's rebellion, which was the principal subject of interest in Massachusetts, and threatened for a time to affect the college. The student in question was a young man in his nineteenth year, who came late to the University, and joined the junior class March 15, 1786. He had a fair share of youthful crudities, but was as free from extreme prejudices as could be expected from a young

[1] The diary of John Quincy Adams.

man of his age, while his manner of looking at things occasionally betrayed a mind which had come into closer contact with grown and educated men than with people of his own age.

The student applied for admission to the junior class, in the third term of the junior year, when more than half the year's work was done. His examination showed the minimum required by the college after about three years of college education. The examination itself was a formal proceeding, and although the proportion of absolute rejections was small, yet admission was far from a matter of course. In this instance the applicant had a special examination, as he applied for admission at a time when no one else wished to enter.

March 15, 1786. Between 9 and 10 in the morning I went to the President's, and was there admitted before the President, the four tutors, three professors, and Librarian. The first book was Horace, where Mr. James, the Latin tutor, told me to turn to the Carmen sæculare, where I construed three stanzas and parsed the word *sylvarum,* but called *potens* a substantive. Mr. Jennison, the Greek tutor, then put me to the beginning of the fourth book of Homer. I construed————lines, but parsed wrong αλλήλους. I had then παραβλήδεν given me. I was then asked a few questions in Watts's Logic by Mr. Hale, and a considerable number in Locke on the Understanding, very few of which I was able to answer. The next thing was geography, where Mr. Read asked me what was the figure of the earth, and several other questions, some of which I answered, and others not. Mr. Williams asked me if I had studied Euclid and arithmetic, after which the President conducted me to another room and gave me the following piece of English to turn into Latin, from the World: "There cannot certainly be an higher ridicule than to give an air of importance to amusements, if they are in themselves contemptible and void of taste; but if they are the object and care of the judicious and polite, and really deserve that distinction, the conduct of them is certainly of consequence." I made it thus: "Nihil profecto risu dignior quam magni aestimare delectamenta, si per se despicienda sunt atque sine sapore. At si res oblatæ atque cura sunt sagacibus et artibus excultis et revera hanc distinctionem merent, administratio eorum haud dubie utilitatis est." I take it from memory only, as no scholar is suffered to take a copy of the Latin he made at his examination. The President then took it, was gone about ¼ of an hour, returned and said, "You are admitted;" and gave me a paper to carry to the steward.

The examination was not difficult, and the candidate, according to his own account, made no brilliant figure at it. Setting aside Watts and Locke, no longer so important a part of the liberal education as they formerly were, a candidate for the freshman class of to-day would think himself happy to escape with no more severe an examination than this. Yet this examination, so far as concerned the classics, represented not the minimum but the maximum of requirements, not for the junior year, but for the entire college course. Homer, Horace, Terence, and Caesar were all that the student attempted to study. With the junior year, instruction in the classics ended. The following entry shows the condition of classical studies in the University:—

July 5, 1786. Mr. James gave us a piece of Latin to make,—the first the class have had since I have been here. This is the last week that we attend the Latin tutor, and last week we closed with Mr. Jennison (Greek). In the senior year there are no languages studied in college. It is very popular here to dislike the study of Greek and Latin.

All that the student could do in college, in the direction of classical acquirements, was limited within a narrow margin represented by the examination described above. Another extract shows the student's opinion of his classical instruction.

May 10, 1786. We finished the Andria of Terence this morning. The class began it last February. I went through it at Haverhill in three evenings. However, it must be said that they study it only one week in four, and that week only four mornings; but even in that way it has taken thirteen lessons to go through this one play. We recite afternoons the Latin week in Cæsar, but I have had nothing to say this week. The class is so numerous that he (the tutor) cannot hear more than one half of them recite at once, and so he takes turns.

Students dropped the classics at Cambridge in the last century where they begin it in the present one. Homer and Horace, or Terence and a sentence in Latin composition, represented all the classical knowledge that Harvard gave; and beyond the simple construing of the text and the application of elementary rules of grammar, nothing was attempted.

In regard to mathematics, the same rule held. Euclid and arithmetic are no further advanced as mathematics than Homer and Horace as classics, if indeed they are so far; but mathematics were continued through the senior year, and apparently with comparative energy. Any other requirement, with the exception of logic and metaphysics, seems to have been unknown, unless geography were something more than the form which the single question repeated in the diary implies.

So far, then, as the standard of knowledge was concerned, it was low; and to judge from the account of the student, his success in satisfying even this low standard was not brilliant. Yet the best acquirements of the highest scholars in his class were no greater. Among the fifty graduates of his year, no one of sufficient superiority appeared to prevent him from carrying away an English oration at his Commencement,—a prize commonly given only to the best scholars.

The examination being over, the new student was fairly a member of the college. He did not appear at the college exercises until a week after his admission, when he went to the President.

March 22. Immediately after prayers I went to the President, who said, "You may live with Sir Ware, a Bachelor of Arts." I made a most respectful bow, and retired.

To persons who have forgotten this use of the title *Sir*, another extract may be of interest:—

July 19. *Commencement Day.* The new Sirs got quite high in the evening, at Derby's chamber, and made considerable of a noise.

Recitations then began. For one week the class recited in Euclid. The following week it recited in Homer and the Greek Testament; the third week, in Locke; the fourth, in Terence and Cæsar. This was the round of studies; and when the four weeks were passed, the process began again. The weeks were classed as mathematical, metaphysical, Greek, and Latin weeks, and no two of these subjects were ever recited at the same time.

Six recitations in these branches occurred every week. On Mondays and Wednesdays, both morning and afternoon; on Tuesdays and Thursdays, only in the morning. Friday was a leisure day for the whole college, so far as regarded recitations. Saturdays brought one early recitation in Doddridge's Divinity. These were all the recitations. In addition frequent lectures were given, both philosophical and doctrinal, which the students of all classes attended; and literary exercises, as well as a regular exercise in declamation, took place.

May 3, 1786. Wednesday and Monday are our two busiest days in the week. This morning (Wednesday) at 6 we went in to prayers, after which we immediately recited (Homer). This took us till 7¼. At 7½ we breakfasted. At ten we had a lecture on Divinity from Mr. Wigglesworth; it was upon the wisdom of all God's actions, and justifying those parts of Scripture which some have reproached as contrary to justice. At 11 we had a philosophical lecture from Mr. Williams upon the mechanical powers, and particularly the lever and the pulley. At 12½, dinner. At 3, an astronomical public lecture upon the planet Mercury, a very circumstantial account of all its transits over the sun's disk. At 4 again we recited (Greek Testament), and at 5 attended prayers again, after which there are no more exercises for this day, but we are obliged in the evening to prepare our recitation for to-morrow morning. This I think is quite sufficient employment for one day, but the three last days in the week we have very little to do,—Thursdays and Saturdays reciting only in the morning, and Fridays a philosophical lecture.

A modern student would not think this work severe, for except the two recitations nothing required preparation. Perhaps the most curious part of the old arrangement was the subordinate place filled by recitations, and it is certainly interesting to hear a student in 1786, who had but seven recitations a week finding fault with the system:—

September 4, 1786. As we have no metaphysical tutor here at present, we supposed that for the ensuing fortnight we should have no reciting. But the government have determined that we shall continue to attend Mr. Read. This is not an agreeable circumstance. A person who does not belong to the University and hears only the word "reciting," naturally concludes that the scholars are an idle set of fellows, because they are always averse to recitations. Now the fact is just the contrary. A person fond of study regards the time spent in reciting as absolutely lost. He has studied the book before he recites; and the tutors here are so averse to giving ideas different from those of the author whom they are supposed to explain, that they always speak in his own words and never pretend to add anything of their own. Reciting is indeed of some service to idle fellows, because it brings the matter immediately before them and obliges them at least for a short time to attend to something. But a hard student will always dislike it, because it takes time from him which he supposes might have been employed to greater advantage.

A change in the recitations occurred in the senior year. Greek and Latin were dropped, and during the first quarter the seniors recited in mathematics alone, because the tutor in metaphysics had resigned, and his place had not been filled. Only on the 3d of October did the new tutor make his appearance and begin upon Burlamaqui's Natural Law, after which the two studies alternated during the rest of the year. The lectures were continued, and a new course, "very dry," was added, upon language. The principal professor did not satisfy the more zealous students:—

April 5, 1787. At 11 this forenoon Mr. Williams gave us the second philosophical lecture. It was upon the incidental properties of matter, and expecting very few deviations, was expressed in the same terms with that we had last year upon the same subject. Indeed, whether the professor's time is taken up by other studies, or whether he is too indolent to make any improvements in his lectures, it is said he gives every year the same course, without adding or erasing a line.

April 7. Mr. Williams gave us this forenoon a lecture upon motion, the same which we heard a twelve-month past upon that subject.

Except for reading Burlamaqui and writing a large number of literary disquisitions, of a stereotyped and academic class, for college societies and public occasions, the best students had little employment. After the winter vacation, ending in the middle of February, afternoon recitations were dropped in the senior year, and the class had but five recitations a week for nine weeks, when recitations ceased.

This analysis of the college studies leads to the conclusion, enforced by every word of the diary, that for the ordinary enjoyments of University life, the last century was the golden age of the college. The most modest capacity could maintain itself upon such a level. This impression prevailed among the students, for the writer of the diary, speaking of a classmate in his twenty-fifth year, said:—

"He was, as he says himself, too old when he entered the University. From fourteen to eighteen I should suppose the best age for entering.

The studies which are pursued here are just calculated for the tender minds of youth."

One cannot detect a sign of coercion on the part of the college government. An examination of any kind was strange to the college career. Rank was apparently unknown, except so far as it was vaguely intimated in the assignment of parts at exhibitions. These parts, if President Willard was to be believed, were the only incentive to study:—

April 11, 1787. I went down this morning to the President to know the determination of the corporation with respect to a private Commencement, and was told that the petition of the class was rejected, because they supposed that if public Commencements were lain aside, there would be no stimulus to study among the scholars, and they are afraid that by granting our petition they might establish a precedent which the following classes would take advantage of, and claim as a right what we only request as a favor. Another reason which Mr. Willard said had weight, although the gentlemen did not choose to avow it publicly, was the fear of offending the future Governor by depriving him of that opportunity to show himself in splendor and magnificence.

Another extract indicated patriarchal simplicity. On the student's first day in college,—

March 23, 1786. I did not hear the bell ring this morning, and was tardy at prayers. Every time a student is tardy at prayers he is punished a penny, and there is no eluding that law; so that a student must prefer not attending prayers at all to being half a minute too late.

The instructors trusted only their general impressions in awarding distinctions. Misdemeanors, absences, and other shortcomings were punished by fines. The recitations were ordinary school-lessons:

June 13, 1786. This reciting in Locke is the most ridiculous of all. When the tutor inquires what is contained in such a section, many of the scholars repeat the two first lines in it, which are very frequently nothing to the purpose, and leave the rest for the tutor to explain, which he commonly does by saying over again the words of the author.

In regard to vacations and permissions of absence, the college law was not rigorous. In April the students had two weeks holiday by law, but in practice at least three. The summer vacation began July 13, and closed by law August 16, lasting five weeks, but recitations were only resumed on the 21st. Two weeks more were given in October, with the same liberal margin. In the middle of December, 1786, the supply of fire-wood fell short, and as none could be obtained from the country, the students were sent home and enjoyed a vacation of eight weeks, till February 7. Recitations began on the 12th. On the 23d "about half the class" had arrived. Thus in the course of the year the college had seventeen weeks of vacation, and twenty-one weeks of freedom from required exercises. Add to this a liberal interpretation of the rule of attendance, and an equally liberal practice in regard to leaves of absence, and the working terms of the college were by no means unreasonably long or severe. When the exercises were most regular, many interruptions occurred, and the amount of work accomplished, from a modern point of view, was small.

A few extracts will illustrate the college practice:

April 26, 1786. Put my name in at the buttery. At the end of each vacation every scholar must go in person and give his name to the butler. Any scholar who stays away after the expiration of the vacancy, unless he gives good reasons for it, forfeits 1*s*. 6*d*. every night.

April 27. No reciting this day, nor indeed this week. The scholars that live near Cambridge commonly come and enter their names in the buttery, and then go home again and stay the remainder of the week.

April 28. About half the college are now here. The bill at prayers is not kept till the Friday after the vacation ends.

May 1. We recite this week, etc.

August 17. The scholars are coming in very fast.

August 19. Almost all the college have got here now, and the new monitors, who must always belong to the junior class, took their seats yesterday.

August 21. We recite this week, etc.

December 12. The government this morning determined that if more than half the students should be destitute of wood, the college should be dismissed. The President went to Boston to consult the corporation upon the subject, and he informed Little this evening that the students would be permitted to disperse to-morrow morning.

December 13. This morning, immediately after prayers, the President informed us that the vacation would begin at present, and be for eight weeks, and hinted that the spring vacation might on that account be omitted.

The spring vacation was not in the least shortened by the hint.

With these eight weeks the student had a right to do what he pleased; yet since the exertions which were evidently not made in term-time may have fallen on the vacation, the inquiry how the most distinguished students of the oldest standing occupied their two months of winter vacation is not impertinent. The writer of the diary remained in college rooms to devote his time to his work, with less interruption than was otherwise possible.

"As I thought I should be able to study much more conveniently here than anywhere else, I obtained leave to remain in town. Bridge proposes staying likewise, and we shall live together. Bridge engaged for us both to board at Professor Wigglesworth's."

Other young men remained, no doubt for the same purpose, since their names occurred afterward on the list of parts at Commencement, attached to English orations and other honors. They were not without other society:—

December 18, 1786. The young ladies at Mr. Wigglesworth's dined at Judge Dana's. I went down there with Bridge to tea, and passed the evening very sociably. The conversation turned upon divers topics, and among the rest upon love, which is almost always the case when there are ladies present.

Love was not mentioned as one of the college studies; but if it was always discussed when ladies were present, these young gentlemen during this vacation devoted more attention to it than they had paid to Locke or Euclid.

The next day a slight improvement in tone was apparent:—

December 19. Several of the class still remain, and until they are gone it will be impossible for us to study much. As they expect to go every day, they are rather dissipated, and more or less make us so.

December 20. I have been rather more attentive today, and have written considerably.

After this spark of energy came a relapse. Descriptions of young ladies recurred with frequency, while, except for a single reference to Montesquieu, no evidence of absorbing mental application was recorded:—

December 22. Miss———is but eighteen, rather giddy and inexperienced. She has a very fair complexion and good eyes, of which she is sensible. Her face is rather capricious than beautiful, and some of her features are not handsome. Of this she is not so well apprised. Her shape is not inelegant, but her limbs are rather large. She is susceptible of the tender sentiments, but the passion rather than the lover is the object of her affection.

December 26. Mason finally took his leave and left us to ourselves, so that we shall henceforth be able to study with much less interruption than we have hitherto done.

December 27. In the evening we went down with Mr. Ware and Freeman to Judge Dana's. We conversed and played whist and sung till 10 o'clock. The ladies seem to have settled that we are to be in love; but ideas of this kind are very common with the ladies, who think it impossible to live without love.

January 17, 1787. After tea we went down to Mr. Dana's. Miss E. was there, and Miss J. with her. Bridge accompanied this lady home, and after they were gone I had a deal of chat with Miss E., who has a larger share of sense than commonly falls to an individual of her sex. We conversed upon diverse subjects, but I can never give anything but general accounts of conversations, for I cannot always keep this book under lock and key, and some people have a vast deal of curiosity.

January 22. Almy has a larger share of sense than commonly falls to the lot of her sex, and that sense is cultivated and improved,—a circumstance still more uncommon.

March 2. I went to take tea at Mr. Pearson's. I got seated between Miss E. and Miss H., but could not enjoy the pleasures of conversation, because the music was introduced. Music is a great enemy to sociability, and however agreeable it may be sometimes, there are occasions when I should wish it might be dispensed with.

By that time the vacation had expired, and the student returned to the labors of five recitations a week. Besides the "Spirit of Laws," he had read, so far as can be gathered from his diary, Watson's "Chemical Essays," Sheridan's "Lectures on Elocution," a volume of the "Idler," and some algebra, in two months. He had also developed an uncommonly strong fancy for the study of female character,—a study not embraced in the official college curriculum, either then or afterward.

The 7th of February began the new term. On the 12th recitations began, one every day, except Friday. On the 15th a ball was given, at which Miss E. headed the list of ladies. The young gentlemen, among whom were most of the first scholars, retired to bed "at about four o'clock," and "rose just before the commons bell rang for dinner, quite refreshed, and not more fatigued than I commonly am." The dances became nearly as frequent as the recitations. On the 23d, "about one half the class are here." On the 27th, "almost all our class have arrived." Among other lectures, March 5 "Professor Pearson gave a lecture with which he concluded his observations upon the article. I did not hear many of them;" but the same evening there was a meeting of the Φ B K at Cranch's chamber, at which a dissertation was read, of which the text is preserved, on the erudite question, "Whether love or fortune ought to be the chief inducement to marriage." This essay was done with much reflection and knowledge of the human heart, but was not a college exercise. March 7 he went to Haverhill, and returned on the 10th. On the 12th the parts were distributed for the next exhibition, and he received an English "Conference," with Freeman and Little, upon the Comparative Utility of Law, Physic, and Divinity.

March 14, 1787. Was employed almost all day in thinking upon the subject of my Conference. Wrote a few lines with much difficulty. Did not like the subject. Wished the Conference to the Devil.

Little and Freeman were of the same mind. After a week's labor the Conference was written, and the next week was devoted to the voluntary work of calculating the elements for a solar eclipse for May 15, 1836. This was also for an exhibition.

March 30. I have been somewhat idle for several days, and expect to continue so till the exhibition is over, for so long as that is before me I can pay very little attention to anything else. I found this to be the case last fall, and do now still more so; but thank fortune I have only one more trial, at the worst, of this kind to go through, which will be at Commencement, unless we should obtain a private one. Distinctions of this kind are not, I think, very desirable; for besides the trouble and anxiety which they unavoidably create, they seldom fail of raising the envy of other students. I have oftentimes witnessed this with respect to others, and I am much deceived if I have not lately perceived it with respect to myself.

April 9. This is the last week on which our class attend recitations.

If such were the duties of the most distinguished scholars, those students who were not remarkable for scholarship could not have been overworked; but on that point no certain information was given, beyond allusions to gunning, fishing, and an occasional "high-go."

Meanwhile a difficulty occurred.

August 26, 1786. Immediately after prayers we had a class-meeting for the purpose of choosing a Valedictory Orator and Collectors of Theses. When the votes were collected it was found that there was no choice. A second attempt was made, equally fruitless. It was then resolved that the choice of an Orator should be deferred, and that the class should proceed to that of the choice of Collectors. The one for Technology, Grammar, and Rhetoric was first balloted. Abbot 2d was chosen. The second Collector, for Logic, Metaphysics, Ethics, Theology, and Politics, was then chosen. Fiske was the person. The Mathematical part fell to Adams, and the Physical to Johnstone. The meeting at about seven o'clock was adjourned till Monday evening, when we shall proceed to the choice of an Orator.

August 28. After prayers the class met by adjournment. The second ballot was between Freeman, Little, and Waldo. The third was between Freeman and Little, who finally carried it by a considerable majority. The class then all went to his chamber, but did not stay there more than an hour.

August 31. We had a class-meeting immediately after prayers. The committee of the class that was appointed to inform the President of the choice for an Orator, etc., reported that the President had not given his consent to have the Oration in English, because he thought it would show a neglect of classical learning. I motioned that the vote for having it in English should be reconsidered, but there was a considerable majority against it. It was then voted that the President should be informed that the class had determined to have an English Oration or none at all. The former committee all declined going again. Johnstone, Fiske, and Welch were chosen, but declined. It was much like Æsop's fable of the mice, who determined to have a bell tied round the cat's neck; they were all desirous that it should be done, but no one was willing to undertake the performance of it. The meeting was finally adjourned till Monday next.

September 12. We had a class-meeting after prayers for determining the matter concerning a Valedictory Oration. By dint of obstinate im-

pudence, vociferation, and noise, the minority so wearied out those on
the other side that several of them went out; after which a vote was
passed ratifying the proceedings of the last meeting. Johnson, Sever, and
Chandler 3d were then chosen as a committee to inform the President of
the proceedings in the class.

September 18. We had a class-meeting after breakfast. The committee
that was sent to inform the President of the proceedings of the class, informed that he had said he feared he should be obliged to direct the
class to have the Oration in Latin. Notwithstanding this, it was voted by
a majority of two that the class should still persist.

The President carried his point so far that there was no Class
Day. In consequence of this, the members of the class began to
leave Cambridge before the 21st of June, the usual day for separation. The parts for Commencement were distributed May 17.

May 24, 1787. Our class having no college exercises to attend to, and
many of them having now finished their parts for Commencement, are
generally very indolent. Riding and playing and eating and drinking
employ the chief part of their time.

Long before Class Day the graduating students were scattered
in every direction, only to return on the 18th of July to Commencement. Thus, as the result of the half-year since the 13th of December, the students who were to take their degrees had attended recitations at the rate of five per week, for nine weeks, and had further
prepared exercises for one exhibition and Commencement. They
had listened to one course of lectures, which they had for the most
part already heard, and another on "the parts of speech," which the
best of them thought a waste of time. They dispersed in May, without conception that there could be such a thing in the student
world as an examination for degrees.

One or two more extracts, to illustrate the stringency of rules during term-time, must be admitted:—

May 4, 1786. No reciting this morning on account of last night's class-
meeting. This is a privilege that all the classes enjoy, and I am told
there have been in our class fellows so lazy and so foolish as to call a
class-meeting merely for that purpose.

Naturally, class-meetings were frequent.

April 10, 1786. No reciting this day because the government met to examine the reasons of those scholars that are absent, or have been within the last two quarters.

September 22. Mr. Read sent for me this morning; informed me that the exhibition was to come on next Thursday, and offered to excuse me from recitations till then, in case I was not prepared, as the time that had been given for getting ready was so short. But, as it happened, I was not in need of more time.

October 9. No reciting. Mr. Burr is engaged to preach several Sundays at Hingham, and does not return early enough for the next morning recitation.

The rules were not more rigidly applied in regard to required exercises than in other respects, and neither instructors nor students considered themselves to be under any inflexible law.

Students who lived under so mild a government should have had no just cause of complaint, unless that the means of the college did not satisfy the requirements of a liberal education. They might urge that Euclid and Burlamaqui were dry nutriment to satisfy the hunger of a whole year, but they could scarcely maintain that a stepmother's hand, when they cried for bread, threw them husks. Under a system so nearly voluntary, a thorough accord should have existed between the instructors and their best scholars.

The President, Joseph Willard, was a graduate of the year 1765, still a comparatively young man. Many instructive hints as to his character were scattered through this diary:—

"It is against the laws of the college to call any undergraduate by any but his sir-name, and I am told the President, who is remarkably strict on all those matters, reproved a gentleman at his table for calling a student Mr. while he was present."

Again:—

March 24, 1786. After prayers I declaimed, as it is termed; two students every evening speak from memory any piece they choose, if it be approved by the President. It was this evening my turn, and I spoke from "As you like it,"—"All the world's a stage," etc. When I came to the description of the Justice, in fair, round belly, with good capon lined, tutors and scholars all laughed, as I myself truly represented the character. But the President did not move a feature of his face. And indeed I believe it is no small matter that shall extort a smile from him when he is before the college.

September 10, 1786. Cranch and myself dined at the President's. He is stiff and formal, attached to every custom and trifling form, as much as to what is of consequence. However, he was quite sociable; much more so, indeed, than I should have expected.

A portrait of the President in the pulpit was included:—

February 18, 1787. The President preached in the afternoon, when we were improved by a very laborious encomium upon Moses. Whatever the President's literary talents may be, he is certainly not an elegant composuist nor a graceful orator.

June 21, 1786. *Class Day.* This day the seniors leave college. There is no recitation in the morning, and prayers are deferred till 10 o'clock. The class then went down in procession two by two with the Poet at their head, and escorted the President to the chapel. The President made a very long prayer, in which, in addition to what he commonly says, he prayed a great deal for the seniors; but I think he ought to get his occasional prayers by heart before he delivers them. He bungled always when he endeavored to go out of the beaten track, and he has no talent at extempore composition.

April 6, 1786. *Fast Day.* The President preached two sermons; that in the afternoon especially I thought excellent,—no flowers of rhetoric, no eloquence, but plain common-sense, and upon a liberal plan. But the President has by no means a pleasing delivery. He appears to labor and struggle very much, and sometimes strains very hard, and making faces, which do not render his harsh countenance more agreeable.

The description indicated no ill-feeling toward the President; but a man cast in such a mould was not likely to throw life or novelty into the system over which he presided. He was an excellent representative of the old New England school, but he had little immediate connection with the undergraduates. The burden of labor fell on the four tutors, although the tutors were not obliged to perform so much work as would alarm the most lightly burdened tutor of the present day. Six or seven hours a week in the recitation-room, and the simplest instruction in the letter of the text-book represented the full extent of their duties, beyond the charge of the college discipline. A considerable opportunity for usefulness was open to the four tutors, and at least one or two of them might be supposed to impress the students with sympathetic activity. The relations between students and tutors were the subject of frequent comments in the diary:—

May 1, 1786. The Greek tutor is a young man; indeed much too young (A. B. of 1782), as are all the tutors, for the place he occupies. Before he took his second degree, which was last Commencement, he was chosen a tutor of mathematics, in which he betrayed his ignorance often. Last fall he changed departments, and took up the Greek. His own class, the freshmen, were the first that laughed at him in that. He has improved since that, but still makes frequent mistakes. It is certainly wrong that the tutors should so often be changed, and be so young as they are. It would be better to choose a person immediately after he has taken his degree, than as they do; because when a youth leaves college he is obliged to turn his attention to other studies, and forgets a great deal of what he studied at college, whereas when he has lately graduated he has all fresh in his mind. The Doctor affects a great deal of popularity in his class, and with the help of the late disagreement between the classes, he has pretty well succeeded; but he does not seem to care what the other classes think of him.

May 2. Our tutor gave us this morning a most extraordinary construction of a passage in Homer. Abbot 1st was beginning to construe the 181st line of the 6th book.

$$\Pi\rho\acute{o}\sigma\theta\epsilon\ \lambda\acute{\epsilon}\omega\nu,\ \acute{o}\pi\iota\theta\epsilon\nu\ \delta\grave{\epsilon}\ \delta\rho\acute{a}\kappa\omega\nu,\ \mu\epsilon\sigma\sigma\eta\ \delta\grave{\epsilon}\ \chi\acute{\iota}\mu\alpha\iota\rho\alpha,$$

he said,—"a lion before;" but the Doctor corrected him by saying it meant "superior to a lion." Abbot immediately took the hint and made it, "superior to a lion, inferior to a dragon, and equal to a wild boar."

An account of the metaphysical tutor was still less flattering:—

May 15, 1786. We recite this week to Mr. Hale in Locke. This is, upon the whole, the most unpopular tutor in college. He is hated even by his own class. He is reputed to be very ill-natured and severe in his punishments. He proposes leaving college at Commencement, and I believe there is not an individual among the students who is not very well pleased with it. One of my classmates said the other day, "I do not believe it yet; it is too good news to be true." Such are the sentiments of all the students with respect to him.

The writer felt no regard for the mathematical tutor:—

May 22, 1786. We recite this week to our own tutor, in Gravesande's Experimental Philosophy. This gentleman is not much more popular than the rest of the tutors. He is said to be very prejudiced and very vindictive.

He is liked in general by the class, however, and this may be a reason why I have not heard as much said against him as against the others.

He closed the list with a blast of indignation against the Latin tutor:—

May 8. We recite this week in Terence and Cæsar to Mr. James. This is the tutor of the oldest standing in the college; he is very well acquainted with the branch he has undertaken, and persons that are not students say that he is much of a gentleman. But it seems almost to be a maxim among the governors of the college to treat the students pretty much like brute beasts. There is an important air and a haughty look that every person belonging to the government (Mr. [Professor] Williams excepted) assumes, which indeed it is hard for me to submit to. But it may be of use to me, as it mortifies my vanity; and if anything in the world can teach me humility, it will be to see myself subjected to the commands of a person that I must despise. Mr. James is also accused of having many partialities and carrying them to very great length; and moreover that those partialities do not arise from any superior talents or virtues in the students, but from closer and more interested motives. There are some in our class with whom he has been particularly severe, and some he has shown more favor than any tutor ought to show to a student. I wish not his favor, as he may prize it too high; and I fear not his severity, which he can never display if I do my duty.

The "interested motives" were more than a figure of speech:—

May 3, 1786. We had after prayers a class-meeting about making a present to our tutor. It is customary at the end of the freshman year to make a present to the tutor of the class; but it has been delayed by ours to the present time, and many would still delay it and lay it wholly aside. The custom, I think, is a bad one, because it creates partialities in a tutor, because it increases the distinction between the wealthy and the poor scholars, because it makes the tutor in some measure dependent upon his class, and because to many that subscribe it is a considerable expense; but the salaries of the tutors being so low, and it having been for many years an universal custom, I am sorry to see our class so behind-hand, and several who could well afford it and have really subscribed meanly endeavoring to put off the matter from quarter to quarter till they leave college.

A year later the writer became aware that the question had two sides. Speaking of one of his classmates, he said:—

"His spirit he discovers by relating how many times he has insulted the President and the tutors, particularly Mr. Read (the class tutor). He damns Mr. Read for being partial towards those who have always treated him with respect, and against those who have always made it a practice to insult him."

The relations between instructors and scholars were far from satisfactory. Thoroughly cordial these relations never could be so long as college discipline remained in the hands of the instructors. The duty of giving instruction, and the duty of judging offences and inflicting punishment, could never be intrusted to the same hands without injury to the usefulness of the instructor. This evil was conspicuous in the last century. Gentle as the rein was, and mild as were the punishments, hostility between students and instructors was a traditional custom of the college, and the one which created most annoyance to both divisions of the University,—the teachers as well as the taught. The system was wrong. While perhaps more liberal in its forms than any that succeeded it, the assumption of social superiority galled every one subjected to it. The assumption created opposition, and the records of the college showed persistent attempts, on the part of the students, to break down the social barrier. Generation after generation followed the same course. Rebellion after rebellion broke out among the undergraduates. Only in proportion as the college government began to act upon the principle that the student was the social equal of the instructor, entitled to every courtesy due to equals, did these disorders begin gradually to subside. Even then the question of discipline remained a source of incessant uneasiness, and the instructor known as a strict disciplinarian, who attempted to combine his duties as police-officer, judge, jury, and executioner with his duties of instruction, sacrificed no inconsiderable share of his usefulness as instructor.

That the spirit of insubordination so persistently exhibited was not due to distinctions of age, or hostility to the instructing body as such, was proved by conflicts with others than the instructors. Another series of extracts illustrated this point:—

August 21, 1786. This afternoon, after prayers, the customs were read to the freshmen in the chapel. They are read three Mondays running in the beginning of every year, by the three first in the sophimore class, who are ordered to see them put in execution.

March 27, 1786. After prayers the senior class had a class-meeting, in order to check the freshmen, who, they suppose, have taken of late too great liberties. By the laws of the college all freshmen are obliged to walk in the yard with their heads uncovered, unless in stormy weather, and to go on any errand that any other scholar chooses to send them, at a mile distance. But the present freshmen have been indulged very much with respect to those laws, and it is said they have presumed further than they ought to have done.

March 28, 1786. After prayers, Bancroft, one of the sophimore class, read the customs to the freshmen, one of whom (McNeal) stood with his hat on all the time. He with three others were immediately *hoisted* (as the term is) before a tutor, and punished. There was immediately after a class-meeting of the freshmen, who, it is said, determined they would hoist any scholar of the other classes who should be seen with his hat on in the yard, when any of the government are there.

June 14, 1786. The freshmen, by their high spirit of liberty, have again involved themselves in difficulties. The sophimores consider themselves as insulted by them, and in a class-meeting, last evening, determined to oblige all the freshmen to take off their hats in the yard, and to send them. There has been a great deal of business between them to-day. Mr. Hale has had several of them before him.

June 15, 1786. The struggle between the freshmen and sophimores still continues. They have been mutually hoisting one another all day.

July 12, 1786. The freshmen carry their enmity against the sophimores a great deal too far. They injure themselves both in the eyes of the other class and in those of the government. This afternoon, while Cabot was declaiming, they kept up a continual groaning and shuffling and hissing, as almost prevented him from going through.

The freshmen ultimately carried their point, and established their right to social equality; but they were obliged to struggle both against the college system and against their immediate masters. Their disorders were but a repetition, against a different authority, of still greater disorders on the part of older classes, in the attempt to establish social rights against college government.

The habits and manners of the time were not rigorously correct:—

March 22, 1786. As we passed by Milton Hall, we saw the ruins of the windows. On the 21st of March the junior sophister class cease reciting at 11 in the forenoon. They generally in the evening have a frolic. Yesterday they had it at Milton Hall, and as they are not by any means at such time remarkable for their discretion, we saw many fractures in the windows of the hall they were in.

March 15, 1786. The sophimore class had what is called in college a high-go. They assembled all together in the chamber of one of the class, where some of them got drunk, then sallied out and broke a number of windows for three of the tutors, and after this sublime manœuvre staggered to their chambers. Such are the great achievements of many of the sons of Harvard! Such the delights of many of the students here!

The manners indicated by these extracts were certainly free; but such offences were not considered heinous by the college government or by public opinion. The severity of discipline in the college was by no means such as to explain the ill-will between the students and the government. Although students considered such discipline annoying at the time, they learned afterward to accept, without a murmur, punishments which in the last century would have been thought monstrous; and this submission was due to the subsidence of the old antipathy to college government. In 1786 punishments, so far from being severe, were remarkably light, notwithstanding loud complaints against them.

As mentioned above, certain members of the college, on the night of March 15, 1786, indulged themselves in a drunken disturbance in the college grounds:—

March 23, 1786. After prayers the President read a paper to this effect: That on the evening of the 15th it appeared the sophimores had assembled at the chambers of one of the class and had behaved in a tumultuous, noisy manner; that at length they sallied out and were very riotous, to the disturbance and *dishonor* of the University. But as their conduct till then had been such as deserved approbation, and was submissive, and as they early shew a proper repentance for their fault, having presented an humble petition to be forgiven,—therefore it had been voted that no further notice should be taken of it; but it was hoped the students would not abuse the lenity of the government, but rather show that they were deserving of it. The freshmen, who are always as a class at variance with the sophimores, thought the government had been partial; and the consequence was that Mr.————, the tutor of the sophimore class, and who was supposed to have favored them, and to have been the means of saving them from severe punishment, had four squares of glass broken in his windows. Such was the effect of the lenity which was to induce the students to do their duty.

A more curious case was the following:—

May 23, 1786. This morning a number of the seniors were sent for by the President to go to his house at 8 o'clock. They went, and the parts were distributed thus: Thompson, English Oration, A. M.; Champlin, Latin Oration, A. M.; Fowle and Gardner 2d, each a Poem; Blake, English, and Andrews 1st, Latin Orations, P. M.; Harris, Dwight, Hubbard, and Parker, a Conference; Bigelow and Crosby, Lowell and Taylor, Loring and Sullivan, Forensics; Lincoln and Warland, a Greek Dialogue; Bradford, Norton, Simpkins, and Wyeth, respondents in Syllogistics, and all the rest opponents to the same. These Syllogistics are very much despised by the scholars, and no attention seems to be paid to them by the company at Commencement. The scholars in general think that the government in giving them those parts write on their foreheads D U N C E in capital letters. Notwithstanding this, some of the most learned men in the country had Syllogistics when they graduated here. The good parts, as they are called, are more numerous this year than they have ever been. Before this there has been only one English and one Latin Oration, and no Poems. It is a doubt whether they intend to establish this as a precedent, or whether it is only a distinguished favor to the present class, who pretend to be the best class for learning and genius that ever graduated here. It is said that the parts have been exceedingly well distributed, and all the college are pleased. However that may be, the Syllogists all got together this evening and drank till not one of them could stand straight, or was sensible of what he did. A little after 9 they sailed out, and for a quarter of an hour made such a noise as might be heard at a mile distant. The tutors went out, and after a short time persuaded them to disperse. Mr.————had two squares of his windows broke.

May 24. It is feared that some bad consequences will ensue from the high-go of the Syllogists last evening. Borland, it seems, was the most active of them all; he collared Mr.————and threw a handful of gravel in his face, and was rather disrespectful to Mr.————. He went this morning to the former to make an apology for his conduct, but was told it could not be received, as the matter was already laid before the government. Thus those fellows play the tyrants here; they have no regard, no allowances, for youth and circumstances. They go out when they are almost certain of being insulted, and then bring the scholar for a crime of which he knew nothing under public censure. They cannot with any face say that a scholar ought to be so severely punished for depriving himself of his senses. For there are here in college persons who have seen —————as much intoxicated as Borland was yesterday and behaving quite as ill. But compassion is too great a virtue ever to be admitted into the breast of a tutor here. It is supposed, however, that Borland's punishment will not be very severe, because it requires a unanimous vote among the governors of the college to punish a student, and they are said to be at such variance one with the other that they can very seldom all agree.

May 25. Government met and were assembled almost all this day to determine what punishment to inflict upon Borland. He was informed of it in the evening, and the class petitioned that it might be mitigated, but probably without much success.

May 26. This morning after prayers Borland was called out to read an humble confession, signifying his repentance of his conduct, etc. The President read the votes of the government; the affair was stated, and it was said that Borland had insulted, in a flagrant manner, two of the governors of the University. Whereupon it was voted, that he read a confession; and secondly, that he be degraded to the bottom of his class, and that he take his place there accordingly. The other scholars were warned by this example not to run into such excesses, and to behave respectfully. I wanted, I think, neither of these warnings, but the event has warned me to alter my opinion concerning—————. I thought him the best of the tutors, but now I do not think he is a jot better than the rest.

Six weeks afterward Borland was restored to his regular place in class.

No student of a later day would have dreamed of calling such a penalty severe. Any undergraduate of the nineteenth century who indulged in the agreeable but dangerous amusement of collaring an unpopular tutor and rubbing gravel in his face, would have accepted the extremest penalty of the law without a murmur, recognizing the fundamental principle of society, that no man can violate the law and enjoy it at the same time; while the notion that drunkenness is anything but an aggravation of the offence hardly commends itself to modern New England.

Such difficulties were common under this *régime;* occasionally they were due really to the instructors. The following may have been such a case:—

May 31, 1786. *Election Day.* There is a custom among the scholars here which some of the classes follow and others do not. It is choosing a governor and lieutenant-governor for the class. They commonly take some rich fellow who can treat the class now and then. The seniors this morning chose Champlin governor, and Lowell lieutenant-governor. The lieutenant-governor treated immediately, and they chose their other officers. At Commons they all went into the hall in procession. Thomas, who was appointed sheriff, marched at their head, with a paper cockade in his hat, and brandishing a cane in his hand instead of a sword. He conducted the governor and lieutenant-governor to their seats, made his bow, and retired to the other table, for which Jackey Hale punished him four shillings. However, he performed his part so well that the spectators were much pleased, and clapped their hands. Hale happened to see Baron, the junior, clapping, and sent orders for him to go to him after Commons. Baron, not happening to go before 2 o'clock, was punished five shillings for impudence, and four for disobedience. That is the way these modest tutors tyrannize over us. As there was a little noise in the hall, Hale struck the handle of his knife three times on the table to still it, but instead of that almost every knife in the hall was struck on the table three times. At last the tutors rose, and as they were going out about half-a-dozen fellows hissed them. They were enraged, turned round and looked as if they would devour us; but they did not discover one person, which made them look silly enough. When they turned their backs again, there was nothing but hissing and groaning and clapping hands and stamping heard in the hall, till they got into the yard, where a few potatoes were sent out to meet them.

A difficulty of such a kind would probably in later times have been avoided by good-nature and forbearance on the part of the tutor; but the student of 1786 cared little whether he was in the right or the wrong. The true grievance lay in the position of semi-hostility to the students taken by the college officers, who refused to acknowledge them as entitled to active assistance and sympathy. The manner, not the act, of discipline was the cause of the evil. Hence the mildest punishments were made a cause of as much complaint as arbitrary vexations.

March 14, 1787. The junior class being displeased with the distribution of parts for exhibition, so far as respected their class, assembled this evening at Prescott's chamber and made a great deal of noise.

March 17. The government met this forenoon to make inquiries concerning the noise at Prescott's and at Wier's chamber.

March 19. This morning the juniors Prescott and Wier were publicly admonished for having had riotous noises at their chambers last week. The sentence is considered all over college as uncommonly severe, and by many as wholly unmerited, at least on the part of Prescott.

March 22. In consequence of the late severity of the college governors there has been, yesterday and this day, a subscription paper handed about among all the classes to promote a meeting of the whole college to-morrow evening in the chapel, every person having a pipe, a glass, and a bottle of wine, and there to convince the government that the students are possessed of "a noble spirit,—a spirit which shall nip the bud of tyrannical oppression." They will get as drunk as beasts, and probably break every tutor's windows in college. This absurd and ridiculous plan has found so many votaries that a large majority of every class, except ours, have already subscribed; but I am happy that in our class there are but few who have joined the association, and as it is to take place only upon condition that there be a majority of every class, the plan will most probably fail.

At the risk of serious injury to the dignity of history, already compromised by this sketch, the extreme leniency of the government in the punishment inflicted in this case shall be shown by a final extract from the diary so often quoted. Some verses, not absolutely contemptible, represented the impression made by the different members of the government on the students more exactly than the regular entries of a prosaic diary could do. The verses were entitled

LINES UPON THE LATE PROCEEDINGS
OF THE COLLEGE GOVERNMENT

BY A STUDENT

> The government of college met,
> And Willard ruled the stern debate.
> The witty Jennison declared
> That he had been completely scared.
> "Last night," says he, "when I came home,
> I heard a noise in Prescott's room.
> I went and listened at the door,
> As I have often done before.

I found the juniors in a high rant;
They called the President a tyrant;
They said as how I was a fool,
A long-eared ass, a sottish mule,
Without the smallest grain of spunk;
So I concluded they were drunk.
From Xenophon whole pages torn
As trophies in their hats were worn.
Thus all their learning they had spread
Upon the outside of the head;
For I can swear without a sin
There's not a line of Greek within.
At length I knocked, and Prescott came;
I told him 't was a burning shame
That he should give his classmates wine,
And he should pay a heavy fine.
Meanwhile the rest grew so outrageous
That, though I boast of being courageous,
I could not help being in a fright,
For one of them put out the light,
And 't was, as you may well suppose,
So dark I could not see my nose.
I thought it best to run away,
And wait for vengeance till to-day;
For he's a fool at any rate
Who'll fight when he can rusticate.
When they found out that I was gone,
They ran through college up and down,
And I could hear them very plain
Take the Lord's holy name in vain.
To Wier's chamber they repaired,
And there the wine they freely shared.
They drank and sung till they were tired,
And then they peacefully retired."
When this Homeric speech was said,
With drawling tongue and hanging head,
The learned Doctor took his seat,
Thinking he'd done a noble feat.
Quoth Joe: "The crime is great, I own
Send for the juniors one by one!
By this almighty wig I swear,

Which with such majesty I wear,
And in its orbit vast contains
My dignity, my power, and brains,
That Wier and Prescott both shall see
That college boys must not be free!"
He spoke, and gave the awful nod,
Like Homer's Dodonean God.
The college to its centre shook,
And every pipe and wine-glass broke.
Williams, with countenance humane,
Which scarce from laughing could refrain,
Thought that such youthful scenes of mirth
To punishments should not give birth;
Nor could he easily divine
What was the harm of drinking wine.
But Pearson, with an awful frown,
Full of his article and noun,
Spoke thus: "By all the parts of speech
Which with such elegance I teach,
By all the blood which fills my veins,
By all the power of Handel's strains,
With mercy I will never stain
The character which I maintain.
Pray tell me why the laws were made,
If they are not to be obeyed."
James saw't would be in vain t' oppose,
And therefore to be silent chose.
Read, with his two enormous eyes
Enlarged to thrice their common size,
And brow contracted, staring wild,
Said government was much too mild.
"Were I," said he, "to have my will,
I soon would teach them to be still.
Their wicked rioting to quell,
I'd rusticate, degrade, expel;
And rather than give up my plan,
I'd clear the college to a man."
Burr, who has little wit or pride,
Preferred to take the strongest side;
And Willard soon received commission
To give a public admonition.

With pedant strut to prayers he came,
Called out the criminals by name.
Obedient to his dire command,
Before him Wier and Prescott stand:
"The rulers, merciful and kind,
With equal grief and wonder find
That you should laugh and drink and sing,
And make with noise the college ring.
I therefore warn you to beware
Of drinking more than you can bear.
Wine an incentive is to riot,
Destructive of the public quiet.
Full well your tutors know this truth,
For sad experience taught their youth.
Take then this friendly exhortation!
The next offence is rustication."

Von Holst's

History of the United States

For almost four years after the publication of "Harvard College" Henry Adams was too busy to write anything but short reviews for the magazine he edited. He was married in 1872 and went abroad for a year with his wife, travelling and making the acquaintance of European scholars with whose work he had lately become familiar. On his return, teaching and research came to absorb more and more of his energies. Not content with the series of courses he had established in medieval history, he branched into American history in its colonial and early national periods, while at the same time he conducted Harvard's first graduate program in History and baked its first "batch of doctors of philosophy." What with editing and occasional diversions into politics, these years were far too active and exploratory to permit any large-scale literary production. But they marked Adams' complete involvement in the world of ideas, the beginning of the intellectual activity that was to result in the great writing of his later years.

The review of Von Holst's book contains Adams' first learned attempt at a generalization concerning American history. Though the review was intended as a collaboration of sorts for which Adams and his editorial assistant, Henry Cabot Lodge—who was also one of his doctoral candidates—were to write separate pieces and then "take what is best out of each and roll them into one," Adams had the final and decisive hand in its composition. The last two pages, *furthermore, which he called "my centennial oration," are entirely his own, and they are particularly interesting for the intense satisfaction one finds expressed there in the "majesty and force of [America's] national movement." This movement was destined to occupy Adams' thought for many years and to become a major subject of his magnificent* History of the United States . . . *during the* Administrations of Thomas Jefferson and James Madison.

1. *Verfassung und Demokratie der Vereinigten Staaten von Nord America*. Von Dr. v. Holst, A. O. Professor an der Universität Strassburg. 1. Theil. Staaten-souveränität und Sklaverei. Düsseldorf, 1873. New York: E. Steiger.

2. *The Constitutional and Political History of the United States*. By Dr. H. von Holst, Professor at the Universiy of Freiburg. Translated from the German by John J. Lalor and Alfred B. Mason. 1750-1833. State Sovereignty and Slavery. Chicago: Callaghan & Co. 1876.

AT length the great work of Dr. v. Holst makes its appearance in an English dress. It is far from creditable to the American public that so long a time should have been allowed to elapse before producing a translation of what is certainly the best book which any foreigner has yet written on the United States, if indeed it be not the best book which has ever been written on that subject, whether by foreigner or native. What Dr. v. Holst claims in his German preface, not given in the translation, is strictly true: "So far as I know, there is as yet no work of the like range for which an equal amount of material has been collected, and in which that material has been so consciously worked." It is equally true that no other historian has followed out the main lines of our historical develop-

[From the *North American Review*, CXXIII (October 1876), 328-361. Signed by Henry Adams and H(enry) C(abot) Lodge.]

ment with so keen a logic or so independent a spirit; and more than this, the book is a model of simple treatment and vigorous style.

Such a work was greatly needed, and it is mortifying to be obliged to confess that we know of no American who could have done it equally well. After the flood of trash which England and France have poured out with little variety for a century past on America and her institutions, it is beyond measure refreshing to find at last a man who knows what he is talking about and who attacks his subject in a way that commands respect. We commend the book without reserve to all American students; they will find in it an example of faithful study. We commend it to members of Congress; it is not too deep for their average comprehension. We commend it to such of our professional politicians as may not be above the painful processes of self-instruction; for them it will be healthy diet. We commend it to our Fourth of July orators; without disrespect to them, we are free to say that Dr. v. Holst has written a far better centennial oration than any which the centenary has produced. We commend it to our clergy; they will find in it some healthy views on the subject of public morality. We commend it to our lawyers and our law professors; even they are not so complete masters of the science but that they may learn something from Dr. v. Holst. This book deserves to be and will doubtless become the recognized handbook for all serious students of American history.

If we praise for the moment without reservation, it is because such drawbacks as will be noticed hereafter are not of a nature to diminish the usefulness of the work to American readers, who are sure to make a liberal allowance for a foreigner's failure to admire their institutions, and who may be trusted to be sharp-sighted enough when there is any question of injustice done or attempted. They will find an amusement and a healthy intellectual exercise in seeking out for their own satisfaction the instances in which Dr. v. Holst has erred and where he shows the influence of prejudices which he has been at no pains to conceal.

Even American critics will however find it difficult to convict the author of any serious misstatement. Dr. v. Holst is, on the whole, in spite of prejudices, surprisingly accurate. He is a striking instance of the advantage of education in a good school. Only Germany can teach such method. He has lived long enough in America to understand, if not to sympathize with, the ordinary American tendencies of mind. It is true that even the Professor's wildest admirers can hardly claim for him a sense of humor that is absolutely acute, and his touch is not altogether that of Sainte-Beuve. His true German "sobriety of mind" condemns the American habit of meeting serious matters with a jest, and translates it into his book as a lack of moral sense. Perhaps he is right, and perhaps we Americans have in fact no very acute sense of moral duties, and kick against the prophets, including foreign moralists. If so, this book will do good by the healthy rigor of its moral standard. If, on the other hand, this apparent want of convictions is only superficial, we may wrap ourselves up in our virtue and treat criticism with good-humor. In any case it would be in the last degree foolish for us to quarrel with Dr. v. Holst merely because that writer has, from an unfortunate superficial acquaintance with the exterior of Tammany Hall, imbibed some prejudices against our code of public morality, which we may hope would have yielded to a more intimate knowledge of the beneficent workings of that institution. Indeed, even among our own citizens, there are some who in the heat of political controversy are in the habit of saying as much if not more than Dr. v. Holst has said or intimated, in regard to a possible majority of their fellow-citizens, and, what is even worse, it is much to be feared that they mean what they say.

If then we have any objection to offer in regard to Dr. v. Holst's manner of meeting his subject, it is not that he has done us injustice. It is rather that, after a repeated reading of his work, in a spirit of faith which we rarely concede to the perusal of anything but "original sources," we are still in doubt what he means. In his preface to the American edition he says: "Several European critics of my work have been of opinion that my judgment of the American system of government and its working is an almost unqualified condemnation, and I do not doubt that some American readers will receive the same impression." But when we expect to hear the author go on to deny the justice of such an impression, and take pains to correct so unfair an inference, we find that he does nothing of the kind, but leaves us to grope our way in the dark as best we can. As a matter of fact, the book abounds in sharp criticism, not indeed unreasonable, but by no means flattering; in frequent allusions to

American shortcomings which are rarely counterbalanced by equally spontaneous praise; in very liberal and even copious administrations of justice which are rarely tempered by mercy. Hence it is unquestionably true that the general effect left on the reader's mind is that of unqualified condemnation, as the foreign reviewers seem to have thought. Nine readers out of every ten would at once say that to them Dr. v. Holst represents that class of European critics which patronizes American history; which considers Washington, Hamilton, Jefferson, Madison, Marshall, the Adamses, Clay, Calhoun, and Webster as very well-meaning men, and as men of very respectable parts though of limited acquirements; and which speaks of the American Constitution as an interesting political phenomenon in its way; but always with the reservation implied or expressed that, as compared with the political development of Europe during the same period, say under the guidance of Friedrich Wilhelm III., v. Stein, v. Metternich, v. Brandenburg, v. Manteuffel, and v. Bismarck, that of America has little to show; her statesmen have been hardly more than respectable, and her development of political principles has been feeble, to say the least. Dr. v. Holst himself nowhere says this, and he says very much which to our minds implies quite a different opinion. There is nothing in his book, setting aside a certain occasional asperity of criticism, which could lead any careful reader to charge him with it. But by setting up an absolute political standard so high that no people of any age or country have ever approached it, he suggests the conclusion that America has proved a lamentable failure, and he has taken no pains to warn his readers from drawing such a conclusion. They have accordingly done so, as he himself has shown. This is, however, a matter of very little consequence to Americans, who are quite able to draw their own conclusions. And indeed the same thing may be said of Dr. v. Holst's own views, should criticism succeed in deducing them from the context. The value of this work does not consist, to American readers, in the author's political theories, whatever they may be, but in his thorough mastery of his subject; the sure hand with which he excludes all that is irrelevant, and the clear statement of all that is important in fact or principle; the rigid application of the laws of logic and morality to historical personages and phenomena; the keen analysis of character; the even-handed if sometimes unnecessary severity with which justice is dealt out to parties and to party expedients. If the standard set up is somewhat too high for human nature, at least in the morally abandoned wastes of America, and if individual judgments are sometimes those of a German professor rather than those of a politician who is forced to act within the limitations of the possible; if when tested by the same instruments, the political history of other countries on which the sun of the moral law shines with more force than it does here, would appear a mass of inconsistencies and impurities not much preferable to our own; yet there is this to be said for Dr. v. Holst's point of view, that foreigners may well be permitted to judge sharply, since it is pretty certain that natives will judge with foolish lenity, and we may fairly excuse ourselves for going abroad for our morals, seeing that as yet history has failed to inculcate any moral at all at home.

Another criticism on Dr. v. Holst's book, which will be further treated in the sequel, is that after granting the justice of his criticisms so far as they go, yet they do not go far enough to justify the fault he finds with the system of government. As a matter of fact, Dr. v. Holst shows no sufficient reason for his apparent conclusions. Perhaps this portion of his demonstration is reserved for a future volume. The misfortune is that the author, who brings overstrained complaints against the character of one political period, detracts from the effect of the criticisms which he has to make on the character of another. The experience of the last ten years has done much to arouse in Americans a sense of the weaknesses of their political system, and sensible criticism from any source is now very welcome to them. It would perhaps be unjust to say that the old boastfulness and arrogance, so disgusting to Dr. v. Holst, are wholly laid aside; but they are for the most part abandoned in practical usage and reserved for show, like other curiosities. It may even be doubted whether the readers of this Review would now be greatly edified by the remark quoted from its columns with so much disapprobation by Dr. v. Holst, that "the American government has its distinctly providential element. It was God's saving gift," etc. Such confidence in what the Abbé Correa, with more good-humor and more wit than Dr. v. Holst, used to call "the special providence over the United States and little children," appears of late to have been more or less abandoned by sensible Americans; and if one may judge from an indistinct recollection of certain telegrams of the present Emperor of Germany during the late French war, a fair share of this youthful self-confidence seems to have fallen to the infant confederation of which Dr. v. Holst is a subject. All the more, therefore, is it necessary that criticism should be restrained from exaggeration. Its effect will be greatest where it is seen to be most free from captiousness and the imputation of ulterior motives.

With this preamble, the American reader cannot do better than to sit down in the spirit of meekness and forgiveness of injuries, and go through Dr. v. Holst's book, chapter by chapter, to draw from it the lessons that it can give.

Dr. v. Holst's intentions can only be learned from the German preface, which, for some not very obvious reason, has not been given in the translation. His original idea was to write a book on the actual social and political condition of the United States, but he very soon decided that this could not be properly done without first writing the constitutional history. This he has divided into two parts, the political and the legal. The whole work, therefore, is planned on the most comprehensive scale. The political history of the Constitution will form the first part; its complement, the legal history, the second; and the original disquisition on the present condition of the United States, the third. The volume before us is, therefore, the first instalment of the first division. It is very earnestly to be hoped that the author will carry out in its full extent his original intention.

This volume begins by a very clear statement of the political situation which preceded the formation of the Constitution, and of the inherent difficulties with which the attempt to form the new nation was surrounded. Of all these difficulties, the most serious was that the Revolutionary statesmen themselves were not clear in their ideas of what constituted a nation:—

"Particularism had become to such an extent part of the flesh and blood of the native-born colonists that it could not be renounced; nay, that it became a measure of necessity to acknowledge its supremacy after the first moment of excitement was over, and the separate interests of the States came in conflict, whether really or only apparently, with the general welfare. John Adams affords the strongest proof of this. Reason compelled him to adopt the national view, and he defended it with great zeal so long as his feelings did not get the better of his understanding. The moment, however, that he allowed his affections to have sway, he gave evidence of his leaning towards the doctrines of the particularists. . . . One man alone [Alexander Hamilton] saw clearly from the first that it would have been as profitable to rack one's brains in the vain endeavor to square the circle [as to make one nation by means of a confederation]. The American statesman's dictionary was written in double columns, and the chief terms of his vocabulary were not infrequently inserted twice: in the right-hand column in the sense which accorded with actual facts, and was in keeping with the tendency towards particularism; in the left in their logical sense, and the sense which the logic of facts has gradually and through many a bitter struggle brought out into bold relief, and which it will finally stamp as their exclusive meaning. Nothing but the bitter experience of many years has been able to make American states- men even partially conscious that they have been using this double- columned political lexicon. The nature of the state was to such an extent a seven-sealed enigma to them, that they, *bona fide* and in the very same breath, used the same word in the most opposite senses, and employed words as synonymous which denoted ideas absolutely irreconcilable."

The first attempt to weld the thirteen "sovereign" States into one nation, made in the form of a Confederation, was therefore neces- sarily a failure. Only a general conviction, reached in 1786, that a desperate crisis had been reached, brought about the second experi- ment, which resulted in the Constitution of 1787:—

"The masses of the American people, in their vanity and over-estimate of themselves, are fond of forgetting the dreadful struggle of 1787 and 1788, or of employing it only as a foil for the 'divine inspiration' which guided and enlightened the 'Fathers' at Philadelphia. In Europe this view of the case has been generally received on faith as correct, and 'the iso- lated fact' in history has been held up to admiration, that thirteen States loosely bound together as one confederate body did not see in the sword the only hammer with which their political machine, which was falling to pieces, could be welded together, but met in peaceful consultation and actually united to transform a confederacy of States into a Federal state of masterly construction. In America this is an inexhaustible theme for Fourth of July orations, and in Europe it is only too frequently used as a text for doctrinarian politico-moral discussions. With history, however, it has nothing to do. The historical fact is, that the Constitution had been 'extorted from the grinding necessity of a reluctant people.'"

The influence of Europe was not without its share in confusing political ideas:—

"It were folly to say that Rousseau's writings exercised any influence on the development of things in America. But the same spirit which gave birth to Rousseau's philosophy, and made it of such importance to Europe, was, long before Jefferson grew intoxicated even to madness with it in Paris, rampant in America. It indeed received its full development here only through the French Revolution, but a series of fortunate circumstances prevented its development to its ultimate consequences. It appeared in the New World in a modified form, but was not wanting there. And here for the first time it became clearly evident that the civilized New World was not separated from the old one by any broad unbridged gulf. They are not only governed by the same historic laws, but the great intellectual revolutions which take place in the one act simultaneously in the other, although in accordance with the existing natural conditions they never manifest themselves precisely in the same manner, or make their influence felt to exactly the same extent. One needs only to read the Declaration of Independence to be convinced that but one more impulse was needed, even in America, to permit these crude theories to be openly advocated, which, disregarding that which had prescriptive right on its side, in virtue of its history, would endeavor to sap the foundations of all things, to lay down their arbitrary premises as unquestionable truths, and which would have willingly, in a night, overturned the state and the established order of society, to make them accord with the ideas which they were wont to call 'natural right.' "

In the second chapter, Dr. v. Holst goes on to comment on the remarkable fact that the Constitution, from being an object of the bitterest attack and of only lukewarm defence, became the political bible of the whole people:—

"It is possible for us to trace the earliest beginnings of the worship of the Constitution. At first it was looked upon as the best possible Constitution for the United States. By degrees it came to be universally considered as a masterpiece, applicable to every country. This was preached with so much unanimity and honest conviction, although internal quarrels were raging all the time, that the propagandism of the new faith reached even Europe. In the United States this conviction grows steadily stronger, although parties not only differ concerning the advisability of certain practical provisions of the Constitution, but have been from the first diametrically opposed to one another in their understanding of the principles on which it is founded. From the close of the century, that is, from the time when the opposing principles assumed a fixed form, the Constitution has been the political bible of the people. The child sucked in with his mother's milk the conviction that this was the light in which he should regard it. The paternal *sic credo, stat fides mea pro ratione,* was a guaranty for the rightfulness of this conviction. What should be deduced from the Constitution in the future was quite another matter. The wilder the war of tongues, the louder the cry of the Constitution was raised on every side, and the more energetically did every one swear not to deviate from it even by a hair's breadth. For four years the people of the United States tore one another to pieces in the most frightful civil war recorded in history, each camp thinking in the best of faith that it was following the standard of the Constitution. The time will come when it will be difficult to conceive how even Europe, which it did not concern, could, in view of the seventy-five years of contest over it, have so universally and so emphatically united in the non-critical laudations the Constitution has received. . . . The Constitution has found many learned and intelligent commentators; but they have all considered its excellence to be an undoubted and universally admitted fact. What should have been only the result of their investigation, they made the premises of their arguments; and these arguments have been confined to the interpretation and to the bearings of the separate provisions of the Constitution. Much ingenuity has been spent in showing how its several provisions might be harmonized with one another and with the peculiar ideas of their authors on the nature and purpose of the general government. There has been no attempt as yet to consider the several provisions as parts of a whole, or to subject the whole to an objective critical examination in the light of history. The abler commentators, like Story, have now and then been forced upon conclusions from which it is but one step to such a course of treatment; but they have never carried out their chain of thought to that extent. They always break off at the decisive point, and proceed to the next question."

Dr. v. Holst himself gives no analysis of the Constitution, and leaves his readers to draw their own inferences from his story. From expressions scattered here and there, and from the general tone of his comments, it may be gathered that there were fundamental defects in the instrument, and that the most fatal of these was the countenance it gave to State rights. Meanwhile he points out that the result of this fetish worship, as he calls it, was to turn away the public attention from the study of constitutional principles to a study of technical construction. The tendency to the creation of political dogmas kept pace with the development of democracy.

"A problem of this kind was then, and would be to-day, of much greater practical significance in the United States than, for instance, in England or in Germany; because, in some respects, the political thought of the Americans is much more superficial and immature. In political questions of a concrete nature, the Americans are, on an average, more competent judges than any people on the Continent of Europe. The political institutions of the country, its social and especially its economical relations, educate them from the cradle to independent thought on all questions involving material interests, and encourage them to summon their whole intellectual strength for their solution. But in the wearing struggles of daily life new problems of this character continually arise, and almost exhaust their intellectual strength. Their energy of mind is not in consequence great enough to give much depth to their thoughts on political problems of a general nature. The disposition towards generalization is sufficiently developed, but their observations are neither various nor long, nor reliable enough to warrant inductions of any real value. Half-true and vague ideas are, therefore, raised by them to the dignity of unimpeachable principles. These are appealed to on every occasion, so that they rapidly rise to the dignity of sovereign laws. And the more they assume this character, the stronger does the conviction become rooted that they are the stars by which the ship of state should be steered."

Dr. v. Holst's idea appears to be that, in the process of converting the Confederacy into a nation, the Constitution made a convenient battle-ground on which the two old parties, States-rights men and Nationalists, could fight out their battle within a sort of self-imposed limit, much in the manner of a tournament. Under cover of the fetish worship, the old tendencies lived and throve, merely interpreting the Constitution to suit their fixed ideas.

"Almost from the very day on which the new order of things was inaugurated, the conflict between the opposing tendencies broke out anew, and before the close of the century it reached a degree of violence which suggested very serious fears. . . . The view which afterwards became more general, that during the first years of the existence of the Republic the thought of separation was never seriously entertained, is a historical misrepresentation made in the interests of party. Until the first part of the nineteenth century, the dissolution of the Union was a standing element in political speculation; and both previous to and after that period, it was repeatedly considered possible, and even probable, in moments of excitement, by either party, that it would be necessary to resort to this radical remedy. . . . These views are, to a great extent, very different from those which are prevalent on the subject; but they must accord with historical truth, for only in such case is the political history of the United States rational and explicable. Calhoun and his disciples were not the authors of the doctrine of nullification and secession. That question is as old as the Constitution itself, and has always been a living one, even when it has not been one of life and death. Its roots lay in the actual circumstances of the time, and the Constitution was the living expression of these actual circumstances."

During the administration of Washington the particularist tendencies were mostly quiet or organizing their strength. Only the disturbances commonly known as the Whiskey Rebellion threatened to develop into serious opposition to the power of the central government, and these were suppressed by Hamilton with a strong hand. But the retirement of Jefferson from Washington's Cabinet gave solidity to the opposition, and the accession of John Adams to the Presidency let loose all the passions of the old provincial jealousies. The first great storm was roused by the condition of our Foreign Affairs. Under the stress of imminent war with France, a Federal Congress enacted the alien and sedition laws. Thereupon Jefferson, with his masterly touch of a true political leader, caused the Kentucky and Virginia legislatures to issue what was to be the definition of constitutional principles for the Republican party. These famous resolutions declared the States to be the judges of infractions of the Constitution, and claimed for them the right to "interpose," or, in other but not essentially different words, to "nullify" the national laws. Already the Virginians went so far as to make arrangements to seize the United States armory, and kept Dark's brigade in readiness to support their plans with military force.

"It is not possible to say whether, or to what extent, these preparations were directly incited by Jefferson and Madison. The suspicion resting on Jefferson is obviously the greater, as Madison was, from first to last, more cautious in his steps. Nor can any definite answer be given to the question how far Madison recommended more moderate measures, or how far a different interpretation of the Constitution lay at the foundation of these recommendations. Every move of his was made with anxious deliberation, and his native cautiousness, which sometimes degenerated into weakness and indecision, contributed beyond doubt to cause him to advise a milder and more tentative procedure. Besides, it may be that the internal struggle between his State and national patriotism, in both of which he was equally honest, hindered him from explaining to himself the 'interpose.' Perhaps he desired to leave open to himself, as well as to the legislatures of the other States, all possible ways of coming to a substantial agreement. It may be, too, that he entertained some real doubt whether the letter and spirit of the Constitution quite justified the last conclusion in the Kentucky resolutions of 1799, drawn from the correct principles (correct in his opinion), which were the common basis of the Virginia and Kentucky resolutions. Whatever estimate of the relative weight of these two motives may be made, the rôle played by Madison in the constitutional conflict which culminated in 1798 and 1799 throws much light on the real character of the Constitution itself and on the history of the development of the national spirit during the last decade. Much weight is not to be attached to the fact that Jefferson read the Constitution in such a way that the union of the States was, in principle, perhaps, a looser, certainly not a firmer one than it had been under the Articles of Confederation. It was not a difficult matter for Jefferson to act in opposition to his own theories; and it was still easier for him to reconcile himself to a contradiction between his words and his deeds. Ambition was the sovereign trait in his character. He was always ready to sacrifice much of his favorite theories to his feverish thirst for power and distinction, the more especially as his eminently practical instinct caused him often to doubt the tenableness of his ideal systems. Moreover, as he, partly from interest and partly because misled by his idealistic reveries, concealed his ambition under the mask of the greatest simplicity, stoical indifference, and even of disinclination to accept any political honor or dignity, so, too, his conscience was not precisely what would be called tender in the weighing and measuring of words, whether his own or those of others. Such a character could scarcely always resist the temptation to make ink and paper say what, in his opinion, they ought to say. His mode of thought, which was a mixture of about equal parts of dialectical acuteness and of the fanaticism of superficiality, as short-sighted as it was daring, made this a matter of no difficulty. Hence it is that not the slightest weight should be attached *a priori* to his interpretation of the Constitution.

"The direct contrary of this is true of Madison. His was not a character so thoroughly and harmoniously constituted and developed as Washington's. He, too, concealed the depth of his ambition under a plain and modest exterior. When it or his over-sensitiveness was wounded, he too could be unjust to his opponents. The violence with which the party struggle was conducted by degrees carried him also so far away that he played a more covert game than can be entirely justified by the excuse of political necessity. And when it was a question of opposing a measure in too great conflict with his own party programme, he could descend to the letter and to petty quibbling, if he could not give his attack the necessary energy from the higher standpoint of the statesman. Spite of this, however, there was nothing of the demagogue about him. He is a purely constituted character, spite of the fact that his moral principles did not so unconditionally govern him as to leave his judgment entirely uninfluenced by his desires. It cannot be charged that he ever consciously approached the Constitution with the intention of discovering in it a word which he might make to serve his purpose by dialectical legerdemain. . . . But it can be shown that he now read the Constitution in such a way as to find in it something essentially different from what he had advocated in Philadelphia, and from what he thought he saw in the completed draught of it. If it be conceded that he did not read the Constitution now so as intentionally to introduce anything new into it, and this will scarcely be denied to-day, these different interpretations can be explained only on two assumptions: without sophistry the terms of the Constitution must admit of essentially different meanings, and Madison's political proclivities and judgment must have experienced a radical change since 1787 and 1788."

The election of Jefferson to the Presidency stopped the further development of particularist tendencies in the Southern States, for the time. But although parties changed their ground, the situation remained essentially the same. On the one hand, Jefferson became the great centralizing influence, and interpreted the Constitution to suit his own momentary policy in that sense. His attitude in regard to the constitutional questions involved in the Louisiana purchase was a "frivolous way of dealing with his own convictions"; it was "audacious contempt of the Constitution." On the other hand, the Federalist party became particularists, and dabbled in small schemes of separation. Dr. v. Holst measures out a tolerably even share of severe condemnation on both parties for their foreign policy between 1806 and 1815, and for the domestic consequences which that policy entailed. He sees in the embargo only "one of the best illustrations of the tenacity with which this practical people hold, in the face of experience, to political theories, once they have accepted them as true." And he looks upon the War of 1812 as solely the work of two or three reckless young Congressmen, who had personal objects to gain. They reduced Madison to the position of a tool of their ambition.

"Clay was elected a member of the House of Representatives [in 1811] and was chosen Speaker. He used the disproportionately great influence of his position with masterly skill and astounding recklessness [for war]. He appointed Calhoun, who had been elected to Congress for the first time, the second member of the important Committee of Foreign Affairs, of which he soon became the head. The first month of the session had not yet passed when the two young zealots had brought it to such a pass that they could proclaim as a fixed resolution what, a year and a half before, Clay had given expression to as an eventual wish. . . . Randolph had said, in his great speech of the 10th December, that the committee had gone further than the President. Madison was indeed far from being able to master the situation. Endowed by nature with a clearer insight into matters of state, and with a much finer moral constitution than Jefferson, he became like wax in his hands when the Republican party had once obtained the permanent mastery in Virginia. The gift of persuasion which he possessed in an eminent degree, and which made him an invaluable ally, became ruinous to himself. When rocks stood in the way of his ambition, which his moral sense would not permit him to go round, his own judgment was then corrupted by a logic as sharp as it was insinuating. The impulse in this direction he always received from others. To him were wanting the independence and energy of will which are the indispensable requisites of a great political leader. He remained, therefore, always a political attorney [*Sachwalter*] of extraordinary capacity, but never raised himself to the height of the statesman. These were qualities which eminently qualified him to serve as the right-hand man of his predecessor in the Presidency. But when he was himself placed at the head of the state, he found himself entangled in a terrible net, which he had wrought with his own hands. He was not the man to tear it in pieces with quick resolution, and his share in the production of the ruinous work was so great that he could not see that the net could be unravelled with success only on condition that the labor was begun without delay, with a firm hand, and in accordance with a well-considered plan. But even if he had seen it, he would scarcely have taken such a resolution, for in doing so he would have been passing judgment, not only on Jefferson, but on himself. Besides, now that the decision rested with him, his real nature got the upper hand. Moderate in his thought and judgment, he had always cautiously felt his way towards a middle course, where he had followed solely his own inclinations and judgment. Under the pressure of responsibility this commendable moderation now became painful uncertainty. Whatever was positive in the programme devised by Jefferson day by day crumbled away like baked sand in his hands. Every day the situation demanded more imperatively a decided initiative; but not only were the necessary qualities wanting in the man whose duty it was to act, but his whole programme, like that of the opposition, became more and more a purely negative one. Under such conditions, the field belongs, in a popular state, to those who have the courage to decide and to act. The *homines novi* in Congress had the courage, and therefore Madison became their tool. Their unsatisfied ambition expected to pluck in war, in rich abundance, the laurels which the questions of internal politics seemed to offer them little prospect of winning in the near future, because the democrats had an overwhelming preponderance. That there had been for years sufficient cause for war, is unquestionable; but it was, nevertheless, the work of a small, ambitious party in Congress. The country was dragged [*hineingezerrt*] into it, although the opposition party condemned it in a manner and to an extent which roused fear of forcible resistance and of treason; although the bearer of the executive authority and the head of the dominant party did not want it; and although only a small minority thought it really inevitable and demanded it with unaffected enthusiasm. This is a remarkable instance how little self-government there is, under given circumstances, even among peoples which, by law, enjoy the most unlimited self-government, and how sharply facts often give the lie to the principle of the rule of the majority in republics. The war party obtained the majority in Congress, because vanity and the party interests of the majority forbade them to acknowledge their former mistakes. They had imposed every kind of restriction on commerce, and all that they had accomplished was to seriously damage their own interests. If they would not acknowledge that the idea which lay at the bottom of these restricions was a false one, they were obliged to hold to the principle that there was no choice between these and war, and that policy and morals demanded a decision in favor of the lesser evil, so long as by this means the attainment of the wished-for end still seemed possible. From this it directly followed that war was not only justifiable but must also be declared necessary. The same burden of logical consequences, drawn from premises which he had himself made, weighed upon Madison. The enthusiasts in favor of war were in a condition to make another influence felt, and this decided the issue. The Presidential election was impending, and the war party made the unconditional adoption of their policy a *conditio sine qua* of his renomination. That the threat could be carried into effect was to be looked upon as certain, for Monroe and Clinton were already prepared to accept the nomination from the war party, and this party could not therefore be at a loss for candidates. Madison was not a man of such rigid moral firmness that his convictions should have withstood such a temptation. He fell a victim, like others before him, and like men of the greatest political talents after him, to the Presidential fever. Clay and Calhoun, who had especially abetted him in this trade, made at the cost of the country, afterwards wasted away under the same incurable malady."

The States of Massachusetts, Connecticut, and Rhode Island refused to call out their militia, and thereupon the President complained to Congress that if these States were right in their interpretation of the Constitution, the Union was "not one nation for the purpose most of all requiring it."

"The complaint was only too well founded; but what party was it that for twelve years long had toiled with restless energy to unravel thread by thread, or even to cut the national ties which the Constitution had been created to knit together? By what right did the anti-Federalists imagine they could assume that the old proverb would not apply to them, that he who sows the wind shall reap the whirlwind? Had not Madison stood for ten years in the front rank of those who preached and strove against further national consolidation with such zeal as to make it possible now for the original national party to lay hands on the roots of nationality in its most vital part?"

The Hartford Convention brought the Federalists squarely upon the ground taken by Jefferson and Madison in the Kentucky and Virginia resolutions fifteen years before.

"The programme of the Convention was throughout a party programme, and this party programme adopted on the fundamental constitutional issue the position formerly chosen by the radical wing of the party opposed to them. Ultra Federalists and ultra Republicans met on a constitutional principle whose logical consequence was the dependence of the national existence on the free pleasure of every single State."

From these early contests, the author now turns to the subject of slavery, and narrates the compromise of the Constitution, which he unqualifiedly condemns.

"The principle was bargained away for the sake of the Union, and hence every new demand dictated to the slavocracy by the impulse of self-preservation presented to the North the alternative of yielding and thereby separating itself one step further from the true principle, or of endangering the Union. . . . The longer men shrank from the test, the more dictatorially was the South certain to speak; the more she was sure to ask, the more must be conceded, and the more must the peculiar slavocratic interests dominate over the interests connected with the Union."

Then follows an account of the infamous legislation in regard to free colored men.

"Can all history furnish a second example of a nation flinging so great a lie with equal impudence in the world's face, as the United States, with its belief in the principles of the Declaration of Independence, did for almost a century?"

He then comes to the Missouri Compromise, and sums up the result of the dispute as follows:—

"Three constitutional questions—two of them of cardinal importance —had been discussed. Men had fought shy of all three for the moment, and for this reason the originators of the compromise claimed that they had postponed the decision to the Greek calends. From a legal point of view only one positive result had been reached, and this was on a point concerning which no legal question existed. The Northern majority had indirectly renounced the right of Congress to forbid slavery, as far as the territory lying south of the line of 36° 30′ was concerned, and it had agreed to this renunciation because the Southern minority had renounced on its side its claims to having the questions of law involved decided *now* in its favor, provided its concrete demands, which it based on its interpretation of the Constitution, were complied with. This was the true nature and the substance of the 'compromise' which gave Henry Clay the first claim to the proud name of 'the Great Peacemaker.'"

This is followed by an account of the dispute in regard to the Panama Congress and a sketch of the character of Henry Clay.

"No one will deny Clay's capacity for statesmanship; but he yielded too readily and too earnestly to the lead of his vigorous fancy. He had to thank it for many fruitful thoughts, but it often prevented his weighing the nature of his plans and the chance of their realization with the necessary soberness. The vast extent and the uncivilized condition of the young West, whose most distinguished representative he was, mirrored itself strongly in his thoughts. He dazzled his hearers by the splendor of his projects, won them a hearing by his fiery, alluring eloquence, and helped himself and his followers over the difficulties in the way by a glittering sketch of the consequences which must result from the development of the ideas. His fancy's flight was towards the sun, but it bore him so high that mountains and valleys began to melt into a plain, and the foot resting on earth stepped uncertainly and insecurely. Moreover, his boldness in decision and action, when every-day circumstances created great and momentous problems that imperatively demanded a thorough solution, did not correspond with his boldness in planning. At such times he could not even entertain an energetic wish for a solution, partly because he did not subject the question of its necessity to proper inquiry, and partly because traditional dogmas and a lack of moral courage made him start with the supposition of its impossibility. Bargaining was then the sum of his wisdom, and his activity degenerated into obstinacy in chaffering. An idealist who wasted the best part of his creative power in impracticable projects, and a politician who was an unsurpassable master of the art of solving great and unavoidable problems by little expedients,—these are the most notable traits in Clay's political character. They do not give his picture in full, but they mark the tendency of his influence upon the fate of the Union. His other qualities and achievements did not lift him above the level of ordinary politicians."

The author now proceeds to recount the collision between the younger Adams and the State of Georgia, in which he dwells upon the fact that the so-called victory of the national government was a barren victory which bore the same fruits as defeat, and he concludes his volume with a recital of the nullification struggle with South Carolina and a sketch of the character of Calhoun.

"Calhoun was a true son of the soil from which he sprang, and he therefore possessed in a high degree the characteristic traits of the Protestant population of the North of Ireland, to which he belonged by descent; that peculiar primitive energy, in which an enthusiasm more idealistic than ideal is strangely linked with stubborn consistency. The blood flowed in his veins not less hotly than in those of any other

Carolinian; but a piercing intelligence and a soaring ambition held it sharply in check when great questions were to be weighed and decided. He had not the breadth of view that characterizes the statesman, but he had extraordinarily keen vision. From the sole of his foot to the crown of his head a speculative politician, he was wholly unaware of the results to which his policy would inevitably lead; but the practical instinct of the American race, and a political activity extending over many years, enabled him to find ways and means for bringing the burning questions of the day to such a solution that he constantly brought his doctrines nearer and nearer to practical realization. He was not idealist enough to delude himself with the hope of an immediate accomplishment of his whole programme, and not to reconcile himself to the withdrawal of half his stake if it appeared that he could then win the game, and must otherwise lose it entirely. But he was enough of a fanatic to allow nothing to interfere with his will if the choice between going forward and a partial sacrifice of the *principles* of his doctrines was once set before him. In such cases he was capable of making 'bend or break' his motto, and this not merely in moments of the highest excitement. His attitude remained the same even when the struggle continued for years. If he had been a visionary whose system was built up in the air, he could scarcely have done this; the material interests which formed the broad basis of his doctrines gave him the needed strength; yes, made this course a necessity. The Constitution and the history of its origin gave him only the formal foundation for the development of the doctrine of State rights, and its development with him and with the whole people did not rest upon *a priori* reasoning. He was originally by no means inclined to this opinion. The slavery question drove him into the path, and with the increasing development of the slaveholding interest he followed it on to the furthest consequences. By the light of slavery and in accordance with the laws of logic, he worked out the constitutional law of a democratic federative republic, and the logically correct result was a systematization of anarchy. He failed to recognize this fact because the doctrine was to him a means to an end, and his whole political reasoning became in time so completely identified with the prosecution of the one aim that the means became to his mind its own end. His inborn firmness, and the self-reliance that had been distorted into haughtiness under the influence of slavery, thus became obstinacy. It was not possible for him to place himself under the orders of a leader; but the one-sidedness of his political reasoning and striving, and especially the readiness, almost genius, with which he mastered in an instant the whole range of questions which lay within his narrow circle of view, made him unfit to be the leader of a great party; at the same time his talent and character marked him out for the head of a faction of extremists. But a growing ambition kept his eyes fastened upon the White House, which he could never hope to reach through a fraction, however devoted to him."

After an analysis of Calhoun's doctrines, showing that their very strength rested on the fact that they advanced no new principles, Dr. v. Holst comes to the compromise of 1833.

"The whole history of party up to that time had not seen stranger bedfellows than Clay and Calhoun were at that instant. They had begun their political career as brothers in arms, but now they had so thoroughly fallen away from each other that they did not even speak together. Even now no change was made in their personal relations. Party spirit and personal enmity have used this circumstance in order to stamp Calhoun as a 'coward.' Benton relates that Calhoun accepted Clay's conditions after he had been told by Letcher, a Kentucky representative, that Jackson wished to hear of no 'negotiation,' but was resolved to have him imprisoned and tried for high treason. Clayton, senator from Delaware, also declares that Calhoun's motive was fear lest Jackson should have him 'hung.' In this case, too, persistent repetition has sufficed to make the assertion of extreme partisans become in the popular mind an historic fact. It has never once been asked whether it was in any way possible for Jackson to 'hang' the 'arch-traitor.' Jackson was enough of an autocrat not to let Americans, proud of their freedom, look back with too great satisfaction upon this chapter of their history. They need not at least boast, upon the most dubious testimony, that he had not an evil pleasure in acting as President with the same arbitrary brutality that he had shown as a general in hunting down Indians. Yet the law and Jackson's will were not always absolutely identical; and however certainly Calhoun, according to European ideas of public law, may have been guilty of high treason, it would have been difficult to have convicted him of it under the provisions of the Constitution. Calhoun was well enough acquainted with the decisions of the Supreme Court in the cases of Burr and Bollman not to be as much frightened by the first dark threat which came to him, at third or fourth hand, as, after a truce was agreed upon, his bitterest opponents affirmed. Only the partisan and the special pleader can lay weight on bits of history which have happened in the night and without a witness."

The volume closes with an analysis of the compromise measure in which "South Carolina had not obtained all that she at first demanded, but the Union had lost much and won nothing."

"Robbins of Rhode Island had rightly called the tariff bill in the Senate a practical recognition of the right of nullification, and John Quincy Adams had cried out in warning to the House that the result of paying such a premium for rebellion against the law must infallibly be the dissolution of the Union. As facts began to prove the truth of this prophecy, the most unreserved admirers of Jackson and the most conservative Democrats recognized the fact that the Carolinian, whom they had seen in spirit already hanging on the gallows, had wrung victory from the 'iron man.'

"It was a terrible victory; the vanquished have been shockingly scourged for the defeat suffered through their own sin, and the victors have been shattered in pieces by the consequences of the accursed triumph. But victors and vanquished brought down the punishment upon themselves, because there was one thing they did not understand, or, if they understood it, would not live up to it: 'Sovereignty can only be a unit and it must remain a unit,—the sovereignty of law.'"

The recapitulation of all the successive concessions to the slave power, all the steps by which that power slowly converted the national government into an instrument of its own will, is a terrible one. It is with a shudder that one turns the last page of this tremendous indictment, and yet the volume ends at the threshold of the antislavery struggle; the worst humiliations are not yet touched.

After devoting so much space to the reproduction of Dr. v. Holst's own words, commentary upon them must be brief and condensed. We will place ourselves so far as possible in Dr. v. Holst's own point of view and accept his premises as correct. It is true that he goes too far in saying as he does that the solidarity of interests among the American provinces rested mainly on the fact of their geographical isolation from the rest of the world. Similarity of language, and for the most part of race, were quite as essential elements, as is shown by the fact that Canada, although equally isolated, stood quite outside the range of American political ambition. But this is a trifle. The essential is that Dr. v. Holst has laid down in the clearest language the problem which lay before American statesmen for solution, and the difficulties which stood in the way of any solution at all. That problem was how to weld thirteen "sovereign States" into a nation without appealing to force.

It is characteristic of a European thinker that the greatest difficulty of all should be considered to lie in the confusion of ideas in the American mind in regard to the nature of the State. Americans would say that this confusion of ideas was itself, so far as it existed at all, the expression of a simple historical fact which European theorists seem never to be able to comprehend, that the thirteen colonies had a history, and were so many entities, which were then and are still believed to be in themselves good. The American statesman was not a French doctrinaire, and he was faced by a fundamental fact which he had to deal with as he could. The process was necessarily tentative, and some time was needed before it became quite clear what was the extent of the sacrifice that would be required of the State governments; but so soon as this was ascertained, American statesmen went to work again in a perfectly practical spirit to adjust the balance. The question is whether the adjustment they made was satisfactory.

It is hardly worth while to defend the American statesmen of the last century further from the charge of confusion of mind. It was not their minds but the facts that were confused, and it is very much to their credit that they did not attempt to attack the subject from a standpoint of *a priori* theory, but all of them, even Hamilton, whom Dr. v. Holst admires so much, and who, according to him, alone comprehended the situation, rejected every thought of attempting to break rudely with the past. They were compelled, as a condition of the problem, to provide for the existence of two supreme powers in the nation. Dr. v. Holst seems to treat the very idea with contempt. But what says Hamilton, who is to Dr. v. Holst the sole representative of political perspicacity in that day?

"That two supreme powers cannot act together is false. They are inconsistent only when aimed at each other or at one indivisible object. The laws of the United States are supreme as to all their proper constitutional objects. The laws of the States are supreme in the same way. These supreme laws may act on different objects without clashing, or they may operate on different parts of the same common object with perfect harmony."

Right or wrong in their solution of the apparently insoluble problem, both the problem and its solution were eminently practical, and cannot be satisfactorily treated from the standpoint of mere theory.

In this connection a similar criticism may be made on Dr. v. Holst's theory of the influence of French philosophy on the American mode of thought. He reduces that influence to a minimum, it is true, but he still overlooks the essential point that Americans were not Frenchmen. What with the latter was an eminently practical idea was to the former simply a speculative opinion. This point can be best illustrated by an example drawn from another foreign critic, who, as being himself a Frenchman, was apparently struck by this national peculiarity. If there was one man in America who was run away with by the French philosophy, it was Jefferson. If his political theories had been put in practice when he had the power to put them in practice, the result would have been very much what the result of similar experiments was in France, with the difference that disintegration instead of despotism would have ensued. But Jefferson wanted to put his theories in practice only at such time as he had not the power, and when he had the power he carefully abstained from theorizing. The following picture, drawn by one of the first of French critics, gives an amusing sketch of our philosopher statesman as he appeared among the philosopher statesmen of Paris in 1788 and 1789:—

"Il était aussi maladroit en matière de gout et d'idées que judicieux en fait de conduite et d'affaires d'état. Il est plaisant de voir sa galanterie. Il veut être gai, gracieux, et il est balourd; il fait penser à cet Allemand qui pour se donner l'air léger se jetait par la fenêtre. . . . Figurez vous des gens du monde et d'académie, parés, poudrés, beaux diseurs, gracieux, sensible, qui munis de phrases et d'élégies, essayent de défaire et de remonter une machine énorme et compliquée à laquelle ils n'ont jamais mis la main; voilà les Français du temps. Ce constructeur mécanicien qui leur arrive d'Amérique, et qui essaie de copier leur dissertations et leur costume, peut faire rire par son exagération et son manque de tact. Mais demandez-lui son avis en matière d'engrenages et de poulies; à coté de lui tous les autres sembleront des bavards. . . . D'un coté le roideur et les audaces du théoricien, de l'autre la flexibilité et les atermoiements de l'homme d'action."[1]

This, however, is a mere parenthesis. The American statesmen had no doubt their own theories on the subject of natural rights;

[1] [Hippolyte Taine, "Jefferson," *Nouveaux Essais de Critique et d'Histoire*, 9th ed. (Paris, 1909), pp. 211, 213, 215. This essay was first published in the *Journal des Débats*, 3 Sept., 1861.]

but the Constitution is simply an expression of the utmost compromise that could be effected between two actual facts,—that of a common nationality recognized by all, and that of local independence equally recognized by all. True it is that this compromise was at last "extorted from the grinding necessity of a reluctant people." But we are utterly at a loss to understand why that fact should be used by Dr. v. Holst to diminish the credit of the act, which consists in the good sense which the Americans showed in perceiving that necessity, and the good temper they showed in acting upon it. If Dr. v. Holst finds it difficult to understand the reason for the "laudation" which this act of the American people has called forth, we will venture to suggest to him an illustration of the opposite course. The German people have now for one thousand years or more felt the "grinding necessity" of political union; but as yet they have, in spite of one lamentable effort to imitate the United States, "seen in the sword the only hammer with which their political machine, which was falling to pieces, could be welded together."

The same answer may be made to Dr. v. Holst's comments on what he calls the fetish-worship with which the American people came to idolize their Constitution. The fact of this idolization cannot be denied. It was one of the first developments of that national feeling which the Constitution was created to develop, and to that extent it was a demonstration of the success of that instrument. But the feeling of veneration for the Constitution was wrong, not because it was veneration, but because it was veneration from mistaken reasons. In the same way the English-speaking people have idolized Magna Charta, to say nothing of other great documents with which they have marked the various stages of their political progress. No one of these has fully satisfied the theoretical requirements of the political situation, but they have all met the exigencies for which they were framed, and have worked sufficiently well until they have been succeeded by something better. Their practical success is the strongest evidence of the English genius for government, and it is the practical success of the Constitution which must be the test of the wisdom of its creators. Let us then proceed to examine the weight of Dr. v. Holst's criticisms from a practical point of view.

As Dr. v. Holst clearly points out, the object of the founders of the Constitution was to weld thirteen "sovereign" States into one nationality. In the words of the preamble to the Constitution itself, it was "to form a more perfect union." He is quite right in his assertion that nullification and secession were not the creatures of the slavery question, but run through the whole century of our history as its particular ear-mark. Yet it is difficult to comprehend why he should consider this fact as a fault of the Constitution. Had there been no particularist feeling, there would have been no need of a closer union; the task of the Constitution would have been already performed. The only real question is, how the Constitution has performed its work of union in the face of these particularist tendencies; how it has answered its purpose in controlling them. It is perfectly true that Jefferson and his party interchanged places with the extreme wing of the Federalists; that each in turn belied its own principles according as each was in power or in opposition. Let history judge them as individuals and as parties for their inconsistencies, and visit on them what condemnation it thinks meet. But the fact which the constitutional historian has to bear in mind is, not what were the inconsistencies of individuals, but what was the effect of these inconsistencies on the government. And it is a part of Dr. v. Holst's own reproach that when the opposition party was vested with a public trust, it followed precisely the same course as its opponent. What was established as law by Washington was respected as law by Jefferson. The precedents established by the Federalist administrations were accepted and enlarged by the Republican administrations. That Jefferson should have exercised as President powers more questionable than any of those which he had triumphantly assailed his predecessors for wielding, may prove that Jefferson was an unscrupulous politician, but it also proves, what is of far more consequence to the world, that the American political system was stronger than the individual, and that the Constitution vindicated its energy in its working. That J. Q. Adams should have been driven from power nominally because he advocated the application of national money to internal improvements, and that the application of national money to internal improvements should have continued with accelerated pace from that day to this, is only another instance of the operation of the same law. The very charges of Dr. v. Holst against Jefferson, Madison, and Jackson are founded on the assumption that, as a matter of fact, they consistently carried out the national theory of the Constitution, at the expense of their own private consistency. In their hands, as in those of Washington and the two Adamses, the authority of the Executive was not only maintained but consistently enlarged, although jealousy of the Executive had been one of the fundamental articles of faith among the opponents of the Constitution.

If this be the case with the Executive, the first great constitutional agency, the argument is still stronger in regard to the second repository of political power, the legislature. Dr. v. Holst is very severe upon the repeated change of front which characterized the attitude of the legislature and of parties on the subject of a national bank. He is very justly shocked at the somersaults turned by Clay and Calhoun on the subject of constitutional powers, and few sensible American critics will care to defend the consistency of those gentlemen. But their inconsistency is in itself the strongest proof that the system was working out, with almost excessive energy, the results which it had been created to attain. That the legislature should construct a national bank; then should allow it to expire on the ground of its unconstitutionality; then almost immediately reconstruct it because experience proved it to be necessary, and therefore constitutional; then allow it to expire again because the President of the day chose to say that he considered it unconstitutional; that thereupon it should organize, step by step, a sub-treasury system, issue treasury notes to an unlimited extent, give these notes the character of legal tender, and so assume entire control over the standard of values, raising or lowering that standard at will from day to day; and finally should mass all the private banks in the country into one huge banking organism, subject to the simple will of the national legislature, and acting on politics with far greater force than ever the Bank of the United States dreamed of doing; that the legislature in the course of eighty years should do all this, proves that constitutional theories fluctuated in appearance, but that the authority of the national legislature grew, in fact, with a degree of rapidity that bade fair soon to justify the fears of George Mason, of Patrick Henry, of Samuel Adams, and of Thomas Jefferson, whom every European theorist insists upon branding as blockheads, because they thought they saw in the State organisms a protection against the uncontrolled despotism of the central government.

And if it be an indisputable fact that the Executive and the legislature worked with almost too great force and steadiness for the establishment of that "more perfect union" which they were called into existence to develop, what shall be said of the last great branch of our government, the judiciary, the most original and the most carefully planned of all the portions of our constitutional machine? It would be unfair to forestall what Dr. v. Holst may have to say on this subject, but it will be interesting to see whether Marshall, too, is to be adjudged a failure, and whether the Constitution from this point of view also is to be overthrown.

If then, starting from Dr. v. Holst's own postulates, it must be conceded that the Constitution as a practical machine has fulfilled the purpose of its creation, and has really formed a more perfect union and welded thirteen sovereign States into one nationality, we conceived that his objections to it fall to the ground. Americans are under such circumstances fully justified in their veneration for it, and the "Fathers" may rest in peace in their graves, without fear that their children will join in attacking them for not doing what it was utterly out of their power to do.

There remain now two serious subjects to deal with, in regard to which Dr. v. Holst has been excessively severe. The first of these is the War of 1812, into which the nation was "dragged against its will," and which offers "a remarkable instance how little self-government there is even among peoples who by law rejoice in the most unlimited self-government, and how often facts give the lie to the principle of the sovereignty of the majority in republics."

Either this is merely a somewhat pompous way of saying that the majority are commonly controlled by the men of the strongest will, or it is an assertion that self-government is impossible in republics, because the people do not directly decide every question by a popular vote. Dr. v. Holst is not given to preaching shallow platitudes, and we will not insult him by supposing that he meant here to proclaim one. What, then, does he mean by denying the possibility of self-government, merely because the representatives of the people, in the regular exercise of their trust, acting within the strict limits of their constitutional powers, and under a full sense of responsibility, decide to adopt a measure which a majority of their constituents may not at once approve? One of the most bitter charges brought by Dr. v. Holst against the American political system is that it destroyed the idea of representation, and degraded representatives into mere mouth-pieces of their immediate constituents. And now he takes the broad ground that self-government is impossible because a majority of the legislature, influenced thereto by a few strong-willed men, did what he is violent against them for not habitually doing, that is, adopted a measure without waiting for a mandate from their constituents. If we supposed that this paragraph was intended to be read in America, we should conclude from it that the author was merely incapable of correct reasoning. But from internal evidence it seems probable that the sentiment is intended solely for a German audience, and that its aim is to demonstrate that Prince v. Bismarck is essentially as good a representative of self-government as Washington and Madison. If so, we have nothing to say in regard to it, beyond the mere suggestion to Dr. v. Holst, that however bad an institution Tammany Hall may be, it at least did not corrupt our American universities, nor pervert the moral sense of our historians.

And now in regard to the War of 1812, which arouses feelings of such deep hostility on the part of Dr. v. Holst. We have no intention of fighting that celebrated war over again, but, in the face of the pure doctrinaire views of the German professor, we may, perhaps, state what is conceived to be the concrete view taken of the subject by the vast majority of Americans at the present day. The statement that the country was dragged into that war to satisfy the ambition of two young Congressmen may be best met by a quotation from Dr. v. Holst's own words in another place: "The history of the United States is a too serious and instructive chapter in the world's history to be brought into the domain of trifles by the explanation of its most significant phases of development as due to the pettiest and most grovelling impulses of single individuals, permitted by circumstances to play a part in them." Calhoun and Clay had, in themselves, no weight whatever, except so far as they were representative men.

The truth is, that as the present century began, the fruit of the Constitution began to ripen. A new generation of men came on the stage, whose principal characteristic was an intense sense of nationality. The first of these was J. Q. Adams, whose passionate devotion to this ideal may be seen by any one who will cast a glance into his Diary, or any of his controversial papers; the second was Clay; and the youngest, Calhoun. Dr. v. Holst does small justice to Clay in this respect. From the beginning to the end of Clay's long career, devotion to the dignity, the prosperity, and the harmony of the Union was his one rule of action. Calhoun fell away from him on one side, and Adams on the other. Both these men had a clearer insight than he into the heart of the situation. But Clay remained to the last what he had been at first, the unconditional supporter of nationality.

For years before the War of 1812, the younger portion of the community, especially in the West and Southwest, had been wrathful at the ignominy of the situation into which the two old parties had brought the country. Between the timid and undignified policy of Jefferson on the one side, and the narrow factiousness of the remnant of the Federalists on the other, they found no vent for that energetic self-assertion which belonged to their age and their situation. It was the rebellion of this youthful, and, no doubt, arrogant and reckless, spirit against the domination of what it considered an unpatriotic and cowardly party rule which brought on the War of 1812. Clay and Calhoun were able to force the declaration of war, simply because they represented that spirit, not because they were ambitious. And their power was itself a very fair measure of the extent to which the Constitution had succeeded in its work of building up a strong sense of nationality in the people.

As for the share that Madison had in the declaration of war, and the motives that impelled him to it, Dr. v. Holst is hardly to blame for taking a view which has been almost universally taken by Americans themselves; yet it would seem as though he might have applied for the benefit of Madison the same principle of political criticism which he has very properly adopted in regard to Calhoun; and this with the more propriety because Madison, of all the leading characters in American history, was the one who felt most keenly the burden of responsibility, and who was most sincerely conscientious in his public acts. To attribute his course to a desire for re-election to the Presidency, when it is perfectly reconcilable with the most patriotic motives, is, in Dr. v. Holst's words, "to bring history into the domain of trifles."

Finally, in regard to the War of 1812, it ought to be said that, so far as that war has still an interest to Americans, it represents now, as it did then, the self-assertion of a young and proud people just becoming conscious of their own future. Opinions will always differ very greatly as to the policy of such a war, and the motives of the individuals who were most active in causing it to be declared; but, so far as the nation is concerned, we state a mere fact when we say that of all pages in American history since 1789, the one which most Americans would be least willing to efface is this same War of 1812. And this for good and sufficient reasons. The American is by no means proud of his military appearance during that war, and the glories of Lundy's Lane and Chippewa have faded. It is not on account of military glory that this war is still popular. Nor is it even on account of naval glory, though it must be confessed that there are probably very few Americans now living to whom it is not to this day a subject of occasional rejoicing that on the 19th August, 1812, the British flag was hauled down from the stump of the "Guerriere's" mizzen-mast, and so some at least of the long series of British insults and outrages were at last atoned for. Nor is it merely because that war probably exhausted the national resentment, and so prevented other and more bloody collisions. The reasons why the War of 1812 is and always will be popular are, in the first place, because there is such a thing as self-respect in a nation, and that war was, in its essence, simply a rough and somewhat clumsy assertion of that self-respect, for the first time in the national history; and, in the second place, because it did more to strengthen the national feeling than all the twenty-five years that had preceded it. And yet it is quite true, as Dr. v. Holst asserts, that it was a party war. Perhaps he will explain how it could have been anything else than a party war, when, on his own postulates, nationalism was always the single great issue in politics, and the party out of power was necessarily a particularist party. Any war in those days must have been a party war, but the advantage of this one was, that it taught one part of the country a lesson of national feeling which, to this day, is keenly felt. New England learned then, once for all, not to trifle with the Constitution and with the Union.

It would be well if we could dismiss with equal peremptoriness the criticisms to which the political influence of the slave power gave rise. Unfortunately this is a chapter of American history which admits of no defence or palliation. Slavery warped the Constitution itself in a manner that for the time amounted to absolute perversion. Yet from a constitutional point of view we have a right to require the historian to be true to his own creed. Dr. v. Holst sets out with the assertion that the clew to our history during the last century is the struggle between nationalism and particularism. He considers the leaning of the Constitution towards State rights a fatal defect. The object of his book is to demonstrate this abstract proposition. He must then hold to his thesis.

The framers of the Constitution had difficulties enough to encounter, but there was one difficulty which they had no reason to foresee and never could have provided for. Had they contemplated the probability of such a development of the slave power as subsequently took place, they would certainly have abandoned their task in despair. The Constitution was not intended to be subjected to such a strain. Nor is this any fault of "the Fathers." As Dr. v. Holst has correctly pointed out, the great development of the slave power in politics was due to economical causes which were of a later origin, and the original concession made to the slaveholders in the Constitution was made on the theory that if there was any truth in the fundamental principles of human liberty, that truth was sure to vindicate itself by steadily undermining and destroying slavery. The principle was correct, although it worked itself out in an unexpected way. From their point of view the compromise was wise and proved the practical good sense of the parties to it. Their business was "to form a more perfect union." This they did, leaving the future to demonstrate the truth of their fundamental principles, so far as necessity compelled a temporary departure from them at the outset. Economical causes subsequently gave to slavery a prodigious development. It became a power in politics. For the first twenty-five or thirty years the Constitution had been subjected to the full strain of its State-rights tendencies, under conditions more unfavorable than were ever likely to recur, and had not only made head against them, but had fairly conquered and bound them, so that there seemed to be no reason to apprehend further danger from that side, when suddenly, under the guidance of Calhoun, the slave power seized upon the old and almost exploded theory of State rights, vamped it up, gave to it a superficial varnish of logic, and so breathed into it new life. But that life was due not to the "inherent defect" in the Constitution in countenancing State rights, but to the unexpected development of the cotton industry. What Calhoun really defended was, not State rights, but the slave power; and what the North really had to fear was, not State rights, for if Calhoun had become President he would in all probability have been as strong a centralizer as Jefferson, but the perversion of the Constitution to the interests of slavery instead of those of freedom.

The concessions of the North to the slave interest are again a very fair measure of the success of the Constitution in doing its work of forming a more perfect union. No doubt it is true that more and more as time went on the finer sense of political principle was sacrificed to the growing passion of nationality: but for all that the Constitution was doing its work, and considering that it was now called upon to vindicate its existence against a greater enemy than its founders had ever dreamed of; considering that this simple declaration of certain practical rules of government was now the only instrument for preserving the nation from a peril so colossal and so terrible that one now stands aghast at it, and our foreign critics can actually taunt us with having "torn each other to pieces during four years in the most frightful civil war recorded in history"; considering that as a matter of fact the Constitution did its work and that the nationality it created was so tremendous a force that at the first moment the slave power ventured to raise its hand against it, that moment the North suffocated the slave power in its own blood, —surely we may, as Americans, venture to hide the wounds which the Constitution suffered during those years when it was our only hope, and still retain for it that veneration which, if not idolatry, is, we are bound to confess, something very near it.

We have no intention of deprecating foreign criticism or of excusing inexcusable faults; but we have a right to claim and we do claim that the Constitution has done its work. It has made a nation. It has thoroughly vindicated the good sense and practical statesmanship of its framers. And more than this, in spite of the many shortcomings and petty drawbacks which are so well catalogued in this book, the people of the United States, as they pass further and further from the vital struggles which characterize this first period of their national history, are quite right in believing that, above all the details of human weakness and corruption, there will appear in more and more symmetry the real majesty and force of the national movement. If the historian will only consent to shut his eyes for a moment to the microscopic analysis of personal motives and idiosyncrasies, he cannot but become conscious of a silent pulsation that commands his respect, a steady movement that resembles in its mode of operation the mechanical action of Nature herself. As one stands in the presence of this primitive energy, the continent itself seems to be the result of agencies not more unlimited in their power, not more sure in their processes, not more complete in their result, than those which have controlled the political system. And if it be true that the moral of our history is correctly expressed in the aphorism quoted from the Prince v. Bismarck, that "sovereignty can be only a unit and it must remain a unit,—the sovereignty of law," then the history of the United States during its first century is surely entitled to the credit of having developed that principle with a rigor and on a scale which is not without its majesty and pathos.

The "Independents"

in the Canvass

Henry Adams' last serious venture into politics occurred in 1875 and 1876 when he tried to reorganize the Independent party which had been virtually wiped out after the nomination and defeat of Horace Greeley in 1872. He had no confidence in the Independents' ability to put up another candidate in 1876, but he hoped, at least, "to organise a party of the centre and to support the party which accepts our influence most completely." The Independents might control the balance of power between Democrats and Republicans, and thus force the choice of better candidates than the two major parties would naturally incline to.

The results of Adams' efforts are related in the following article which was written in collaboration with his brother Charles. The Independents showed their weakness as soon as the regular party nominations were made, and "that rope of sand, the Independent party," dissolved precisely as the Republican managers hoped it would. The bitterest blow among all these events, although it is carefully disguised in the article, was the reversion of Carl Schurz to party regularity. "I cannot help laughing to think how, after all our labor and after we had by main force created a party for Schurz to lead, he himself, without a word or a single effort to keep his party together, kicked us over in his haste to jump back to the Republicans." As if in repudiation of his lost leader, Adams decided to come out for the Democratic candidate, Samuel J. Tilden.

This decision, and the political attitudes in general that were given full play in the October, 1876, number of the North American, *brought about a rupture between Adams and the publishers of the* Review, *James R. Osgood and Co. Adams was glad to be relieved of the editorship which had become burdensome to him, and the publishers were forced by his resignation to bring out the obnoxious issue as he had left it. They eased their consciences by inserting the following disclaimer on the table of contents page: "The editors of the 'North American Review' having retired from its management on account of a difference of opinion with the proprietors as to the political character of this number, the proprietors, rather than cause an indefinite delay in publication, have allowed the number to retain the form which had been given it, without, however, committing the Review to the opinions expressed therein."*

Just before the first meetings intended to have a bearing on the Presidential nominations for the campaign now going on were held, Mr. W. M. Evarts[1] one day remarked to Carl Schurz[2] that the Republican party in its then condition reminded him of nothing so much as of an army whose term of enlistment had expired. Mr. Evarts is justly famed for the witty and incisive way in which he expresses what other people think, but he has not often had the good fortune to hit off a happier simile than this. It included in ten words a pamphletful of political insight, and accounted at once for that large amount of individual action which is such an essential feature in the present canvass. The field is full of stragglers.

On the slavery issue the Republican party enlisted for the war. So far at least as the loyal States of the Union were concerned, it numbered among its leaders or in its ranks a very considerable pre-

[From the *North American Review*, CXXIII (October 1876), 426-467. Unsigned.]

[1] [William Maxwell Evarts, Attorney-General in the administration of Andrew Johnson 1868-69; Secretary of State during the administration of Rutherford B. Hayes 1877-81. He defended President Johnson in the latter's impeachment trial, and served as counsel on the American side in the Geneva arbitration of the *Alabama* claims.]

[2] [Republican senator from Missouri 1869-75; one of the leaders of the Liberal Republican movement and of its convention of 1872 that nominated, against his wishes, Horace Greeley for the presidency. His support of Hayes led to his appointment as Secretary of the Interior in the Hayes administration.]

ponderance of the political virtue and intelligence, and of the disinterested public spirit of the community. It mustered, of course,
its train of camp-followers and stragglers and adventurers,—those
who joined its ranks at the eleventh hour, and even just before the
striking of noon,—who were as loud-mouthed and repulsive a set
of political vagabonds as ever canted about principles or hungered
after loaves and fishes. For a number of years this element, as a
whole, retained its proper position at the rear. In proportion, however, as the objects for which the party was organized became accomplished facts, it assumed a greater and greater prominence,
until at last it secured for itself an almost undisputed ascendency.
This was not unnatural, but it none the less indicated the close of
a term of service. Accordingly, about the time when those who
never knew what a principle was had pushed their way to the front
and were confidently appealing to a glorious record, those who had
made the party and inspired its policy through its years of active
life found themselves once more pondering over new issues and
striking out in independent action.

With the Democratic party the case was somewhat different. The
very completeness of success which deprived the Republican party
of its occupation in great degree re-created an occupation for the
Democracy. That party, as such, had, anterior to the war, been long
and laboriously formed as the Northern ally of the slaveholding
oligarchy of the South. Into it had naturally drifted the great mass
of the political ignorance, corruption, and venality of the free
States, and, throughout the Rebellion, it constituted simply a cowardly and traitorous opposition, always gravitating heavily towards
its ancient allies, but utterly unable, from want of that direction to
which it was accustomed, to originate a policy or to conduct a respectable opposition. A lifedom of leading-strings had wholly
unfitted it for independent political action. The close of the war did
not at once restore to it either a lead or a policy. The old slave
oligarchy was utterly ruined, and it took time for the new South
either to organize a policy or develop political leaders. The lapse
of eight years, however, supplied that need, and at the elections of
the year 1874 it became apparent that the South, as such, was once
more a political power, though no longer cemented and welded to-

gether by the one overshadowing interest of a property in slaves. In place of this, however, there was a new and temporary bond of common action,—the desire and determination on the part of the white population in those States to recover their political independence in the Union, and to throw off the odious rule of the enfranchised Africans. This, on the other hand, it had been the whole aim and object of the reconstruction policy to prevent. Thus gradually but surely the South once more became a political unit, and, as it did so, the Democratic party of the North, true to its instincts and traditions, gravitated towards it and assumed at last the shape of a coherent opposition. The Republicans had restored to it a mission. It is always so in revolutionary times. It was so in England in 1649, and in France in 1793. Moderation and wisdom in the use of victory won through civil strife are rarely given to individuals, almost never to parties. In our own case, when the Republican party undertook, as the phrase went, to "reconstruct" the South, it fairly overstepped the bounds of moderation, and went to work to reorganize a thoroughly disorganized social, political, and industrial system on preconceived theories which were wholly at variance with actual facts. By more than accomplishing their own work, they thus made work for their opponents. Accordingly the party which had been so skilfully organized by the dominant South to be its faithful political ally, after fifteen years of demoralization and defeat found itself once more rising into prominence as the protector of a struggling and dominated South. Thus the presidential election of 1876 finds the deep ground-swell of the great rebellion storm only slowly subsiding. The blow is over and will not revive; the South is a wreck in pressing need of repairs, and to insure her getting them is the present work of the Democratic party, while it remains for the Republican party to see that in the process the great results of the war are not disturbed.

So far, therefore, as the momentous political issues of twenty years ago are concerned, little remains over which to struggle. During the present canvass issues, side-issues, and after-issues will, indeed, be manufactured out of it; sometimes by very honest and very dull men who, having once learned to talk on a certain subject, have no faculty of speech on any other; and sometimes by very cunning and unscrupulous men, who will work on the old passions and the old hatreds as long as they can possibly hope to get themselves into office, or to keep themselves there, by so doing. In all this, however, there is something very uninviting and even repulsive to men who look upon politics as anything more than an occupation, and upon office-holding as anything more than a means of support. The continued dwelling upon the last phases of a stale excitement is neither a philosophical nor an ennobling pursuit. It is small matter for wonder, therefore, that the number of those who act independently of all party affiliations is continually increasing. The wonder rather is that the majority still cling to the ruts. Meanwhile it is now proposed to discuss, as temperately as may be, the considerations likely to influence the former class either in voting or abstaining from voting in the present election.

It was the action of these men in holding a conference at the Fifth Avenue Hotel in New York, on the 15th of May, which constituted the first important act of the campaign, and in no small degree gave a character to it. Political conferences are always dangerous things to meddle with. Not infrequently they produce results directly opposite to what is desired by their originators. It was somewhat thus with that which gathered in New York in May upon the call of Mr. Schurz and his friends. The assemblage was large, miscellaneous, earnest, and intelligent. Made up of men who cared little for office and who were deeply dissatisfied with existing political conditions, it was apparent enough that circumstances might easily arise which would impel them to a united action. Nor in such case was it at all improbable that their action would exercise a decisive influence on the results of the campaign. The difficulty in their way arose from the fact that the men there gathered were thoroughly representative men,—that they actually had behind them a large constituency,—and they represented that constituency most directly in that they asserted a perfect independence of all party organizations. They were in fact a company of Independents; only, as such, they happened to be just as independent of each other as they were of the party "machines." Accordingly they agreed only in negatives. They did not even attempt to suggest, much less did they think of laying down, any positive line of action. Indeed, hardly any two were there with the same purpose.

Some desired to force the nomination of Mr. Bristow[1] upon the Republican party; others that of Mr. Tilden[2] on the Democrats. There was a general and determined feeling of hostility to Messrs. Blaine, Conkling, Morton, and Hendricks, which in case of their nomination wished to have everything prepared for an organized and emphatic opposition, independent if need be. This result, indeed, was by some secretly hoped for; though the majority undoubtedly stood ready to accept from either of the regular parties any nomination which carried with it a reasonable assurance of reform. The pressure it was sought to bring about was on the conventions at Cincinnati and St. Louis. Measures looking towards independent action were regarded with suspicion and simply as a last resort.

Having adopted a vigorous and ringing address, and appointed an executive committee to insure action in certain contingencies, the conference dispersed. The Independent Voters had retired to their homes, and now it remained for the party managers either to conciliate their support or drive them into a movement of their own. The two conventions were then held, and resulted, the one in the defeat of Mr. Blaine, and the other in the nomination of Governor Tilden. The result was in neither case all that the Independent Voters as a class could have desired, but, on the other hand, both parties had placed themselves in a position which made outside action practically impossible. In other words, the nominations made and platforms adopted at St. Louis and at Cincinnati were in neither case the best, but in each case they were good enough. There was nothing from which an appeal could be taken to the country at large, with any prospect of success. They

[1] [Benjamin H. Bristow, appointed Secretary of the Treasury by President Grant in July, 1874. He acquired considerable reputation as an independent and a reformer after his smashing of the Whiskey Ring which, however, led to a personal conflict with Grant and Bristow's resignation in June, 1876. He was a prominent candidate at the Republican convention of 1876, but was bypassed in favor of the less controversial and less known Hayes.]

[2] [Samuel J. Tilden; elected Governor of New York in 1874, he had a distinguished record as a reformer. Nominated by the Democrats for the presidency in 1876, he received a majority of the popular votes, but lost the election when the contested electoral votes of Oregon, Louisiana, South Carolina, and Florida were awarded to Hayes by a Commission specially appointed by Congress.]

were, in a word, perfectly calculated to satisfy the average voter. Accordingly, no sooner were they announced than those who had met in the Fifth Avenue Hotel in May seemed in an agony of impatience to declare their adhesion to the one side or the other. In this respect they displayed only that lack of discipline and absence of leadership which is almost invariably the fatal defect in such attempted combinations. Could they have held together, or acted upon the party organizations with any degree of concentration, it can scarcely be doubted that before the campaign was over they could have forced their own issues to the front and dictated their own terms of adhesion. As it was, however, the instant the nominations were made the members of the conference resembled nothing so much as a group of discreetly clad clergymen caught out in a thunder-storm without any umbrellas. There was something absurdly ludicrous in the haste with which they got themselves under cover. The papers were full of their telegraphic despatches, and wherever two or three were gathered together an Independent was among them defining his position. Mr. Schurz speedily appeared with a manifesto on one side, and Mr. Godwin[1] on the other; while the body of the Independent vote, which it had been the object of the conference to concentrate, found itself free to make its own choice of candidates and platform, with only one thing absolutely certain, that in neither case were they wholly satisfactory, and that injudicious haste had rendered the action impossible through which alone an improvement could be compelled. Though any positive or united line of conduct has, therefore, ceased to be possible, the principles which may be expected to control the individual course of those who now hold themselves aloof from party lines are none the less worthy of consideration. The average politician to the contrary notwithstanding, there is a hereafter to every election. Whichever party succeeds in electing its candidates, the Independent Voter will have political duties of some sort to perform. In the first place, so far as the present campaign is concerned, he must make up his mind whether he will follow Mr. Schurz into the support of Governor Hayes, or Mr. Godwin into that of Governor Tilden; or whether he will, declining to sup-

[1] [Parke Godwin, son-in-law of William Cullen Bryant and associated with him in the editing of the New York *Evening Post*.]

port either candidate, quietly stay at home and abide the development of events, the course of which he can neither plainly discern nor greatly influence. Having decided this question for himself, it yet remains for him to have his mind clear as to the course it will be his duty to take, whichever party comes into power.

In considering these questions it is well in the first place to try to get a perfectly clear perception of the issues involved in the campaign. That he may do this it is absolutely necessary for an intelligent being to close his ears to the discussion generally carried on. In that, words supply to an altogether inordinate degree the place of ideas. Of the three elements, therefore, into which every campaign discussion may be decomposed,—rubbish, formalities, and essence,—it is here proposed to devote very few words except to the last. Under the head of campaign rubbish may, in the present case, safely be classed all the rambling discussion of the war records of the several candidates, and their opinions prior to the Rebellion or the Mexican War; also the charges and counter-charges made as to their transactions in mules, their stealing railroads, plundering widows and orphans, "dodging" taxes, issuing "shin-plaster" currency, the number of watches they own, and the date at which they may have purchased pianos. Personally all the candidates are respectable gentlemen. They have passed their lives before the communities in which they live, and been honored and trusted. As to the views they may have entertained twenty years ago, it is to be remembered the War of the Rebellion closed in the year 1865. The issues at stake between the years 1848 and 1860 are now just as much settled beyond the peradventure of reversal as those involved in the War of 1812 or the Revolution. The records of Governor Hayes and of Governor Tilden anterior to 1861 have, therefore, sentiment apart, just about as much bearing on the living issues of this campaign as their opinions on the Hartford Convention or the Darwinian theory of evolution. No one can deny that the mass of trash and rubbish of this description—constituting, as it does, nine tenths of the campaign literature—has its influence. Unhappily, mud-flinging is to a very large class of mankind one of the more enjoyable features of every canvass; and, as there are said to be German counties in Pennsylvania where votes are regularly at each election cast for General Jackson, so a not inconsiderable portion of the community now does, and for the next fifty years will, measure every candidate, not by his acts of the day, but by what he said or thought in 1860, or did or did not do during the Rebellion. Citizens of this description unquestionably cast votes, and it is only proper, therefore, that a fair proportion of the discussion of every campaign should be devoted to them. They are, however, not entitled to the whole of it.

Excluding, therefore, all these topics from consideration here, there yet remain the formalities of the campaign and its essence. Among the formalities should be classed the proceedings of the party conventions, including those meaningless arrays of platitudes which are regularly dignified by the name of platforms, and are supposed to beguile unthinking and inexperienced voters; and in this class belong, also, those ponderous campaign speeches of the great party "statesmen," in which, at regular intervals, they define their own positions and demolish "the other man." In the essence of the campaign are the personal characters and surroundings of the several candidates, their letters of acceptance, and their party associations; everything, in fact, which throws any reliable light upon the probable tone of the incoming administration, the line of policy likely to be adopted by it, and its practical ability to carry that policy out.

And in the first place, as respects the formalities of the campaign. Certainly there is in the present case little enough either in the action of the conventions, the framing of the respective platforms, or the ponderous eloquence of the party "statesmen" to excite enthusiasm or to influence the calmer judgment. Estimated by their professions merely, there would seem to be absolutely no ground of choice between the parties. There has been nothing like the canvass in this respect since 1852, when Whigs and Democrats vied with each other in servility to the slave oligarchy. An intelligent foreigner, coming here now and reading the two platforms in order to get an idea of what the election hubbub was about, would assuredly be most reminded of Swift's "big-endians" and "little-endians." Throughout, the two declarations of principle are so curiously identical that, with one minor exception and the omission of the regular campaign denunciation, they might just as well be exchanged and each party accept the other. Especially is this the case in regard to what are called the great results of the war. One party insists on their unconditional acceptance, and the other party accepts them unconditionally.[1]

[1] In support of the correctness of this proposition, the declarations contained in the two platforms on the prominent issues involved in the canvass are set forth below in parallel columns. In view of the savage denunciation for utter political profligacy in which partisan organs have indulged towards those who professed themselves ready to act with either party which put certain men in nomination, these extracts supply a good deal of food for reflection.

CONSTITUTIONAL AMENDMENTS

Republican Platform

"The power to provide for the enforcement of the principles embodied in the recent constitutional amendments is vested by those amendments in the Congress of the United States; and we declare it to be the solemn obligation of the legislative and executive departments of the government to put into immediate and vigorous exercise all their constitutional powers for removing any just cause of discontent on the part of any class, and for securing to every American citizen complete liberty and exact equality in the exercise of all civil, political, and public rights."

Democratic Platform

"We do here reaffirm our faith in the permanence of the Federal Union, our devotion to the Constitution of the United States, with its amendments universally accepted as a final settlement of the controversies that engendered civil war."

["If the duty shall be assigned to me, I should not fail to exercise the powers with which the laws and Constitution of our country clothe its chief magistrate, to protect all its citizens, whatever their former condition, in every political and personal right."—*Governor Tilden's Letter*.]—Author's note.

SPECIE PAYMENTS

Republican Platform

"In the first act of Congress signed by President Grant, the national government assumed to remove any doubts of its purpose to discharge all just obligations to the public creditors, and 'solemnly pledged its faith to make provision, at the earliest practicable period, for the redemption of the United States notes in coin.' Commercial prosperity, public morals, and national credit demand that this prom-

Democratic Platform

"We denounce the failure, for all these eleven years of peace, to make good the promise of the legal-tender notes, which are a changing standard of value in the hands of the people, and the nonpayment of which is a disregard of the plighted faith of the nation.

"We denounce the financial imbecility and immorality of that party which, during eleven years of peace,

So far as words count for anything, therefore, there is not on this last point a hair's breadth of difference between the parties, and the issue becomes merely the practical one,—Under which organization in power will the wounds caused by the war soonest close?

ise be fulfilled by a continuous and steady progress to specie payment."

[A motion pledging the party to the Resumption Act of January, 1875, was rejected on a *viva voce* vote, without a count.]—Author's note.

has made no advance towards resumption, ... and, while annually professing to intend a speedy return to specie payments, has annually enacted fresh hindrances thereto. As such hindrance we denounce the resumption clause of the act of 1875, and we here demand its repeal."

CIVIL-SERVICE REFORM

Republican Platform

"The best interest of the public service demands. . . . that senators and representatives, who may be judges and accusers, should not dictate appointments to office. The invariable rule in appointments should have reference to the honesty, fidelity, and capacity of the appointees."

Democratic Platform

"Experience proves that efficient, economical conduct of the governmental business is not possible if its civil service be subject to change at every election, be a prize fought for at the ballot-box, be a brief reward of party zeal, instead of posts of honor assigned for proved competency and held for fidelity in the public employ; that the dispensing of patronage should neither be a tax upon the time of all our public men, nor the instrument of their ambition."

On certain other points, which must, in the eyes at least of embodied party wisdom in convention assembled, be of great public moment, if we may judge from the prominence always given them, the resemblance of sentiments would be enough to convict an author of plagiarism.

SOLDIERS AND SAILORS

Republican Platform

"The pledges which the nation has given to her soldiers and sailors must be fulfilled, and a grateful people will aways hold those who imperilled their lives for the country's preservation in the kindest remembrance."

Democratic Platform

"The soldiers and sailors of the Republic, and the widows and orphans of those who have fallen in battle, have a just claim on the care, protection, and gratitude of their fellow-citizens."

Of course those whose whole political stock in trade lies in stimulating sectional hate and in repeating the noisy watchwords of the war—the Boutwells, the Logans, and the Mortons—will insist to the end of this century, and, should they live so long, to the end of the next, that it will always be an act of madness to trust the great results of the war in any hands but their own. Some weight, however, ought in reason to be given to practical experience in coming to a conclusion on this point; and practical experience teaches a very different lesson. It is an indisputable fact that peace and quiet and good-will between the races has been restored in the South exactly in proportion as the States formerly in rebellion have passed into Democratic hands; hatred, outrage, and the dreaded color line have been perpetuated exactly in the degree that the administration at Washington has succeeded in bolstering up the "reconstructed" State governments. Judging by the experience of the last eight years, it would seem that the one great boon the

---

RAILROAD LAND-GRANTS

Republican Platform	*Democratic Platform*
"We reaffirm our opposition to further grants of the public lands to corporations and monopolies, and demand that the national domain be devoted to free homes for the people."	"Reform is necessary to put a stop to the profligate waste of public lands, and their diversion from actual settlers by the party in power, which has squandered two hundred millions of acres upon railroads alone."

It is useless, however, to extend this curious collection of "principles." The real distinction seems to come down to this,—the leaders of both parties confess to a close similarity of sentiments, but the Republican leaders assert that the Democrats *will* not carry out their professions; to which the Democrats, with some force, reply, that the Republicans *have* not carried out theirs. But it is when the Republicans "charge the Democrats" with "treason," with "repudiation," with "imbecility," with "incompetence," and solemnly warn "the country against trusting a party thus alike unworthy, recreant, and incapable"; and when the Democrats "denounce" the Republicans for "improvidence," "financial imbecility and immorality," "profligacy," and divers other more especially enumerated "abuses, wrongs, and crimes,"—it is then, in the utter demolition of "the other man," that the fight waxes hot, and the lines of demarcation are sharply drawn. It is all very funny in its way, and irresistibly suggestive of the famous Eatonswill election, and the tremendous controversies between Mr. Pott of the "Gazette," and Mr. Slurk of the "Independent" [in Dickens' *Pickwick Papers*].

sensible negro at the South should pray for would be to be let alone by his "protectors" at Washington,—to be allowed to assume, as quietly and speedily as he can, those natural relations to which, in spite of everything, he must at last come with the community in which his lot is cast. Certainly, wherever this has taken place his position and prospects are infinitely preferable to what they are confessed to be where it has not taken place. During eight long years the United States government has meddled and muddled in the affairs of South Carolina and Mississippi and Louisiana, with results over which the least judicious cannot but grieve. It is now nearly as long since it lost all practical power to interfere in Virginia, in North Carolina, and in Georgia; and now could Mr. Morton or Mr. Boutwell or Mr. Logan even pretend to assert that the condition of affairs as respects the colored race is better in South Carolina than in North Carolina, or in Louisiana than in Arkansas? The usual reply to this argument is, not a denial, but a gloomy reference to the order which reigns in Arkansas as compared with that for which Warsaw was once renowned. The question, however, for reasonable men to decide, is not whether the existing condition of affairs is perfect,—that we know it neither is nor, under the existing condition of affairs, can be,—but is it better in North Carolina than in South Carolina, in Arkansas than in Louisiana? The answer does not admit of doubt. When, therefore, the Independent Voter is told that he must vote for Governor Hayes lest perchance the existing condition of affairs in South Carolina and in Louisiana may not be perpetuated for yet another four years, and those States may become even as North Carolina and Arkansas, it may fairly be asked whether he is not justified in regarding such an argument as an insult to his intelligence. So far, therefore, as the condition of the South is concerned, the less the leaders of the Republican party have to say on the subject, except in the form of appeals to passion, hatred, and prejudice, the better. With their impotent system of protection which did not protect, and of meddling which only aggravated prejudice, they have themselves during the last six years been the most dangerous enemies the freedmen have had. The argument on this issue is overwhelmingly in favor of that organization which can set up Virginia against Louisiana and Georgia against South Carolina.

Practically, however, though exercising an immense influence on its result, this question is not at issue in the present canvass. Whichever party gains the ascendency, the South will in the future be left to work out its own destiny undisturbed by national interference. The Republican leaders have small desire to repeat the blunders of Louisiana, and Mr. Boutwell's proposal to remand Mississippi into a territorial condition stands not much better chance of adoption than would a counter proposal from Mr. Ben. Hill to take the same course towards Massachusetts. The Southern question in its present phase is consequently doing duty in the canvass as a powerful and well-understood campaign tonic,—a species of "Plantation Bitters," calculated to revive a flagging public interest. Abandoning the further discussion of it, therefore, to those by whom it is prescribed, it remains here to consider the formal attitude of the two parties on the questions practically at issue in the immediate political future of the country.

There are three great phases into which all political movement resolves itself,—the revolutionary, the constructive, and the administrative; and these three also necessarily succeed each other in the order in which they have been named. Within the last sixteen years it is apparent that this country has passed through two, and the more momentous two, of these phases, and is now entering upon the third. The period between 1861 and 1865 was one of unquestioned revolution; that since 1865 has been one of construction, which, well or ill done, will be complete as soon as South Carolina and Louisiana are permitted to reach the position of rest towards which they are irresistibly tending. That time cannot long be deferred. Meanwhile, naturally enough, as the special work of each period taxed all the energies and absorbed all the attention of the country, its administration fell into greater and ever greater abuses. At last, during the first administration of President Grant, the abuses which had gradually crept into the currency, the tariff, and the civil service began to excite the public attention. After the tremendous issues and excitements of the war, however, these purely administrative questions seemed almost trivial. Large bodies, also, move slowly, and for a time the great mass of voters went quietly and smoothly along in the old established party ruts. It was only necessary for the leaders to raise the familiar slogan, and at once the clan was all excitement; while, for the rest, a well-rounded platform declaration answered every purpose. This state of affairs cannot, however, last forever. A period during which questions of administration only will be at issue and engage public attention in this country is, in the natural order of things, near at hand. The time must soon come when a formal enunciation of platitudes by party conventions will cease to be accepted in lieu of the faithful observance of pledges of administrative reforms. The progress of the canvass now going on,—the emphatic summoning of the war issues to the front and the relegation of the new issues to the rear,—the suspicious prominence of the vagabond element in party control, and the loud and ominous creaking of the two political "machines" as they grind out a result,—the success with which the political Bourbons have again succeeded in distracting the public attention from the abuses of the present by reviving the passions of the past,—all these unmistakable indications show that the time has not yet come. To hasten its arrival would seem to be the object the Independent Voter should have most at heart. That he may contribute to that end he must, in the first place, so far as in him lies, hold parties to a rigid and absolute adherence to their professions; and when they fall short of those professions, he must do what he can to defeat them, regardless of consequences. If he is not prepared for this, he may as well at once acknowledge his political impotence and satisfy himself with a constant perusal of his Bible.

Apart from the condition of the South, which has already been sufficiently referred to, there are at this time three living questions before the country: these are the matters of reforming the civil service, the currency, and the tariff. Among the Independent Voters there are those who give the palm as respects importance to each of these issues, and to each of them the conventions addressed themselves. So far as the formal utterances contained in the platforms are concerned, it is not too much to say that, judging by the experience of the past, no observing man will attach the slightest weight to them. Take the clauses in the Republican platform, for instance, relating to the currency or civil-service issues, and compare them with the expressions on the same subjects contained in the platforms of the same party four and eight years ago. They are certainly no stronger; they assuredly offer no new guaranties. As respects the Republican party, the case needs but to be stated. With an assurance which would be comical were it not insulting, that party which, throughout six of the last eight years, has had complete and absolute control of every branch of the government, and during that time has not made even a decent pretence of carrying out its solemn pledges, now comes forward and unblushingly asks to be intrusted with a new lease of power on the strength of more pledges. Neither can the party lay its shortcomings as respects the currency and the civil service at the door of the President. It was the party,—the party leaders,—and not the President, who was responsible there. It was the Republican Congress which, in the face of its party pledges, passed a bill to inflate in time of peace a fraudulent paper currency; and it was that same Congress which contemptuously broke down its President's single weak attempt at civil-service reform. And, after doing this, the party convention puts forward a claim to be retained in office on the ground that it has nominated a new man to succeed President Grant, and that, though it fulfils no pledges, its "tendencies" and "impulses" are good! Twice in eight years has it dealt in noble professions; continuously through those years has it mockingly refused to make them good; and now when it proffers them again—*credat Judæus Apella!*

Neither is it much better with the Democrats. On one of the three living issues, that of the tariff, they certainly promise better than the Republicans, who in that respect are simply hopeless. Thoroughly believing in the Chinese system, no inroad into the outrages and absurdities of protection can be hoped for from that quarter. It is not easy, therefore, to see how any person who gives a prominence to free-trade among the living issues of the day can vote a Republican ticket. As to the Democrats, they promise well, but can they be relied on to make their promises good? Judging by the wretched fate of the admirable tariff measure introduced into the House by the chairman of the Committee of Ways and Means during the last session of Congress, they cannot. So, also, on the currency and on the question of civil-service reform. Democratic platform promises can be had to order and in quantity to satisfy the most eager; but as for performance, the votes of the

Democratic House of Representatives and its action as respected its officers were not reassuring.

It is, however, hardly better worth while to waste time over empty political formalities than over unadulterated rubbish. Declarations of principles adopted by Presidential conventions are not intended by those who frame them to express intentions, and should not be so construed; they indicate "tendencies" and "impulses." The profound indifference with which the platforms adopted at Cincinnati and St. Louis were received by the outside world afforded excellent evidence that this fact was generally appreciated. The lessons of the last eight years were not wholly forgotten. Passing on then to the essence of the campaign, the candidates are first to be considered.

In this respect unquestionably the *prima facie* advantage is with the Democrats. If there is one thing wholly opposed to the spirit of our institutions and the earlier and better usages of the country, it is the political trick of nominating unknown and untried men, on the ground that, being unknown and untried, they have no "record" to defend. Every voter is thus left free to imagine what he pleases, and, of course, *omne ignotum,* etc. In such a matter as this, it is best, perhaps, to try to see ourselves as we would see others, and as others must see us. As practical men, priding ourselves on our capacity for self-government, what would we Americans say if we saw, for instance, the Liberal party of England, on a defeat of the Disraeli Ministry and a dissolution of Parliament, select as their candidate for Premier, not Gladstone, not Forster, not any well-known or experienced leader, but some unknown, untried Lord Lieutenant of Canada, who had been a colonel in the Sepoy insurrection, and a silent member during one short Parliament? In the days of Washington and Jefferson and Madison we should have smiled, not without just pride, and remarked that, republicans though we were, we at least did not make a farce of our government. Yet this is exactly what was done by the Republican party in the case of Governor Hayes. Of that gentleman all that is known is to his credit; he seems to have been a gallant and meritorious officer during the war; a faithful though uninfluential member of Congress after its close; and more recently a respectable, though not brilliant, governor of Ohio. Since his nomination, the verdict of those most intimately acquainted with him has been decidedly in his favor, and they have joined in warmly recommending him for the Presidency. All this, however, ill supplies the place of long public service. To fill the Presidential chair with success a man must have a great deal more than those good purposes, fair talents, and high character which serve to make him locally respectable. He must have judgment, firmness, insight, and, above all, experience in a much more than ordinary degree; and that he has these is only shown by trial. Even the most enthusiastic supporters of Governor Hayes can hardly, as yet, claim that his election would be anything more than a political experiment; more of an experiment than the election of James K. Polk in 1844, for he had at least been nationally prominent as chairman of the Committee of Ways and Means, as Speaker of the national House of Representatives, and as governor of Tennessee before he became a Presidential candidate. Governor Hayes's nomination, so far as the previous reputation of the candidate is concerned, is just about on a level with the nomination of Pierce by the Democrats, in 1852, or that of Fremont by the Republicans, in 1856; and it is infinitely below that of Lincoln by the Republicans, in 1860, for he had brillantly sustained himself through the most trying canvass in the history of the country against the ablest and most unscrupulous of all the Democratic leaders. It is, therefore, difficult to see why Governor Hayes does not fall within that class of candidates who were so well pictured in the address adopted by the Fifth Avenue Hotel conference, as candidates whom Independent Voters could *not* support; men "who, however favorably judged by their nearest friends, are not publicly known to possess those qualities of mind and character which the stern task of genuine reform requires; for the American people cannot now afford to risk the future of the Republic in experiments on merely supposed virtue or rumored ability, to be trusted on the strength of private recommendations."

The Democrats, on the other hand, whatever may be thought of the men, unquestionably have put in nomination candidates both of whom were among their most prominent party leaders,—men

with whom and whose records the whole country was thoroughly
familiar.[1] That, on certain essential issues, and especially that of
the currency, these two leaders were at variance is indisputable,
but this merely proved that they were party leaders, and all who
considered such variance a good ground for refusing to support
the ticket had full notice of the fact, and could shape their course
accordingly. Good or bad, the candidates were tried men, and the
whole country knew how to measure them; the appeal was to
facts, not to fancy; to the record, not to the imagination. And this
is the only sound practice. In so far, therefore, the Democratic
party has in this campaign approached much more nearly than
its opponents to a correct usage; its record may be bad or otherwise, but it has at least nominated the most distinguished reformer
in its ranks.

Passing from the individual candidates, it is now necessary to
consider the letters in which they accepted the nominations. For,
recognizing as if by common consent the utter contempt into
which convention platforms have fallen, each candidate went to
work at once to form a platform of his own, upon which, and which
only, it was universally understood he would be expected to stand.
These letters of acceptance were also received by the public as
alone setting forth the distinctive issues of the campaign. Of the
letter of Governor Hayes it may fairly be said that it was in every
respect more satisfactory, far more manly, honest, and outspoken,
than the platform of the convention which nominated him. It
breathed, indeed, a refreshing atmosphere of frankness and almost of ingenuousness. On the other hand, to those who have heard
and read of the dark ways of American politics, this very honest
freshness of tone is suggestive of some unpleasant doubts. And
here is the difficulty in substituting a letter for a record of trial.
Any ingenuous boy can write a letter full of high purpose; but
to carry out that purpose in the Presidential chair requires a full-
grown, stalwart man. For reasons presently to be shown, Governor

---

[1] [Tilden's running mate was Governor Thomas A. Hendricks of Indiana. He
had been a leader of the Democratic opposition in the Senate from 1863 to
1869, and was elected Governor of Indiana in 1872, one of the first Democrats
elected to a northern governorship after the war. He ran again for the vice-
presidency in 1884 on the ticket with Grover Cleveland, this time successfully.]

Hayes's letter seems more calculated to inspire in the mind of the Independent Voter a belief in the good intentions of the writer, than a faith in his knowledge of men or his practical acquaintance with the difficulties of the position he may be called upon to assume. In other words, in reading his letter the mind instinctively goes beyond the programme laid down in it, to dwell upon the circumstances under which the writer must try to carry that programme out.

If elected President of the United States, Governor Hayes will not be, as many seem to suppose, an autocrat ruling the nation through four years by his own supreme will, but a chief executive officer merely, with very limited powers, who must look somewhere for support, if his administration is not to result in ignominious failure. Now Governor Hayes's letter was to the last degree outspoken in two respects: first, as regards a radical reform in the civil service, and, secondly, on the question of a return to specie payments. Upon each of these issues he went far in advance of the stereotyped and intentionally meaningless phrases which had long, to the grim delight of the party leaders, done harmless platform service, and placed himself directly on the line of the most pronounced reformers. Indeed, so outspoken was he that it has been more than once publicly suggested that the portions of his letter relating to these two issues were inspired, if not directly written, by Mr. Schurz. Be this the case or not, the question yet remains whether the man who, as candidate for the Presidency, wrote, or adopted in his letter of acceptance, the language referred to, can appreciate the circumstances by which, in case of his election, he must be surrounded. Facts are proverbially stubborn things. A President has got to encounter them, and must measure his language accordingly. If he does not so measure it, he will probably find in the end that it is not the facts which suffer. Now, what are a few of the probable facts of President Hayes's administration?

First, as respects the currency. An act of Congress passed in January, 1875, provides for a resumption of specie payments at the United States treasury on the first day of January, 1879. If Governor Hayes is elected President, his first Congress will meet in December, 1877,—less than thirteen months before the process of resumption is to begin. In his letter of acceptance Governor Hayes gallantly says: "I regard all the laws of the United States relating to the payment of the public indebtedness, the legal tender notes included, as constituting a pledge and moral obligation of the government, which must in good faith be kept. . . . If elected, I shall approve every appropriate measure to accomplish the desired end, and shall oppose any step backward";—thus fully committing himself to carry out to the letter the provisions of the act of 1875. This was certainly most creditable to Governor Hayes's heart; but how does it speak for his head? Is it possible that any man competent not to occupy but to fill the Presidential chair can believe that the long and cautious process absolutely essential to a quiet resumption of specie payments in this country can be compressed into the brief space of thirteen months? It involves, somehow or other, a very considerable contraction of a much-inflated currency, a very considerable accumulation of gold, and consequent disturbance of exchanges and values. At least it involves all these, unless previous experience is wholly at fault. Can all this be accomplished in thirteen months, even though a thoroughly docile Congress seconds the exertions of an earnest President? That when the act of 1875 was passed, specie payments might have been resumed by this country, to its own great relief, by January, 1879, or even before that date, no student of financial questions for a moment doubts. But neither does any such student doubt that long and cautious preparation will be found an essential preliminary to resumption, whether it is to take place on the 1st of January, 1879, or any other day. A quiet and easy resumption is a port into which this country is destined neither to drift nor to drive; it has got patiently to beat there, in the face of wind and tide. That the United States, by the act of its constituted authorities, is pledged to pay its notes in specie on the 1st day of January, 1879, is indisputable; that not to fulfil the pledge will be a discreditable act of semi-repudiation is no less true than mortifying; and that, for this humiliating condition of affairs, the party which nominated Governor Hayes is responsible, is most undeniable of all. It was that party, in full and unchecked control of the government in all its branches which passed the Resumption Act of 1875, and refused even to consider the supplementary legislation which could alone make that act effective. Before Governor Hayes so implicitly pledged himself to carry out the provisions of the Resumption Act, would it not have been wise for him to consider whether the time in which it was possible to do so had not already passed? Should he not in common prudence, while announcing himself as opposed to any step backward, have insisted on the early passage of the legislation necessary to make resumption possible, and declared that the day for resumption should be deferred with his consent only after an honest effort to resume had at least been made and failed? As it is, Governor Hayes has pledged himself to ignore facts. He has placed himself in an apparently impossible situation, from which he will have to recede; he has pledged himself to the act of resumption at a near date, instead of to the means by which resumption is to be made possible at any date. He has thus got himself into a false position to begin with, from which nothing but almost a miracle of good luck can save him. The Senate may, in case of his election, good-naturedly relieve him by passing the House bill repealing the date fixed for resumption, before his accession to office; but unless they do this, the chances are heavy that one of President Hayes's early acts will be to affix his signature to a measure repealing or at least deferring that date to which he now stands so explicitly committed.[1]

So also as respects a reform of the civil service. Far be it from any reflecting citizen of the Republic to deny that the present national system of civil service is a disgrace. Founded as it is upon the principle that the national offices constitute, not a sacred trust, but a rich mass of plunder, the prospect of securing which will incite opposing factions to use their utmost exertions, it has become a standing peril to our institutions. The work of reforming a corrupt system which has been in use now for fifty years, and to which every bad and active element in the country is thoroughly wedded, is no trifling task. On this point, however, something must be said at greater length in another part of this paper. In the present connection it can receive no justice. Recognizing the magnitude of this evil, however, every intelligent voter must respond to those portions of Governor Hayes's letter of acceptance in which he says that it is the question of "paramount interest" that "at first the

[1] [Resumption of specie payments was actually carried out on the date set by Congress.]

President, either directly or through the heads of departments
made all the appointments, but gradually the appointing power, in
many cases, passed into the control of members of Congress. The
offices in these cases have become not merely rewards for party
services, but rewards for services to party leaders. This system . . .
is felt, I am confident, by a large majority of the members of
Congress, to be an intolerable burden and an unwarrantable hin
drance to the proper discharge of their legitimate duties. It ough
to be abolished. The reform should be thorough, radical, and com
plete. . . . If elected, I shall conduct the administration of the
government on these principles, and all constitutional powers vested
in the executive will be employed to establish this reform."

Yet brave as these words are, they cannot but suggest to any
one not wholly ignorant of our political system and its workings
grave doubts as to the practical capacity of the candidate who
wrote them. They are so very ingenuous! They seem to evince such
a painfully simple faith that Messrs. Cameron and Conkling and
Morton and Blaine and Howe and Sherman and Logan will at once
see the matter in its correct light, and will gently and submissively
accept the situation; yielding their dearly prized patronage, for
the pure love of reform, without a murmur, much less a thought of
resistance! It may be so; but if it is, then will the Afric indeed have
changed his skin and the leopard his spots!

A thorough and correct appreciation of circumstances and an
accurate adjustment of means to end is generally looked upon as
a first essential to human success. Don Quixote performed, perhaps, a very gallant feat of arms when he ran a tilt with the wind-
mill; but he came out of his tournament badly damaged none the
less. It is surely to be supposed that Governor Hayes appreciates
the fact that, if he is elected President of the United States, his
powers as such will be limited, and his administration can be saved
from lamentable and utter failure only through the hearty and
united support of some organized party. No President in this
country can carry on an administration to suit himself on senti-
mental or guerilla or Ishmaelite principles. He has got to have a
party behind him, or fail. Not only this. Common-sense, as well
as political usage and party courtesy, always dictates to the President-elect who are to be his confidential advisers and whom he

can look to for effective support. These are, in the first place, his unsuccessful competitors in the nominating convention; and, in the second place, those who brought about his nomination and subsequent election. Not only does this usage exist in our political system, but it is a sound one. Through it alone can a responsible, in place of a personal, administration be secured. President Grant, looking upon his Cabinet as a sort of civic staff, ignored the usage, picking up his heads of departments as he met men he fancied in the cars, at dinner-tables, or in the club-rooms; and the result became known as "Grantism." Lincoln always recognized it, and it saved his administration. In the early days of the Republic no President thought of disregarding it. In the case of Governor Hayes, who are the advisers thus designated to him in advance? His chief competitor in the convention was Mr. Blaine; his rivals, who secured his nomination over Secretary Bristow, were Messrs. Morton and Conkling. Senator Sherman from Ohio first named him prominently as a candidate;[1] Secretary Cameron manipulated the Pennsylvania delegation in his favor at the decisive moment; and Secretary Chandler is the head of the national executive committee which is organizing the campaign for his election. Under these circumstances, how is President Hayes to form a Cabinet in sympathy with his views as respects the civil service? Upon his inauguration he will find Messrs. Cameron and Chandler holding from his predecessor the portfolios of War and of the Interior. No names in the country are perhaps so thoroughly identified with the idea of a debauched, "machine" civil service as those of Cameron and Chandler. The first is own son to his father;[2] and the last has always delighted in heaping his coarse and clumsy ridicule on every sug-

[1] [Sherman was named Secretary of the Treasury by Hayes.]

[2] [The father, Simon Cameron, was political boss of Pennsylvania for many years. He was Lincoln's Secretary of War during the first year of Lincoln's administration, but was removed for his corrupt and political management of the office. From 1867 to 1877 he was a member of the Senate, resigning his seat and, with the help of a compliant legislature, passing it on to his son, Don Cameron, when Hayes refused to keep the younger Cameron in his cabinet as Secretary of War. Don inherited his father's position in Pennsylvania affairs and was re-elected to the Senate in 1879, 1885, and 1891. In later years Adams and Don Cameron became friends, and Cameron's second wife, Elizabeth, a niece of Senator John Sherman, was perhaps his most intimate correspondent.]

gestion of civil-service reform. These two prominent contributors to his election President Hayes must unceremoniously eject from the Cabinet or his professions will assume a very hollow sound. Having disposed of them, who is to be his Secretary of State? If usage is to be observed, it must be Mr. Blaine. But the name of Blaine is at the present time very far from being pleasantly associated in the minds of conscientious reformers. To put it very mildly, his nomination as Secretary of State would fail to inspire confidence.[1] Nor is the case any better as respects Messrs. Conkling and Morton, Governor Hayes's other competitors. Their entrance into the Cabinet could and would receive but one interpretation. Yet these are the party chieftains without whose active support in the Senate President Hayes's administration must be from its very inception a foregone failure. He cannot ignore them without destroying his party; he cannot be guided by them without tacitly abandoning all his brave professions. Yet the issue is one he has got to meet on the threshold of the White House. Frankness is not always wisdom; honesty is not always identical with capacity. Mr. Bristow had been tried and had a record; no declarations from him would have been needed. The country knew what he could do. Governor Hayes promises well, but he has not been tried, and he seems somewhat disposed to ignore stubborn facts. The proof of the— But, as Hamlet remarked, "the proverb is something musty."

The same ingenuous simplicity which has been referred to in connection with other portions of his letter shone out in the self-denying ordnance at its close, as respects a re-election. It was simply puerile. If Governor Hayes does not know, he should know,

[1] [Blaine's unsavory financial relations with railroads interested in legislation during the years of his membership and speakership in the House had been under investigation by a Congressional committee earlier in the year. He had received, without payment, large amounts of stock from the Little Rock & Fort Smith Railroad, and his name was mentioned in the expense accounts of a lobbyist employed by the Union Pacific. Blaine never satisfactorily explained his dealings with these corporations, nor were the sources of his private income ever very clear. The House investigation ended inconclusively when Blaine was appointed Senator from Maine. Adams always had a peculiarly intense distaste for Blaine; refused to meet him socially; and used him as the model for Senator Silas P. Ratcliffe in his novel *Democracy*.]

that if he proves but in a small degree the man his friends claim him to be, if he carries out but in part the great reforms he suggests, his re-election for a second term will be a matter of such transcendent public consequence, that no pledge he could now give would or should for an instant stand in the way. In fact, there is something about this whole proposition for disqualifying Presidents from re-election which to a reflecting man is thoroughly exasperating. What, again, would the American people say of a European community which, after a short fixed period of administration, forever disqualified its Gladstones and Disraelis and Thiers and McMahons and Bismarcks and Cavours and Nesselrodes,—turned their most experienced servants neck and heels out of the direction of public affairs at just the time they had proved themselves qualified for it?—and that, too, on the avowed ground that public and private virtue were so weak that those whom the people chose could not be trusted with power, lest they should abuse it to their private ends! Undoubtedly we should say that such a people made a farce of government, and were only fit to live under the effete sway of an hereditary ruler. In the present campaign both candidates give countenance to this childish expedient to secure reform, and Governor Tilden even goes so far as to suggest a constitutional disqualification. He fails, however, to explain why he limits his reform to the Presidency. He is now governor of a great State, and as such disposes of a large amount of patronage. He or his successors may use it to secure a re-election. Would it not be well, therefore, while about it, to institute a wider reform, and to solemnly disqualify for re-election every executive officer in the Union, down to the village mayors? This, at least, would lay the axe at the root of the evil. It is such contemptible tinkering as this which brings the whole system of written constitutions into contempt. It is suggestive of nothing so much as of trying to extinguish a first-class conflagration by squirting on it with a syringe. If the political virtue of our community and our public men has indeed fallen to so low an ebb that disqualification has become necessary to prevent a breach of trust, then the end is not far off, and the depriving ourselves of the power to re-elect a Washington, a Madison, or a Lincoln will not help us much. Governor Hayes probably meant all that he said in his letter on this subject; as to

Governor Tilden, he, doubtless, reiterated the jargon in another form, not without some sense of shame, and simply because his opponent had set the bad example.

If the marked peculiarity of Governor Hayes's letter was its simple directness of tone, Governor Tilden's was chiefly noticeable for its extremely labored character. It plainly showed throughout that the writer felt himself placed by the circumstances of his nomination in a false position, from which he was trying to extricate himself, and with no very marked success. His position was indeed a false one. The currency question and administrative reform are Governor Tilden's two battle-horses, and as regards both the action of the St. Louis Convention greatly aggravated his difficulties. In the first place, the Convention had insisted on denouncing the Specie Resumption Act of January, 1875, as a fraud, and demanded its repeal. As governor of New York Mr. Tilden had, however, distinctly identified himself with the Specie Resumption Act, and had gone out of his way to cause it to be re-enacted by the State Legislature. Consequently, however much others might denounce that law as a sham and a fraud, it did not lie in his mouth to do so. The act was not only denounced, but its repeal was demanded, and, so far as the Democratic House of Representatives was concerned, obtained; thus going as far as the party then could to establish the principle that in America there is no such thing as a national faith which all parties respect, but that the nation's pledge is binding only so long as the party in control of the government at the time it is given remains in power. A more humiliating experience for a Presidential candidate would not have been easy to imagine. Not only did Governor Tilden have to renounce his record before he began his campaign, but he did it very awkwardly. He might well, it would seem, have declared his adherence to every position he had assumed, and again insisted that a resumption of specie payments in January, 1879, had been perfectly feasible in January, 1875, though it had wholly ceased to be so in July, 1876; and that the national disgrace and long-continued business depression involved in the repeal of the Resumption Act belonged, not to him nor to the Democratic party, but to that other party, which, though in power, had named only a day of resumption, and had then wantonly and ignorantly refused to make any preparation to meet that day. In reluctantly assenting to the repeal of the date of resumption, he did, therefore, but recognize and bow to that inevitable necessity for which his opponents only were responsible. This would all have been perfectly true and thoroughly tenable. But this position Governor Tilden did not take. To the thorough believer in hard currency his letter was at once most entertaining and most reassuring reading. It was so, however, from the fact that it contained a body of most admirable doctrine at great length, and yet the writer never once distinctly said what he meant. In this respect his utterances were the exact counterpart to those of Governor Hayes. He showed by what he said that he understood his subject, and by what he did not say that he fully appreciated the difficult circumstances by which the end he had in view was surrounded. Accordingly he preached contraction at great length, and never once named it; he strongly advocated resumption, but denied that it was necessary to fix any day for it. He quietly ignored his own record on the act of January, 1875, and, while he certainly did not greatly conciliate the inflation and paper-money element of the West, he succeeded in alienating a very considerable portion of the hard-money sentiment of the East.

Notwithstanding all this, however, it would be very difficult for any well-informed man to read Governor Tilden's letter of acceptance, or his earlier official utterances on the subject of the currency, without being satisfied that he is thoroughly master of it. He is by nature a financier, and a strong one. Unless the record of his life belies him, it is not unsafe to predict that if elected President he will practically be his own Secretary of the Treasury, and a successful return to specie payments will be the one great aim and monument of his administration. There is, also, another side to this question worthy of the careful consideration of those who believe that a return to specie payments is the one thing now needful to an early and complete restoration of national prosperity. The great obstacles in the way of that result have hitherto been an utter lukewarmness on the part of the Republican party and the dead opposition of the Democrats. To bring the thing about, therefore, not only has the Democratic opposition got to be neutralized, but a real life must be infused into the Republican support. If it did nothing else, the election of Tilden would spike the whole inflationist battery; for, through him, the friends of a sound currency could and would take possession of the Democratic organization, and through its agency could spur the Republicans up to something remotely resembling a fulfilment of their pledges. For the last eight years each party on this subject has tried to make its record as little objectionable as possible to the paper-money element,—the Democrats promising everything that was bad, and the Republicans doing nothing that was good. It is very hard to see how matters in this respect would be bettered by Governor Hayes's election. He, certainly, by himself and through his Secretary, could do no more than has been done by President Grant and Secretary Bristow. He would apparently meet in Congress the same negative support and the same positive opposition. The presence of a hard-money Democrat in the Presidential chair would, however, at once destroy this equilibrium of forces. Unless a Republican opposition was utterly wanting to every pledge, it would have to oppose any specie-resumption measures proposed by President Tilden on the ground, not that they went too far, but that they did not go far enough. This would at once change the character of the struggle. The bidding would tend upwards instead of downwards. Then at last something might be hoped for.

The currency question is, however, one comparatively easy of solution. The country has been through that experience many times before, and, like certain forms of physical disease, it is disfiguring, weakening, and painful, but it never kills; somehow or other we always struggled through before, and we shall do so now. The civil-service issue is, however, quite another matter. That, as an attempt will presently be made to show, is unsettling the very foundations of the government, and on that the position of Governor Tilden and his supporters is far from an ideal one. Governor Tilden, it is true, has sought especially to identify himself with the popular demand for administrative reform, and to-day in the public mind he personifies it to a very considerable extent. Nevertheless, what reason is there to suppose that Governor Tilden even knows what administrative reform is? Does he not confound it with thief-catching and ring-smashing? These are, it is true, very admirable occupations in their way, and that Governor Tilden has achieved remarkable results in them will be denied by no one who will take the trouble to read the article entitled "An Episode in Municipal Government" in the present number of this Review.[1] Nevertheless, though the requirements and consequent usages of the last few years have carried us very far in that direction, it may yet be questioned whether the qualities of a chief of police are exactly the qualities which would be most strongly developed in an ideal President of the United States. It cannot be too freshly borne in mind that a reform of the civil service to be worth anything means a return to the earlier and better usages of the Republic,—to the system in vogue before Andrew Jackson debauched it,—to the time when the word "patronage" conveyed no idea of plunder, and men held office under the government in the same way they now hold it in banks or insurance companies. Does Governor Tilden, when he talks of administrative reform, mean this? Does the party behind him mean it? Are they really prepared to cut down and eradicate, root and branch, the atrocious spoils system originated by their great idol, President Jackson? Or, instead of this, does Governor Tilden mean a vigorous system of thief-catching and ring-smashing under and supplementary to the spoils system? That he should mean a thorough, radical, genuine reform seems scarcely possible; and it is ludicrously evident that his associate on the ticket, Governor Hendricks, means nothing of the sort. That gentleman is perfectly willing to talk of civil-service reform, but he premises that, before entering upon it, "no man shall be retained [in office], on any consideration, ... who has furnished money to corrupt the elections." As this convenient test would, under the present system, notoriously cover all existing office-holders who have been "assessed,"—and who among them has not been?—one more "clean sweep" appears to be in Governor Hendricks's mind a necessary preliminary to the work of reform; which seems to be very much the system which President Jackson inaugurated.

In attempting to forecast his probable action on this subject, it cannot be forgotten that Governor Tilden has passed his life in the most thoroughly corrupt political atmosphere in the New World; that he is a Democrat dyed in the wool, and that, since the days of

[1] [The article, by Charles F. Wingate and Charles F. Adams, Jr., described the overthrow of the Tweed ring in New York City, an action in which Tilden played an important part.]

its origin, no one good or honest thought or act respecting the civil service has ever come out of the Democratic party. To reward partisans, and to catch them if they stole, has been the highest level as respects the use of public office to which that organization has ever risen. It there any good ground on which to rest a confident belief that either party or candidate has now at last risen to a higher level than this?

It is, however, the very doubt, or rather the absence of all doubt on this point, which brings the reflecting Independent Voter to the very heart of the issue in the present canvass. As respects a radical reform of the civil service, there is no ground to hope that the question is yet ripe for solution, and matters must apparently be a great deal worse before they can be materially better. In what respect are the Republicans better than the Democrats? True, they did not introduce the vile system, but they were apt pupils; nor has the country witnessed a greedier or more disgusting scramble for office than took place when the "party of reform" came into power in 1861. Since then they have only not completely sacked their own camp. The truth is, neither party is in the least degree sound on this question; nor have the party leaders on either side the slightest intention of making thorough work of it. The country is not educated up to it, and does not yet demand it; and until it is educated up to it, and does demand it, the thing will not be done. Under these circumstances, the very worst which could happen would be just such a half-way measure of reform as Governor Hayes might, by his utmost effort, succeed in exacting from an unwilling party,— that wretched degree of reform which just neutralizes action by making a radically bad system externally endurable.

It was Horace Mann who one day exclaimed, in despair over the slowness of the educational movement, "The fact is that I am in a hurry, and God Almighty isn't!" The great difficulty with the civil-service reformers is, that they have been and still are in such a pressing hurry. Governor Hayes, for instance, in his letter of acceptance, contemplates curing a disease of fifty years' growth, imbedded all through our political system and woven into its every fibre, in a single term of four years. In the same spirit, Mr. Schurz confidently predicts, in the event of the election of Governor Hayes, "the employment in the government service of not one more party agent;

the abolition of the spoils system; opposition to these reforms on the part of the spoils politicians in Congress; the overthrow of this opposition at the next Congressional elections." In Mr. Schurz's judgment, therefore, one half of President Hayes's single term will suffice for the whole work. Of course, if these two gentlemen do not underrate the magnitude of the task, there is nothing more to be said on the subject. It is a comparatively trifling work, and will be accomplished in a short space of time. If, however, the evil is of that portentous magnitude which others equally qualified to form an opinion have supposed, if it is, indeed, sapping the foundations of the government, then two things may safely be predicted of its cure: first, that it will not be effected in any one Presidential term; and, secondly, that it will be the work of a party specially organized to do it, and not of a party formed to do other work and which assumes this one merely because its so doing may induce a half-in-earnest country to retain it in power.

In America almost every one, even reflecting men, seems to suppose that nothing can be done except by a party in power; that the opposition has no functions to perform, can exercise no influence in the grand result. Accordingly, the advocate of administrative reform is now told that he must vote for Governor Hayes, because he is committed to it; and he must vote against Governor Tilden, because he has no conception of it. Admitting the premises, the conclusion is very far from following. Let everything that can be said against Governor Tilden and the Democratic party, with their record, and in favor of Governor Hayes and the Republican party, with its "tendencies" and "impulses," be conceded for the sake of argument; let it be acknowledged that the success of the former in the pending election would be followed by a "clean sweep" and a revolting scramble for office, ending in a carnival of jobbery and corruption; let it be further conceded, though in the face of all experience, that the "tendency" of the Republican party is to reform, and that from those acting with that party only can reform ultimately be hoped for,—though all this be conceded, yet none the less the genuine, patient, thorough-going civil-service reformer would, in the present campaign, have good cause to cast his vote for Tilden. Before doing so he would probably argue thus. This question is one of necessarily slow solution. It goes back in its history to the beginning. It involves the whole subtle question of the allocation of powers under the Constitution,—a question infinitely better understood eighty years ago than now. The present phase of the issue itself originated more than half a century ago. Briefly stated, the difficulty is, that a strong President then perverted the entire patronage of the government into a mass of plunder, with which to reward his partisans; since then, still regarding it as plunder, the legislative has usurped the executive patronage out of the hands of weak Presidents, and, accordingly, we now have the legislative dispensing, as its own, the plunder of the executive. Any real measure of reform, therefore, involves, in the first place, a long and doubtful struggle between the executive and the legislative, in which the former will seek to recover the power which legitimately belongs to it, and of which it has been deprived. A collision between the executive and the Senate will be the first stage of the struggle, and to overcome an oligarchy like the Senate will require a vigorous executive. We are now electing a President, not for life, but for the short term of four years, and deciding merely whether the Republican or Democratic party shall, during that time, control the executive department. During the last eight years the Republican party has been, with the exception of two years only, in absolute control of every department of the government. They went into it with the fairest professions in regard to the civil service, every one of which they have treated with contempt and ridicule. They have not even made a pretence of regarding them. And yet, notwithstanding all this, in that party, and in that party only, are found those active elements through which a thorough administrative reform can be brought about. The difficulty, however, is an obvious one. The party has never, on this subject, passed through that preliminary hardening and solidifying of opinion which is gained only in opposition. No party organized for other ends ever did, or ever will, accomplish any considerable new work until, educated up to it in opposition, it goes back into power prepared and pledged to accomplish it. Certain necessary preliminary stages have to be passed through. In keeping the Republican party in power, therefore, the friends of civil-service reform, in so far as they have contributed to that result, have simply, after the manner of men, been good-natured, credulous, and impatient; they have magnified each four years into an eternity. After all, the longest way round may, in this case also, prove the shortest way home. There are limits to good-nature as well as to human patience, and men who are really in earnest do not like to be nourished too long on a somewhat insipid diet of "tendencies" and "impulses." It has sufficed for eight years, but before the end of twelve it may chance to grow monotonous. A wholesome defeat, followed by four years of life in opposition, might have a quickening tendency; it might ripen "tendencies" into intentions, and "impulses" into action, and promises into perform-ance. Judging by experience, it is very certain nothing else will.

The remedy, then, is a simple one. Remembering the broken promises of 1868 and of 1872, the would-be "party of reform" must be held to an absolute and unrelenting responsibility for them, and must go out of power, no matter who comes in. During the next four years it can be of far more service in opposition than in office; and, even if the corruption and abuses of the coming four years ex-ceed those of the last four,—a most improbable contingency, by the way,—it will but convince the people of the absolute necessity of reform and render the return to power of the reorganized Republi-can party a certainty of the future. After all, four years is, at most, a somewhat brief period of probation. In the case of the Democrats, sixteen have failed, as yet, to bring forth works meet for repentance. And, arguing thus, who could blame any determined civil-service reformer if he cast his vote for Governor Tilden, even though in so doing he voted also for Governor Hendricks?

Nor is this the whole argument in the case, nor, indeed, the strongest side of it. It must ever be borne in mind that the greatest present danger to be apprehended from the corrupt civil service arises, not from the fact of the spoils system, or the scandal of rota-tion in office, but from the utter subversion already suggested of a fundamental principle of our government, through the usurpation by the members of the Senate of the appointing power of the Presi-dent. In plain language, therefore, as a necessary preliminary to any effective measure of civil-service reform, the Senate has got to be compelled to surrender back to the executive its usurped powers. This it requires no very deep insight to know that body will never willingly do. Governor Hayes must have clearly foreseen the direct issue he was making when he said, in his letter of acceptance, that the control of the appointing power by members of Congress was an abuse which "ought to be abolished. The reform should be thorough, radical, and complete. . . . If [I am] elected . . . all constitutional powers vested in the executive will be employed to establish this reform."

In writing those words, could the Republican candidate for the Presidency have fully appreciated the nature of the struggle he was challenging? If so, how was it possible that he should have supposed that a single Presidential term would suffice for the work? The Republican party controls the Senate. That body is, indeed, the cerebral centre of what is best described as the Republican "machine." No matter who is elected President, the Senate will remain Republican. When President Hayes lays an exclusive hand on the patronage, he will lay a heavy, hostile hand on the whole famous "Senatorial group," and from that moment he divides his own camp, and exposes himself naked to his enemies. With Governor Tilden as President the case would be wholly different. In a struggle with an opposition Senate he would be backed to the bitter end by his whole party strength, and in all probability by the country too; for the Senate is not a popular body. As Jackson, supported by the House, broke it down once, Tilden might hope to do it again. The real friend of civil-service reform might well, therefore, be content to devote the next four years to the work of reducing, through the action of a Democratic President and House of Representatives, the Senate to its proper constitutional functions. The further work of reform might then be quietly and safely postponed to a later period. One thing at a time is enough, so that thing be done.

Against this it is usually argued that it will not be safe to trust the Democratic party in office, even for the brief term of four years, in view of the possible mischief it might accomplish in that time. The deprivation of the blacks of all civil rights, the payment of the rebel war debts, the pensioning of Confederate officers and soldiers, and numerous other similar visions of terror, are conjured up. With an argument of this character it is almost humiliating to be called upon to deal. Again, the existence and obstructive power of an organized opposition, this time controlling the Senate, is ignored; and that, too, by the leaders of a party which, in complete control of the government in its every department, through six years out of eight, piteously claims that its utter failure during all that time to fulfil any of its pledges was due to the presence of a contemptible minority. Experience is, however, after all, the best of guides, and experience is not without its lights on this subject. The "ins" always do, and always have, unanimously averred, with a fervor which can only spring from heartfelt conviction, that the incoming of the "outs" will be shortly followed by the final crack of doom. A good many credulous people, from force of habit chiefly, can always be relied on, also, timorously to accept this view of the subject. Two years ago it was nervously argued by the party leaders, in the same spirit, that the country could not be so rash as to elect a Democratic House of Representatives; to trust, etc., etc. Yet, looking over the field, and judging by the record, no truly Independent Voter could probably now be found who would not admit that the existence of an opposition majority in one branch of Congress has been, during the last year, a piece of national good fortune; and, also, that the record of that opposition body will, as a whole, compare more than favorably with the records of either the Republican Senate or the Republican executive. No party, however, ever enjoys an exclusive possession of all the political virtue and intelligence of the country; and, as a rule, where parties are at all equally divided, they enjoy these desirable qualities in about an equal degree. In the present case, in spite of the alarming irruption at the front of individuals of a class designated by Judge E. R. Hoar as "bummers," there is undoubtedly some reason to suppose that the Republican organization, under the strong impulse of its great start, does still contain somewhat more than its relative share of the better elements of our political life. The triumphant nomination of men of so low a political type as General B. F. Butler and his like, in some of the most intelligent of the Congressional districts of Massachusetts does, it is true, make the assertion either a little ludicrous or very melancholy; but none the less it is probably true. And yet, practically, what does the difference amount to? During the last eight years not a few States, North as well as South, have been under Democratic rule. What evidence is there that they have been worse governed than their Republican sisters? Governor Gaston administered the affairs of Massachusetts quite as satisfactorily as either his Republican predecessor or successor. So Governor Tilden has administered those of New York, and Governor Hendricks those of Indiana, not less creditably, so far as the world knows, than Governor Hayes did those of Ohio. The United States government has of late years passed through some very considerable political trials, and, remembering them, it surely cannot be classed as an act of rashness to venture the prediction that in these piping times of peace its perpetuity will not be greatly endangered by four years of Democratic ascendency. A sufficiently vigorous opposition, in control of the Senate, may at least save our institutions from any absolutely irreparable injury until the people can, two years hence, again come to the rescue. No! There are abundance of good arguments ready at hand to justify any intelligent man in voting for Governor Hayes, but this shambling appeal to the absolute wickedness of the other side is not one of them.

It is clear, then, from what has been said, that the interests of the Independent reformers are not, in the long run, the interests of the party organizations. It is clear that the reformers cannot honestly join either party organization except to obtain a special and temporary purpose. It is clear that they must pass from one organization to the other according as one or the other offers the best chance for obtaining reform. And it is clear that there are points of the most weight in the eyes of reformers in respect to which they have no choice but to struggle, as best they can, against the weight of both party organizations combined.

Let us then attempt to state as simply and distinctly as possible the reform platform. And since the reform here intended means, not currency reform, not revenue reform, not administrative reform, but all these only so far as they tend to result in political reform; since the common ground on which all honest men can meet is not that of restoring a sound basis to exchanges, or freedom to commerce, or decency to the executive, but that of purifying the political system and correcting the vices of political practice,—it is inevitable that reformers who mean to work together for any practical object and with any but visionary hopes of success should lay aside their peculiar hobbies and abstain from insisting upon individual theories. The field of reform is in itself so vast, and the hopes of reformers are so faint, that the least they undertake is likely to be beyond their force.

The single great end to which all reformers, whatever their private theories may be, must look is distinct enough; it is to overcome the tendency of our political system to corruption. All political systems, no doubt, have some tendency, greater or less, towards corruption. The peculiarity of ours is that it moves, and for fifty years has moved, in that direction with accelerating pace, and it has now arrived at a point where even the blindest patriots see that, unless the evil is checked, our political system must break down and some new experiment must be substituted in its place. The ground, therefore, and the only ground on which all honest men can unite and insist with one voice upon reform, is that of resistance to the corruptions of our political system.

These corruptions are the growth of the last fifty years. Previous to that time there were no doubt numerous cases of legislative and official dishonesty, some of which were fully as disgusting as any of the "carpet-bag" revelations. But there was no systematized political corruption, none that was more serious than the ordinary frailty of human beings, until about fifty years ago the present system of party organization, bred in the gutter of New York politics, was adopted by the entire nation. These party organizations, growing up outside the Constitution, wielding a power never dreamed of by the framers of the Constitution, began by assuming as their own property the patronage of the national as well as the state and municipal governments. Fortified and consolidated by this great and rapidly increasing source of pecuniary and political power, these organizations have steadily proceeded to other and even more corrupting acquisitions, until at length there is in the entire range of national, state, and municipal politics, with few exceptions, no considerable interest dependent upon legislation which does not pay or has not paid its tax to the support of a party organization; and, what is the most fatal of all symptoms, there are few interests engaged in secret evasions or violations of the law, robbing the public treasury and making private honesty impossible, which have not, as a condition of their existence, been made to contribute to the same political system. From such a state of things no result is possible except destruction, because it can generate nothing but corruption.

The problem of reform is then to devise such a system of measures as shall if possible cut up these evils by the roots. These meas-

ures, however, in order to stand even a remote chance of success
must be perfectly practical and not too far in advance of public
opinion and public prejudice.

It is obvious at a glance that currency reform, or return to specie
payments, is not so closely connected with this issue as some other
measures. A debased and fluctuating currency is rather a social
than a political evil. Party organizations may indeed at some future
day find means here too of drawing nutriment from treasury issues
but as yet it is the individual and not the party which looks to profit
from that source. Yet it is undoubtedly true that whatever tends to
shake the foundations of public morals, tends also and very strongly
to increase the power of party organizations. The reformer, how
ever, requires a return to specie payments most of all because until
the public can be brought to acknowledge principles of common
honesty, there is not the shadow of a hope that it can be persuaded
to grapple with points of political expediency.

Next to the question of returning to specie payments, nothing has
more keenly seized on public attention than the contests of the
Treasury Department under Secretary Bristow with the Whiskey
Ring. These were in fact contests of the national government with
creatures of its own creation. The strength of the Whiskey Ring
consisted in the extent to which it had succeeded in identifying it
interests with those of the party organizations. It is idle to suppose
that mere administrative reform can effectively deal with this evil
Administrative reform can do much. A careful and thorough revi
sion of the revenue laws, diminishing the inducement offered to
dishonest evasion and distributing the taxes over objects which car
neither be concealed nor are matters of discretion, will do more
But the utmost skill of administration, and the utmost care in fram
ing the laws, will at best cut off only one source of party support
It is true that this source is the most scandalous and the vilest; but
if reform is to be limited to this result, it will be a reform of the
slightest kind. If our modern statesmen stop here, they are mere
mountebanks. The evil will revive with the next turn of the political
wheel.

Tariff reform is of the same nature. It is a matter of course that
every true reformer must require a return to specie payments, a
revision of the internal-revenue laws, and a revision of the tariff
from any administration that claims his support. An entire abandon

ment of the theory of protection is essential to the purification of politics. Nor is it a matter of much consequence whether individual reformers accept or reject this article of their creed. If one part of the old system goes, all must go, and the reform movement will either be fruitless or it will carry out its principles to the end.

All these measures of reform, necessary as they are, attack merely the outposts of corruption. They would, if successful, considerably reduce the resources of the political organizations; but when it is considered how infinite the ramifications of these party supplies are, and how extraordinary the skill with which new sources are constantly developed, it is ridiculous to suppose that these measures, even if adopted to their utmost extent, would offer any permanent cure for the radical evils of our political system.

No serious impression can ever be made on those evils until they are attacked at their source; not until the nation is ready to go back to the early practice of the government and to restore to the constitutional organs those powers which have been torn from them by the party organizations for purposes of party aggrandizment. The fabric of party must be reduced to a size that corresponds with its proper functions. The relation between the party system and the constitutional system must be reversed.

The peculiar difficulty, the almost desperate character of this reform, arises not so much from the intrinsic strength of the parties whose wealth and power are to be attacked, as from the extent to which they have twisted their roots round and among the organs of the Constitution itself. Fortune or popular feeling may perhaps rescue the executive from their grasp. Not impossibly the more popular branch of Congress may follow the executive in abandoning such hold as it has on the patronage of the government. But the case is much more serious with the Senate. That body, if it had been created for the purpose, could not have been more ingeniously constructed to serve as the fortress of party organization and the focus of party intrigue. Such it has been from the earliest days of the Republic; such it must be until that government is in its grave. The long tenure of the senatorial office; the small number of Senators; their peculiar importance as the constitutional advisers of the executive in many cases where their advice is equivalent to command; their constitutional right to a share in the appointing power; their inevitable position, a consequence of their peculiar power, as heads

of the party organizations in their own States; and the equally inevitable consequence of bringing together in one small body the
principal heads of the local party organizations,—all combine to
make the Senate an almost if not quite irresistible agent of political
corruption.

To wring from the grasp of the Senate its established control over
the national patronage implies a struggle between the Senate and
the executive which may well shake our political system to its centre. It is this struggle to which all the clearest and coolest heads in
the country have looked forward as the next great political issue
since the close of the Rebellion. It is this struggle which our last
President shrank from and which our next President must inevitably
face.

The simplest form in which the least possible demands of reform
can for the time be met and satisfied is that of a law enacting that
all officers, except heads of department and their assistant secretaries, and such as may be specially provided for by the Constitution, shall hold their appointments during good behavior. That such
a law would be within the constitutional powers of the legislature
may be considered as established by the Tenure-of-Office Act. Objection on this score could have little weight. The only questions
that would seriously interest reformers are whether such a law
would be commensurate with the evil; whether its provisions could
be enforced without evasion; whether it might not end in still further disorganizing the government by giving to officials the unlimited right to intrigue against the President, at the very moment
it deprived the President of the power to protect his own administration by enforcing necessary discipline; whether, in short, it is
possible to adopt such a law without enacting also that any interference, direct or indirect, by any office-holder in the management
of party politics, or any attempt on his part, direct or indirect, to
control elections, shall be deemed a violation of good behavior, and
when proved to the satisfaction of the President, it shall be the
President's duty to remove such official from office.

The propriety of such a law is perfectly recognized by every
man who has watched the atrocities of the last four years, and the
cynical contempt with which office-holders, in open control of a
corrupt and venal party organization, have laughed in the face of
every decent remonstrant, and throttled every honest political opin-

ion within their party lines. The case may not be improved by encouraging them to defy the President also. The time, it is to be hoped, will come when conduct such as is now the rule among the servants of the people will be punished with some sharper penalty than removal from office; but so long as the American public crouches, in a sort of good-natured ignorance of its dignity, under acts of its officials which even in France would rouse forcible resistance, the utmost that reformers can hope is to obtain a recognition of the simplest principle, without insisting upon what is as yet unattainable.

This series of great measures implies, under the most favorable circumstances, many years of incessant struggle, and probably more than one serious political crisis. And even after all these measures have been adopted, if adoption is possible, there remains still a greater mass of corruption at the bottom of our political system than has ever been known in the party organizations of other constitutional governments. No national legislation can deprive parties of the absolute control of state governments, state patronage, and state legislation in party interests. No political wisdom has yet even suggested a satisfactory solution of the difficulties of municipal government; and so long as there are ignorant and vicious multitudes, so long there will be Tweeds and Sweenys to organize and manage the political machinery of the caucus and the convention. No professional skill can so frame legislation as to exclude the possibility of profitable fraud; and so long as there is money to corrupt, there will be parties to hide the corruption and to receive their reward. The struggle is to be one, not of our own day, but for an indefinite future, and the utmost that can now be hoped is not to destroy, but only to make head against, the political disease; not to expel it from the system, but to drive it from the national government back to its strongholds in the States and municipalities.

If the supremacy of party organizations is to remain unshaken, it matters comparatively little which of the two great parties is to conduct the government. Both are founded upon the same system, and both must lead to the same results. The hopes of reform lie entirely with the Independent voters and thinkers. One by one the great organs of public opinion have assumed the Independent position. One by one the honester and abler leaders of thought have followed and are following the same irresistible tendency. On this steady growth of Independent opinion the hopes of reformers are built, not on the momentary triumph of any party or of any party leader. And whichever party may in the impending election be elevated to power will command the active support of Independents precisely in that extent to which it shall initiate and honestly support the reforms here set forth.

Whether the Republicans or the Democrats succeed in electing their candidates, it is evident already that whoever is inaugurated President in March, 1877, will enter upon the duties of his office pledged to measures of reform. Then will come the time of trial, and just so long as the next President, be his name Hayes or Tilden, be he Democrat or be he Republican, respects his pledges, and honestly tries to make them good, so long will he be entitled to the uncompromising and earnest support of every honest Independent Voter. If Governor Hayes should be elected, there is reason to hope that Mr. Schurz may represent the Independent reform element in his Cabinet, side by side, perhaps, with Bristow, Evarts, or Curtis. In such an event it will surely be remembered that Mr. Schurz is the natural leader of the Independent Voters; that he, more than any other man in the country, personifies that which they wish to see introduced into politics; that he is the spear-head to which they are but a shaft. Nor is his constituency likely to fail him. It is not unsafe to say that, if President Hayes summons Mr. Schurz to be of the number of his advisers, every member of the Fifth Avenue conference, whether he voted for Hayes or for Tilden, or stayed at home, will give his administration an earnest and unqualified support as long as Mr. Schurz remains in it. His record is evidence that he would not long remain in it when the promises of 1876 had begun to prove as barren of results as those of 1872. On the other hand, if Governor Tilden is elected, it is probable that he, too, will summon to his councils some representative man like Mr. Wells or Mr. Godwin or Mr. Sherman, and, in that case, while he abides by his professions, no one who knows Mr. Schurz can for a moment doubt that he will yield him a cordial and loyal support. It is hereafter—when the election, with its fair words, is over, and the administration, with its hard acts, is begun—that the real struggle is to take place, and the Independent intelligence of the country must make itself politically felt.

Primitive Rights of Women

The immediate stimulus for Adams' essay on the "Primitive Rights of Women" is unknown, but there is a great deal of evidence to show that during much of his life he was drawn to women by a special sympathy and was deeply concerned with the question of their role in society. "The American woman of the nineteenth century," he said, "was much better company than the American man," yet her superiority to the man had not saved her from taking a path that threatened not only her own identity but the very existence of society. This was the path of imitation which had been forced on her by the man's refusal to honor her in her own sphere and by his complete absorption in the world of business and machinery. "The typical American man had his hand on a lever and his eye on a curve in his road . . . He could not run his machine and a woman too; he must leave her, even though his wife, to find her own way, and all the world saw her trying to find her way by imitating him." To Adams' view, then, modern industrialism and technology were breaking down, in America faster than elsewhere, the most ancient element in civilized human life, the family, "strongest and healthiest of all human fabrics."

The sexual equality that Adams was at pains to establish in "Primitive Rights of Women," therefore, was not intended as a contribution to the suffragist movement or the campaign for "women's rights." Adams' wish, rather, was to help in the redefinition of a true *feminine dignity on grounds more secure than those afforded by the "equality" of modern democracy. These grounds were present in woman's original character which was distinguished not by submissiveness or moral purity but by the power derived from sex. Her "monopoly" of reproduction—"the greatest and most mysterious of all energies"—gave her a claim, through the family, to an equality rooted in nature. She had but to believe in her own claim, or else become "sexless like the bees" in a "future reserved for machine-made, collectivist females."*

According to the generally accepted opinion of writers on Primitive Institutions, the original position of the married woman was one of slavery, or akin to slavery. By this phrase is meant not merely subjection to superior force, but to legalized force. In all ages, the weak were the victims of the strong, and were often treated with severity not essentially different from the treatment of slaves; but the exercise of force by the strong over the weak did not constitute slavery, even in the most barbarous societies. Unless the law declared men or women to be slaves, they were, in the view of the law, free, notwithstanding their inability to obtain redress.

The common view of marriage as a primitive institution implies in the man more than arbitrary superiority, such as he exercised over the child, which still remained free. The woman's slavery was assumed to be for life. As a child she was subject to the absolute authority of the male parent, extending over life and death. Her marriage originated, according to the most recent scientific historians, either in purchase or in capture; and in either case the woman was the property of the man. The wedding ring was the symbol of marital power. The right of the husband to sell his wife still survives in the popular traditions of England; the forms of capture are still common in barbarous society, and may be seen even in highly civi-

Revision of a lecture delivered at the Lowell Institute, Dec. 9, 1876. [Printed in *Historical Essays*, 1891.]

lized countries; while the forms of purchase are thought to be well-nigh universal. "While wives were captured, if there was any sense of property at all, wives would be regarded as property. When, at a later stage, they came to pass from the houses of their birth into alien houses by purchase, they would still be property."[1] The recorded history of early society offers numberless illustrations of the unbounded power which the husband exercised over his wife, and the Roman law was especially emphatic in extending over her the *patria potestas*, in which the Romans blended their conceptions of the family relation. "The family was based not upon actual relationship, but upon power; and the husband acquired over his wife the same despotic power which the father had over his children."[2]

Starting from the assumption that the wife was in origin a slave, either by capture or by purchase, the commonly received theory of her escape from this degradation assumed a gradual rise in the moral standard of civilized society, and finally attributed the complete triumph of women to the influence of Christianity, with its high moral ideals and its passionate adoration of the Virgin Mother.

Such seems to be the doctrine of modern investigators. In theory they have carried back the origin of society to a stage anterior to the institution of marriage,—a stage of communism. The original community is believed to have had no idea, or only a rudimentary idea, of private property; and as men emerged from the condition of animals, they possibly held all things in common within their communal association. Theoretically, men and women, like all else, in the earliest stage of society were communal property. No tie connected individual men and women together. No man had the right to appropriate any one woman to himself, nor had any woman the right to appropriate to herself any one man. Such communities were large families and small States, with a strongly democratic organization and an elected chief or chiefs. All their members were equal, for all were brothers and sisters. Mothers there were, but fathers were unknown. Where no permanent tie existed between men and women there could be no conception of paternity and no

[1] McLennan's Studies in Ancient History, pp. 136, 137. Edition of 1886.
[2] The Early History of the Property of Married Women. A Lecture delivered March 25, 1873, by Sir H. S. Maine. See the Early History of Institutions, p. 312.

notion of paternal authority. The mother alone was important in the parental relation. The earliest family therefore, so far as it could exist at all, was a system of relationship through women; and the germ of the future family organization was embodied in the mother, not in the father.

Such pure communism, if it ever existed in real life, ceased at a very early time. No such communal society,—that is to say, no society in which communal marriage was practiced,—has been found or is recorded as existing in times past; nor is it essential to history that precisely such an institution as communal marriage should ever have existed in the strictness of its forms. A mass of evidence has been collected, which leaves no reasonable doubt that the first organized human society approximated more or less nearly to this type. In all countries and through all ages its traces have been found; and in this respect the primitive tribes of Africa, of Asia, and of America, both north and south, unite in telling a common tale. In its day this social organization was a step in the progress of the race. Under the shelter of communal society man found such protection against the dangers that beset his first steps as to cause its development over the world. If primitive communism had not been beneficent in its results, it could never have attained such development. Wild as man was, and disgusting as the more degraded tribes and communities were, the best of them, and all those from which further advance came, were marked by good qualities, or they could never have risen to a higher stage. Many communities were doubtless mild in manners and not unhappy in their modest range of interests. Where the conditions of life were favorable and wilder hordes remote, these communities cultivated their common fields from year to year, from century to century, from era to era, and did no conscious wrong. They had wars, and these were no doubt cruel; they had superstitions, which were no doubt both cruel and gross; their range of thought was narrow and their mode of life low; their relations with the world beyond their tribal connection were those of war; but within the bounds of their own society they succeeded in constructing a social fabric that compared with any that succeeded to it for successful adaptation of means to ends. After it had long passed away the world still looked back to it with regret, and not a few of the prettiest and tenderest verses of the classical poets recalled that idealized golden age when men lived together as brothers, when peace and content reigned on earth, when mankind was not devoured by the thirst for gold, when all were of one family, and all the products of the earth or of industry were held by brothers in common.

Assuming that any typical form of primitive communal society ever existed, no long time can have elapsed before some communities must have begun to depart from the normal type; and in some cases this departure must have taken that direction which the strongest human instincts pointed out. Of these instincts few if any are more energetic than the instinct of property. Man loves most that which is his own; and that which he most loves he is most anxious to have for his own. Here and there in the rudest human society passions must have developed which are recognized even in animals. Probably this development went on simultaneously in many centres, and worked in many different lines. In this respect the characteristics of all the great races were already sharply marked at their first appearance in recorded history. We cannot know what special influences caused some to throw off more completely than others the old habits of communism, to substitute the practices of private property; but enough remains to show that the distinctions between races were to no small degree founded upon this difference of policy.

Probably the institution of marriage had its origin in love of property. Both men and women were united in this,—that whatever they loved best, they wished to possess. The usual theory holds that the communal system would not permit the gratification of this desire at the expense of communal rights, and that therefore men were driven to gratify their passion by purchasing or by capturing women from neighboring and hostile tribes. In support of this doctrine the extraordinary frequency of the forms of purchase and capture is relied upon as conclusive evidence; but if so, the position of the purchased or captured wife must have been regulated by laws very different from those that controlled the disposition of other purchased or captured property.

American students of primitive history have one great advantage. To them archaic communistic society is not, or at least need not be, a mere historical theory. The entire race of American Indians from

Behring's Straits to the Straits of Magellan were, and to a certain extent still are, in the stage of communism. The American Indian is the best representative of the social system to which he belonged. Communism in Europe and Asia has been disturbed or affected by subsequent complicated developments; in America it was subjected to no such strain. If it be assumed, as is becoming inevitable, that the American Indian was a branch from a primitive stock, from which it became separated at a very early day, and thenceforth pursued a course of development little influenced from without, institutions common to American Indians must have been inherited from that primitive ancestry which belonged to them and to Asia alike. This is the more probable, because the communism of the North American Indian and the general character of his institutions were but one or two steps more primitive than those of the Germans when the Germans first came into the light of history.

Every Indian tribe was subdivided into clans, and the first remarkable characteristic of the clan was that it simulated the supposed form of the primitive commune. The men were classed as brothers, the women as sisters; but what was most suggestive, marriage between them was prohibited as incestuous, and, unlike many of the prohibitions of archaic law, the rule was rigidly enforced. Men and women married only into other clans than their own.

Marriage was the rule of Indian customary law, and every form of primitive marriage common elsewhere was common among the Indians; but the apparent historical relation between these forms was not what European writers have adopted in explanation of their so-called marriages by capture, purchase, and other modes, implying slavery or absolute property in the woman.

The formal Indian marriage, and probably the oldest of all legal forms, was "marriage by legal appointment;" that is, the selection and allotment, by the elders of the clans, of some woman belonging to one clan, to live with some man belonging to another.[1]

This form of marriage often took the appearance of purchase. The parents of the woman received gifts from the suitor, according to the advantages of the match.[2] In some tribes the practice grew into an abuse, as private property became more common; girls were

[1] Annual Report of the Bureau of Ethnology, 1881-1882, lix.
[2] Dorsey's Omaha Sociology; Report of Ethnological Bureau 1881-1882, p. 258.

sold, and custom authorized the sale;[1] but in its origin the so-called purchase was only a detail of the primitive formal marriage, as appears from its legal consequences. A true sale would have deprived the woman of her position in the clan; but in law the Indian woman remained after such a marriage as before a member of her family and tribe, entitled to her rights and proper protection, like any other woman or any man. Nothing but her own misconduct could deprive the woman of her position in the tribe, and even her misconduct rather affected her social position than her legal rights. She could assert her rights as long as she had friends. Indians have been known to sell their wives; but such an abuse, like similar abuses among other races, left the woman still free, with her customary rights intact, and by no means trifling in extent.

Marriage by legal appointment, with gifts, was the formal customary Indian marriage; but primitive law, after recognizing the rigor of custom, commonly privided for legalizing violations of the strict code. Equitable processes existed by the side of formal processes for most acts that required the sanction of the clan, whether in America, Asia, or Europe. Several irregular forms of marriage were recognized and sanctioned by Indian custom.

1. Elopement, which was evidently in some degree a protest against constraint of the woman's choice. Any runaway couple, escaping to the forest, living there until the next regular day of limitation, might then return to their clans, and their marriage was held to be valid. Every tribe usually fixed a day of limitation for such offences against strict forms, at least one in each year, when pursuit or punishment of offenders must cease.

2. Capture, not as an act of war or from another tribe, but always from a clan of the same tribe. If the attempt at capture was successfully resisted, it could not be repeated in the particular case. If it succeeded, the man kept the woman, the marriage was valid, and no punishment was allowed.

Such a form of capture affected in no respect the rights of the captured woman in the Indian community. She became neither a slave nor property, but remained as before, in most cases, a member of her own family and clan; her children followed her line of descent, and the husband belonged to her as much as she belonged to

[1] Clark's Indian Sign-Language, pp. 243-246.

her husband. In some tribes the husband seemed to belong to the wife even more than the wife to the husband.

3. Capture in war. So little had the form of capture to do with creating in the captor a right of property in the woman captured, that when women of enemy tribes were taken in war, they were necessarily adopted into some clan before they could be appropriated as wives. Captives could live only as brothers or sisters of some group. They became, by the act of adoption and marriage, members of clans, with the rights of other members. Slavery was unknown to the great families of Indians between the Atlantic and the Rocky Mountains, and no such social institution was recognized in their customary law. Captives were either killed or adopted.

4. Another more curious form of irregular marriage was by duel. Under certain conditions, not precisely explained, a young man without a wife might challenge a man to whom more than one wife had been assigned; and if he succeeded in the combat, he had an admitted right to the woman.

All these forms of marriage had the same legal effect. In certain respects the woman came under the power of her husband; in other respects she retained rights of no little importance. She had the right of divorce, and might return to her own family, or dismiss her husband. She could, if she preferred, claim the protection of her own family against her husband; and her claim was effective, if she had relations strong enough to enforce her rights. Her murder was atoned for or avenged, like that of any other member of the tribe. In most cases she was the head of the family; her husband usually came to live with her, not she with him, and her children belonged to her clan, not to their father's.

The line of inheritance and descent was commonly through females; titles descended through females. The property of the husband and wife was usually kept distinct during marriage, and held in separate ownership; in case of separation each took his or her effects. A striking illustration of the position of the Indian women was offered by the well-known custom that when an Iroquois sachem died, and a council was held to elect his successor, this council consisted of all the adult male and female members of the tribe; and among the latter the mother of the deceased ruler exercised a decisive influence.

The marriage relation was of a very shifting kind, but the wife, as such, was neither a slave captured in war nor purchased property, nor property of any kind in the strict sense; she was a free member of her own tribe and clan. The rule among the Indian race was that the family meant the mother's family; but as if to show that even in the extreme antiquity of society all the great lines of development had already been seen and marked out, according to Mr. Morgan there were tribes in Central America, and those naturally the most advanced, which had adopted the conception of relationship through the father, and founded their polity on this principle.

From the American Indians turn to the oldest records of European and Asiatic society. To Egypt of course we look first for light; and though the field of Egyptian history has been as yet barely touched, the most superficial examination shows evidence sufficient for the present purposes. No one can enter an Egyptian Museum without seeing the weakness of any theory which assigns to Egyptian women, even in extreme antiquity, the position of slaves. On the contrary, the further one's inquiries are carried into the remotest regions of Egyptian history,—even into that age of the pyramid-builders, so remote that Egyptologists hesitate to fix for it a date within a possible error of some thousands of years,—the evidence which proves the social position of women to have been highest in the ages most distant becomes more convincing. The female line of descent was followed regularly if not invariably among Egyptians, as among American Indians. The queen sat on the throne with her husband; her statue rests in the tomb by his side. At all periods the sister and the wife were held in the highest respect, and a trace of the old communal society remained in the well-known Egyptian custom by which the sister frequently if not habitually became the wife. "The Egyptian woman," says Mariette Bey, "occupied a large place in the family. The rights which were hers by birth were not absorbed in those of her husband, and she transmitted them intact to her children. At certain epochs the family tables often name the mother to the exclusion of the father. In the most ancient inscriptions the love between husband and wife is sometimes expressed in delicate and touching language."

The position taken by woman in the Egyptian philosophy and religion is more curious and still more decisive. Among the commonest Egyptian monuments are the famous triads or trinity of deities. This trinity represents a man, a woman, and a child. The male deity, most widely known under the name of Osiris, appears to have represented the creative power, the principle of light struggling with darkness, and overcome by it only to be brought again to life through the aid of the woman. Osiris was the generator,—the fructifying force of Nature; the sun with its mysterious energy which called life into being. By his side sat the woman, Isis, the sister, the wife,—that mysterious power which according to the physiological ideas of that day gave only shelter and protection to the germ of being, resembling the earth teeming with life under the beams of the sun. The third member of the Egyptian trinity was the child, Horus or Ra, who completed the mysterious circle, returning again to the father, never designated as the son, but represented as the father self-engendered; for in the Egyptian trinity, as in the Christian, the father and the son were one,—the insoluble mystery of generation, insoluble then as now, ever returned upon itself.

In so elevated and philosophic a system of theology where shall we look for the degradation of the woman? Not surely in the mere fact that the place assigned to the mother was of secondary importance, inasmuch as the father and not the mother was considered as author of the child's existence. The mother was as essential to the trinity as the father or the son. Isis stood on the same plane as Osiris. Never from the beginning to the end of that marvellous history whose records still remain the most astonishing monuments of human development, can we find reason to suppose that the family sprang from the exercise of force, and that the wife was a slave or the descendant of slaves. The Christian philosophers of a later period, probably influenced by their close connection with Alexandria, adopted the trinity, and in adopting it, dethroned the woman from her place. Yet even then, notwithstanding this degradation, the irresistible spread of Mariolatry, the worship of the Virgin Mother, proved how strongly human nature revolted against the change.

The races of Western Europe showed tendencies more strongly marked. In all branches of what is commonly known as the Aryan

stock,—Celt, Roman, Greek, German, and Scandinavian,—are in
dications that at some period antecedent to recorded history, a
social rebellion against the old communal system had been felt. The
institution of marriage, the law of descent in the male line, the im
portance of the family and the authority of the father, are charac
teristics so distinct in the whole Aryan group as to countenance
the idea that this was in fact the real origin of the race, and that the
primitive Aryan stock broke away from the original communal so
ciety with no other distinctive principle. Perhaps the institution o
the family was the means of their extraordinary success, and of the
domination which they established wherever they set their feet
Historically, the family is but an example of the energetic realiza
tion of those natural affections and that passion of property which
lie deepest of all passions in humanity. The race which followed thi
path with the most vigor must have been the strongest race and the
best fitted to conquer. Such a race had a natural instinct for law
its taste for the acquisition of private property required develop
ment of legal principles; its faculty of adopting reforms in society
proves its intellectual versatility; and what are all these but the
same characteristics which appear again ages afterward, in the
greatest of all the works of their descendants,—in the civil law o
Rome, and in the common law of England?

Turning to the Greeks and to their literature, unmistakable
traces prove the existence at no very remote time of the same class
of institutions as those of the American Indians. Descent and inherit
ance through women to the exclusion of men; subjection of the
persons of women to obligations which seem to have had their
origin in the old communal ties; even distinct efforts to force them
back under the burden of those obligations after they had once
freed themselves,—all these are recorded, and all point in one di
rection. Yet it may be doubted whether these were any part of pure
Greek civilization. Probably they belonged to the races which the
Greek overran and ruled; and if traces of the old communistic sys
tem are found in Greek literature or history, they crept in, as after
ward the corruption of the East crept into the society of Rome
Fortunately something is known of the heroic age of the Greeks
The Homeric poems are a monument of early Greek society; and

the peculiarity of the Homeric poems which causes them to stand in sharp contrast with later Greek literature is, that they invariably treated women and the marriage contract with respect which subsequent literature of no country or age can show. If marriage were really the child of force, if the wife were a captured or a purchased slave, we should find a trace of it here; but no such trace exists.

Ulysses in one of his accounts of his origin said,—

> "It is my boast that I am of the race
> Who dwell in spacious Crete,—a rich man's son,
> Within whose palace many other sons
> Were born and reared, the offspring of his wife;
> But me a purchased mother whom he made
> His concubine brought forth to him.
> And yet Castor Hylacides from whom I sprang
> Held me in equal favor with the rest."

The wife, in contrast with the purchased mother, was always a free woman, with rights which her husband could not disregard. The whole story both of the Iliad and the Odyssey is little more than a running commentary on the Greek law of marriage. I will not stop to discuss the legal status of Helen of Troy, although her position offers some remarkable illustrations of law; but the Odyssey offers little else. This poem opens with an account of the state of affairs at Ithaca after Ulysses had been absent twenty years. The neighboring chiefs, assuming Ulysses to be dead, made common cause to compel his widow Penelope to choose a second husband. They came in a body to the abode of Ulysses, and there seated themselves with the formal intention of eating Penelope and her son Telemachus out of house and home if she did not accede to their wish. In this case what was the legal status of Penelope, the assumed widow? Was she a slave? Was she under the authority of her husband's family, or of her own son? Or had she fallen back under the authority of her own family? What were her legal rights, if she had any? How did the suitors show their sense of her inferiority as a woman to their dignity as men? How did they expect to compel her to carry out their wishes?

It was not the beauty of Penelope which brought the suitors to her house with a system of wooing so energetic. Homer represents

Penelope as still handsome, but she could hardly have been less than forty years old, and most if not all her suitors were young enough to have been her sons. Distinct evidence is given that not merely her youth and beauty caused her to be so ardently sought; she possessed attractions independent of these, and more potent to fix the affections of the Achaian suitors. Penelope was the widow of the chosen chieftain of all the Ithacans; she was wealthy in her own right; she carried with her to her future husband a certain claim to the coveted position of chieftain which her husband had held, and this too in face of the claim by inheritance which belonged to her son Telemachus.

Telemachus was the heir to his father's wealth; he was the owner of the house in which his mother lived; he was head of the family in his father's absence; but his property was encumbered by his mother's claims, and he could not pay off these claims without reducing himself to the position of a comparatively poor man. He would have been well pleased had his mother settled the difficulty by accepting and marrying one of the suitors, even on the chance of his father's return. He would have been still better pleased had his mother consented to go back to her own father, and so relieve him and his estate; but he did not dare to send her back, since such an act on his part would have been an infraction of the terms of the marriage contract between Ulysses and Penelope, and would have subjected Telemachus to the claims of his mother's family for large damages on her behalf,—claims that would certainly have been enforced. Penelope was mistress to decide what to do, and she preferred to make no decision. We are left to surmise her motives. What hindered her from at once dismissing the suitors and insisting upon maintaining her widowhood? Possibly she feared their resentment; but probably the Greek custom, which amounted to law, required that the widow should marry again, if not too old. At all events she did not decide, and the suitors, to the disgust of Telemachus, went on eating day by day the flocks and herds which were the bulk of his wealth. Between his mother and the suitors Telemachus was in despair; and the second book of the Odyssey shows him calling a public council to force a solution of the difficulty. The story continues, in the words of Mr. Bryant's translation:—

"He took the seat
Of his great father, and the aged men
Made way for him. And then Ægyptius spake:
    'Hear, men of Ithaca, what I shall say.
No council, no assembly have we held
Since great Ulysses in his roomy ships
Departed from our isle. Who now is he
That summons us?'
    As thus he spake, Ulysses' son rejoiced
In his auspicious words, nor longer kept
His seat, but yielding to an inward force
Rose midst them all to speak, while in his hand
Pisenor, the sagacious counsellor
And herald, placed the sceptre. Then he turned
To the old man Ægyptius, speaking thus:
    'O aged man, not far from thee is he
Who called this council, as thou soon shalt know.
Mine chiefly is the trouble; I have brought
No news of an approaching foe, . . .
Nor urge I other matters which concern
The public weal; my own necessity,
The evil which has fallen on my house,
Constrains me. It is twofold: first, that I
Have lost an excellent father, who was king
Among you, and ruled o'er you with a sway
As gentle as a father's. Greater yet
Is the next evil, and will soon o'erthrow
My house and waste my substance utterly.
Suitors, the sons of those who in our isle
Hold the chief rank, importunately press
Round my unwilling mother. They disdain
To ask her of Icarius, that the king
Her father may endow her, and bestow
His daughter on the man who best may gain
His favor; but with every day they come
Into our palace, sacrificing here
Oxen and sheep and fatling goats, and hold
High festival, and drink the purple wine
Unstinted, with unbounded waste; for here
Is no man like Ulysses to repel
The mischief from my house. Not such are we

As he was to resist the wrong. We pass
For weaklings, immature in valor; yet
If I had but the power assuredly
I would resist, for by these men are done
Insufferable things, nor does my house
Perish with honor.' ". . .

To this speech Antinous, one of the suitors, made the following significant answer:—

" 'Telemachus, thou youth of braggart speech
And boundless in abuse, what hast thou said
To our dishonor? Thou wouldst fix on us
A brand of shame. The blame is not with us,
The Achaian suitors; 'tis thy mother's fault,
Skilled as she is in crafty shifts. . . .
          . . . Now let the suitors make
Their answer to thy words, that thou mayst know
Our purpose fully, and the Achaians all
May know it likewise. Send thy mother hence,
Requiring that she wed the suitor whom
Her father chooses and herself prefers.
But if she still go on to treat the sons
Of Greece with such despite, too confident
In gifts which Pallas has bestowed on her
So richly, . . . so long will we consume
Thy substance and estate as she shall hold
Her present mood. . . . She to herself
Gains great renown, but surely brings on thee
Loss of much goods. And now we go not hence
To our affairs nor elsewhere till she wed
Whichever of the Greeks shall please her most.'
    And then rejoined discreet Telemachus:
      'Antinous, grievous wrong were it to send
Unwilling from this palace her who bore
And nursed me. . . .
And should I of my own accord and will
Dismiss my mother, I must make perforce
Icarius large amends, and that were hard.
        . . . Think not I
Will ever speak that word.' "

The conference broke up, and a temporary suspension of hostilities was effected. Telemachus on the one hand was determined to drive out the suitors, and even to kill them if he could; while the suitors were well disposed to forestall him by putting him to death at once, and sharing his estate among themselves, while the succession to the throne should be decided by the choice which Penelope should make of a husband. In their deliberations, the suitors expressed their intentions with frankness, especially Antinous, their most active leader:—

> "Let us be first to strike
> And slay him in the fields or on the way,
> And taking his possessions to ourselves,
> Share equally his wealth. Then may we give
> This palace to his mother and the man
> Whom she may wed, whoever he may be."

The father and the brothers of Penelope counselled her to wed Eurymachus, the wealthiest and the least objectionable of the suitors, and it was understood that she would carry to him the rank which Ulysses had held. The widow's choice would in this respect decide the election; and Telemachus distinctly admitted that this solution would be satisfactory to him if it relieved his estate quickly from the impending ruin.

In the face of all this, Penelope paid no attention to the opinions or wishes of any one. She regarded the desperation of her son with as little sympathy as she did the cool advice of her father and brothers and the too marked attentions of her suitors. Her action was contrary to the advice and wishes of her relatives and connections on both sides. She was perfectly independent. She relied on her legal rights, which until the death of her husband was formally ascertained were sufficient to protect her; and according to the poem these rights were respected. Neither the suitors nor Telemachus, nor any of the family of Ulysses, nor her own family, ventured to restrain her independence of action.

This is but one example from many which Homer offers of the position of women in the earliest Greek society. Turning next from Greece to Rome, the inquiry is checked by the difficulty that Romans were not a very poetic or a romantic people. No great monument of their primitive condition, like the Homeric poems, is extant; probably none ever existed. Hardly a vestige of their early history has survived in an authentic form. The most primitive of their extant laws belongs to a period of development far in advance of that now in question. Moreover, the Romans threw themselves into the reaction against primitive communism with a degree of energy, not to say of violence, which went far beyond anything known in other branches of the Aryan stock. The Roman family not only exaggerated the characteristics of the wide-spread hostility to old communistic ideas, and asserted in the strongest manner the principle of relationship through males, but it went even to the extravagance of annihilating relationship through females; not only did it make the father the head of the family, it absorbed the family in the father; not only did it raise the authority of the husband over the wife, it asserted the astounding principle that the wife was the daughter of her husband. Alone among Aryan races the Romans, with their extravagant logical sequence, inferred from the premise of paternal headship the conclusion that that headship carried with it the rights of absolute property; and if of absolute property over the chattels of the family, why not also over the children; and if over the children, then since the father, in giving his daughter in marriage, conveyed with her to her husband all the rights which he himself enjoyed, it necessarily followed that the wife stood toward her husband in the position of a daughter, and that his power over her was unlimited.

This was already the theory of the law when the law first becomes known; but this theory was limited and controlled in practice by influences which were also peculiar to the Romans. In no country has the family been so serious and so sacred a thing as among the Romans at the time when this theory of their law prevailed. The sanctity with which it was invested, elevated and dignified the position of wife and child in spite of the perverted letter of the law. No complaint comes from Roman history of the abuse of the enormous power thus vested in the father. Nowhere has the family been so intimate and so united a fabric as in Rome. Almost from the first the Romans seem to have felt that their family law was not defensible in practice, and was inconsistent with the theory of the State. During a long series of years the Roman jurists continued to devise new expedients for evading the consequences of their own legal doctrines. Step by step they emancipated the wife; they emancipated the son; they tried to explain or to smooth away the extravagances of their own creation, until at last they did it so successfully that not only was the husband's authority over the wife destroyed, but the whole family organization was shaken to pieces.

In any case the authority conferred upon the husband by the Roman law did not prove the degradation of women. Whatever that authority was, it was exercised over the wife, not because she was a woman, but because she was a daughter. To the paternal power the man as well as the woman was subject; and no matter what age the man had attained, he was, during the lifetime of his father, under the same domestic rule as his sister or his mother.

There remain to be considered the institutions of the great German race from which we more directly claim descent. Like the other branches of the Indo-European stock, the German founded his society firmly on the family, with its masculine peculiarities; but the German family was still, as compared with the Roman, a loose and flexible structure, and more than one suggestion is to be found in the early German law pointing to that communal society so evidently the starting place of human institutions.

Like the Greeks, some of the German tribes had strong romantic tendencies and poetic instincts. Little of the pure German poetry which has survived illustrates the subject now under discussion, but the rudest and least Romanized branch of the German race left some extraordinary literary monuments; and among the northern barbarians who struggled most desperately against the civilizing and centralizing influences of their day were portions of the Scandinavians, who, when their power was at last finally broken, and their country lay helpless at the feet of their conqueror, still refused to accept the fate of war, and abandoning their homes, betook themselves to the sea, with the resolution to accept life only on the condition of preserving undiminished those rights which consisted principally in recognizing no one as master, and in waging private war on their private enemies. One considerable mass of these men, carrying their families with them, crossed the ocean, and a thousand years ago found the absolute freedom which they sought in a spot where they were little likely to be disturbed.

They established a commonwealth in Iceland; and there they lived, and after their own manner flourished for many years in the complete enjoyment of all their archaic liberties. Their society was in many respects remarkable, but in none more so than in that of its literature. Iceland alone among western countries has left an heroic poem, which, for historical interest if not for artistic merit, can stand by the side of the Odyssey. The *Njalsaga*, as it is called, is a piece of pure, or nearly pure, and authentic primitive history, and offers an invaluable picture of Scandinavian society, at a period of development not very unlike that described in the Odyssey.

The *Njalsaga*, like the poems of Homer, turns on the character of a woman, and I will use the language of Mr. Dasent's translation in order not to lose the vivacity and quaintness of the original. Hallgerda was her name. She was fair-haired, and had so much of it that she could hide herself in it; but she was lavish and hardhearted. A suitor named Thorwald asked her of her father in marriage. The father warned his future son-in-law of her temper; but his answer was: "Lay down the terms of the match, for I will not let her temper stand in the way of our bargain." Then they talked over the terms of the bargain; and Hauskuld, the father, never asked his daughter what she thought of it, for his heart was set on giving her away, and so they came to an understanding as to the terms of the match. Hauskuld then told Hallgerda of the bargain he had made, and she said: "Now that has been put to the proof which I have all along been afraid of, that thou lovest me not so much as thou art always saying, when thou hast not thought it worth while to tell me a word of all this matter. Besides, I do not think this match so good a one as thou has always promised me."

Hauskuld's reply indicates the power which the father in almost every period exercised over his daughter's choice of a husband. "I do not set so much store by thy pride as to let it stand in the way of my bargains; and my will, not thine, shall carry the day if we fall out on any point."

Hallgerda gave way, and the marriage took place. But she revenged herself upon her husband by her intolerable temper, until one day within the first year of their marriage her husband was stung by an insult to such anger that he gave her a blow on the face that drew blood. That same day she caused him to be murdered, and then she rode home to her father. He was obliged to pay the legal atonement for the life of his son-in-law to the family of the murdered man, while Hallgerda took up her residence again in her father's house, and her property accumulated till it had reached a great sum.

After a time another suitor appeared. His name was Glum. This time the father was better advised than to dispose of his daughter without consulting her. They sent for Hallgerda and she came thither, and two women with her. She had on a cloak of rich blue wool, and under it a scarlet kirtle, and a silver girdle round her waist; but her hair came down on both sides of her bosom, and she had turned the locks up under her girdle. She sat down; greeted them all with kind words and spoke well and boldly, and asked what was the news. After that she ceased speaking.

Then Glum said: "There has been some talk between thy father and my brother and myself about a bargain. It was that I might get thee, Hallgerda, if it be thy will as it is theirs; and now, if thou art a brave woman, thou wilt say right out whether the match is at all to thy mind; but if thou hast anything in thy heart against this bargain with us, then we will not say anything more about it."

Hallgerda said: "I know well that you are men of worth and might, ye brothers; I know too that now I shall be much better wedded than I was before; but what I want to know is, what you have said already about the match, and how far you have given your words in the matter. But so far as I see of thee, I think I might love thee well, if we can but hit it off as to temper."

So Glum himself told her all about the bargain and left nothing out, and then he asked Hauskuld and Hrut whether he had told it right. Hauskuld said he had, and then Hallgerda said: "Ye have dealt with me so well in this matter, my father and Hrut, that I will do what ye advise, and this bargain shall be struck as ye have settled it."

After that Hallgerda's goods were valued, and Glum was to lay down as much against them, and they were to go shares, half and half, in the whole. The marriage took place, and Hallgerda kept her word. She lived happily with her husband for a time; but her want of heart was again the cause of her second husband's murder by the same hand which had slain the first. Hallgerda went back again to her father's house, and was there in the course of time married to a third husband, one of the heroes of the story. He was a wise and high-minded man. His wife made his life miserable, and developed the utmost ingenuity in the effort to embroil him with his friends and neighbors in quarrels of every sort; but he succeeded for the most part in keeping his temper and in warding off the dangers caused by her conduct. Even toward her his patience seemed inexhaustible, until one day he detected her in a peculiarly base theft; and in his wrath at the disgrace she had brought upon him, he slapped her face. She said she would bear that slap in mind, and repay it if she could. As usual she was as good as her word. Gunnar, her husband, was at last attacked in his house one night, and was hard pressed by the attacking party. He wounded eight men and killed two, but his enemies succeeded in cutting his bowstring, and he could not hope to hold them at bay unless he could procure another string.

Then Gunnar said to Hallgerda: "Give me two locks of thy hair; and ye two, thy mother and thou, twist them together into a bowstring for me."

"Does aught lie on it?" said she.

"My life lies on it," he said; "for they will never come to close quarters with me if I can keep them off with my bow."

"Well," she said, "now I will call to thy mind that slap on the face which thou gavest me and I care never a whit whether thou holdest out a long while or a short."

She sat by, all that night, and saw her husband slowly exhausted by one wound after another, until at last his enemies could come near enough to kill him; but he did not turn his hand against her, and Hallgerda lived to enjoy the wealth acquired from her three murdered husbands, and to bring more misery and death on her friends.

Surely a woman of this stamp was no slave, no descendant of slaves, no possible connection of slaves. All the fierce and untamable instincts of infinite generations of free, wild animals were embodied in her. Nor were her legal rights those of a dependant. No Norse pirate, no Danish jarl, enjoyed more completely than she the legal rights of a free citizen. Marriage is described as a sale, and this passage might be quoted to prove that the father sold his daughter to her first husband without her consent; but what sort of a sale was that which carried with it no rights of property over the thing sold? The father conveyed to the husband no more than the father himself had, and the *patria potestas* was no part of Scandinavian or German law. The father conveyed to the husband simply the rights of guardianship, not rights of property,—the right to act as her representative, with the corresponding duties; the right to the control and charge of her property while she remained his wife, and certain rights of inheritance in case of her death, though these apparently depended in each case on the terms of the contract. In that stage of society the rights of the husband over the wife were less extensive than they now are. Her position was more independent; her ability to hold property was quite as complete; her protection against ill-treatment, if anything, was more effective than it is now.

One final resource the wife always had. The Scandinavians were not yet much advanced beyond the Indians of America in their view of marriage as a voluntary association, which might be terminated at the will of either party. Another passage of the *Njalsaga* throws light on the Scandinavian law of divorce. Unna, wife of Hrut, was dissatisfied with her husband and wished to leave him. She took counsel with her father, who on hearing her reasons was satisfied with their force, and being the best lawyer in Iceland advised her as to the proper way of securing her divorce without risk of opposition or of personal constraint. She was to throw her husband off his guard by appearing happy and good-tempered, and then when he was absent from home in the summer on necessary business, and when all the men of the district had ridden away to the annual meeting of the Thing, or popular assembly and court of law, she must summon her own people to ride with her to the Thing; and when she was ready to start she must, in the presence and with the witness of the men who were to bear her company, go before her marriage bed and declare herself separated from her husband by such separation as would hold good before the laws of the land and the judgment of the great Thing. At the door of the house she must take the same witness. After this she must make her way as safely as she could to her father at the Thing.

All this she did, and successfully joined her father at the Thing. Then she went to the hill of laws and declared herself separated from Hrut, her husband; and this proceeding constituted a full and valid divorce according to Scandinavian law. Her husband came home, and on learning what had happened, knit his brows and held his peace. He saw that the divorce was accomplished, and that he could do nothing to invalidate it. The affair did not end there. Unna had carried a marriage portion to her husband, of which he during the marriage had the possession and management. Naturally Hrut was not disposed to be generous in a case where he had been so ungenerously treated, and he therefore took no steps to return the property. His wife's father consequently brought a suit against him to compel surrender. Hrut met and defeated the suit by challenging the father to the wager of battle,—a challenge which the father's age and inferior strength made it folly to accept. This broke off the suit so far as the father was concerned. Unna, however, the divorced wife, was still the rightful owner of the property, and could recover possession whenever she could find a representative whose physical strength and legal knowledge were sufficient to overcome Hrut. This she ultimately did, and the affair ended in the recovery of the property and the maintenance of the divorce.

The sole legal inferiority of women to men consisted in their subjection to guardianship. This limitation of their legal capacity seems to have been due to their physical inability to perform the public duties of men. A woman could not go to war. She could not act as her own champion in the inevitable wager of battle. She had to act through her next of kin, or through some person whom she appointed as her legal representative; but one of the most firmly established principles of society obliged her family to protect her in such cases, and until such a protector or representative was found, her rights simply lay dormant.

This is not the place to enter into any elaborate examination of the other codes of northern law to find light on this subject. The same principles will be found to underlie the whole fabric of northern society. That women as a weaker class suffered from violent deprivation of their rights, and that in many cases, perhaps habitually, they were treated without much regard to them, may be true; so doubtless were children; but violation of law never was law. One must look back beyond the records of history for any condition of pure force among the races from which modern institutions and theories are derived. Among these races can be found no evidence of a lawless stage of society. If one may judge from the faint indications that remain, their faculty for instituting progressive laws gave them their superiority over rival races.

A favorite theory has insisted upon regarding the wedding ring as a badge of servitude or a symbol of purchase. This idea cannot be maintained. The wedding ring appears in its origin to have been merely the earnest money which bound the contract of marriage between the father and the husband, and was not the only symbol of the kind in early custom, although no other survives in modern use. The ring proved, not that marriage was a sale, but that marriage was a civil contract executed according to the strict formalities of contracts in the primitive law; it proved, not that women were deprived of rights, but that their rights were secured to them in marriage by the most careful provisions known to early society.

On a world made up of the two great elements of Roman society, with its ruined family system and its debauched morality on the one side, and Germany, with barbarism resting on a strong family organization, on the other, the Christian church began its work of creating a new unity and a new morality for mankind. For more than a thousand years the Church profoundly affected and even controlled the conditions of social existence and the ethical tendencies of law. On no branch of law did it exercise a more marked influence than on the law of marriage. Historians, aware of this influence, have naturally assumed that the elevation of women from what was supposed to have been their previous condition of degradation and servitude was due to the humanitarian influence of the Church. In truth, the share of the Church in the elevation of women was for the most part restricted to a partial restoration of rights which the Church herself had a principal share in taking away from them. The Church was a Roman church; it rose to power under the intense moral reaction against the corruptions of the Empire; and of all the corruptions of the Empire none had been more scan-

dalous and more fatal than the corruption of the women. For sufficient cause the women of the later Empire found little favor in
the eyes of the Church. In the early days the ascetic principle was
strong in religion, and women as such, even the best of women,
were not sought by men whose present existence was as nothing in
their eyes, and to whom the price of eternal happiness lay in the
avoidance even of temptation to worldly life. Next to the purification of morals, and indeed as one principal means toward it, the
Church felt with most intensity the necessity of discipline and obedience in society, and taught that lesson with only too much earnestness and success. The rise of Christianity marked the diminution of
women's social and legal rights both in the old imperial world and
in the new Germanic race, which flung itself with all the ardor of its
fresh enthusiasm into the ideas of the new religion. A long time
elapsed before the pure humanitarian influences of Christianity got
the upper hand, and began to struggle with the manifest injustice
toward women which the Church had either stimulated or permitted.

In the mean time church doctrines were more frequently calculated to inculcate the duties than the rights of women. The moral
aspect of marriage and its religious meaning were pressed with em-
phasis, which did not often stop to weigh the immediate importance
of the legal and temporal contract. The Church regarded as of
greater consequence to the happiness of mankind, here and hereafter, that women should be obedient to their bishops and their
husbands than that they should be encouraged to protect themselves. Perhaps anything that tended to depress the legal status
and the civil rights of women, tended at the same time to make
them more and more dependent on the Church, and to turn their
minds more passionately toward the one channel through which
consolation and protection came.

The Church ultimately made persistent and partly successful efforts to protect women from the inevitable results of its own policy, but these efforts could never have gone to the point of restoring
them to the independent position they held either under the Roman
or the German law. The Church, for example, frowned upon divorce
and sternly forbade it; yet which was likely to suffer most under an
enforced yoke, the man or the woman,—and why was the law not

as competent then to make a contract that should protect the woman, as the Church was to intervene by a purely ecclesiastical principle? The Church felt with reason that society should be taught to obey; and of all classes of society, the women who were least in need of learning that lesson were obliged to learn it most thoroughly. The Church established a new ideal of feminine character. Thenceforward not the proud, self-confident, vindictive woman of German tradition received the admiration and commanded the service of law and society; not the Hallgerdas, the Brunhildas, the Fredegundas, were the women whose acts were chronicled and whose will was obeyed. Such women were the horror and the shame of the Church, unless, like the great Countess Matilda of Tuscany, they paid to the Church that obedience which they refused to their husbands. In reprobation of these the Church raised up, with the willing co-operation of the men, the modern type of Griselda,—the meek and patient, the silent and tender sufferer, the pale reflection of the Mater Dolorosa, submissive to every torture that her husband could invent, but more submissive to the Church than to her husband. For her and such as her was the kingdom of heaven reserved, while a fate of a very different kind was in store for the defiant heroine of the heroic age.

These mediæval conceptions belonged to a time when the most pressing necessity of society was concentration, and when discipline was the chief lesson to be learned. The process by which the free and democratic German world had to be trained was long and painful. The wretchedness of feudal tyranny was succeeded only by the sharper inflictions of concentrated power. For centuries the most intelligent part of society set its heart on building up a social fabric which should rest not on human but on divine authority. The principle of authority was essential; and authority, when not resting on the will of society, could find no other logical support than the divine will. The conditions of their existence precluded the Church, the arbitrary monarch, the feudal noble, and the husband of that day from resting the claim of authority on the consent of society. Thus the family, like the State, took on the character of a petty absolutism; and to justify in theory the sacrifice of rights thus surrendered by the wife and children, whether in the form of the harsh provisions of the law toward women or the even harsher rules of primogeniture, men fell back on what they called the patriarchal theory, and derived the principles they required from a curious conglomeration of Old Testament history and pure hypothesis.

England was the country which carried these theories to the most extreme conclusions in her law; but England was also the country which resisted their application most successfully. Luther led the way by overthrowing in northern Germany the divine authority of the Roman church. England struck the first blow at the whole system in her rebellion against the theory of divine right in the State. Luther and Cromwell were conservatives in a wider sense than they imagined. They represented more than the protest against religious or political absolutism. The movement which they led could not come to a legitimate end without effecting a readjustment of the whole social balance, which the exigencies of a pressing immediate necessity had for a thousand years thrown from its natural equilibrium.

Future history can hardly produce any new experience which has not its prototype in the past. If modern society is destined to move at all, it can only move on the same lines which have already and repeatedly been followed out to their conclusions. If it carries the tendency toward the independence of women to its logical extreme, it will find that Rome has already travelled that path. If it reacts toward a re-establishment of the family in sterner aspect, it will find that this reaction has again and again told its whole story. If it seeks a moral from which to draw all the light that history can throw on its true interests, this moral is obvious and trite. All new discoveries in the record of human development point to the familiar facts that the most powerful instincts in man are his affections and his love of property; that on these the family is built; that no other institution can be raised on the same or on equally strong foundations; that for this reason the family is the strongest and healthiest of all human fabrics; that it always has and probably always will trample every rival system under its feet; and finally, that just in the measure that society has on the one side carried the theory of the family to an exaggeration, or has allowed it to fall into contempt, has been the violence of the reaction.

The

Declaration of Paris. 1861

In 1877 Henry Adams left Harvard and returned to Washington where he was to live for the rest of his life. "The fact is," he wrote, "I gravitate to a capital by a primary law of nature. This is the only place in America where society amuses me, or where life offers variety." Whatever political ambitions he may once have entertained, however, were as good as dead; now he was purely and simply the historian, occupying a desk in the State Department for the sole purpose of historical research.

The thirteen years following Adams' removal from Cambridge were highly productive ones. A biography of Albert Gallatin, Jefferson's Secretary of the Treasury, and a three-volume edition of Gallatin's papers; a life of John Randolph; and two novels, Democracy and Esther—all these appeared by 1885. And during this time Adams was steadily at work on his great history of the Jeffersonian era which was finally published in nine volumes from 1889 to 1891. In the latter year, too, he brought out a collection of some of his shorter writings under the title Historical Essays. *This volume ranged in its material from "Captaine John Smith" to the second "Session" and included a couple of new essays, one of them "The Declaration of Paris," which apparently had been written in periods of diversion from his main work, as exercises, so to speak, in the weaving of small historical patterns.*

Of course, "The Declaration of Paris" must have had its personal

361

meanings for Adams too. When he speaks of the American legation standing "in an attitude of anxiety not easy to realize" during the year 1861, his own memory more than the historical record is the source of his knowledge. He was, in fact, fascinated all his life by the diplomatic struggle he had witnessed in the early period of the war between his father and the British Foreign Secretary. Fifteen years after the Historical Essays, *in* The Education of Henry Adams, *he went once more over the ground covered by "The Declaration of Paris," exposing the contradictory acts and motives of the British Government and the unforgotten "double-dyed rascality and duplicity of Lord Russell."*

AT THE outbreak of the Crimean War in 1854, Great Britain and France agreed to respect neutral commerce, whether under its own flag or under the flag of an enemy. Great Britain expressly limited the concession to the special emergency: "To preserve the commerce of neutrals Great Britain is willing for the present to waive a part of the belligerent rights appertaining to her by the law of nations. . . . Her Majesty will waive the right of seizing enemy's property laden on board a neutral vessel unless it be contraband of war."

At the close of the Crimean War the Congress of Paris adopted, April 16, 1856, a Declaration embracing four heads,—

1. Privateering is and remains abolished.

2. The neutral flag covers enemy's goods, with the exception of contraband of war.

3. Neutral goods, with the exception of contraband of war, are not liable to capture under enemy's flag.

4. Blockades in order to be binding must be effective; that is to say, maintained by forces sufficient really to prevent access to the coast of the enemy.

Great Britain, France, Prussia, Russia, Austria, and Turkey adopted this mutual agreement, and pledged themselves to make it known to States not represented in the Congress, and invite their accession

[From *Historical Essays*, 1891.]

363

to it, on two conditions,—(1) That the Declaration should be accepted as a whole, or not at all; and (2) That the States acceding should enter into no subsequent arrangement on maritime law in time of war without stipulating for a strict observance of the four points. On these conditions every maritime power was to be invited to accede, and had the right to become a party to the agreement. Accordingly nearly all the States of Europe and South America in course of time notified their accession, and became, equally with the original members, entitled to all the benefits and subject to the obligations of the contract.

The government of the United States was also invited to accede, and like the other Powers had the right to do so by simple notification. Secretary Marcy notified the French government, July 28, 1856, that the President could not abandon the right to use privateers, unless he could secure the exemption of all private property, not contraband, from capture at sea; but with that amendment the United States would accede to the Declaration. The French government made no objection to the Marcy amendment; Russia favored it; Prussia, Italy, and the Netherlands were friendly to it. Great Britain was understood to oppose it.

Before the negotiation was fairly begun, President Pierce was succeeded, March 4, 1857, by President Buchanan, who directed the negotiation to be arrested for the purpose of enabling him to examine the questions involved. During the four years of Buchanan's administration the subject remained untouched; and when, March 4, 1861, President Lincoln began his term of office, his Secretary of State found the Declaration of Paris among the most important of the unsettled subjects calling for attention.

At that anxious moment, when the fate of the Union depended on many uncertain forces, any step which promised to conciliate Europe and convince Great Britain and France of the advantages they might expect from a Northern rather than a Southern influence in the United States, seemed to President Lincoln and his Cabinet good policy.[1] They decided to give the accession of the United States to the Declaration of Paris. The decision was taken early, and promptly acted upon. About six weeks after the inauguration, Secretary Seward sent a circular despatch, dated April 24, 1861,

[1] Seward to Dayton, July 6, 1861. Infra, p. 257.

to the American ministers in Great Britain, France, Russia, Prussia, Austria, Belgium, and Denmark, instructing them to ascertain whether those governments were "disposed to enter into negotiations for the accession of the government of the United States to the Declaration of the Paris Congress, with the conditions annexed by that body to the same; and if you shall find that government so disposed, you will then enter into a convention to the effect, substantially in the form of a project for that purpose herewith transmitted to you,—the convention to take effect from the time when the due ratifications of the same shall have been exchanged."

Meanwhile the subject attracted the attention of the British government. Lord John Russell, the Foreign Secretary in Lord Palmerston's Ministry, wrote to Earl Cowley, the British ambassador at Paris, May 6, an important despatch,[1] which began by announcing that her Majesty's government considered the Confederacy of the Southern States as a belligerent, invested with all a belligerent's rights and prerogatives. As both belligerents, North and South, were about to enter on maritime operations, Lord John Russell suggested to the Emperor Napoleon that they should be invited "to act upon the principles laid down in the second and third Articles of the Declaration of Paris of 1856, which relates to the security of neutral property on the high seas."

The form thus suggested was somewhat peculiar. Scarcely five years had then elapsed since April 16, 1856, when the plenipotentiaries at the Congress of Paris, including the representative of England, signed the protocol to the proceedings of that day:—

"On the proposition of Count Walewski and recognizing that it is for the general interest to maintain the indivisibility of the four principles mentioned in the Declaration signed this day, the plenipotentiaries agree that the Powers which shall have signed it, or which shall have acceded to it, cannot hereafter enter into any arrangement in regard to the application of the rights of neutrals in time of war, which does not at the same time rest on the four principles which are the object of the said Declaration."

In 1856 England and France pledged themselves to enter into no arrangement with each other or any third Power unless it started

[1] Russell to Cowley, May 6, 1861; Papers presented to Parliament, 1862; North America, No. 3, p. 1.

from the indivisible four Articles. In 1861 England invited France to do the thing which both Powers had pledged themselves not to do.

The act was the more significant, because under ordinary circumstances, as a matter of courtesy, the adhesion of both belligerents to the Declaration as a whole should have been first invited, previous to suggesting their adhesion to half the principles involved. The discourtesy was not due to any peculiar interest of England in the two principles thus put in the foreground. Russell's wish went no further than to secure the immunity of the British flag when covering belligerent goods, and of British goods under the belligerent flag. The abandonment of privateering and the definition of a binding blockade seemed equally important to neutrals, but to these points Russell made no allusion.

Earl Cowley had an interview, May 9, with M. Thouvenel, then Foreign minister of Napoleon III., and wrote[1] the same day to Lord John Russell that the Imperial government concurred entirely in the views of the British government, and was prepared to act jointly in asking from the belligerents "a formal recognition of the second and third Articles of the Declaration of Paris." Thouvenel suggested that a friendly communication should be made to both governments in the same language, "that the governments of Great Britain and France intended to abstain from all interference, but that the commercial interests of the two countries demanded that they should be assured that the principles with respect to neutral property laid down by the Congress of Paris should be adhered to,—an assurance which the two governments did not doubt they should obtain, as the principles in question were in strict accordance with those that had been always advocated by the United States."

Lord John Russell acknowledged the receipt of Cowley's despatch May 13, and on the same day the new minister of the United States to England arrived in London. A few days intervened before Mr. Adams could begin upon business,[2] and these were actively employed by Russell in fixing the attitude of England beyond re-

---

[1] Cowley to Russell, May 9, 1861. Papers No. 3, p. 3.
[2] Adams to Seward (No. 1), May 17, 1861; Papers relating to Foreign Affairs; Diplomatic Documents, p. 69.

monstrance. The Proclamation of Neutrality, recognizing the Confederate States of America as belligerents, was signed May 13, and published May 15; while Russell wrote to Cowley, May 16, transmitting to the French government the draft of a despatch requesting the accession of the belligerents to the second and third Articles of the Declaration of Paris.[1] The draft sketched the history of the subject, showing that the United States government had in principle acceded to the second, third, and fourth Articles of the Declaration, and withheld its assent only from the first, which regarded privateering. On that point, Russell announced that Great Britain must hold any government issuing letters of marque responsible for losses sustained in consequence of privateers which did not respect the established laws of war.

Lord Cowley reported, May 17, that Thouvenel concurred entirely in the draft, and had already written in the same terms to the French minister at Washington, M. Mercier.[2] Cowley's report reached Russell May 18, and Russell immediately, on the same day, sent the despatch to Lord Lyons, the British minister at Washington, together with instructions for his action.[3] The personal instructions contained matter not included in the formal despatch intended for communication to the United Sates government:—

"I need not tell your Lordship that her Majesty's government would very gladly see a practice which is calculated to lead to great irregularities, and to increase the calamities of war, renounced by both the contending parties in America as it has been renounced by almost every other nation in the world; and therefore you will not err in encouraging the Government to which you are accredited to carry into effect any disposition which they may evince to recognize the declaration of Paris in regard to privateering, as her Majesty's government do not doubt that they will, without hesitation, recognize the remaining Articles of the Declaration to which you are now instructed to call their attention. You will clearly understand that her Majesty's government cannot accept the renunciation of privateering on the part of the government of the United States if coupled with the condition that they should enforce its renunciation on the Confederate States, either by denying their right to

[1] Russell to Cowley, May 16, 1861; British Papers, No. 3, p. 3.
[2] Cowley to Russell, May 17, 1861; Papers No. 3, p. 4.
[3] Russell to Lyons, May 18, 1861; Papers No. 3, pp. 4-6.

issue letters of marque, or by interfering with the belligerent operations of vessels holding from them such letters of marque, so long as they carry on hostilities according to the recognized principles and under the admitted liabilities of the law of nations."

At noon, Saturday, May 18, before these despatches could have left the Foreign Office, Adams appeared at Pembroke Lodge, Lord John Russell's country house nine miles from London, to claim an interview with the minister.[1] Their conversation was long and serious; not till toward its close did Adams reach the subject of the Declaration of Paris. Then he said that he had the necessary powers to negotiate, "together with a form of convention" which he would submit if the British government was disposed to pursue the matter. Lord John Russell did not express a wish to pursue the matter in London, nor did he ask to see the draft of convention, "but he seemed to desire to leave the subject in the hands of Lord Lyons, to whom he intimated that he had already transmitted authority to assent to any modification of the only point in issue which the government of the United States might prefer. On that matter he believed there would be no difficulty whatever." Under these circumstances Adams postponed further action until he should receive new instructions.

Russell reported the substance of this conversation in a short despatch to Lord Lyons,[2] dated May 21, that may be quoted in full:—

"In the course of our conversation on the 18th, Mr. Adams told me that his Government was disposed to adhere to the provisions of the Declaration of Paris, and that he had powers to negotiate upon that question; but upon my saying that both Great Britain and France had given instructions to their ministers at Washington upon this subject, he thought it would be well not to pursue the matter here, but to leave it in the hands of the Secretary of State."

These two reports of what was apparently a brief and clear exchange of views, differed in effect. Russell understood Adams to suggest leaving the subject to be treated at Washington. Adams understood Russell to prefer that course, with the addition that the

[1] Adams to Russell, May 21, 1861; Diplomatic Documents, p. 74.
[2] Russell to Lyons, May 21, 1861; Papers No. 3, p. 6.

British government had already transmitted "authority" to assent to any modification of the article on privateering, "the only point in issue," which the United States government might prefer. "On that matter he believed there would be no difficulty whatever." That Adams should have misunderstood Russell was highly improbable, the more so because Russell's language, as reported, harmonized with the language of his despatch to Lord Lyons, which he signed only an hour or two before or afterward.

The next step was taken by Mr. Dayton, the United States minister at Paris. Dayton notified the French government, May 25, that he was fully authorized to enter into a convention on the points of the Declaration of Paris. In conversation, May 28 or 29, Dayton added that he was authorized to accept the four Articles, although he preferred to make the offer in the first place with the addition of Marcy's amendment.[1] Thouvenel, according to his own report to the British *chargé,* replied that the Imperial government would be glad if that of the United States acceded "purely and simply" to the Declaration of Paris.[2] He gave Dayton no reason to suppose that France was opposed to the Marcy amendment; but after three weeks of delay and consultation with the British government he replied that the American proposition must be addressed jointly to all the Powers associated in the treaty. In other words, Thouvenel, like Russell, evaded the offer of the United States government. After consulting Russell, Thouvenel no longer wished that the United States should simply accede to the four Articles.

Between May 18, when Lord John Russell had his first interview with Adams, and June 20, when Thouvenel made his reply to Dayton, the governments of England and France changed their attitude. Before learning that the United States offered pure and simple adhesion, both Governments expressed a wish or willingness for that result; after learning it, both Governments evaded an answer.

The misunderstanding in the case of Thouvenel was greater than in the case of Russell. Thouvenel sent word to the British government that Dayton had made him two propositions,[3]—

[1] Dayton to Seward, May 30, 1861; Diplomatic Documents, p. 200.
[2] Grey to Russell, June 14, 1861; Papers No. 3, p. 7.
[3] Russell to Grey, June 12, 1861. Grey to Russell, June 14, 1861. Papers No. 3, p. 7.

1. That the United States should adhere to the four Articles with the addition of the Marcy amendment. To this, Thouvenel replied, according to his story to the British government, that it was out of the question. Dayton on the contrary affirmed that Thouvenel never made such a reply.

2. Thouvenel represented Dayton as asking "that privateering being abolished by the adoption of the first Article of the Declaration of Paris, amended as proposed, the privateers sent out by the so-called Southern Confederacy should be considered as pirates." Dayton declared that he never made such a proposition. He certainly never did make it.

Another complication then occurred. Lord Lyons wrote from Washington, June 4, a letter received June 17, saying that Adams would propose adhesion to all the Articles of the Declaration of Paris.

"There is no doubt," added Lyons,[1] "that this adherence will be offered in the expectation that it will bind the Governments accepting it to treat the privateers of the Southern Confederacy as pirates. . . . It seems to be far from certain that the United States Congress would ratify the abolition of privateering, nor do I suppose that the Cabinet will abide by its proposal when it finds that it will gain nothing toward the suppression of the Southern privateering by doing so."

The animus of Lord Lyon's remarks was evident; and he was clear in the opinion that President Lincoln, after the recognition of Southern belligerency, would not renew his offer to accept the four Articles.

Ten days afterward, June 15, Lord Lyons and M. Mercier waited together on Secretary Seward at the State Department, to communicate the joint action of their Governments in regard to neutral flags. As their proposed communication was founded on the assumption that the Southern States were to be regarded as belligerents, Seward declined to receive it, and complained that England and France should concert, and announce their concert of action on such a subject. He asked them to leave their instructions with him informally, that he might understand the views of the two governments and found his despatches on clear apprehension. They

[1] Lyons to Russell, June 4, 1861; Papers No. 3, p. 8.

did so, and the discussion closed. Lyons reported the result to his Government, June 17, and in another despatch of the same day added that Secretary Seward seemed to have concluded, from a despatch he had received from Minister Adams, that Lyons had received authority to enter into a separate negotiation on the offered adhesion to the treaty or Declaration of Paris. When Lyons undeceived him, Seward said he thought he had reason to complain of the want of notice taken by the governments of Europe of the offer to adhere; but he should authorize Adams to renew it without delay.[1]

Few Secretaries of State would have borne such treatment with such temper. When Minister Adams in London learned what had occurred at Washington, he was still less favorably impressed by the manner in which he and his Government had been treated by Lord Russell and M. Thouvenel. He too kept his temper, but the affair made a lasting impression on his mind, and shook his faith in the straightforwardness of the British government. When he received renewed instructions from Secretary Seward, dated July 1, repeating the order to accede to the Declaration of Paris, he wrote to Seward expressing his "profound surprise" at the remarkable series of misunderstandings that had occurred, of which he then knew only a part; and he added that he had already written to Lord John Russell a letter intended "to bring this matter to a distinct issue."[2] He meant to trust no longer to oral communications.

The note was dated July 11, and brought the matter "to a distinct issue."

"I certainly understood your Lordship to say that the subject had already been committed to the care of Lord Lyons at Washington with authority to accept the proposition of the government of the United States, adopting three Articles of the Declaration of Paris, and to drop the fourth altogether."

As Lord Lyons was not authorized to enter into a convention, Adams offered to present his own project of convention to Russell at any moment he should appoint.[3]

[1] Lyons to Russell, June 17, 1861; Papers No. 3, p. 10.
[2] Adams to Seward, July 12, 1861; Diplomatic Documents, p. 97.
[3] Adams to Russell, July 11, 1861; Diplomatic Documents, p. 99.

To this letter Russell replied, July 13, in language undoubtedly chosen with care:—

"In the first conversation I had the honor to hold with you, on the 18th of May, I informed you that instructions had been sent to Lord Lyons to propose to the government of the United States to adopt the second, third, and fourth Articles of the Declaration of Paris, dropping the first altogether. You informed me that you had instructions on the same subject; but I understood you to express an opinion, in which I fully concurred, that it would be well to leave the question in the hands of the Secretary of State at Washington. Lord Lyons had instructions to make an agreement with the government of the United States, but he had no express authority to sign a convention."

Lord John next said that the States which had adhered to the Declaration of Paris had done so by notes or despatches. He did not expressly say that the United States had, by the terms of the Declaration, the same right to adhere to the four Articles by a simple notification,—no such admission was required, since no one questioned the right; but, he added, as Mr. Adams was instructed to present a convention, he might do so the same day at the Foreign Office at three o'clock.

Evidently Lord John, with his usual spirit, meant to meet Adams's issue as distinctly as it was made; but the note of July 13 was still an extremely curious paper, and caused Adams much perplexity, which time increased rather than diminished.

Comparison of the note to Adams of July 13 with the despatch to Lyons of May 21 shows that Russell evidently referred to the earlier paper to refresh his memory while writing the latter. He could hardly have done otherwise. No minister could venture to write a second report of conversation without referring to his first. The despatch of May 21 was before Russell's eyes when he wrote the note of July 13; but the despatch of May 21 was unknown to Adams; and could not at that time be appealed to. Russell was at liberty to make any changes that suited his purposes or position, without immediate danger of criticism. Conversely, every change he thought proper to make must have been made with the object of suiting some purpose.

In the letter of May 21, Russell began by saying: "Mr. Adams told me that his Government was disposed to adhere to the provisions of the Declaration of Paris." In the letter of July 13 he represented that the subject was not introduced by Adams, but by himself: "I informed you that instructions had been sent to Lord Lyons. . . . You informed me that you had instructions on the same subject." In the letter of May 21, Russell said that both Great Britain and France "had given instructions" to their ministers at Washington. In the letter of July 13 he said that instructions "had been sent to Lord Lyons." In strictness, the instructions dated May 18 might perhaps be said to have been "given," but they had certainly not been "sent;" and in both cases the intention was obvious to conceal from Adams that the instructions were not yet sent. In those days the Foreign Office despatch-bag, like the despatch-bag at the United States Legation, was closed and sent Saturday evening to go by messenger to Queenstown for Sunday's steamer. Russell could hardly have said at three o'clock Saturday afternoon, May 18, that despatches had been "sent" which were still in the Foreign Office, if not on his own table, and could not start for America till nine o'clock that night or thereabout.

The next divergence was more significant. The note of May 21 gave Adams's words: "Mr. Adams told me that his Government was disposed to adhere to the provisions of the Declaration of Paris, and that he had powers to negotiate upon that question." The note of July 13 ignored Adams's proposal. "You informed me that you had instructions on the same subject." For some reason not expressed, Lord John preferred that the nature and extent of Adams's proposal should not be repeated to Adams in the note of July 13.

At three o'clock the same afternoon of July 13, Adams promptly appeared at the Foreign Office with the draft of a convention in his hand. Lord John took and examined it; then, in the language of Adams's report,—

"The first remark which he made was that it was essentially the Declaration of Paris. He had never known until now that the government of the United States was disposed to accede to it. He was sure that I had never mentioned it. To this I assented."

Apparently Adams's memory deceived him, and he allowed too much credit to that of his opponent. Russell's report of May 21 proved that Adams had mentioned it, and Russell's suppression of that report, only two or three hours before he made the assertion, proved that Russell had motives for not recalling it to memory. Within two or three hours of writing to Adams the note of July 13, which was but a copy of the despatch of May 21, with the inversion of one fact and the suppression of another, Russell affirmed that he never had heard of the fact he himself suppressed.

If this were all, Lord John's reputation would repel the charge; but this was not all. Russell told Adams, July 13, that "he had never known until now that the government of the United States was disposed to accede" to the Declaration of Paris,—he had never know a fact of newspaper notoriety. A few months afterward he himself published for Parliament a blue-book containing the official letters on this subject, and among these was the despatch from Lord Lyons, dated June 4, marked as received June 17, and containing the passages already quoted:—

"It is probable that Mr. Adams may, before this despatch reaches your Lordship, have offered, on the part of his Government, to adhere to Article 1 of the Declaration of Paris as well as to the others, and thus to declare privateering to be abolished. There is no doubt that this adherence will be offered in the expectation that it will bind the government accepting it to treat the privateers of the Southern Confederacy as pirates. . . . It seems to be far from certain that the United States Congress would ratify the abolition of privateering; nor do I suppose that the Cabinet will abide by its proposal when it finds that it will gain nothing toward the suppression of the Southern privateering by doing so."

Lord John Russell was then near his seventieth year, and at that age failure of memory is common; but whatever was the true cause of his inversion and perversion of truth in this instance, no European diplomatist with whom he had ever come in contact during his long public career, would have hesitated in regard to the interpretation to be put on his conduct. Diplomacy cannot afford, and never has admitted, the possibility of accidents like these. Statesmen who made such slips were always, in European diplomacy, understood as meaning to deceive. American diplomatists in Europe could do nothing else than accept European rules. When Adams learned these contradictions, as he did within a few months, he was obliged to infer that Russell had intended to mislead him.

Two months had then elapsed since Adams's arrival in London, and during that time the British government had done no act which impressed him as honest or straightforward. Russell's reception of the project of convention, July 13, was as little calculated as all the other acts of the British government to inspire confidence.

An American would have supposed that any British minister must welcome an offer from the United States government to adhere to the Declaration of Paris. So great was the concession, that, as Lord Lyons justly said, Congress would probably have rejected it. So strong was the feeling against it among Americans abroad that Dayton, the United States minister in Paris, refused to carry out Secretary Seward's order, and gave the British and French governments a pretext for a misunderstanding, by coupling the Marcy amendment to the offer of adhesion. By no device could Great Britain have gained so much from the United States, at so little cost, as by accepting on the spot Adams's offer of adhesion pure and simple. Had Russell signed Adams's convention on the spot, he would have gained what nine Americans in every ten regarded as a great advantage over the United States.

Russell showed no such understanding of the matter. Taking the copy of the project "for the purpose of submitting it to the consideration of his colleagues in the Cabinet," he said he would let Adams know when he should be ready for another meeting. There the matter rested five days, till July 18, when Lord John wrote a formal note, beginning with two remarks: (1) That hitherto States had adhered to the Declaration by simple notice of adherence; and (2) That the Declaration was not an insulated engagement between two Powers only. Her Majesty's government were willing to waive objection to the form, but should be assured that the United States were ready to contract with all the parties to the Declaration as well as with Great Britain. As much time would be required for these communications, "her Majesty's government would deem themselves authorized to advise the Queen to conclude a convention on this subject with the President of the United States so soon as they shall have been informed that a similar convention has been agreed upon, and is ready for signature, between the President of the United States and the Emperor of the French, so that the two conventions might be signed simultaneously and on the same day."

Once more the British government insisted upon acting only in union with France, on a matter that concerned France much less than England. The persistency of this attitude of suspicion or compulsion toward the United States could not be mistaken. Adams felt it, as it was meant to be felt, but wrote immediately to Dayton at Paris, asking to know whether the joint action was within Dayton's authority. This letter was sent July 19, and on the evening of July 24 Dayton himself arrived in London to help Adams in solving the mystery that had hitherto baffled comprehension.

Meanwhile Seward at Washington made every effort for the same object. He wrote a long despatch[1] to Dayton, July 6, to overcome Dayton's objections, and gave him the positive order to make the offer of adhesion to the four Articles, without raising a question about the belligerent rights of the Union over the States in rebellion. Dayton had feared that after the recognition by France and England of belligerent rights in the rebel States, accession to the Declaration of Paris would cause a serious injury to the Union and a sacrifice of considerable advantages, not merely for the benefit of England and France, but especially for the rebel government. "If I understand the view of these foreign governments," wrote Dayton,[2] "such accession by us would merely bind our hands as respects privateering; it would not at all enlarge our rights as against a belligerent power not a party to the treaty. If they admit the Confederate States as a belligerent power, and recognize them for even commercial purposes, which, I take it, is what they mean to do, our accession to the Treaty of Paris will not change their action on this question." The soundness of this opinion was obvious; but Seward's action rested on different views.

"The United States," wrote Seward to Dayton, "have never disclaimed the employment of letters of marque as a means of maritime war. The insurgents early announced their intention to commission privateers. We knew that friendly nations would be anxious for guarantees of safety from injury by that form of depredation upon the national commerce. We knew also that such nations would desire to be informed whether their flags should be regarded as protecting goods, not contraband of war, of disloyal citizens found under them, and whether the goods, not

[1] Seward to Dayton, July 6, 1861; Diplomatic Documents, p. 215.
[2] Dayton to Seward, June 7, 1861; Diplomatic Documents, p. 204.

contraband, of subjects of such nations would be safe from confiscation when found in vessels of disloyal citizens of the United States."

The object to be gained by Seward was evident, but it had nothing to do with Dayton's fears. Seward wished to quiet foreign Powers and exclude them from interest in the war. He regarded the abandonment of privateering as not practically important to the United States, and he was undoubtedly right; but he believed that the Union was vitally interested in precluding every excuse for interference by Europe. The conduct of Great Britain was already demonstrating to him, and every other American, that there again he was right, and that at any sacrifice of small interests the vital interest of the Union must be protected,—if, indeed, protection was still possible. The attitude of England and France became more equivocal every week.

On the same day of writing the long despatch to Dayton, Seward called on Lord Lyons and tried to remove obstacles on that side. Lyons, like his French colleague Mercier, made little disguise of his leanings, and no one was ignorant that the whole social weight of both Legations was thrown in the scale against the Union. Lyons had no faith in the success of the national government, or in its professions; and his influence with his own government was exercised in that sense. Seward struggled to win him over. The visit of July 6 had no other object than if possible to draw Lyons into a friendlier attitude.

Seward had been obliged to take a strong measure in refusing to receive the joint action of the two Powers, or to recognize their concession of belligerent rights to the rebel States. He exerted himself to assure the two ministers that the United States government, though evidently unable to admit or even to discuss a denial of its own sovereignty, would ignore the action of England and France. Seward asked only that England and France should not insist on forcing their measures upon the attention of the United States government. He assured Lyons that if Europe would but consent to let the President shut his eyes, the President would not open them. The Declaration of Paris was the test. Evidently to influence British opinion, Seward told Lyons of Dayton's fears and of his own course, and in effect begged him to prevent the raising of obstacles.

"Now," Mr. Seward went on to say, "if, on the one hand, the government of the United States declared that they held their accession to the Paris Declaration to impose an obligation on France with regard to all the States of the Union, the disloyal as well as the loyal; or if, on the other hand, the government of France announced that it did not intend, by accepting the accession of the United States, to contract any engagement affecting the States in revolt,—then Mr. Dayton's apprehensions might be well founded. But if nothing was said on either side concerning this particular point, the accession of the United States might be given at once, and accepted, and the effect of it in regard to the States in revolt be determined afterward."

Lyons understood, as he was intended to understand, that Seward wished his assistance to deter the governments of England and France from preventing the adhesion of the United States by imposing any condition that should imply recognition of the Southern Confederacy. Everything else the United States would do to please England, but recognize the rebels they could not.

Lyons listened to Seward's remarks without further comment than to say that he supposed the accession of the United States would be received with great satisfaction by every government. He then reported the conversation to Lord John Russell. His report, dated July 8, closed with the following paragraph:[1]

"Notwithstanding the opinion expressed by Mr. Seward, I continue to think it very important, with a view to preventing serious disputes in future, that Great Britain and France should not accept the accession of this government to the Declaration of Paris without stating to it, formally and distinctly beforehand, the effect which their so doing is intended by them to have with regard to the seceded States."

Lord Lyons knew that his advice, if followed, would prevent the United States from acceding to the Declaration of Paris. His motive, as he explained it, was to prevent serious disputes in future. In his mind the advantages to be gained by the adhesion of the United States were outweighed by the risk of disputes.

In these complications certain points gradually became clear. That the governments of Great Britain and France were unwilling that the United States should accede to the Declaration of Paris

[1] Papers No. 3, p. 14.

pure and simple, was evident. Under the Declaration of Paris they were bound to invite the United States government to adhere to the four Articles in their entirety, and were especially pledged to enter into no other arrangement. In violation of the pledge, they invited the United States government to enter into another arrangement, and did not invite it to accede "purely and simply." They persistently ignored, evaded, and postponed attention to the offer of pure and simple adhesion. Lord Lyons, when requested by Seward to use his influence to facilitate the accession pure and simple, acted in the opposite sense, and pressed his Government to impose a condition which he was warned would prevent accession. France acted only as the ally of England, and was guided by the wishes of the British cabinet. Palmerston and Russell were the chief agents in the affair, and their wish to prevent the United States from acceding was the cause of the whole difficulty. The mystery that neither Seward nor Adams could penetrate was the motive that actuated the British cabinet. To that point Adams directed his attention.

Dayton having arrived in London, July 24, had an interview with Adams, July 25, and "under the circumstances felt it his duty to say to Mr. Adams that there need be no delay on his account." [1] Dayton asked only that before offering accession pure and simple, Adams should obtain from Russell a distinct refusal to entertain the Marcy amendment. Adams accordingly wrote to Russell, July 29, informing him of Dayton's wish to be assured on that point, and promising that as soon as he should receive an explicit assurance that the Marcy amendment was inadmissible, Dayton would apprise the French government of his intention to accede to the Declaration of Paris pure and simple.

Russell replied July 31, giving the required assurance, and adding that he was ready to carry on the negotiation so that the convention should be signed simultaneously at London and Paris. His note closed with a significant phrase: "I need scarcely add that on the part of Great Britain the engagement will be prospective, and will not invalidate anything already done." [2]

In transmitting this note to his Government, August 2, Adams said: "I must frankly admit that I do not understand the meaning

[1] Dayton to Seward, July 30, 1861; Diplomatic Documents, p. 220.
[2] Russell to Adams, July 31, 1861; Diplomatic Documents, p. 110.

of the last paragraph."[1] The persistent creation of difficulties by Russell caused in Adams an equally persistent determination to force Russell into an avowal of his true position. Adams took no notice of the reservation, and waited for Russell to take the next step. If Russell wished only to reserve the right to disregard future complaints or claims of the United States, this formal notice seemed sufficient. He would in that case sign the convention without more delay.

Russell waited until August 19. Then he wrote to Adams a note enclosing a formal declaration which he meant to make on signing the convention.[2]

"In affixing his signature to the convention of this day between her Majesty, the Queen of Great Britain and Ireland, and the United States of America, the Earl Russell declares, by order of her Majesty, that her Majesty does not intend thereby to undertake any engagement which shall have any bearing, direct or indirect, on the internal difficulties now prevailing in the United States."

On the same day Russell transmitted a copy of this declaration to Paris, and it was adopted by Thouvenel for communication to Dayton.

To Russell's note of August 19 Adams replied in a long and carefully prepared note,[3] dated August 23, recapitulating the story of the negotiation down to the actual moment, when the "novel and anomalous proceeding" of Earl Russell arrested it.

"Obviously," said Adams, "a consent to accept a particular exception, susceptible of so wide a construction of a joint instrument, made by one of the parties to it in its favor at the time of signing, would justify the idea that some advantage is, or may be suspected to be, intended to be taken by the other. The natural effect of such an accompaniment would seem to be to imply that the government of the United States might be desirous at this time to take a part in the Declaration, not from any high purpose or durable policy, but with a view of securing some small temporary object in the unhappy struggle which is going on at home. Such an inference would spoil all the value that might be attached to the act itself. The mere toleration of it would seem to be equivalent

[1] Adams to Seward, Aug. 2, 1861; Diplomatic Documents, p. 108.
[2] Russell to Adams, Aug. 19, 1861; Diplomatic Documents, p. 118.
[3] Adams to Russell, Aug. 23, 1861; Diplomatic Documents, p. 120.

to a confession of their own weakness. Rather than that such a record should be made, it were a thousand times better that the Declaration remain unsigned forever. If the parties to the instrument are not to sign it upon terms of perfect reciprocity, with all their duties and obligations under it perfectly equal, and without equivocation or reservation of any kind on any side, then it is plain that the proper season for such an engagement has not yet arrived. It were much wiser to put it off until nations can understand each other better."

To this note Russell replied at equal length, August 28,[1] evidently feeling that his position was seriously assailed. His defence of the proposed declaration was contained in a few sentences:—

"It would follow from the position taken by the United States that the privateers of the Southern States might be decreed to be pirates; and it might be further argued by the government of the United States that a European power signing a convention with the United States declaring that privateering was and remains abolished, would be bound to treat the privateers of the so-called Confederate States as pirates. Hence instead of an agreement, charges of bad faith and violation of a convention might be brought in the United States against the Power signing such a convention and treating the privateers of the so-called Confederate States as those of a belligerent power. . . . It is in this spirit that her Majesty's government decline to bind themselves, without a clear explanation on their part, to a convention which, seemingly confined to an adoption of the Declaration of Paris of 1856, might be construed as an engagement to interfere in the unhappy dissensions now prevailing in the United States."

This explanation was remarkable for admitting the correctness of Adams's criticism; but it raised doubts of another kind, which could not but strengthen the growing conviction in the minds of all Americans who followed the negotiation, that behind the British evasions and excuses some unavowed motive was still concealed.

The ostensible plea was clear. Lord Russell wished to avoid the vortex of American wars. Equally clearly the proposed declaration would not answer that purpose, even though the American government had accepted it. It could not be a part of the four Articles of the Declaration of Paris. The United States government could at any moment, by merely writing a formal note, accede to those

[1] Russell to Adams, Aug. 28, 1861; Diplomatic Documents, p. 128.

Articles as they stood, and Great Britain was pledged to accept the adhesion unconditionally. Adams asked for a convention because the Senate must have some instrument to ratify in order to make it valid at home; but had the United States government chosen to act directly, it could have done so, as far as regarded foreign Powers, without the possibility of condition or refusal from Great Britain.

The proposed declaration was merely a notice given by Earl Russell that the British government would follow a certain course; but the notice would bind the United States in no way, and left President Lincoln still free to call upon Great Britain to fulfil all the obligations of the four Articles, whatever they were. In that case the British government, with or without the declaration, stood in the same attitude. The declaration merely warned the United States that Great Britain, in case of a demand to fulfil certain duties resulting from the treaty, meant to refuse compliance; but it could not prevent the demand if the United States government chose to make it.

Lord Russell knew that the United States always had considered Great Britain bound to treat the Southern cruisers, whether public or private, as pirates, on grounds altogether separate from the Declaration of Paris, though in American eyes much stronger. The British ministry had emphatically refused to do so by recognizing them as belligerents. The act, unfriendly to the United States at best, had been made more so by its adoption on the day when Adams reached London, as though Russell wished to preclude discussion. President Lincoln had not acquiesced in that decision, but had not made it ground of quarrel. Russell showed extravagant bias against the United States government if he supposed that President Lincoln meant to seek a contest over the Declaration of Paris, when Lincoln had made every effort to prove that he did not mean to quarrel over the proclamation of Southern belligerency. The Declaration of Paris was a side issue. The main issue was the belligerency of the rebel States; and the British government had already by proclamation given formal and sufficient notice, by creating them belligerents, that Great Britain did not intend to treat Southern privateers as pirates.

The proposed declaration was superfluous as far as concerned its ostensible object; it was discourteous, for it implied that the United States government was laying a trap for Great Britain; it had no binding power on the United States; and it was a measure which Russell knew, through the warning of Seward to Lyons, would prevent further proceedings on the part of the United States.

As a matter of history the story stops there. The motives of the British government were not further avowed, and its action led to no apparent consequence. Earl Russell's course in 1861 was all of one character; and whether in a single point it was controlled by fear of Seward's supposed tricks or by unavowed motives, is immaterial. In either case it was equally unfriendly. History abstains from imputing motives and adopting uncertain conclusions; but what history avoids, diplomacy is obliged habitually to do. No diplomatist in the service of a European government ever received such treatment as was received by Adams and Dayton without searching for unavowed reasons to account for it. Least of all would an English diplomatic agent have been satisfied with the official explanations in this case; for among diplomatists the English, not without excuse, were always most prone to act on the assumption that truth was an English virtue, and that falsehood was a diplomatic profession. During the year 1861 the United States Legation in London stood in an attitude of anxiety not easy to realize; and in the face of hostility or distrust so openly avowed by Earl Russell, no member of that Legation could afford to pass over so extraordinary an experience without framing some explanation that could be used for guidance through the darkness and danger that surrounded him.

When Adams arrived in London, May 13, 1861, the American Union was universally supposed to be at an end. Not one Englishman in a hundred took a different view. The possibility of a civil war, believed to be necessarily futile, irritated Englishmen against President Lincoln and his supporters. Never in the history of human events had a revolt of such a nature and extent been repressed by force; and even the friends of America shrank for a moment from the realization that a million lives might have to pay the price of Union. This state of public opinion was natural, and not a subject for complaint so much as for correction. Within a few months it was corrected, and within a year the British government could have adopted no unfriendly measure without meeting vigorous resistance from its own ranks; but during the summer of 1861 the United States government could count on no support in England. Not until Bright, Cobden, and Forster had fully entered the lists and shown a temper almost resembling that of the American combatants, did the American Legation in London draw a free breath.

The conviction that the Union was at an end lay at the foundation of every act adopted by the British government during the spring and summer of 1861. The assumption that the United States government existed only in form was evident in Russell's attitude toward Adams from the moment of his arrival until the following year. Russell intentionally fixed, as far as he was concerned, the position of Adams before he arrived, as the representative of half an empire, and afterward showed without concealment his intention to hold Adams in the position fixed for him.

The Declaration of Paris was the first battle-ground between Russell and Adams. For the Declaration itself Adams cared as little as Russell or Dayton; but the evident intention to prevent Adams from giving his Government's adherence to the Declaration of Paris, and the extraordinary equivocations to which Russell resorted in the effort to take from his course the appearance of outrage, exasperated Adams to the point of pressing the British government as far as it could be induced to go in discovering its true intentions. Evidently the British government, for some reason not clearly understood, shrank from saying how far it meant to go. Russell said only enough to show that in due time he meant to say more.

The story has shown that Russell and his colleagues recognized the rebels as belligerents before Adams could arrive to remonstrate; that they effected a practical alliance with France against the United States at the same time; that they induced the French government to violate the pledge given in the protocol of the Declaration of Paris in order to offer to both belligerents a partial adhesion, which must exclude the United States from a simple adhesion, to the Declaration of Paris, while it placed both belligerents on the same apparent footing. These steps were taken in haste before Adams could obtain an interview. When Adams by an effort unexpected to Russell obtained an interview at Pembroke Lodge at noon of Saturday, May 18, and according to Russell's report of May 21 said that the United States were "disposed to adhere to the Declaration of Paris," Russell evaded the offer, saying that he had already sent sufficient instructions to Lyons, although the instructions were not sufficient, nor had they been sent. When this evasion was afterward brought to his notice by Adams, Russell, revising his report to Lyons, made such changes in it as should represent the first proposal as coming from himself, and the evasion to have come from Adams. When at last obliged to read the American offer, Russell declared that he had never heard of it before, although he had himself reported it to Lyons and Lyons had reported it to him. When compelled to take the offer for consideration, Russell, though always professing to welcome adhesion pure and simple, required the co-operation of Dayton. When Adams overcame this last obstacle, Russell interposed a written proviso, which as he knew from Lyons would prevent ratification. When Adams paid no attention to the proviso, but insisted on signature of the treaty, Russell at last wrote a declaration in the nature of an insult, which could not be disregarded.

Lord Russell's motives for this conduct were his own affair. The United States Legation in London could not undertake to say certainly what they were, nor did it greatly care for an explanation, since no conceivable explanation could have excused the Legation for acting on any principle but one of distrust. By the necessities of the case, Adams had no choice. Russell's acts, whether straightforward or not, bore every external appearance of covert hostility. Adams could do nothing else than draw inferences from every step in Russell's progress. From the first,—Russell's disregard of the pledge of indivisibility in the protocol to the Declaration of Paris,— the American minister was obliged to infer that England no longer thought her interest to require that the United States should be a party to the whole Declaration. From the second,—Russell's wish for accession to the second, third, and fourth Articles,—it was clear that the first Article, or the whole in conjunction, in some manner clashed with British interests after the dissolution of the Union. From Russell's evasion of Adams's offer, May 18, Adams could only conclude that the offer was in some manner inconvenient for the

British government, which had motives for joining France in acting at Washington. From Russell's misstatement of the interview of May 18, it appeared that he wished to conceal, or not to avow, the motives of his action or the action itself. From the delays interposed by Russell, Adams must conclude that the British cabinet was trying one device after another to evade the proposition; and finally, from the written declaration of August 19 he could draw no other inference than that Russell had resorted to the only defensive weapon left him, in order to avoid the avowal of his true motives and policy.

Just or not, these were necessary conclusions for any minister of the United States in 1861, who had to shape a course of conduct in the face of universal ill-will. In such a situation the business of a diplomatist was to account in some way for the mysterious acts of his enemies in order not to be taken by surprise when the blow should come. A little study of the history of the Declaration of Paris suggested motives which might offer a clew not only to Russell's strange conduct in May and July, but to the danger it threatened to the United States.

The Declaration of Paris while purporting to add four principles to international law, did in fact offer only two. The principle that neutral goods were not liable to condemnation under enemy's flag, and the other that blockades to be binding must be effective, were then and had always been acknowledged maxims of law, as well established as any of the common rules of a little respected code had usually been. Only two of the principles involved new points. One was that privateering should be abolished; the other was that the neutral flag covered enemy's goods.

Of the two new principles the first was indisputably advantageous to Great Britain, and never met with opposition from her. Earl Russell could have no objection to the abandonment of privateering by the United States. The secret of his evident unwillingness to the adherence of the United States on any terms to the Declaration of Paris could not be found in the Article on privateering; but if it was not there in Article 1, or in Articles 3 and 4, it must be sought in Article 2, that the neutral flag covered enemy's goods.

Considering that England was about to become a neutral, the idea of her hostility to a provision so favorable to neutrals was apparently unreasonable; but in April and May, 1861, the American Union was supposed likely to fall apart without serious trouble, and the permanent interests of Great Britain as a belligerent still outweighed her momentary interests as a neutral. The principle that the neutral flag covered enemy's goods was a neutral and American interest against which Great Britain had fought with something like desperation.

This second Article of the Treaty of Paris was always regarded as hostile to British power, and was accepted by England only as a sacrifice under motives sufficiently strong to justify it. Russell himself objected to it and opposed it, and the whole conservative spirit of the kingdom uniformly maintained that Great Britain had "a great and preponderating interest in maintaining the legitimate rights of belligerents, and cannot afford to sacrifice such legitimate exercise of belligerent power as is justified by the law of nations."

The Ministry of 1854 decided to concede the sanctity of the neutral flag for reasons well understood. One of these reasons was that by this concession England obtained the abandonment of the practice of privateering. The other reason was given by Lord Palmerston officially from his place on the Treasury Bench in the House of Commons on the night of March 18, 1862. He said that had the Government not taken the course it did take in 1854; had it insisted on maintaining the right of search and seizure of enemy's goods in neutral ships,—such persistence would within six months have added a war with the United States to the war they were then waging with Russia. According to Palmerston, the British government was forced by the great and growing power of the United States into an unwilling assent to principles which it held to be dangerous to the maritime power of England.

The continuance of the later policy was naturally dependent on the continuance of the motives that led the British government to adopt it. If fear of the power of the American Union produced the leniency toward neutrals, the removal of this fear would remove the motive to persevere in the leniency. The same men and the same ideas ruled England in 1861 as in 1856; and both Palmerston and Russell were statesmen of the old school, whose views of the United States had not essentially changed since the War of 1812.

The dissolution of the American Union was foreseen from the

moment of Abraham Lincoln's election as President in November, 1860. After five months of doubt and preparation, the civil war broke out beyond restraint, April 12, 1861, and the news reached England, April 20. Three agents of the insurgent government were already on the spot,—Yancey, Rost, and Mann,—and Lord John Russell admitted them to an interview, May 4, in which they urged at great length the cause of their new republic. Only two days afterward, May 6, Russell wrote to Cowley at Paris, directing him to invite the French government to join in an effort to obtain from the two contending parties in America their adherence to the second, third, and fourth Articles of the Declaration of Paris. Only two days after the British government had reason to know officially the rupture of the American Union, it began to disregard its pledge given five years before in the Treaty of Paris, under the avowed idea that the power of the United States was too dangerous to be thwarted. The plan of Lord John Russell was merely to provide a temporary arrangement protecting British neutral rights while saving British belligerent practices. He proposed "to invite the two contending parties to act upon the principles laid down in the second and third Articles of the Declaration of Paris." He did not propose to enter into any arrangement for adopting principles, or for acting on them beyond the time of hostilities. At the close of hostilities the proposed arrangement was to terminate, and the British rights of belligerency were to remain at all times intact.

The United States were required to promise only that belligerent rights should not, during the coming hostilities, be used against British commerce; while Russell and Palmerston retained the right to revive at any future time the exercise of those belligerent rights against the enfeebled and divided States which they expected to survive the civil war. Had the United States been permitted to accede to the Declaration of Paris pure and simple, Great Britain would have lost her belligerent rights beyond recall, the more effectually because the United States were obliged by their Constitution to record their accession in the form of a treaty, whereas Great Britain had entered with other Powers into a mere agreement, which was binding, as Lord Malmesbury declared, only so long as it was convenient to respect it.

The British government had no reason to suppose that the United

States would lay aside their objections to the Declaration of Paris, and Seward's offer to do so disconcerted Russell. In his second despatch to Lyons, of May 18, he made no suggestion of adhesion pure and simple, but he said that he could not accept the renunciation of privateering on the part of the United States, "if coupled with the condition that her Majesty's government should enforce its renunciation on the Confederate States;" yet when the United States offered to renounce privateering without coupling to it any condition whatever, Russell introduced conditions on his part which he knew would prevent President Lincoln from carrying out his purpose.

Whether these were the motives of Russell or not, they were the motives that the American Legation in London was irresistibly obliged to impute to him. After the manner in which Russell received the advances of President Lincoln, no American minister in London could safely act on any other assumption than that the British government meant, at the first convenient opportunity, to revive the belligerent pretences dormant since the War of 1812.

Count Edward de Crillon

For a time after the publication of his History *Adams intended to continue his research in order to be able to make revisions in a possible future edition. But the disappointing reception given the* History *and the shift of his mind to other interests soon discouraged the carrying out of this plan. Only the following paper on the adventurous and disreputable Count Edward de Crillon resulted from Adams' original intention. He contributed it to the first issue of the* American Historical Review, *where it was surrounded by the most solid academic dignity, and flavored its Stendhalian quality with a deliberately provocative and somewhat malicious little disquisition on the fallibility of historians. The gesture is reminiscent of the young Washington writer twenty five years before who loved nothing better than to bring "all the respectable old fools of the country down on me."*

Aᴄᴄᴏʀᴅɪɴɢ to mathematicians, every man carries with him a personal error in his observation of facts, for which a certain allowance must be made before attaining perfect accuracy. In a subject like history, the personal error must be serious, since it tends to distort the whole subject, and to disturb the relations of every detail. Further, the same allowance must be made for every authority cited by the historian. Each has his personal error, varying in value, and often unknown to the writer quoting him. Finally, the facts themselves carry with them an error of their own; they may be correctly stated, and still lead to wrong conclusions. Of the reader's personal error nothing need be said. The sum of such inevitable errors must be considerable. At the most moderate estimate the historian can hardly expect that four out of five of his statements of fact shall be exact. On an average every history contains at least one assertion of fact to every line. A history like that of Macaulay contains much more than one hundred and fifty thousand assertions or assumptions of fact. If the rule holds good, at least thirty thousand of these so-called facts must be more or less inexact. In regard to events of earlier history or of less familiar societies, the necessary error must be much greater.

The historian is properly responsible only for his own personal error, but this he can never calculate, since it is hopelessly con-

[From the *American Historical Review*, I (October 1895), 51-69.]

fused with the conditions of his education, his society, and his age. His personal tricks of thought or manner he may sometimes recognize. One can imagine that Gibbon and Macaulay might even have been greatly annoyed by their own mannerism, had they been of a nervous temperament; but their personal error would have remained the same. Some historians are more, some less, inaccurate; but the best must always stand in terror of the blunders which no precaution and no anxiety for truth can save him from committing.

This subject acquires serious interest to any one who undertakes to teach or write upon History, because, of all objects of study, human beings are the most complicated and least easily understood. They do not even understand themselves. They habitually deceive themselves about their own motives. The most respectable and the most honest are seen in politics engaged in transactions which, from another point of view, seem to imply the want of a moral sense. Their evidence is rarely conclusive. If, to this confusion of error, the personal error of the historian is added, the result becomes an inextricable mess. Almost every great criminal in history has been defended with more or less force, and almost every example of lofty virtue has been more or less successfully attacked. After two thousand years of hot dispute, society to-day is still hotly disputing the characters of the Gracchi, of Cicero, of Brutus, and of Julius Cæsar, while that of Oliver Cromwell shakes the credit of a ministry.

Conscious of the pitfalls that surround him, the writer of history can only wait in silent hope that no one will read him,—at least with too much attention. He knows the worst. He has taken some patriot at his own estimate, and condemned some traitor at the estimate of the patriot! He has misread some document, adding his own blunder to the deception intended by the author of the document! He has accepted, as authority, an official statement, made, for once, without intent to deceive; and thus, thrown off his guard by the evident absence of dishonest intention, he has fallen into the blunder of taking a government at its own low estimate of itself.

One of these blunders, which is fortunately of so little consequence as to allow of attaching a story to it, will be found in Volume II., page 186, of the *History of the First Administration of Madison*.

Special students of American history may remember the curious episode of John Henry in 1812, who got fifty thousand dollars from Mr. Madison for revealing the intrigues which the Boston Federalists had not had with the British government. Opinions differed then, and probably differ still, as to the value of John Henry's papers, but few persons would differ about the value of John Henry himself. He was a political blackmailer; an adventurer; and, like a good many of his political superiors, more or less of a liar; yet, on the whole, want of truth was not one of his strongest peculiarities. Indeed, except for the overestimate of his own services, the statements made by Henry were reasonably exact. The *History* has no quarrel with him.

A person who more interested society at the time, and is more amusing still, than John Henry, was an extraordinary Frenchman, who appeared suddenly, as Henry's patron, in Washington society, and figured conspicuously at the White House, at the French and British Legations, and before a Congressional committee, disappearing as suddenly as he came, and leaving only the conviction that he was a rogue, and general perplexity to account for his presence in such a part of the world. The world naturally inferred that Savary, Duke de Rovigo, Napoleon's Minister of Police, was in the secret. The Frenchman was an agent of Napoleon's secret police. This inference became the accepted version of history. Among the French secretaries at Washington who knew the so-called Count Edward de Crillon was the Count Georges de Caraman, who published, forty years afterwards, in the *Revue Contemporaine* for August, 1852, an account of the affair,—an account authorized by Serurier, who, in 1812, was the French minister in Washington. Caraman, who might be supposed to know, expressly said that the man who called himself Crillon was found to be an agent of the Emperor's secret police. From Caraman's memoirs, the statement slipped naturally into the *History of the Administration of Madison,* where it stands on the page already cited.

In spite of Caraman's assertion, and in spite of the apparent safety of taking for granted that he knew what he said was known, the so-called Count Edward de Crillon seems not to have had any authority to act as a police agent. In that character he appears only as a volunteer. The French police were frequently in pursuit of him, but are not known to have availed themselves of his distinguished services. The statement made in the *History* should therefore be struck out, and, as no further conclusions were deduced from it, the error, unlike many other similar mistakes, stops there. Yet the correction, slight as it is, leads to another inquiry, which has little to do with the history of the United States, but opens a curious chapter of the social history of the world at the beginning of the century. If Count Edward de Crillon was not a secret agent of the French police, who was he, and how did it happen that he appeared and disappeared so dramatically in the diplomatic drama of the War of 1812?

A volume of the archives of the French Foreign Office, overlooked in the original search for documents relating to the United States, contains some papers relating to this matter, which seems at the time to have perplexed the French government almost as much as it annoyed Mr. Madison. The first of these papers is a letter from the Prefect of the Department of the Gers, in the south of France, written four years after Crillon's adventure in America, and directed to the Minister of Foreign Relations at Paris.

THE PREFECT OF THE DEPARTMENT
OF THE GERS

TO

MONSEIGNEUR [THE DUKE DE RICHELIEU] THE MINISTER OF FOREIGN RELATIONS.[1]

PREFECTURE OF THE GERS,
Auch, 1 March, 1816.

Monseigneur:

The nomination of M. Hyde de Neuville to the Legation of the United States has suggested to me the idea of putting under your Excellency's eyes some papers which were seized at the domicil of a St. Soubiran of Lectoure, and a knowledge of which may interest the mission of His Majesty's ambassador.

This Soubiran is an intriguer of the first order, who, being son of a goldsmith of Lectoure, has successively played the roles of Colonel, Consul, Ambassador, and Chevalier of all the Orders. Pursued by the imperial police whom he had disturbed from Spain to Hamburg by his

---

[1] *États Unis,* Supt. 2, 103.

political or financial expedients, he finished by reaching the United States, where he contracted a kind of intimacy with an Irish major named Henry, whose name your Excellency will doubtless remember to have seen figure in the quarrel of the United States with England. It seems that this Major, having been charged with some political exploration by the chiefs of the English army, sold the secret of his mission to President Madison, and the memoir of Soubiran seems to show him as intermediary in that negotiation, of which he doubtless allotted to himself a good part of the price, since he returned to France with 70,000 livres of bills of exchange from Consul Lescallier, who treated him with intimacy, as did also M. Serurier, then Minister of France in the United States.

As all this medley [*tripotage*] seems to me to have some relation with the respective efforts of the two American parties which then respectively cultivated or combatted the envoy of France, I have thought necessary to communicate to your Excellency the verbose and romantic memoir of Soubiran, in which the simple or impudent avowals may, to a certain point, offer a presumption of truth.

I am with respect, Monseigneur, your Excellency's very humble and very obedient servant,

The Prefect of the Gers,
BROCHET DE DESIGNY

If exactness of translation matters little, exact dates would be convenient, but the Prefect unfortunately did not mention whether Soubiran's papers had been just seized, or whether the seizure had taken place at some previous time. None of the papers seem to have been written later than 1814. The first is the memoir which the Prefect correctly described as verbose and romantic, but which he thought might to a certain point offer a presumption of truth. Most of Soubiran's papers offer only a presumption of untruth, but his account of the episode of Henry's documents can, to some extent, be tested by other evidence.

MEMOIR OF SOUBIRAN[1]

The Last Two Years of My Life

The 1st August, 1810, after having sold furniture, I set out for Baréges. My health had no need of the mineral waters, but my purse had need of supplies. In consequence, I left Baréges for Bagnères, where, two hours after my arrival, I sacrificed to the *Tapis vert,* and, deceived for

---

[1] *États Unis,* Supt. 2, 102.

the hundredth time in my hopes, I saw myself a victim and was immolated on this stage of fortune. Nevertheless, I had the courage to remain until October 15, and, after having borrowed 600 francs from the Prefect Chazal, I quitted this place which had been so often disastrous to me and returned to my country. I arrived at Lectoure with 54 francs and a valet de chambre. My project was to pass the winter there, but when I learned that I was under suit for a bill of exchange from Paris, I determined to go to offer my services in Moldavia to the hospodar (Prince ———), with whom I had relations; and I remained only a few hours at Lectoure.

On arriving at Agen I had drawn 18 francs on my fund, and I had hired a small boat to Bordeaux for 72 francs, when my faithful valet came to join me at Port Ste. Marie, and to my great astonishment, brought me six double Louis that he borrowed of a certain lady whose loyal conduct will never be lost in my grateful heart.

A high and puissant seigneur, I reached Bordeaux, where I received the most amiable reception from all my friends. I left it, always filled with my great project. I stopped at Blois, where for two years I had maintained a correspondence with a charming woman (Madame de Lajonquière). I wanted to find out whether amiability or trickery [*rouerie*] formed the essence of her character; and, in consequence, a carriage was harnessed, and four post-horses conducted me to the Chateau de la Savonière, whither a note and my Gilbert had already preceded me.

On leaping from my carriage, I was met by a man who seemed to me frank, loyal, and generous. "M. de Soubiran," he said to me, "how glad I am to see you, and how happy I should be if my wife, who is waiting for you in the parlor, could enjoy the same pleasure! but for twenty years past she has been blind! What happiness for us to receive among us him who protected our son in Spain—that poor Albert! He is prisoner in England! He was taken in the affair of Ta— Ta— eh! yes! Talavera!"

I knew nothing about it! No matter! We arrived in the salon, where I found Mme. de Latour with two priests, a perfect contrast with the master of the place. A face gentle, angelic; an air of dignity; the tone, the bearing of candor and of modesty; which would have inspired me if I had not every moment been recalled to my gay humor by M. de Latour, who appeared like a Jean Bart, a De Ruyter. "Monsieur," said he, "if you listen to Madame, she will talk to you of all the noblesse of the Vendômois, of the Orléanais, of the Gâtinais, of the Court of Guise, and of Francis the First. She knows thoroughly her French history; but I beg you!— This affair belongs to these gentlemen. As for us, let us talk of war!" "But, monsieur," I said to him, "how is Mme de la Jonquière?" "She has been, for a month past, with Mme. de Staël. I have sent to inform her of your arrival, and if we do not all sup together this evening, to-morrow morning we shall breakfast together." Thereupon, supper was announced. "Monsieur is served," said Gilbert, who had already taken the direction of the household. But three or four great blows of the knocker announced the goddess of the chateau, who, after having embraced her mother, turned to me with the most proper and amiable tone and said: "Colonel, you will not be surprised at my impatience to come and receive at home the man who has deigned to protect that poor Albert, that good brother, tenderly cherished. Promise me to pass some months with us, and I shall believe that happiness has not totally deserted the Chateau de Savonière." I answered as I best could her charming politeness, but I could not weary of admiring her who spoke to me. In truth, I was transported; I was among the angels; I thought myself in fairyland. My costume suggested the adventurer a little [*prêtait un peu à l'aventure*] and my Frontin showed an alacrity for Madame which made it clear to the priests that he thought he was serving the future wife of his master. At length, the conversation turned on the Church. I edified everybody and became the idol of the mother. I made loud responses to the prayer, while Gilbert prayed like the rest, and we were on the road to canonization.

Soon I was presented to all the neighboring gentry, and I always ordered a post-chaise which seated Monsieur and Madame and Gilbert. Everybody talked of our future marriage, but I knew there was nothing in it. Finally, after having finished my projects, and colored with a pretext a loan of which I had need, I set out post for Paris.

The next day I arrived at the capital. I feared to remain there. My debts frightened me. I feared that my creditor there would prove less magnanimous than the noble family at La Savonière. I set out for Senlis, leaving Gilbert behind with two notes for two charming women, Mlle. Millières and Mme. Éléonore. They accepted my invitation and I spent for them 240 francs out of the sixteen louis that remained to me. It mattered much to me that two women *à la mode* should say in the *grand monde* that I was always generous and full of good graces. From there I went to Saint Omer and then to Roye, where my faithful Gilbert made acquaintance with the driver of a coach who was taking to Brussels Mme. de Mirecour, former canoness, who had just gained a lawsuit at Paris. Without telling me anything beforehand, Frontin woke me at four o'clock in the morning, by crying out: "Monsieur, they are harnessing the horses!" I get up; the bill is paid; and I seat myself in a handsome carriage by the side of a heavenly woman. I saluted her so modestly that she afterwards told me the impression it had made on her. I will not enter into a longer detail; it will be enough to know that her house became my hotel during a fortnight that I remained in Brussels. For my journey in Holland I had to accept a cabriolet, a box of wine, and Gilbert had 50 louis that were lent him for me.

I arrived at Amsterdam, where my stay offered nothing remarkable. Frontin went to visit Mme. de Ménoire. He promised to bring me to her, and was presented with a hundred ducats of which he said that I had need. I visited Groningen and arrived at the seashore; there I found Admiral Devanter, who was my intimate at Paris. I saw, and was presented by him to General Miollis. He gave me letters for the generals of brigade who were at Emden, where I was received as Prince Frederick would have been if the garrison had been Prussian. I was lodged with the richest merchant; I gave fêtes; the generals and all the officers came to them; the music of the regiment played all night, and I lost harmoniously all my money. That honest banker offered me some; I accepted it; and after two weeks' stay I came to Oldenburg, bearer of a letter for General Soligny. I passed there two days and dined alternately with the General and with the Prince, who sent me in one of his carriages as far as Bremen, where I had calculated a stroke of contraband which would have brought me 80,000 francs. But the secret ways of Providence confound the projects of mortals. Accordingly I had to quit Bremen and go to Hamburg. The evening of my arrival I gained a thousand ducats; the next day I won again, so that my stay in that city was the subject of every conversation. I was summoned by the Governor,—the antagonist of the Prince of Sweden. "I am on my way to Stockholm," I told him, "to claim or solicit service." "Where are your orders?" "I am going to deserve them." My answers did not appear to him conclusive; he ordered two gendarmes to keep watch on me. The evening of the next day I shook off the yoke, abandoning at midnight my wardrobe and my money. I took without knowing it the road to Copenhagen; I made ten German leagues on foot, and hired a carriage which took me to Kiel, where I presented myself to the Maréchale de Lowendal. Some recommendations for Copenhagen, and 250 guineas, put me in condition to continue my journey. I visited Stockholm without succeeding in my projects. I came to Gottenburg, and from there to Frederikstad. I visited devoutly the tomb of Charles XII.; and the 15th March I embarked for Carolina. Hardly ten days at sea we were taken by the *Formidable*, an English seventy-four. I was a passenger, and Spanish, I said; so I obtained liberty to go to London. I recalled to mind that the man, who, two days before quitting in 1801 the city of Paris, had won from me 30,000 francs, and who the next day, having lost £10,000, ran away without paying me,—I recalled, I say, that he lived in London, and I resolved to make him fight, or to obtain an indemnity. I called on the father of the young man; I made my demand, and complained of his want of delicacy with so much force that the son took it up with insolence. On my promise to fight a duel with him the father gave me an order on the bank, at sight, begging me not to pay attention to his son, or he would call in the police. "I am all right, sir," I said, "and here is my permit of residence in London." Then I showed him my Spanish permit, which luckily he did not read. The next day I was waked by order of this brave young man who waited me in the park. I loaded him with insults, and my quarrel changed object. I put a pistol-ball through his shoulder, and got as recompense the order to quit London under penalty of transportation. I made nothing of it, and came to Brighton.

I was on the point of departure for the United States when M. de Crillon Partorias, with whom I had relations, begged me not to abandon him. I was entirely master of his mind; I read him the Holy Scriptures, more devout than the Grand Inquisitor. Soon he had gout in his stomach and made me heir, by testament, of his name, of all his property, and of twelve hundred quadruples [doubloons]. This adventure made some noise. The ambassador wanted to have the will broken, but it was in good form.

Then I quitted Brighton and went to the Isle of Wight, where I remained incognito until the moment when I sailed for the continent of America. I made acquaintance with the passengers. Of this number was Major Henry, a young Irishman, a very handsome man, but with an air of melancholy showing some secret trouble. Soon our acquaintance became intimate, and after some weeks of voyage we confided in each other our most secret thoughts.

"For twenty years," said he, "I have lived in America, where I was taken under the care of a rich and powerful uncle named Keane. Quite early I pronounced against republics. The English government was not slow in offering me employment. Young, ambitious, I seized the opportunity, and at first went to Quebec, where I agreed with the Governor of Canada on my plan of conduct. I had served in the American army; I had many partisans there. Since my marriage I had studied law; and I was about to succeed in dividing the five States of the north,—in separating them from the American Union,—when the affair of the *Chesapeake* occurred. After that event I returned to England, where I was invited to go back and continue under George Prevost what I had commenced under his predecessor; but my enthusiasm was destroyed. I had visited Ireland, and seen her destruction; our palaces turned into prisons, our mansions into barracks, and our best citizens loaded with the chains of despotism."

I profited by this avowal. I discovered the discontent that seemed to animate him, and I turned to the profit of France what was intended to destroy her cause. I neglected neither promises nor hopes, and at last, master of all the correspondence, of the official despatches, I reached the continent of America. Arrived at Boston, I wrote to the ambassador my situation and the treasure of which I was depositary. I received from him the most flattering letter and the invitation to go to Washington, the seat of government. I arrived there and was at once presented to the President and all the ministers. The French Legation became my hotel, and when the government offered a million to possess the treasure, I offered it for nothing.—"Restore me to France! Let me die in my country—close the eyes of my old mother—there is my recompense, one that no treasure could equal!" All was solemnly promised me. I fought with Thompson, with Derby. I saw the Embargo decreed which was to famish the army of Portugal; and, made bearer of despatches by the government and by the French ambassador, I set out to present myself to the Duke de Bassano. After a long but fortunate passage, after having burned at sea several English and Spanish vessels, I was set ashore at Santander. I deposited my despatches with the French Consul, and put to sea again to reach Sauterne(?). A column of two thousand men escorted me in safety to Bayonne, where, when I was stepping into my carriage, I was recognized by a vile saddler whom I had the bad luck not to employ. Gendarmes seized my despatches, my gold, my effects, my servants; and I was alone, flying persecution, tyranny. When I looked for the highest recompense, I found myself naked, despoiled, and prevented from rendering account to his Majesty of the important situation of the United States, of the wishes of the Canadians, of the inhabitants of Nova Scotia; and a warrant issued against me obliges me to appear a criminal or a coward when I am far from either of these hypotheses.

Mr. Dervilliers, never could an agent of England have served his ministry better!!! What is to be done! I groan and I suffer. I wait an answer from the government, and I must add this loss to those I have already suffered. The American government will indemnify me; but I fear that it may turn its arms, and that its system, reuniting itself with the English system, may make the imbecile agents of so many disasters repent. This is what pains and afflicts me, and what destroys the fruit of my labors beyond the Atlantic. The wretches, dividing my spoils, will dig the tomb of the French cause in America, and I shall cry out with truth (since they believe me to be loaded with gold): *Auri sacra fames, quid non mortalia pectora cogis!!*

Conclusions

I left Lectoure with 54 francs and I have travelled like a prince, covering more than 7000 leagues in the two worlds. Except one apostolic day, I have always had a good carriage and at least three domestics. During my residence in America, I always had a deposit of near $40,000 in the Bank of the United States. There remained to me, after having finished my operations, a carriage valued at 11,000 francs, at least; before my disaster at Bayonne, effects or money, 50,000 francs; in letters of change, one of 69,000 francs, the other of 84,000. Total, 214,000 francs, with which I was withdrawing to my country, happy to have served it, and hoping from the French government a reimbursement of 200,000 francs that I had spent, without ever having received a sous from any government whatever. Who will undertake an equal task and obtain the same success? It will not be I! Nevertheless, I leave, still, friends and claims on the continent. Yet I am here, unhappy and without a sous. I have been wrecked in port, like a bad pilot; but I can only admire the secret ways of Providence, and in my ecstasy, I cry, *O Altitudo!!!*

Soubiran was a lineal descendant from that society which the Spaniards called *picaresque,* and which had a literature of its own. The French adopted it from Spain, and *Gil Blas* made it famous throughout the world. Soubiran was a Gascon, and must have been a more or less plausible rogue; for, although his stories contradicted themselves in every other sentence, and were so numerous, so long, and so detached that he could, with the best of memories, hardly have repeated any one of them accurately, he lived in an age of adventurers far more successful than himself, and seems never to have been publicly exposed in the good society whose scrutiny he challenged. At Washington, he went directly to his minister, Serurier, who should have penetrated his character at once, yet Serurier wrote despatch on despatch about him, without once seeming to appreciate that the man was merely a common swindler. Serurier's letters were hardly less amusing than Soubiran's impostures.

No. 45.   Washington, 8 Feby., 1812

Monseigneur:

I received, some time ago, a letter dated from Boston, signed Édouard de Crillon, in which this traveller informed me that he had escaped from England, that he had just arrived in the United States, and that on his journey he had had the good fortune to form an acquaintance with a person employed by the English government in a secret mission to New England; had become master of his secret, of his papers, and that they were of a nature to produce an immediate explosion between America and Great Britain; and that he had sworn to make me their depositary. The letter was of a style somewhat romantic, and although the traveller's name was certainly very fine and very French, it might cover a trap, and I thought that everything which came from England should be received by me with great circumspection. The traveller begged me to send my answer to New York under cover to the Consul General, whom he would see in passing. I wrote to M. Lescallier to examine the new arrival; to send him to me if he was in fact M. de Crillon; and in the contrary case to dissuade his coming. M. de Crillon arrived here ten days ago. He came to see me. He talked to me with enthusiasm of his Majesty the Emperor; of the happy times when he had the honor of serving him; of his own faults; of the wrongs of which he felt himself the object, and which, reducing him to despair, had led him to fly to England in want of a better asylum. He told me that there he had received letters from his family which made known to him the just anger of his Imperial Majesty, and which gave him to understand that he could hope for no pardon unless he quitted that enemy's country and went to wait, in America, the return of the imperial favor which his family would not cease to implore; that when in London he had met Baron d'Ebeut, aide-de-camp of the Prince Regent, whom he had formerly seen in Germany, and who, having recognized him, made him every sort of caress and the offer, difficult to refuse in his position, of presenting him to his Royal Highness. He says that the Prince Regent received him with every possible kindness, and, judging that in his disgrace he might be disposed to change sides, offered him the command of the Legion of Estremadura. M. de Crillon had in his hands the letter in which M. d'Ebeut reiterates to him this offer, in the most flattering terms. M. de Crillon says that he answered the Prince Regent (in the impossibility of giving a positive refusal, which would very certainly

[1] *États Unis,* Supt. 2, 95.

have compromised his safety) that he would reflect on the proposition that his Royal Highness deigned to make him, and that he would at once let M. d'Ebeut know his decision. From that moment M. de Crillon says he had no other thought than flight; no other intentions than that of obeying the views of his family and the inspirations of honor, which did not permit him to make a longer stay among the enemies of his sovereign. A famous hunt [*chasse*] was preparing in Scotland; he announced that he would be there; he hired an apartment in London for six months, and profiting by the security which these demonstrations should inspire, he went secretly to the Isle of Wight, where he knew that a ship was going to sail for America, and he embarked. . . .

To some extent, Serurier was blinded by his own suspicions. He could imagine no theory to account for this extraordinary personage who bore one of the best names in France, except that he was a British political agent. The British minister, Foster, could see in him only a French agent. The idea that he might be merely a private gambler and swindler was so improbable that they did not readily grasp it. As for Madison and Monroe, whose knowledge of such characters was small, and who found themselves in the hands of two adventurers at once, when one would have been more than enough, they seem to have taken Soubiran quite seriously. Even Gallatin made no apparent protest. They were blinded, in their turn, by the unquestionable genuineness of Henry's documents. Crillon asked nothing, and professed sublime unselfishness. He seems, in fact, to have contented himself with only a thousand dollars of the fifty thousand which Henry got from the United States Treasury. The rest of his money must have come from other sources, and perhaps was really gained, as he said, by making an imbecile old man sign a will in his favor. Probably there was a certain amount of truth in his representation that his chief object was to obtain readmission to France. Harebrained as such adventurers are apt to be, he may have hoped to win the favor of the French police by rendering a service to French diplomacy. He certainly won Serurier's favor, who did his best to help the man, and, to judge from Caraman's version of the story, was ashamed of it afterwards. Serurier obliged Crillon to narrate a foolish farrago about the cause of his disgrace with the Emperor, and gravely reported it all to his government. Serurier himself added something very near a recommendation to favor:—

SERURIER TO THE DUKE DE BASSANO[1]

No. 46   WASHINGTON, 18 FEBY., 1812

. . . This, Monseigneur, is what M. Crillon has been willing to reveal to me. Your Excellency will understand that I have no means of verifying it. Moreover, I see no absolute necessity for verifying it, as M. Crillon asks nothing of me. Why should I have taken a trouble of that kind? Only in France can one know what truth there is in his version, and only there can it be judged. . . . I have presented him nowhere. I have publicly declared that the motive of my reserve in this respect was that he had not, according to usage, brought letters from your Excellency. I have made this declaration before the whole ministry; but as he has been received and dined [*accueuilli, fêté*] at the President's and by all the ministers, I have thought that, in order not to discredit the offer he made to the administration, I should occasionally receive him myself. I have, therefore, received him, but at the same time repeating that it was not as a Frenchman, since I could not do so owing to my official ignorance of his position as regarded my Court; but as a man who, as the government of the Republic declared to me, had rendered it a signal service.

On arriving at Washington, M. Crillon, to escape better the suspicions of Mr. Foster, thought proper to call upon him. He even dined there, but this British minister, who had probably been informed of his brusque flight from England, said to the other guests, at the moment he left the room: "There is a spy of the Emperor!" This was told to M. de Crillon, who wrote on the instant the harshest and most insulting letter to Mr. Foster that ever was read. The latter answered with a moderation assuredly very rare. This correspondence being shown by M. Crillon to all the ministers has made Mr. Foster ridiculous in all eyes. Since that time M. Crillon has never set foot in his house, and has kept up the same line of conduct. He always speaks with the same enthusiasm of the Emperor, of his love for France and his family with the liveliest tenderness. He appears to regret his faults, whatever they may be. I received him at first with extreme distrust and put myself quite beyond reach of any trap, giving nothing in writing and sending him to the Secretary of State. But I must admit that I believe now in the sincerity of M. Crillon's regrets. Not but that there is always something of romance in his stories, sometimes contradiction in the details of his adventures. But it seems to me very hard to doubt the substance. The man has such an exaltation of brain, he shows so delicate a sense of honor, that one cannot suppose him engaged in a double intrigue. Moreover, it could be only the American

[1] *États Unis,* Supt. 2, 98.

government that could be deceived. I have declared to Mr. Monroe that I guaranteed nothing; that it was for him to verify the documents that I have not even asked to see, and to establish their authenticity. Every verification has been made. They have compared the English seals and the known handwritings. Mr. Pinkney, Attorney-General, recently arrived from England where he was Minister of the Republic, has been called in. He has verified everything. The greater part of the facts contained in that correspondence were known to him, and there remains no doubt in the mind of the administration.

. . . The bargain was concluded on the 7th. The papers are in the hands of Mr. Monroe. Mr. Henry at first asked £25,000 sterling, and the Secretary of State granted it; but on examining the affair afterwards with the Secretary of the Treasury, it appeared that the President could not dispose of more than $50,000 for secret service. Mr. Monroe offered to give that amount first, and to pay the rest after publication, with the necessary approval of Congress. This clause displeased Mr. Henry, who declared that he would rather burn the papers than haggle over them so. As he is a very violent man, they took alarm. M. Crillon said that he thought the price too high, and that he would persuade his friend to come down to £18,000 sterling, but the same difficulty remained for the £8000 in excess of the $50,000. Mr. Monroe put the whole negotiation into his hands. Mr. Henry remained inflexible. M. Crillon announced that he would supply this deficit by his estate of St. Martial in Spain which he valued at 200,000 francs, and which he ceded to his friend. As I found this proceeding a little too handsome to be natural, and as I showed some astonishment, M. Crillon told me that he considered the success of that affair as the only means of recovering the good graces of his Majesty, and that, with this idea, nothing cost too much; moreover, that he thought he could wait until the Republic should indemnify him for this sacrifice. I thought it not my business to exaggerate doubts on such motives, and said no more.

Mr. Henry has gone to New York, whence he is to sail within a few days on a government vessel. He had asked to pass to England, under pretext of business, and to make talk of this event through the channel of his friends. Mr. Monroe communicated this project to me. I told him that this seemed to me too refined for its object; that letters would do quite as well; that Mr. Foster, informed of his arrival here, must have notified them in London, and that I saw no attraction that could make him want to go to a country where, supposing he had acted in good faith here, he would risk being hanged. The project seems to be given up. He will be sent to France. . . . M. Crillon has gone to Philadelphia, where he proposes to pass three or four days with Count Pahlen, last minister of Russia in America, and who has not yet started for Brazil. He knows the Count and announces that he is going to talk about his brother who is in the Russian service. On his return he has promised to hand me the memoir which he addresses to your Excellency by my advice.

Serurier's letter was written February 18. At that time both John Henry and Crillon were in Philadelphia, whither they had gone after concluding their bargain on the 7th, and obtaining the Treasury warrants for $50,000, dated and paid on February 10. Henry went on to New York and sailed for France on the sloop-of-war *Wasp*, March 10. Crillon returned to Washington and wrote letters for France.

SERURIER TO THE DUKE DE BASSANO[1]

Monseigneur:
I have the honor to address to your Excellency the letter that M. de Crillon wrote to M. the Duke of Elchingen. I have thought it best that whatever relates to this affair should pass through your Excellency. For the same reason I permit myself to place under this cover two other letters written by that officer, one to his Highness Monseigneur the Vice Grand Elector, and one to the Minister of General Police.

I am, etc.,
SERURIER.

WASHINGTON, 24 Feb., 1812.

The letter to Ney is a long medley, without present interest, and bearing no date. The letters to Sieyès and Savary are more curious. For some reason best known to himself, Soubiran dated them at Philadelphia,—although on those days he was in Washington,—and signed himself, not Crillon, but Émile Édouard.

SOUBIRAN TO THE VICE GRAND ELECTOR SIEYÈS[2]

PHILADELPHIA, 5 FEBY., 1812.

Monseigneur:
Your Highness had sent me to Malta with Méchin. This was a crime in the eyes of the Directory. The hatred of Barras pursued me; prejudiced Regnaud and Vaubois against me; I was threatened with arrest; I should

[1] *États Unis*, Supt. 2, 100.
[2] *États Unis*, Supt. 2, 94.

have been arrested, and then shot, if my friend Subervie had not warned me. I was then at Cività Vecchia. The unfavorable impressions have followed the subsequent government. Younger, more adroit, I had carried off some mistress from the Director; I had thrashed that scamp Davis, who was his aide-de-camp. *Inde irae!*

Since that time I have been voluntarily in the army. I have been employed there as a superior officer by Belliard and Ney, and I was bearer of a letter from Lannes to be named by King Joseph his confidential aide-de-camp. I arrived. I was, perhaps, not enough of a courtier. I went straight to my new master. The Sasignys, the Jourdans, etc., took umbrage. I was forgotten. My letters remained without answer, and I was dropped. Nevertheless, I was despatched to his Imperial Majesty at Bordeaux. I warned him of the rage of the Spaniards, of their infamous plans, and their audacious courage, the disastrous effects of which tended to nothing less than to plunge France into mourning and despair. I received the order to withdraw, but I enjoyed the indelible happiness of delaying the entrance into Spain, where I had rendered a thousand services to the cause of his Majesty.

Since that time a mark for an infinity of persecutions, I have been obliged to quit France and assume every sort of mask. When shall I obtain the favor of returning to my country? This harrowing idea paralyzes all my actions.

Your attachment to the person of his Majesty obliges me to inform your Highness that there will arrive on the continent an audacious English agent named Major St. Adrien or Major Henry. For more ample information, I shall have the honor to write to your Highness on the departure of the vessel which will carry this savage [*ce barbare*].

I am occupied here in causing war to be declared against the English, in overcoming the apathy of this government, and in making the English minister decamp. What I can do I hope to announce to your Highness within twenty days. I will write you then in great detail. I am obliged at present to do it in a great hurry.

No indiscretion or inquiries! The good that comes in sleep,—one does not inform oneself of the hour it will arrive.

Your very respectful
ÉMILE ÉDOUARD

This secret denunciation of Henry adds another touch to the comedy of Crillon. One is at a loss to understand precisely what idea was in the writer's mind, but probably it was nothing more than to give himself importance in the eyes of the French police; for the letter to Savary, the Emperor's Minister of Police, repeated the warning.

Soubiran to the Duke de Rovigo[1]

PHILADELPHIA, 10 FEBY., 1812

Monseigneur:

I love the Emperor as much as you. I have a thousand times exposed my life, and have never received or required recompense. Your Excellency will recall my letters from Bagnères, my last from Hamburg. I desire that your Excellency should some day bear in mind that nothing is dearer to me than my country, and that I am the most zealous and the most faithful subject of Napoleon the Great.

Confidentially

I have only time to inform your Excellency that there will arrive on the coasts of France a man, agent of England, bearing the name of Major St. Adrien, or Major Henry, about thirty-six years old, blond, about 5 feet 9 inches in height, who must be put under surveillance and severely confined. He knows how to take all colors, and is sent to commit the most frightful crime [*attentat.*]

I dog his steps, and I will inform your Excellency of his determination, of the name of the vessel and of the captain with whom he crosses the Atlantic.

I hope before April 1st to have decided this country to war with England. I shall have the honor to inform you of it. Your Excellency will know how to reward a devoted servant and a faithful subject.

ÉMILE ÉDOUARD

Your Excellency will remember that I was Colonel on the staff and met you travelling; but you will never know to what a point my devotion goes! Above all—discretion! It is necessary that I should succeed, and my confidence has no other interest connected with you than that of interesting you in order that I may be permitted to finish my days in my country when I shall have recourse to your goodness. Any indiscretion on your part destroys my success, and it will be your fault alone that the English party is not entirely annihilated.

Beside these letters, Soubiran wrote another, and a long one, to Maret, Duke de Bassano, Napoleon's Minister for Foreign Affairs. This letter, which is dated Washington, February 22, 1812, con-

[1] *États Unis,* Supt. 2, 97.

tains a further tissue of inventions, but is remarkable for the strange impudence with which the writer challenged his fate with the police. He not only signed himself Édouard de Crillon, but claimed permission to return to France in consideration of the sacrifice he had made of his estate of St. Martial—an estate which the Duke de Bassano, in a few moments, by inquiry from the Duke de Crillon, could and did assure himself never existed; and not content with this, he begged the Duke de Bassano to unite with the Duke d'Elchingen "who has been witness of my military conduct,"—which the Duke d'Elchingen, in still less time, would declare wholly imaginary.

Such was the actual result. Soubiran sailed from New York, May 28, 1812, and on his arrival at Bayonne was promptly arrested. His subsequent adventures are unknown, but among the papers seized by the police at some later persecution of this interesting citizen was the draft of a letter written, or intended to be written, to John Henry in 1814. Apparently both of them were in Paris in the early part of July of that year. Soubiran was dogging Henry, presumably to get money from him, for Soubiran was then penniless and could hardly have had any other object. Nevertheless, through Soubiran's rags, the old tone of Gascon grandiloquence talked as loftily as ever. The nature of the transaction which he proposed to Henry is something for the curious seekers of puzzles to explain if they can; but certainly one would like to know whether Monroe ever gave him the smallest hope of obtaining more money from the United States Treasury.

SOUBIRAN TO HENRY[1]

. . . July, 1814

Sir:

When I wrote to you in America, you were in Paris; this is doubtless the reason why I have never heard from you. I have no need to tell you how much I have been annoyed not to have been able to get an interview with you, although I followed you step by step for more than two hours, the evening of Saturday, July 2, at the moment when you were talking with a woman, doubtless on important affairs,—for I had neither the power nor the faculty to wait longer than midnight. Nor was I sure it was you, since I thought I saw you with a black band over one eye, which

[1] *États Unis,* Supt. 2, 102.

I learned with regret that you had lost. Now I turn to our affairs. When I had the pleasure of meeting you at Ryde in the Isle of Wight, I was in hiding from everybody. The decree of death that Buonaparte had issued against me rested on my head. I had avoided it at Hamburg only by getting rid of a gendarme. Bernadotte refused me an asylum; set a price on my head to please the puissant idol of the world; and I had no doubt that emissaries of that savage would have conceived the plan of destroying me in England if I had been discovered in that situation. Hidden in the shadow of my mother's name, we became friends! You complained to me of the British government. I told you all I had suffered from that of Napoleon; and we conceived the project—you, of revenging yourself on those who had, as you said, outraged your interests; while I found it best, since it enabled me, not indeed to return to favor with a monster whom I have always detested, but at last to reopen the door of that fair France which I never found elsewhere in my travels.

It is useless for me to recapitulate here all I did to obtain the result which brought you fifty thousand dollars. I sacrificed my existence, all that man holds most sacred. You lent me a sum of some thousand dollars, which it is out of my power to repay, since Vigaroux, who kept rather a large amount for me, died my debtor, and I can obtain none of it. In this situation you set out for Europe, and I remained exposed to all the vexations of the two parties; a mark for all their sarcasms. I had to fight with Willing, with Colonel Roussel, and I was nearly assassinated in New York by an English party.

You were at Paris when I sailed, bringing an order enclosed in Monroe's despatches for Barlow to pay me 84,000 francs; but instead of coming to Paris, I was arrested on landing; all my effects were seized; my properties were sold; and my brother was thrown into prison, whence he came out only a few weeks ago. In this frightful situation, I did not know to what saint to turn. England could not offer me an asylum; yet I was constrained to go there, after being shipwrecked at Gibraltar; and on my arrival, though I travelled under my own name, I was recognized, and Foster instructed the government of all my movements. I was taken at Abbé Roufigny's, Castle Street, and thrown into the prisons of Tothillfields, where I remained 213 days because I refused to tell what would have irrevocably destroyed you (even at Paris). Returned to my country, deprived of all assistance, I learn that you have complained of me; and of what, I pray? Because I have not destroyed you in England? because I have caused you to get fifty thousand dollars in America? finally, because I still persist in my loyal conduct towards you? Oh, if it is those thousand dollars that you gave me when you were gorged with gold! then I shall say to you: *Ad impossibile nemo tenetur,* since I have no longer a sous; but if you want the despatches that I had saved with the order of Monroe to count me down that sum, even if you want to return to America, I offer it to you, and, in offering it, I do all I can do, since I have never mixed in your affair except to gain a right to return to my country, which the return of my sovereign has incontestably restored to me.

This is, sir, all I can do in this affair, and you will have the goodness to return me the effects of mine which you have, and my declarations of relinquishment. On my part, I should have crossed the Atlantic only to preserve the most flattering idea of you; but if, contrary to my expectation, you reject this arrangement, do not blame me for taking the step of publishing my situation with all your letters, notably that in which you tell me that I am an extraordinary man since I have decided those wretches, that you have seduced, to keep their word, and that all your ambition is that we may meet in Paris to laugh at the expense of these wretches, who tremble for a bagatelle of ten thousand pounds sterling!— What a government!!!

I am much of your mind; but I think, too, that nobody will blame me for the course which I should be obliged to take, and which I have till now refused to take, for considerations which were personal to you and were equally repugnant to my delicacy and my honor.

Obliged to quit Paris for some time, I have charged M. ———— with my full powers to terminate this affair. When I return to the city, I shall be happy to renew an acquaintance formed under very unfortunate auspices, but such as have always opened for the future the perspective of what one may attain when one is aided by your counsels and your genius. I beg you never to doubt the distinguished sentiments entertained for you during life by

Your very, etc.,

E.

The Tendency of History

Although Adams' History failed to make an impression on the general public, among professional historians it quickly achieved and still retains a very high reputation. In recognition of his pre-eminence, the American Historical Association elected Adams, in absentia, its president for the year 1894. But by this time he had grown to dislike every form of public life. The death of his wife by her own hand in 1885 had destroyed his inclination to participate actively in the affairs of society, and his increasing bitterness toward "the present evils of the world" confirmed him in his attitude of "silence." When, therefore, the time approached for the customary presidential address at the end of his year's tenure in office, Adams wrote the following letter to the Association, designated it as coming from Guadalajara, Mexico, and departed Washington in a southerly direction.

"The Tendency of History" was Adams' first open avowal of his belief that the study of history must become a science exactly comparable to the physical sciences. The idea had been in his mind for a long time, but it was probably crystallized by conversations he had in the summer of 1893 with his brother, Brooks Adams, who was then at work on his book, The Law of Civilization and Decay. *Brooks was trying to formulate a law of historical change that would "correspond," as he put it, "with the laws which are supposed to regulate the movements of the material universe," and Henry was*

deeply impressed by his efforts. Henry later told Brooks that "The Tendency of History" had been written as a kind of introduction for The Law of Civilization and Decay *in order to prepare the way for it among hidebound teachers of history. Whether or not this was so, the short paper was a landmark in Adams' intellectual career. It was the first step toward the writing of his later years, most notably* Mont-Saint-Michel *and* Chartres *and the* Education, *and the first sign of what was to become almost an obsession with the problem of a science of history.*

Communication from Henry Adams, President of the Association

GUADA'-C-JARA, December 12, 1894

DEAR SIR: I regret extremely that constant absence has prevented me from attending the meetings of the Historical Association. On the date which your letter mentions as that of its first decennial I shall not be within reach. I have to ask you to offer my apology to the members, and the assurance that at that moment I am believed to be somewhere beyond the Isthmus of Panama. Perhaps this absence runs in some of the mysterious ways of nature's law, for you will not forget that when you did me the honor to make me your president I was still farther away—in Tahiti or Fiji, I believe—and never even had an opportunity to thank you. Evidently I am fitted only to be an absent president, and you will pardon a defect which is clearly not official, but a condition of the man.

I regret this fault the more because I would have liked to be of service, and perhaps there is service that might be usefully performed. Even the effort to hold together the persons interested in history is worth making. That we should ever act on public opinion with the weight of one compact and one energetic conviction is

[From the *Annual Report* of the American Historical Association for 1894, pp. 17-23.]

417

hardly to be expected, but that one day or another we shall be compelled to act individually or in groups I can not doubt. With more anxiety than confidence, I should have liked to do something, however trifling, to hold the association together and unite it on some common ground, with a full understanding of the course which history seems destined to take and with a good-natured willingness to accept or reject the result, but in any case not to quarrel over it.

No one who has watched the course of history during the last generation can have felt doubt of its tendency. Those of us who read Buckle's first volume when it appeared in 1857, and almost immediately afterwards, in 1859, read the Origin of Species and felt the violent impulse which Darwin gave to the study of natural laws, never doubted that historians would follow until they had exhausted every possible hypothesis to create a science of history. Year after year passed, and little progress has been made. Perhaps the mass of students are more skeptical now than they were thirty years ago of the possibility that such a science can be created. Yet almost every successful historian has been busy with it, adding here a new analysis, a new generalization there; a clear and definite connection where before the rupture of idea was absolute; and, above all, extending the field of study until it shall include all races, all countries, and all times. Like other branches of science, history is now encumbered and hampered by its own mass, but its tendency is always the same, and can not be other than what it is. That the effort to make history a science may fail is possible, and perhaps probable; but that it should cease, unless for reasons that would cause all science to cease, is not within the range of experience. Historians will not, and even if they would they can not, abandon the attempt. Science itself would admit its own failure if it admitted that man, the most important of all its subjects, could not be brought within its range.

You may be sure that four out of five serious students of history who are living to-day have, in the course of their work, felt that they stood on the brink of a great generalization that would reduce all history under a law as clear as the laws which govern the material world. As the great writers of our time have touched one by one the separate fragments of admitted law by which society betrays its character as a subject for science, not one of them can have failed to feel an instant's hope that he might find the secret which would transform these odds and ends of philosophy into one self-evident, harmonious, and complete system. He has seemed to have it, as the Spanish say, in his inkstand. Scores of times he must have dropped his pen to think how one short step, one sudden inspiration, would show all human knowledge how, in these thickset forests of history, one corner turned, one faint trail struck, would bring him on the highroad of science. Every professor who has tried to teach the doubtful facts which we now call history must have felt that sooner or later he or another would put order in the chaos and bring light into darkness. Not so much genius or favor was needed as patience and good luck. The law was certainly there, and as certainly was in places actually visible, to be touched and handled, as though it were a law of chemistry or physics. No teacher with a spark of imagination or with an idea of scientific method can have helped dreaming of the immortality that would be achieved by the man who should successfully apply Darwin's method to the facts of human history.

Those of us who have had occasion to keep abreast of the rapid progress which has been made in history during the last fifty years must be convinced that the same rate of progress during another half century would necessarily raise history to the rank of a science. Our only doubt is whether the same rate can possibly be maintained. If not, our situation is simple. In that case, we shall remain more or less where we are. But we have reached a point where we ought to face the possibility of a great and perhaps a sudden change in the importance of our profession. We can not help asking ourselves what would happen if some new Darwin were to demonstrate the law or the laws of historical evolution.

I admit that the mere idea of such an event fills my mind with anxiety. When I remember the astonishing influence exerted by a mere theorist like Rousseau; by a reasoner like Adam Smith; by a philosopher, beyond contact with material interests, like Darwin, I can not imagine the limits of the shock that might follow the establishment of a fixed science of history. Hitherto our profession has been encouraged, or, at all events, tolerated by governments and by society as an amusing or instructive and, at any rate, a safe and harmless branch of inquiry. But what will be the attitude of government or of society toward any conceivable science of history? We know what followed Rousseau; what industrial and political struggles have resulted from the teachings of Adam Smith; what a revolution and what vehement opposition has been and still is caused by the ideas of Darwin. Can we imagine any science of history that would not be vastly more violent in its effects than the dissensions roused by anyone or by all three of these great men?

I ask myself, What shape can be given to any science of history that will not shake to its foundations some prodigious interest? The world is made up of a few immense forces, each with an organization that corresponds with its strength. The church stands first; and at the outset we must assume that the church will not and can not accept any science of history, because science, by its definition, must exclude the idea of a personal and active providence. The state stands next; and the hostility of the state would be assured toward any system or science that might not strengthen its arm. Property is growing more and more timid and looks with extreme jealousy on any new idea that may weaken vested rights. Labor is growing more and more self-confident and looks with contempt on all theories that do not support its own. Yet we can not conceive of a science of history that would not, directly or indirectly, affect all these vast social forces.

Any science assumes a necessary sequence of cause and effect, a force resulting in motion which can not be other than what it is. Any science of history must be absolute, like other sciences, and must fix with mathematical certainty the path which human society has got to follow. That path can hardly lead toward the interests of all the great social organizations. We can not conceive that it should help at the same time the church and the state, property and communism, capital and poverty, science and religion, trade and art. Whatever may be its orbit, it must, at least for a time, point away from some of these forces toward others which are regarded as hostile. Conceivably, it might lead off in eccentric lines away from them all, but by no power of our imagination can we conceive that it should lead toward them all.

Although I distrust my own judgment and look earnestly for guidance to those who are younger than I and closer to the movement of the time, I can not be wholly wrong in thinking that a change has come over the tendency of liberal thought since the middle of the century. Darwin led an intellectual revival much more hopeful than any movement that can now be seen in Europe, except among the socialists. Had history been converted into a science at that time it would perhaps have taken the form of cheerful optimism which gave to Darwin's conclusions the charm of a possible human perfectibility. Of late years the tone of European thought has been distinctly despondent among the classes which were formerly most hopeful. If a science of history were established today on the lines of its recent development I greatly fear it would take its tone from the pessimism of Paris, Berlin, London, and St. Petersburg, unless it brought into sight some new and hitherto unsuspected path for civilization to pursue.

If it pointed to a socialistic triumph it would place us in an attitude of hostility toward existing institutions. Even supposing that our universities would permit their professors in this country to announce the scientific certainty of communistic triumphs, could Europe be equally liberal? Would property, on which the universities depend, allow such freedom of instruction? Would the state suffer its foundation to be destroyed? Would society as now constituted tolerate the open assertion of a necessity which should affirm its approaching overthrow?

If, on the other hand, the new science required us to announce that the present evils of the world—its huge armaments, its vast accumulations of capital, its advancing materialism, and declining arts—were to be continued, exaggerated, over another thousand years, no one would listen to us with satisfaction. Society would shut its eyes and ears. If we proved the certainty of our results we should prove it without a sympathetic audience and without good effect. No one except artists and socialists would listen, and the conviction which we should produce on them could lead only to despair and attempts at anarchy in art, in thought, and in society.

If, finally, the science should prove that society must at a given time revert to the church and recover its old foundation of absolute faith in a personal providence and a revealed religion, it commits suicide.

In whatever direction we look we can see no possibility of converting history into a science without bringing it into hostility toward one or more of the most powerful organizations of the era. If the world is to continue moving toward the point which it has so energetically pursued during the last fifty years, it will destroy the hopes of the vast organizations of labor. If it is to change its course and become communistic, it places us in direct hostility to the entire fabric of our social and political system. If it goes on, we must preach despair. If it goes back, it must deny and repudiate science. If it goes forward, round a circle which leads through communism, we must declare ourselves hostile to the property that pays us and the institutions we are bound in duty to support.

A science can not be played with. If an hypothesis is advanced that obviously brings into a direct sequence of cause and effect all the phenomena of human history, we must accept it, and if we accept we must teach it. The mere fact that it overthrows social organizations can not affect our attitude. The rest of society can reject or ignore, but we must follow the new light no matter where it leads. Only about two hundred and fifty years ago the common sense of mankind, supported by the authority of revealed religion, affirmed the undoubted and self-evident fact that the sun moved round the earth. Galileo suddenly asserted and proved that the earth moved round the sun. You know what followed, and the famous "E pur si muove." Even if we, like Galileo, should be obliged by the religious or secular authority to recant and repudiate our science, we should still have to say as he did in secret if not in public, "E pur si muove."

Those of us who have reached or passed middle age need not trouble ourselves very much about the future. We have seen one or two great revolutions in thought and we have had enough. We are not likely to accept any new theory that shall threaten to disturb our repose. We should reject at once, and probably by a large majority, a hypothetical science that must obviously be incapable of proof. We should take the same attitude that our fathers took toward the theories and hypotheses of Darwin. We may meantime reply to such conundrums by the formula that has smoothed our path in life over many disasters and cataclysms: "Perhaps the crisis will never occur; and even if it does occur, we shall probably be dead." To us who have already gone as far as we set out to go, this answer is good and sufficient, but those who are to be the professors and historians of the future have got duties and responsibilities of a heavier kind than we older ones ever have had to carry. They can not afford to deal with such a question in such a spirit. They would have to rejoin in Heine's words:

> Also fragen wir beständig,
> Bis man uns mit einer Handvoll
> Erde endlich stopft die Mäuler,
> Aber ist das eine Antwort?

They may at any time in the next fifty years be compelled to find an answer, "Yes" or "No," under the pressure of the most powerful organizations the world has ever known for the suppression of influences hostile to its safety. If this association should be gifted with the length of life that we all wish for it, a span of a century at least, it can hardly fail to be torn by some such dilemma. Our universities, at all events, must be prepared to meet it. If such a crisis should come, the universities throughout the world will have done most to create it, and are under most obligation to find a solution for it. I will not deny that the shadow of this coming event has cast itself on me, both as a teacher and a writer; or that, in the last ten years, it has often kept me silent where I should once have spoken with confidence, or has caused me to think long and anxiously before expressing in public any opinion at all. Beyond a doubt, silence is best. In these remarks, which are only casual and offered in the paradoxical spirit of private conversation, I have not ventured to express any opinion of my own; or, if I have expressed it, pray consider it as withdrawn. The situation seems to call for no opinion, unless we have some scientific theory to offer; but to me it seems so interesting that, in taking leave of the association, I feel inclined to invite them, as individuals, to consider the matter in a spirit that will enable us, should the crisis arise, to deal with it in a kindly temper, and a full understanding of its serious dangers and responsibilities.

Ever truly yours,

Henry Adams

Index

Adams, Brooks, 415-416
Adams, Charles F., xv, 1, 5 n., 19, 20, 25, 33, 86, 89, 103 n., 366-376, 379-386
Adams, Charles F., Jr., 1, 289, 319 n.
Adams, John, xvi, 95, 103 n., 258, 260, 280
Adams, John Quincy, xv, xvi, xviii, 225-252, 258, 275, 279, 280, 283
Adams, Samuel, 280
Alabama claims, 83-91, 215, 291
Anderson, Major Robert, 6 and n., 10
Arrick, Clifford, 64-65

Bancroft's (George) *History of the United States*, 45-46
Barlow, Francis C., 188 n.
Barnard, George G., 166, 167, 187, 188 n.
Bassano, Duke de, 402, 406, 408, 410
Belden, William, 162, 180, 185, 186
Bingham, John A., 141, 148
Bismarck, Otto von, 258, 282, 287
Blackstone, Sir William, 194
Blaine, James G., 295, 312, 313, 314 and n.
Blair, Montgomery, 26, 27
Boutwell, George S., 108, 109, 169, 171, 173, 177, 178, 191, 198-202, 203, 204, 206, 208, 209, 301, 302, 303
Bradley, Joseph P., 210, 211
Breckinridge, John C., 4, 9, 11
Bristow, Benjamin H., 295, 313, 314, 318
Bristow, Francis M., 21
Brooks, James, 121-122
Brown, Albert G., 118, 120
Bryant, William Cullen, 296 n., 346
Buchanan, James, 5-6, 364
Buckle, Henry T., 418

Butler, Benjamin F., 67 and n., 76, 80, 325
Butterfield, Daniel, 173, 176, 188

Calhoun, John C., 258, 265, 268, 270, 272-274, 280, 282, 283, 286
Cameron, Don, 312, 313 and n.
Cameron, Simon, 313 n.
Caraman, Count Georges de, 395, 405
Cardozo, Albert, 166, 167
Cass, Lewis, 6, 118, 119, 120, 123
Cecil, Lord Robert, 61
Chandler, Zachariah, 313
Chase, Salmon P., 132, 133, 136, 138, 140, 145, 148, 150, 153, 211, 212
Chase, Samuel, 213 n.
Civil service reform, 71-75, 95-128, 300 n., 304, 305, 309, 311-315, 318-326
Clarendon, Lord, 87, 90
Clay, Henry, 258, 268, 270, 271-272, 274, 280, 282, 283
Cleveland, Grover, 308 n.
Clinton, De Witt, 270
Cobb, Howell, 5 n., 6
Collamer, Jacob, 116, 118, 120, 121, 152
Committee of Thirty-three, 5, 13-14, 18-19, 20-21, 25
Congress of Paris, 363, 365, 366
Conkling, Roscoe, 295, 312, 313, 314
Consular pupils, 115-125
Copper Bill, 71 and n.
Corbin, Abel R., 171-172, 173, 174, 175, 176, 177, 178-180, 181, 183-184, 185 n., 188, 196
Correa, Abbé, 259
Cowley, Earl, 365, 366, 367, 388
Crillon, Count Edward de, 391-413
Crittenden, John J., 10-11, 18, 27
Cromwell, Oliver, 360, 394

Currency reform, 75-77, 299-300 n., 309-311, 316-318, 328

Dale, Sir Thomas, 50, 54, 55, 56
Darwin, Charles, 418, 419, 420, 421, 422
Davis, Henry Winter, 15-19, 25, 26
Davis, Jefferson, 11, 27-28
Davis, Reuben, 13
Dawes, Henry L., 204
Dayton, William L., 369-370, 376-377, 379, 380, 384, 385
Deane, Charles, 34, 46, 47 and n., 48, 49, 50, 58, 60
Dickens, Charles, 301 n.
Douglas, Stephen A., 8, 9, 11, 103
Drew, Daniel, 161, 162, 163
Dyer, Alexander B., 64-65

Evarts, William M., 291 and n.
Everett, Edward, 115, 120, 123
Executive powers, 67-69, 101-106, 125-128, 197, 218-219, 322-324, 329-330

Fessenden, William P., 116, 118, 119, 120, 121, 124, 151, 152
Field, David D., 64, 167, 186, 187 and n., 188 n.
Fifteenth Amendment, 66, 71, 77
Fillmore, Millard, 115
Fish, Hamilton, 216, 217, 218
Fisk, James, Jr., 145, 157, 162-163, 164-165, 166, 167, 168, 172, 176, 177, 178, 179, 180, 181, 182, 183-184, 185, 186, 188, 189
Floyd, John B., 5 n., 7-8, 21
Foreign policy, 79-93, 215-218
Foster, Augustus John, 405, 406, 407, 412
Fremont, John C., 307
Fuller, Thomas, *Worthies of England*, 58, 59

Gallatin, Albert, 144, 361, 405
Gallatin, James, 138, 140, 144
Garfield, James A., 76 and n., 157
Gates, Sir Thomas, 50
Gibbon, Edward, 394,
Godkin, E. L., 129
Godwin, Parke, 296, 332
Gould, Jay, 145, 157, 161-162, 163, 164, 165, 166, 167, 168, 169-189
Grand Army of the Republic, 106-108
Grant, Ulysses S., 68-69, 71, 73, 74, 91, 93, 97-101, 105-106, 107, 109, 111, 113, 126, 171, 172, 173, 174, 176, 177, 178-179, 182, 188, 191, 195-198, 199, 202-204, 206, 207, 209, 210, 217, 218, 219, 295 n., 299 n., 303, 305, 313, 318
Greeley, Horace, 289, 291 n.
Grinnell, Moses H., 144

Hale, John, 227, 241, 244, 248
Hale, Sen. John P., 116-117 and n., 120
Hamilton, Alexander, 200, 209, 258, 261, 265, 276
Hamor, Ralph, 53-54, 56; *A True Discourse of the Present Estate of Virginia . . . ,* 53-54
Harrington, Edward, 42, 52
Hartford Convention, 270
Hayes, Rutherford B., 291 n., 295 n., 296, 297, 302, 306-307, 308-316, 318, 320, 321, 323-324, 326, 332
Heine, Heinrich, 423
Hepburn *vs.* Griswold, 212, 214
Hendricks, Thomas A., 295, 308 n., 319, 323, 326
Henry, John, 395, 396, 401-402, 407, 408, 409, 410, 411
Henry, Patrick, 280
Hill, Benjamin, 303
Hoar, Ebenezer R., 109-111, 204, 210, 211-212, 214, 325
Homeric poems, 344-350, 352
Hooper, Samuel, 141, 148
Howe, Timothy, 192, 312
Hunter, Robert M. T., 4, 116, 118, 120

Jackson, Andrew, 101, 102, 274, 275, 279, 297, 319, 324
James, Eleazar, 227, 228, 242, 251
Jefferson, Thomas, xxi, 83, 103, 126, 258, 262, 265, 266, 267, 268, 269, 270, 277, 279, 280, 283, 286, 306
Jenckes, Thomas A., 72 and n., 126, 128
Jennison, Timothy L., 227, 228, 241, 249
Johnson, Andrew, 11, 15, 24, 67 n., 71, 75, 78, 100, 104, 218, 291 n.
Johnson, Reverdy, 89, 121

Kentucky and Virginia resolutions, 265-267
Know-Nothing party, 15, 16, 17

Laplace, Pierre Simon de, 199
Lane, Frederick A., 163, 164, 189
Legal-Tender Act, 129-155, 209

Lincoln, Abraham, 7, 9, 26, 31, 33, 80, 103, 104, 307, 313, 315, 364, 370, 382, 383, 388, 389
Lodge, Henry Cabot, 253, 255 n.
Logan, John A., 107, 301, 302, 312
Lovejoy, Owen, 150
Luther, Martin, 360
Lyons, Lord, 367, 368, 369, 370-371, 372, 373, 374, 375, 377-379, 383, 385, 389

Macaulay, Thomas B., 393, 394
Madison, James, 127, 209, 258, 265-267, 268, 269, 270, 279, 283-284, 306, 315, 396, 405
Mann, Horace, 320
Marcy, William L., 103, 105, 115-116, 118-119, 120, 123, 364; Marcy amendment, 364, 369, 370, 375, 379
Marshall, John, 258, 281
Mason, George, 280
Mason, James M., 4, 118, 120
Massachusetts Bill of Rights, 97, 124, 126
McCulloch, Hugh, 169
McHenry, James, 177
Mercier, Henri, 367, 370, 377
Mill, John Stuart, 199
Missouri Compromise, 271
Monroe, James, 270, 405, 407, 411, 412, 413
Morrill, Justin S., 134, 150
Morton, Levi, 295, 301, 302, 312, 313, 314

Napoleon I, 197, 395, 410, 412
Napoleon III, 365, 366
Native American party, see Know-Nothing party
Necker, Jacques, 194
Nelson, Thomas A. R., 21
Newport, Captain, 36, 37, 43, 47, 48, 49
Newton, Sir Isaac, 199
New York *Times*, 33, 177
Njalsaga, 352-356
North American Review, 61, 129, 130, 167, 290

Osgood, James R. & Co., 290

Palfrey, John G., 33, 35-36, 58
Palmerston, Lord, 82, 87, 90, 365, 379, 387, 388
Pearson, Eliphalet, 235, 236, 251
Penelope, 345-349

Pennington, William, 17 n.
Percy, George, 37, 50
Pierce, Franklin, 115, 307, 364
Pitt, William, 135, 200, 201
Pocahontas, 33, 41, 44-46, 48, 49, 52, 53-57, 58, 59
Polk, James K., 307
Porter, Gen. Horace, 176, 177, 178
Powhatan, 41, 42, 45, 48, 52, 53, 54, 57
Purchas, Samuel, 55-56

Quitman, John A., 116

Randolph, John, 268, 361
Ratcliffe, John, 36, 37, 49, 50
Rawlins, John A., 217
Read, Nathan, 227, 230, 239, 243, 251
Reconstruction, 65-66, 78, 204-205
Reeve, Henry, 157
Revenue reform, 69-72, 206-209, 305, 328-329
Rice, Henry M., 20
Rolfe, John, 54, 55, 56, 58
Rousseau, Jean-Jacques, 262, 419, 420
Rovigo, Duke de, 395, 410
Rusk, Thomas J., 117, 118, 120
Russell, Lord John, 86-87, 90, 362, 365-375, 378, 379-389
Rust, Albert, 13

San Domingo Treaty, 204, 217-218, 219
San Juan affair, 83 and n.
St. Thomas Treaty, 79-81, 82, 216-217
Sainte-Beuve, Charles A., 257
Schenck, Robert C., 69, 75, 77, 208
Schurz, Carl, 289, 291, 294, 296, 320-321, 332
Scott, Winfield, 21
Scrivener, Matthew, 49
Serurier, Jean, 395, 403-405, 406-408
Seward, William H., 1, 12, 19, 21-23, 24, 25, 26, 27-29 and n., 79 n., 80, 82-83, 87, 88-89, 91, 119-120, 123, 215, 364, 370-371, 376-378, 383, 389
Shays's Rebellion, 226
Shearman, Thomas G., 167, 186
Shellabarger, Samuel, 149
Sherman, John, 25, 121, 141, 204, 312, 313 and n.
Sherman, William T., 196, 197
Simons, William, 51, 56; *A Map of Virginia . . .* , 51, 52-53
Smith, Adam, 199, 419, 420

Smith, Captain John, 33-60; *A De-
    scription of New England,* 57; *The
    Generall Historie of Virginia,* 36,
    39-44, 45-46, 49, 51, 52, 57, 58, 59;
    New England's Trials, 57; *A True
    Relation of Virginia,* 34, 37-45, 47,
    48, 49; *True Travels,* 35
Spaulding, Elbridge G., 133 n., 134-
    135, 137-140, 141, 144, 145, 146-
    147, 148, 150, 153
Specie Resumption Act, 309-311, 316,
    317
Stanley, Lord, 83, 87-89, 89-90
States' rights, 204-205, 221-222
Stevens, Thaddeus, 134, 135, 137, 141,
    145, 149
Story, Joseph, 263
Strachey, William, 53, 56; *Historie of
    Travaile into Virginia,* 53, 54
Strong, William, 210, 211
Studley, Thomas, 42, 52
Sumner, Charles, 71, 78, 92, 121, 123,
    152, 204, 205, 218
Sweeney, Peter B., 165, 331
Swift, Jonathan, 298

Taine, Hippolyte, 277 n.
Taylor, Miles, 21
Telemachus, 345-349
Tenure-of-Office Act, 67 and n., 68,
    330
Thomas, Benjamin F., 150
Thompson, Jacob, 5 n.
Thouvenel, Édouard Antoine, 366,
    367, 369-370, 371, 380

Tilden, Samuel J., 289, 295, 296, 297,
    299 n., 308 n., 315, 316-319, 321,
    323, 324, 325, 332
Turgot, Anne Robert Jacques, 200
Tweed, William M., 165, 319, 331

Ulysses, 345-349

Vanderbilt, Cornelius, 161, 189
Vansittart, Nicholas, 200-201

Wade, Benjamin F., 67 n., 118, 121
Walker, Francis A., 129-130
Washington, George, 101, 103, 195,
    258, 265, 266, 279, 280, 282, 306,
    315
Watts, John S., 19
Webster, Daniel, 258
Wells, David A., 69-71, 72, 207
Whig party, 15, 17, 24, 25
Whiskey Rebellion, 265
Whiskey ring, 295 n., 328
Whittier, John G., 29 and n.
Wigglesworth, Edward, 230, 234
Willard, Joseph, 227, 229, 232, 233,
    237, 238, 239-240, 245, 247, 249,
    250, 251-252
Williams, Samuel, 227, 230, 242, 251
Wilson, Henry, 149
Wingate, Charles F., 319 n.
Wingfield, Edward Maria, 34, 37, 47-
    49, 56; *A Discourse of Virginia,* 34,
    37, 47-49